The Foundations of Social Work Practice

D0163809

The

a graduate text

Foundations
of Social Work
Practice

Carol H. Meyer and Mark A. Mattaini

Editors

NASW PRESS

National Association of Social Workers
Washington, DC

Ann A. Abbott, PhD, ACSW, President
Sheldon R. Goldstein, ACSW, LISW, Executive Director

BOWLING GREEN STATE
UNIVERSITY LIBRARIES

Linda Beebe, *Executive Editor*
Nancy A. Winchester, *Editorial Services Director*
Patricia D. Wolf, Wolf Publications, Inc., *Project Manager*
Wendy Almeleh, *Copyeditor*
Louise Goines, *Proofreader*
Annette Hansen, *Proofreader*
Susan Nedrow, *Proofreader*
Robert Elwood, *Indexer*

© 1995 by the NASW Press

All rights reserved. No part of this book may be reproduced or transmitted in any form or by any means, electronic or mechanical, including photocopying, recording, or by any information storage and retrieval system, without permission in writing from the publisher.

Library of Congress Cataloging-in-Publication Data
The foundations of social work practice / Carol H. Meyer and Mark A.
    Mattaini, editors.
        p.   cm.
    Includes bibliographical references and index.
    ISBN 0-87101-237-5
    1. Social service.   I. Meyer, Carol H.,   II. Mattaini, Mark A.
HV40.F683 1995
361.3'2–dc20   95-18028
                                                               CIP

Printed in the United States of America

Contents

Introduction

Carol H. Meyer

WHY THIS BOOK?

During its accreditation by the Council on Social Work Education in 1991, the Columbia University School of Social Work was asked to develop a foundation course in social work practice. This course was to be an introduction to social work practice for graduate students who were preparing to enter one of three advanced curricular tracks, called at Columbia, clinical practice; practice, programming, and supervision; and social administration. After a complex preparatory period, the course was given in over a dozen sections. The faculty who taught the course in the first year met regularly to develop it, learning several things in the process. First, they learned that entering students who are preoccupied with learning skills immediately for fieldwork practice must have an opportunity to study those skills in the classroom. In view of the range of content that had to be taught in this course, time had to be allocated for the development of the skills. Thus, a third classroom hour was added to the normal two-hour class time for this purpose. This course model raised many questions, such as these: How would such a course be organized and arranged in sequence, given the range and amount of subject matter to be taught? What was to be included, and what was to be left for more advanced courses?

Second, the faculty discovered that a graduate-level textbook was needed because the existing texts (Hepworth & Larsen, 1990; Sheafor, Horejsi, & Horejsi, 1994), helpful as they were, were written primarily for undergraduate students. Their concern about a textbook led the faculty to ponder the differences between graduate- and undergraduate-level teaching, even though the bachelor's- and master's-level foundation courses might cover the same subjects. But would the content of the two courses be the same? What were the distinctions in teaching this course on the graduate level, and could they be articulated?

Finally, it became evident that to develop a foundation course, the faculty would have to come to grips with the nature of social work itself to be able to extract its essence and to condense it so it could be presented in an introductory, yet comprehensive, course. This realization raised questions about priorities and ideologies. The choice of what to teach is a professional–political decision, and given that the field has such extensive boundaries, there

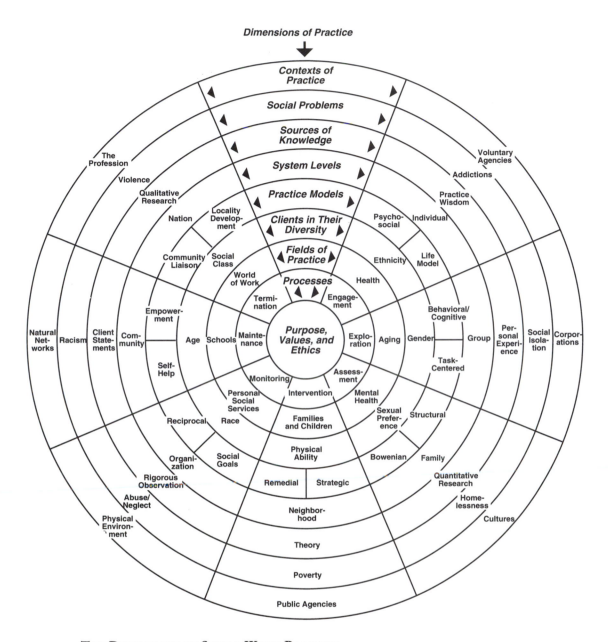

THE DIMENSIONS OF SOCIAL WORK PRACTICE

is no one right answer to what should be emphasized. Fortunately, the Columbia faculty were sufficiently diverse in their philosophical commitments that there was little risk that the course (when taught by over a dozen people) would be monolithic. The primary task was conceptual: to decide on a framework and to select the components of social work that are universally accepted as essential. The next task was to decide how much theoretical difference could be absorbed into an introductory course that was to be a graduate student's first encounter with the real-world professional issues in social work. The process of developing this course came to reflect the wider professional dialogue, thus providing a degree of validity to the character of the course itself.

This book was also written to give the faculty the opportunity to articulate what they had learned about extracting the essentials of the profession and translating them into a course. The results (it was hoped) would affirm that a common framework, purpose, history, knowledge base, commitment to certain values and ethics, and recognizable repertoire of skills define social work practice. This book is intended to provide graduate social work students with the socializing experience of becoming potential professional colleagues in an evolving profession. In this book and the course in which it is used, the students will learn what is known in social work, but, perhaps what is more important, they will become familiar and comfortable with the fact that the profession (like all others) is uncertain in some of its purposes, unfinished in its preferred outcomes, and sufficiently resilient that it can tolerate theoretical conflict within its agreed-on frameworks. For graduate students, the thread of indefiniteness should encourage them to think for themselves, to sort out what works and what does not, and to arrive at their own orientation to practice. If this book does nothing other than expose students to an open system of ideas, then it will have succeeded as a graduate text. Thus, in the sense of this course and this book, "foundations" does not mean basic; it means core, essential, and comprehensive. The foundation course and the book should serve as an icon for social work practice in that what students learn in them will resonate throughout their succeeding courses and fieldwork experiences.

THE COMPLEXITY OF SOCIAL WORK PRACTICE

Social work encompasses a wide range of interests, and its multidimensional focus requires a broad base of knowledge and an equally broad repertoire of methods and skills. The scope of social work reaches from attention to the individual, family, group, and community to the arena of social policy. Social workers work with adults and children of different economic classes, racial and ethnic groups, cultures, and sexual identification in hospitals, clinics, social agencies, schools, institutions, and community centers as well as on the street and at home. Their interventions span the realms of prevention and protection, support and rehabilitation. Among the many social problems in which social workers intervene in the matrix just described are family dysfunction, child neglect and abuse, marital conflict, separation and divorce, adolescent adjustment, problems of aging, adaptation to physical and mental illness, homelessness, substance abuse, unemployment and job training, and child care. This postindustrial, technological society has engendered new lifestyles, a new degree of social isolation, and heightened tensions among cultures and generations, and people have responded differentially with depression, violence, or withdrawal. These responses are reflected in the caseloads of all social workers.

This is the bare outline of the context in which social workers practice, and given the complexity of the tasks, the practice of social work has become equally complex. The typical professional social worker must be skillful in multiple roles as an advocate, therapist, counselor, mentor, case manager, group leader, community organizer, agent of change, program developer, and evaluator. The ability to assume these roles flexibly, under different circumstances as particular cases demand, is not inborn. No one is prepared to assume this level of responsibility for others' welfare without professional education, which includes the mastery of an essential base of knowledge that is relevant to the domain of social work. This knowledge is usually conceptualized broadly as human growth and behavior, social science, social policy, and social work history and philosophy. When broken down into specific categories, it is made applicable to the varied problems and conditions that are reflected in social work cases. The intellectual and experiential demands on social workers notwithstanding, an additional dimension surrounds professional practice: the framework of ethics and values that must be internalized as a permanent guide to professional actions.

Social work is a social institution and, as such, carries certain mandates in the fields or arenas of health, welfare, and education. In each of these fields, whether in family and child welfare agencies, hospitals, or schools (or their extensions in the community), one may say that the social worker's focus is on the psychosocial welfare of clients. Except in the case of family and child welfare, in which social work traditionally has been the primary service, social workers in "host agencies" such as hospitals; clinics; schools; and, increasingly, in the workplace; in institutions for elderly people, children, and people with disabilities; and in correctional institutions carry out similar practices as in family and children's services, albeit with a different focus. These fields and social institutions represent the concerns of the American public and are supported by laws, statutes, and ordinances that provide legal sanction and funding by all levels of government. They are also supported in the voluntary sector by philanthropy and the leadership of boards of directors. The social welfare, health, and educational institutions of the United States are its largest social and economic investment; therefore, it would appear that social work is a mainstream profession.

Historically, the profession has been organizationally based, partially because of the early social assignment and commitment of social workers to work with poor people and partially because the breadth and complexity of necessary social services require organizational support. In other words, given the scope and interconnectedness of all clients' activities and needs, it is efficacious to provide services in organizations. With regard to poor people, whose private resources are severely limited, publicly supported organizationally based services can be the only route to the assistance they need. The notion of bureaucracy may seem anathema to some, but bureaucracies became a permanent fact of life with the rise of industrialism and the urban world. One may as well decry civilization as we know it as wish away bureaucracies. For example, although few people would choose to be a patient in a hospital, one could not imagine any other way to receive modern medical care. Similarly, schools are in great need of upgrading, but one could not imagine organizing a learning community of students in any other way but in schools. Likewise, social agencies that offer multiple services could not function in any other way but to pool their resources within organizational boundaries. Since the 1970s much has been learned by social workers and others about humanizing bureaucracies, both for employees and for consumers of services, and the development of electronic communications is greatly changing organizations for the better by enhancing data collection, analysis, and retrieval.

Social work, like all professions, is not an academic pursuit, but an applied practice, and thus its knowledge and professional roles and values have to be expressed in action. In social work, this action, or methodology, is loosely defined as practice with individuals, families, groups, and communities. All the many approaches that are in use incorporate the components of gathering or exploring the data of a "case," assessing and evaluating the case, and applying interventions differentially. This is the commonly held framework of action in all professional practices. Flowing from this multidimensional context are the actual skills, the moment-to-moment actions carried out by practitioners in their multiple professional roles. These skills are almost beyond counting, for each role that is carried out demands particular skills. Clinically, these skills may be verbal expressions or body language, the right words at the right time, or a touch when it is needed. Advocacy may require a different type of behavior, and organizational activity requires consensus-building skills. All professional skills are embedded in one's understanding of the case one is working with; all skills emanate from the context that shapes their use.

The task of social work education is to prepare social workers for entry-level professional practice. In view of the complexity of the field and the inevitability of specialization in so many requisite areas of knowledge, it is important to have one place in the social work curriculum where "the whole" of social work can be studied. This comprehensive view of the field has been translated into a foundation course whose purpose is to provide students with a place in their education where they can learn about the range and spaciousness of their profession and where they can become comfortable with the connectedness of it all. Like a telescope, the various components just described are embedded in each other, and at the end, when students look through the skills lens, they will understand that this lens is the extension of the context, knowledge, methods, and values lenses to which the skills lens is connected.

THE GRADUATE-LEVEL FOUNDATION COURSE

The master's-level student in social work has taken undergraduate courses in the liberal arts and may have majored in a social science, the humanities, or social work. What, then, is the difference between graduate-level and undergraduate-level education that is rooted in liberal arts and draws heavily from the social sciences and the humanities? First, in graduate-level education, there is the assumption of a common language, in that students should have mastered the basic concepts in sociology and psychology and have become familiar with history and literature. This grasp of the elements of "the foundation" enables the graduate student to go as far beyond the basics as he or she is capable of going. The graduate instructor can then go beyond as well, to the pinnacle of what he or she knows beyond the common language. Second, because the graduate student will know the essentials of certain subjects, the graduate instructor will be free not only to build on the base but to help the student diversify his or her search for more knowledge. Third, on the assumption that undergraduate education has provided the student with the tools for thinking critically, the graduate student will come to a master's-degree program with more questions than answers. This open-mindedness will enable the graduate school instructor to generate more questions, so by the end of his or her graduate education, the student will be adept at critical thinking.

Not only must the foundation course introduce students to the complexity of social work, for that is the real world of practice, but it can begin to help them recognize (and learn to live with) theoretical complexity, diversity, and conflict. This is one of the most important features of the foundation course—that its introduction to the field is forthright in its representation of social work. The profession is fragmented in that practice theories reflect different and often conflicting worldviews and there is no agreement on the contours of specialization: Should it be defined in relation to population groups, problem areas, methods, or fields of practice? Given a field whose boundaries are so flexible that it expands and contracts depending on where practice is located, social workers always have to draw reasonable boundaries around their own roles. One need not know about everything, but where are the limits? How does one balance breadth and depth in both knowledge and skills? In a world in which specialization is valued, what does it mean for social workers whose cases usually require the provision of many kinds of services at the same time? How does the social worker move from advocate to clinician relatively seamlessly? These are but a few of the competing demands on the minds and actions of social work students as they move into their professional careers. The graduate-level foundation course will help to identify these demands and will demonstrate that all the seemingly loose threads and disparate components of the field are indeed interwoven.

Relationship to the Total Curriculum
Because the foundation course is comprehensive and connected to the real world of social work, it must also be connected to the total curriculum of which it is but one part. Each school of social work draws its own configuration of the curriculum, so it is not possible in this text to make definitive connections with every curriculum. However, all schools follow some general guidelines, although the courses they include may have different titles or be taught in combination and in different sequences. The next sections present some of the basic general concepts that all schools include.

Human behavior and the social environment
Social work practice attends to individuals, who relate to each other in intimate groups such as families and extended families; friendship, support, and

interest groups; and neighborhoods. Through these relationships, people find community in private and in public arenas. Social workers' knowledge of the developmental course of life is important for understanding people in their individuality and for adapting professional expectations to the capacities of individuals. Individual development ideally takes place in families, which may take many different forms. The need for relatedness is an aspect of the human social imperative, and depending on such variables as cultural differences, generational interests, and gender and class characteristics, people relate to each other in groups that are small or large, intimate or open. All people belong to communities that may emanate from where they live or work or where they find shared interests. The diversity of people's cultural and sexual orientations and racial and ethnic identities must be recognized and understood as part of their characters and lifestyles.

Society may fail to provide the nutritive supports for people at all stages of their lives, and people may incur deficits in their development owing to genetic or emotional dysfunction or trauma. Thus, social workers must know about acute and chronic illness, both physical and mental, and must recognize and work with lags in physical, social, and cognitive development. Furthermore, they must learn to distinguish clinically defined pathologies, ranging from psychosis to depression, from reactions to problems that are generated by destructive personal or social situations. The psychological, biological, and social sciences describe these essential ("normal" and pathological) features of the people with whom social workers practice, and the foundations course draws heavily on this field of knowledge.

Social policy, social welfare, and history

The profession of social work is not autonomous; it is embedded in the political, economic, and social structures of this country. Social policies govern social work practice through their definitions of social problems and the services that are to be supported by legislation and funding. Social welfare policies deal with child care; child neglect and abuse; and, to some extent, family well-being through policies on economic maintenance, youth, and aging. Related policies in health and education impinge on social work's functioning in those arenas, although their primary focus is on the provision of health care and education. However one defines the policy arena, the fundamental issue for social work practice is that policies govern, and the foundation course frames its content within a policy structure.

The range of services in which social workers are engaged requires such a large amount of knowledge that it is necessary for social workers to specialize because they cannot know everything about everything. One way to specialize is by fields of practice, such as family and child welfare, health and mental health, aging, work, and corrections—a construct that allows for the greatest flexibility. Each field is governed by particular social policies, funding streams, programs, types of problems, and a practice "culture." Although there are other ways for social workers to specialize, this book discusses fields of practice. The reader will find that it is a parsimonious and efficient way of organizing the profession in a framework of policy and programming. This form of specialization allows methodology to be generic and applicable to practice in all fields.

Over a hundred years of social work history have laid the groundwork for the current profession. It is through the study of this history that social workers can find explanations for both the rational and the irrational in social work institutions and programs. Just as social work cannot be understood as separate from the legal and economic frameworks of the society in which it is practiced, so, too, it cannot be viewed in a historical vacuum. Social work carries vestiges of the Elizabethan Poor Laws of the 17th century, as well as of the New Deal of the 1930s and the War on Poverty of the 1960s and 1970s. It has evolved through two world wars and too many lesser wars; it has reflected boom times and depressions, and it has weathered a host of ideological struggles. The curious student will find his or her own connections in this history and will recognize that the foundation course is only the most current expression of over a century of efforts to refine the contribution of social work to the well-being of society. Thus, the foundation course is presented within this context of social policy and history.

Research and evaluation

All professions are accountable to demonstrate not only what they do, but how effectively they perform. Professions are public, in the sense that they are both sanctioned by and are responsible to the public that supports them. It is not enough for the practitioner to claim success from his or her efforts in a case; success has to be confirmed; measured in some way; and, if possible, made replicable. Although social work practice is not a "hard science" and is always only one aspect of the influences in a client's life, which makes it difficult to determine its singular impact, the quest for validation must be pursued. Research in social work has developed rapidly since the early 1980s, and practitioners and scholars are working on ways to adapt research models to the complexities of practice. At the same time, they are creating new approaches to research that will be attuned to the ways in which practice is carried out.

Graduate-level social workers are expected to master the elements of research methodology for at least two reasons: to be able to read and evaluate research that illuminates the problems with which they are working and to be able to evaluate their own practice so they can demonstrate their effectiveness. Those who have further interests in learning more about the practice of social work can use research methodology to assess the needs of groups of clients, families, and communities; to search for the causes of problems that persist in this society; or to test and compare different practice approaches. Whichever route is chosen, the foundation course is framed in such a way that the graduate student will always be able to think about practice with questions framed for further research. That is how professional knowledge and competence will move forward.

Fieldwork

It is well known among social work educators that students believe that their greatest learning occurs in their practicum or fieldwork experience. This is as it should be in that experience with real clients in real organizations is the way one really learns. What is often not recognized is that whereas fieldwork practice is in the foreground, it is knowledge that shapes what the practitioner sees and understands in any case. Although the "doing" of practice skills is always the most exciting for students, it is the context and purpose of those skills that justify their use. The social work curriculum described earlier is not really background: rather, it is ever present—almost as an active participant in practice processes. It is not possible structurally to teach all that must be learned in the fieldwork experience, and it is not a real experience to teach skills in the classroom as a laboratory. Yet, ideally, teaching in both the classroom and the field should combine knowledge and skills as they exist in professional practice. Good field instruction introduces theory, and good classroom teaching of practice introduces skills, or the application of theory. The foundation course attempts to achieve this goal, and this book is ever mindful of maintaining this connection.

How to Use This Book

The table of contents describes the chapters in the book, and chapter 1 explains the book's rationale and sequencing. Because each school will have its own rationale for ordering and teaching the foundation course, the book allows for "mixing and matching." The reader will discover that graphics help him or her to grasp concepts and that different theoretical perspectives can exist alongside each other with ease. The graphic at the beginning of each chapter highlights the practice elements emphasized within that chapter. The elements that are not shaded are those that are emphasized in the chapter. Recalling that social work is a complex field, the book deals with that complexity, and thus is not an "easy read." Yet, the authors have made every effort to write as teachers to help the student reader master the content. The central purposes of the foundation course, as expressed in this book, are to introduce graduate students to the content of social work practice and to ensure that the knowledge and experiences they accumulate beyond this course will strike a familiar note because they read it here.

References

Hepworth, D. H., & Larsen, J. (1990). *Direct social work practice: Theory and skills* (3rd ed.). Belmont, CA: Wadsworth.

Sheafor, B. W., Horejsi, C. R., & Horejsi, G. A. (1994). *Techniques and guidelines for social work practice* (3rd ed.). Boston: Allyn & Bacon.

The Foundations of Social Work Practice

Mark A. Mattaini

The purpose of social work is to enhance adaptations among clients (whether they are individuals, families, communities, or other entities) and the systems within which the clients are embedded—the environment. (A *system* is any organized entity that exists and adapts over time—see chapter 2 for a comprehensive discussion of general systems theory.) Private troubles and public issues (Mills, 1959) reflect difficulties in these adaptations. Although professionals of other disciplines are often interested in some of the same problems, their core professional purposes are different (Meyer, 1993). Medicine, including psychiatry, is concerned with curing illness and enhancing health, essentially an individually focused mission. Psychology is primarily a science; when applied it also tends to focus on the individual, with special emphasis on mental phenomena (although psychology has its own professional struggles, between a "science of the mind" and a "science of behavior," for example). In contrast, social work is, at its core, concerned with the person-in-situation. In early developmental stages of the profession, caseworkers looked at both the person and his or her environment, maintaining a dual focus, in which each aspect was alternately the foreground and the background. It was difficult to find ways of conceptualizing the interactions, of seeing the interconnections between the client and the environment as the foreground, but early social workers tried to do so.

Given the purpose of social work, it is clear that social workers need to understand individuals and environments and how they interrelate; this is perhaps the most complex assignment of any profession. Issues with which contemporary social workers grapple every day (for example, the acquired immune deficiency syndrome [AIDS] crisis or the increasing family breakdown and violence that are associated with drug abuse) clearly demonstrate this complexity, but it has also been true historically. One has only to read the work of Charles Loring Brace (1872/1973) or Mary Richmond (1917) to see that solutions have never been easy.

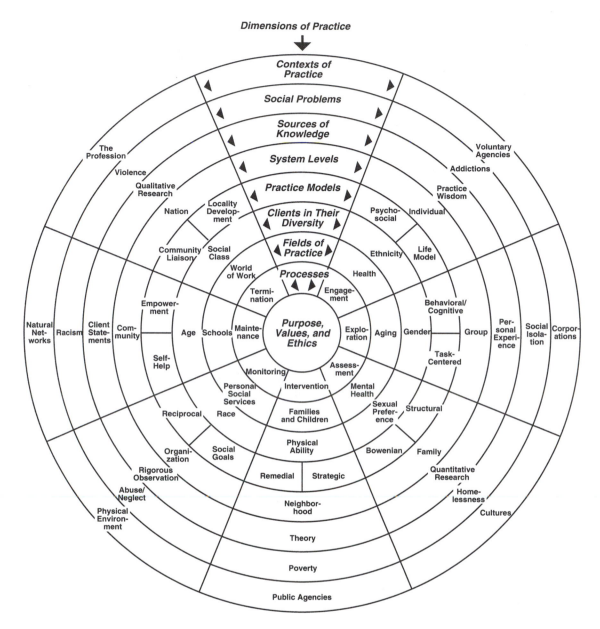

FIGURE 1-1. THE FOUNDATIONS OF SOCIAL WORK PRACTICE
Note: In many dimensions, such as social problems and practice models, the items noted are common examples, not a comprehensive list.

Although many functions of social work practice can be performed effectively by paraprofessionals and bachelor's-level staff, the primary function of the graduate-level social worker is not so much simply to act as to understand the perplexing intricacies of the client's unique dilemma and to develop intervention strategies that are based on that understanding. Therefore, professional practice cannot be based on simple formulas or step-by-step prescriptions. One never knows enough, and as the social worker faces the full complexities of social problems, comprehensive understanding is elusive. The professional social worker recognizes these facts, and still must decide with the client what is to be done, even when there is little that can be done.

It is important to recognize that differences in theoretical and interventive approaches that characterize practice are not just academic. Social workers make decisions that occasionally mean the difference between life and death and that often contribute to the difference between a life of active empowerment and one of pain and unfulfilled promise. For any case, all interventions are not equivalent and interchangeable. For example, in child protective settings, Peile (1993) suggested the adoption of a "creative worldview" in which the social worker "no longer [seeks] to control and predict her effects on [the client] and his parenting behavior" but rather to "create a context that maximizes potential for [the father] to behave creatively with his son" (p. 132). (In the case example that Peile presented, the client had seriously injured his six-year-old child.) In a more traditional approach to the same case, the social worker, as a representative of society, would consider his or her primary responsibility to be the safety of the child (making use of existing empirical knowledge about ameliorating child maltreatment) (see Howing, Wodarski, Gaudin, & Kurtz, 1989). The decision about which way to work clearly matters. Different approaches sometimes lead to very different interventions, which in turn affect a client's well-being in crucial ways, so it is essential for the social worker to know how to distinguish effectively among practice approaches (Meyer, 1983) and theoretical models. (Values must guide such decisions; in general, professional and social values suggest that minimizing the short- and long-term risk to the child ought to be the overriding consideration in child protection.)

The social work practitioner needs to see—and know—everything at the same time. It is not possible to look at and deal first with a client's emotional state, then the possible effects of family dynamics, then the effects of racial and cultural factors. Adequate assessment in social work requires "thinking big"—seeing the full transactional situation all at once (Meyer, 1993). The practice setting, the field of practice, the behavioral roots of the problem, and larger sociocultural factors are among the numerous facets of every case.

Practice can perhaps be seen as a rope made up of many strands, all of which work together to achieve the "purpose" of the rope (see Figure 1-2). These strands include knowledge, skills, values and ethics, and commitment, all of which inform practice decisions. Each strand, in turn, consists of multiple threads. Because all graduate-level social workers need certain core knowledge from each strand, but will pursue specific threads differentially depending on the practice situation and their stage of professional development, no attempt is made here to trace every thread completely. It is not possible to say everything that needs to be said in any book or course or at any point in time. Rather, readers are encouraged to explore and test those areas that are significant to them and their clients in an ongoing, self-directed process of professional education. Throughout the process, remembering that the threads and strands of the profession are always intertwined will help to ground these inquiries.

Not only can a rope be stretched out linearly, it can curve and loop back on itself. This nonlinearity also characterizes practice, and thus it is not surpris-

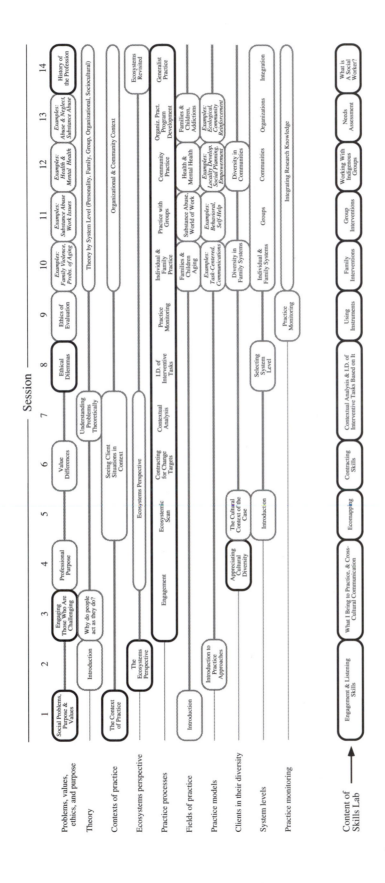

FIGURE 1-2. THE CONTENT OF A COURSE ON THE FOUNDATIONS OF SOCIAL WORK PRACTICE

Note: The content is organized for a 14-week term; this is only one of many possible ways to structure the course. Also note that all strands intertwine, but that they are shown linearly here for simplicity. All strands are implicit in all sessions, but the emphasis varies; metaphorically, the thickness of each strand varies by session. The course is organized around bold units, and major subthemes of each session are also expanded.

ing to find that the chapters that follow include transactional mixes of knowledge, skills, and practice examples. Although the chapters can be read in any order, ultimately the subjects discussed in all of them make up the core of professional practice and are organically connected and indivisible.

CENTRAL METAPHOR: THE WHEEL

The image of the wheel (Figure 1-1) that introduced this chapter is also found, with variations, at the beginning of each of the following chapters. This figure suggests that every practice event involves factors from each ring of the wheel, which conceptually can be rotated independently. In other words, at any moment the social worker may be engaged in, say, assessment or termination with an individual or a family in a school or a child welfare setting, applying a task-centered or a psychosocial practice model, and so forth.

The segments of each ring that are the foreground in each chapter are highlighted in the wheel introducing that chapter, but the others are implicitly present as well. In a chapter on work with families, for example, the reader may find a statement that some family members have been referred for group services. Or, if the chapter on group work emphasizes social work in health and family service settings, it does not mean that much of the content does not also apply to social work in agencies serving primarily elderly people. Deciding what segments can or must be ignored—although they are present—is often as important as deciding what to focus on at each moment.

Note that the wheel is only one way to divide artificially what is, in reality, an indivisible whole; there are many other valid ways that the professional knowledge base could be partitioned. All the rings are introduced (as opposed to summarized—an impossible task) in the sections that follow; subsequent chapters discuss them in greater depth and begin to integrate them into a holistic view of practice.

Professional Purpose, Values, and Ethics

Meyer (1993) suggested that "social work claims as its central purpose the enhancement of adaptations between individuals, families, groups, communities—and their particular environments" (p. 18), referring to a definition of clinical social work developed in 1979 (Ewalt, 1979). She noted that this central focus on the person-in-environment construct is unique to social work, despite interdisciplinary overlaps in "skills and selected knowledge" (p. 18). Notice that this definition is broad enough to include both cause and function, but narrow enough to discriminate social work from other professions. For now, this definition will be accepted as characterizing the core of the profession's identity, recognizing that continued flux is a certainty.

The distinction and balance between *function*—a set of treatment activities carried out with the sanction of the larger society—and *cause*—the organized effort to advocate for oppressed populations (Lee, 1929)—has been an ongoing debate in the profession. Both personal troubles and public issues

(Malagodi & Jackson, 1989; Mills, 1959) have always concerned social workers, even as the level of relative interest in each has ebbed and flowed.

Although the purpose of the profession as a whole may be as was just described, every person begins graduate social work education for his or her own reasons. Thinking these reasons through explicitly and discussing them with peers can help a student clarify his or her personal priorities in ways that are valuable for the conscious development of a professional identity.

As can be seen in Figure 1-1, the central ring of the wheel consists of professional purpose, values, and ethics, with which all practice is imbued. In addition to purpose, common values (for example, a client's right to self-determination and to gain access to what he or she needs to maintain life and dignity) are characteristic of social work, as are common ethics. Values and ethics are not easy to apply in practice. For example, although self-determination seems straightforward, if the social worker recognizes that not all human behavior is under the unconstrained, conscious control of the person, limitations on the potential for self-determination are evident. And when one individual's right to self-determination conflicts with his or her own or another person's right to safety (as when an elderly patient in a hospital setting insists, against the wishes of family members, on returning to an apartment where he or she has been robbed several times before), the social worker must make difficult decisions. These may be further complicated by organizational factors; for example, a high-status physician may forcefully insist on nursing home placement, resulting in potential conflict between the medical and social work departments.

Sources of Knowledge

An organized knowledge base is crucial to any profession. Bartlett (1970) emphasized the centrality of knowledge for practice, explicitly identifying values and knowledge as the "essential elements" in professional social work practice, as opposed to "method," which had historically been seen as the core of practice. Anyone can simply act; the professional is expected to act deliberately, taking the steps that are most likely to be helpful, parsimonious, and consistent with a client's welfare. Deciding on those steps requires an extensive knowledge base.

Among the sources of knowledge relevant to practice are the social worker's personal and professional experiences; "practice wisdom" (often only partially systematized) gleaned from colleagues and supervisors; reports of quantitative and qualitative research; and information obtained by listening to and observing clients. Theory—coherent systems for understanding behavioral and social phenomena—and practice models also provide guidance for practice at a different level. Different sources sometimes suggest conflicting actions. The social worker then must act on the basis of the information that he or she has evaluated as being the most relevant and rigorous. Rigor involves accuracy and objectivity, but even these, as will be seen in chapter 5, are difficult concepts to capture. Nevertheless, practice that is based entirely on intuition or common sense is not only not professional by definition, but what is far more important, is likely to be ineffective. And effectiveness, when it can be achieved, is an ethical mandate.

Client Diversity

The clients that social workers see are highly diverse on many dimensions. Recognizing and learning about this diversity is not a matter of political correctness, but a crucial area of professional knowledge with substantial implications for practice. Clients differ in age, gender, health and physical ability, race, education, occupation, sexual preference, physical attractiveness, intellectual and verbal abilities, behavior, and in many other ways. In addition, individuals play out their lives as parts of multiple cultural entities of all sizes, from families to social classes to ethnic and religious groups. Social workers commonly need to learn to be effective not only within their own group, but across sometimes deep rifts of credibility and trust. (Any social worker's "own" group would include only a small minority of people, considering the dimensions noted here, which is only a partial list.) If our multicultural society is to work, differences must be understood and valued as sources of potentially useful variations for enriching the lives of members of all cultures. Unfortunately, these divisions are often bitter, as a result of various groups' long history of oppression and disrespect in this country; thus, bridging these gaps is a critical professional—and cultural—challenge.

A good deal is known about sensitivity to differences and even, to some extent, about specific approaches that tend to be valuable in practice with members of particular groups (Ho, 1987; McGoldrick, Pearce, & Giordano, 1982; Sue & Zane, 1987). However, every client is an individual, not just an accumulation of various descriptive categories, and levels of biculturalism and acculturation differ, as do personal life experiences. Hence, it is almost paradoxical that although a deep awareness of differences sensitizes the social worker, the essence of culturally sensitive practice is to be able to individualize a case without being blinded by categorical labels (Thyer, 1994).

Fields of Practice

Most social work practice—even private practice—is performed as part of service systems. Social work has been conducted within such "fields of practice" throughout its history. For example, the report of the Milford Conference (*Social Casework: Generic and Specific,* 1929/1974) listed family welfare, child welfare, visiting teaching, medical social work, psychiatric social work, and probation work as recognizable and internally coherent fields. Contemporary fields include families and children, health care, aging, mental health, school-based services, and industrial social work, among others.

Conceptual difficulties in finding the "bright lines" (Ainslie, 1993) that separate fields are many; note, for example, that the partial list just provided includes fields discriminated by setting, developmental stage, and type of problem. Nevertheless, each field has a certain ad hoc coherence because institutional structures, funding streams, and social policies tend to be organized along these lines, and each provides access to clients at important "crossroads of life" (Meyer, 1976). Fields are also continually evolving, with some fading and others emerging at any point in time.

Many professions tend to specialize in similar conceptually inelegant but practically meaningful ways; medicine designates specialties by age (pediatrics), gender (gynecology), method (surgery), body parts (cardiology), and many others, including combinations. Fields also change over time in all professions; for example, law firms specializing in workers' compensation and personal injury expect these areas to decline in importance if universal health care coverage is established and are moving to expand into emerging practice areas.

Social Problems

Social work exists to address social problems (Reid, 1977). Although writers sometimes speak in terms of enhancement, of improving the quality of people's lives, social work's historic mission is related primarily to the severe problems with which people, families, and communities grapple, with ameliorating (or preventing) difficulties and intervening in crises. These problems include violence (domestic and nondomestic), the maltreatment of children, substance abuse, homelessness, poverty, racism, isolation, and mental and physical illnesses.

Social workers know a good deal about many of these problems, about their epidemiology and etiology and about what may be helpful when a client system is faced with them. There is no substitute for in-depth knowledge about the issues one's clients are dealing with, and staying up-to-date with current knowledge is an ethical imperative. For example, there is a substantial knowledge base about which practice strategies are effective and under which circumstances for work with clients with substance abuse problems (Miller, 1980, 1989). For instance, one treatment approach, the Community Reinforcement Approach, has been demonstrated in multiple studies to be substantially superior to traditional treatment for both inpatients and outpatients with serious alcohol (Sisson & Azrin, 1989) and drug problems (Budney, Higgins, Delaney, Kent, & Bickel, 1991; Higgins, Budney, & Bickel, 1994). Although social workers need not apply this approach with every client with a substance abuse problem, if they will be working with such clients, they probably have an ethical mandate to know about it, so that together, they and their clients can reach an informed decision about whether to use it.

Practice Processes

Practice is nonlinear, but it is not random or chaotic. Certain processes must occur if social workers are to be helpful. These processes tend to occur in a rough order, although they are recursive, and social workers will often find themselves cycling backward to move ahead.

First, the social worker must be able to engage the client in a genuine human relationship, not as a separate process, but organically throughout the work. A good deal of research has supported what every skilled worker knows: that the facilitating conditions of empathic communication, warmth and respect, and authenticity are crucial. These principles were first elaborated by

Carl Rogers (Rogers, 1957) and were subsequently explicitly adopted and adapted by social workers (see, for example, Hepworth & Larsen, 1993), who had for many years recognized the centrality of the helping relationship (Perlman, 1979). The social worker who cannot achieve these necessary—but not sufficient—conditions will fail with most clients. A complication is that people are often not the best judges of their own interpersonal skills, so that supervised practice, including feedback, is generally essential for ensuring competence in these skills.

Assuming that a social worker has these basic skills, he or she must then know how to intervene to help. Intervention is always rooted in data about a particular case that are uncovered during exploration and are organized in a coherent way in an individualizing assessment. These processes, central to effective practice, are discussed in subsequent chapters.

Practice Models

Although individual cases, and therefore specific interventions for each, are unique, the social worker seldom must develop overall interventive strategies de novo. Practice models are organized systems of intervention that are designed to be applied in relatively consistent ways across multiple cases (including groups and communities). Not only do practice models permit social workers to apply what has been learned from other cases to the current one, they are valuable in making explicit how the social worker understands the case situation and what is to be done about it. In other words, when using a practice model, the social worker does not depend exclusively on amorphous, unarticulated intuition, which is no doubt always present, but also engages in thoughtful analysis.

Some practice models are rooted in specific behavioral science theories, but others are not. The psychosocial model of practice has traditionally been rooted in psychodynamic thought (including contemporary ego psychology, self psychology, and object relations theory) (Goldstein, 1984), for example, whereas behavioral and cognitive-behavioral models emerged from operant, respondent, and social learning theories (Schwartz, 1983). The task-centered model (Reid, 1992), on the other hand, was designed to be applied regardless of the underlying theoretical base. The life model (Germain & Gitterman, 1980) applies ecological theory, focusing on mutuality in adaptation between the person and his or her environment.

Practice models are valuable because they provide specific guidance to social workers about "what to do." Social workers can appropriately use techniques from different practice models at different times, using crisis intervention for psychosocial crises, techniques from a cognitive approach for some kinds of depression, and psychoeducation when working with clients with severe mental illnesses. At the same time, it is crucial to avoid random eclecticism. Every social worker needs a basic framework for understanding the phenomena of a case: individual behavior, family dynamics, and sociocultural forces. For example, in work with an individual it would be a serious mistake to apply concepts from object relations and behavioral theories in a random mix. Such an approach would generally lead to confusion because each theory defines terms and core issues differently and prescribes often conflicting interventions (Kohlenberg & Tsai, 1991).

The existence of multiple practice models does not mean, however, that social workers have nothing in common. In addition to social workers having common core purposes, values, and knowledge, the person-in-situation construct suggests that all social workers need a way to look broadly at cases that capture the interconnectedness of the cases. The ecosystems perspective (see chapter 2) is a conceptual framework for doing so that has achieved nearly universal acceptance in the profession. This perspective provides guidance about how to look at cases, but not what to do about what one finds. Practice models are designed to do the latter.

System Levels

Social workers are professionally concerned with individuals, groups, couples, families, neighborhoods, formal and informal organizations, communities, and societies. Each of these systems is made up of subsystems and itself constitutes a subsystem of higher-order systems. System levels are organized hierarchically, so a particular system (say, an individual) may at one moment be viewed as the focal system, at another as a subsystem of another (a family). General systems theory (see chapter 2) has proven helpful in identifying what these disparate systems have in common (for example, exchange of resources and energy with their environments across boundaries and the notion of hierarchical organization). At the same time, each level (individual systems, family systems, community systems, and so forth) has its own coherence. What happens in families is the aggregate of what individuals do, but is often best understood at its own level; for example, families establish and maintain regular patterns, their own "cultural practices," which tend to continue over time, even when they may be costly (emotionally, physically, or otherwise) to some or all of the individuals involved. Even a simple parent–child dyad, for instance, can fall into a repetitive coercive spiral, unpleasant for both, which can be understood only if one looks at the pattern of exchanges through an adequate theoretical lens (Patterson, 1976).

To be effective, the advanced generalist (see chapter 12) needs specific knowledge about each system level and how all the levels fit together, but even specialists must know something about each. If the social worker knows only about individuals, he or she is likely to view every case through an individual lens. If, however, he or she has learned to concurrently observe and, when indicated, work with multiple system levels, the available options expand dramatically (Nelsen, 1975).

Contexts of Practice

All practice occurs in a context and the context shapes the practice. Context refers to the systems that constitute the environment of the case, sometimes at a substantial distance. For example, over the next few years national policy initiatives in health care will have a major impact on the way social workers deal with cases. There is likely to be a greater emphasis on managed care networks and less emphasis on a private, entrepreneurial model of care. Therefore, the importance of focused, short-term work, which has been growing for some time, will increase further.

Clients, workers, agencies, and service systems are always embedded in contexts. In work with an individual, for example, family or informal natural networks often are resources for the work, but can also be sources of the problem and obstacles to intervention (Reid, 1992). Contextual factors that influence practice include (but are not limited to) the physical environment, natural networks, institutions, voluntary agencies, corporations, cultures, and the profession itself. In every "case," the potential positive and negative effects of contextual factors must inform the social worker's thought. Obviously, those that are particularly salient in a case are likely to occupy the foreground, but it is important not to ignore others that may have less obvious, but still meaningful, effects on the case. It can also be valuable to think through contextual factors that affect cases within organizational networks, to take a fresh look now and then, and to think about the implications of these forces for achieving the organizational mission.

THE FINAL METAPHOR: THE NET

Imagine that you are working with a neglected girl. It probably makes sense to you that your purpose relates to doing something about the fit between the child and her environment; that factors related to culture and social class, as well as to her mother's mental illness, may be relevant; and that it is important to understand the girl's emotional functioning, the mother's behavior, and the lack of positive exchanges between them. It is also necessary to apply what is known about neglect from research and practice experience to select the best practice model, and to examine agency- and policy-level structures that may affect the case. And while you think about all these factors, you must build genuine, empathic, respectful relationships with the child, the mother, and perhaps a "kinship" foster parent (a relative serving as a foster parent).

The challenge seems clear: You cannot sequentially step through each ring of the wheel until you have established an effective and efficient case plan. All these factors and their interconnections must be present at the same time. Figure 1-3 depicts the sort of conceptual net that is required.

As the social worker carrying the case, you must filter data through this richly interconnected net until the "event shape" (roughly the complex configuration of what is happening in the client's life) (Auerswald, 1987) of the case emerges. As you would expect, it takes a significant amount of time before all these things happen automatically. Visual depictions and simulations of the case can be helpful tools in this process (Mattaini, 1993; Meyer, 1993). Graphic images have a broad bandwidth; they can be seen "all at once." Figure 1-4, for example, is a sequential ecomap (Hartman, 1978; Mattaini, 1993)

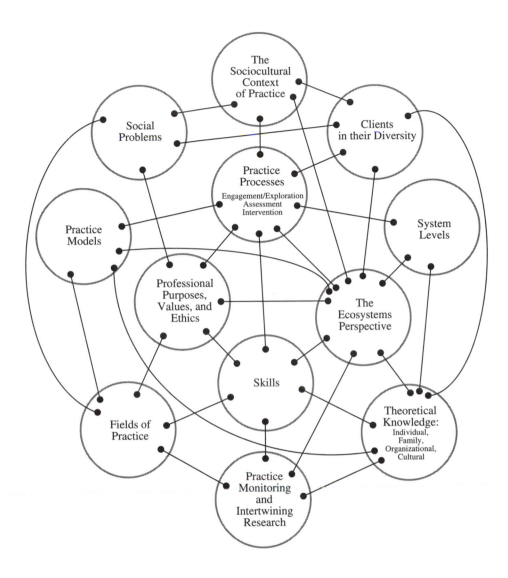

FIGURE 1-3. THE RICHLY INTERCONNECTED CONCEPTUAL MATRIX OF
SOCIAL WORK PRACTICE

portraying changes over time in the case of a 41-year-old depressed single man. Note that at the beginning of the case (the upper-left panel) you can look not only at the particular positive and negative interactions that the client experienced, but at the configuration of the case holistically; overall, the client is isolated and has few meaningful connections anywhere. Moving clockwise, you can observe changes in both the specifics and the broader pattern over time and how they relate to the presenting problem.

Other approaches for seeing the case in its interconnected wholeness with other phenomena are discussed throughout this volume. Although social workers usually find that, over time, it gets easier to recognize what is important quickly (instead of after the client leaves the office), it is always valuable

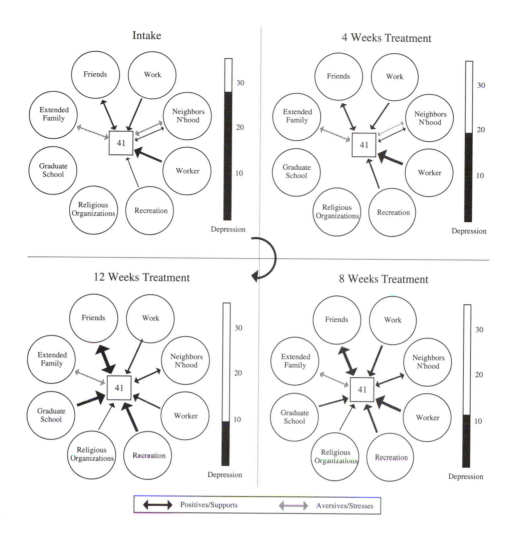

FIGURE 1-4. SEQUENTIAL ECOMAPS PORTRAYING THE CHANGING LIFE SITUATION AND DEPRESSION OF A CLIENT (USING THE BECK DEPRESSION INVENTORY) OVER 12 SESSIONS OF INTERPERSONAL THERAPY
Reprinted from Mattaini, M. A. (1993). More than a thousand words: Graphics for clinical practice *(p. 159). Washington, DC: NASW Press.*

to find ways to remind oneself of the organic manner in which the phenomena of a case are embedded in larger contextual matrices.

REFERENCES

Ainslie, G. (1993). A picoeconomic rationale for social constructionism. *Behavior and Philosophy, 21*(2), 63–75.

Auerswald, E. H. (1987). Epistemological confusion in family therapy and research. *Family Process, 26,* 317–330.

Bartlett, H. M. (1970). *The common base of social work practice*. New York: National Association of Social Workers.

Brace, C. L. (1973). *The dangerous classes of New York, & twenty years' work among them*. Washington, DC: National Association of Social Workers. (Original work published 1872)

Budney, A. J., Higgins, S. T., Delaney, D. D., Kent, L., & Bickel, W. K. (1991). Contingent reinforcement of abstinence with individuals abusing cocaine and marijuana. *Journal of Applied Behavior Analysis, 24,* 657–665.

Ewalt, P. (Ed.) (1979). *Toward a definition of clinical social work*. Washington, DC: National Association of Social Workers.

Germain, C. B., & Gitterman, A. (1980). *The life model of social work practice*. New York: Columbia University Press.

Goldstein, E. G. (1984). *Ego psychology and social work practice*. New York: Free Press.

Hartman, A. (1978). Diagrammatic assessment of family relationships. *Social Casework, 59,* 465–476.

Hepworth, D. H., & Larsen, J. A. (1993). *Direct social work practice* (4th ed.). Belmont, CA: Wadsworth.

Higgins, S. T., Budney, A. J., & Bickel, W. K. (1994). Applying behavioral concepts and principles to the treatment of cocaine dependence. *Drug & Alcohol Dependence, 34,* 87–97.

Ho, M. K. (1987). *Family therapy with ethnic minorities*. Newbury Park, CA: Sage Publications.

Howing, P. T., Wodarski, J. S., Gaudin, J. M., Jr., & Kurtz, P. D. (1989). Effective interventions to ameliorate the incidence of child maltreatment: The empirical base. *Social Work, 34,* 330–338.

Kohlenberg, R. J., & Tsai, M. (1991). *Functional analytic psychotherapy: Creating intense and curative therapeutic relationships*. New York: Plenum Press.

Lee, P. R. (1929). Social work: Cause and function. *Proceedings of the National Conference of Social Work*, pp. 3–20.

Malagodi, E. F., & Jackson, K. (1989). Behavior analysts and cultural analysis: Troubles and issues. *Behavior Analyst, 12,* 17–33.

Mattaini, M. A. (1993). *More than a thousand words: Graphics for clinical practice*. Washington, DC: NASW Press.

McGoldrick, M., Pearce, J. K., & Giordano, J. (1982). *Ethnicity and family therapy*. New York: Guilford Press.

Meyer, C. H. (1976). *Social work practice: The changing landscape* (2nd ed.). New York: Free Press.

Meyer, C. H. (1983). Selecting appropriate practice models. In A. Rosenblatt & D. Waldfogel (Eds.), *Handbook of clinical social work* (pp. 731–749). San Francisco: Jossey-Bass.

Meyer, C. H. (1993). *Assessment in social work practice.* New York: Columbia University Press.

Miller, W. R. (Ed.) (1980). *The addictive behaviors.* New York: Pergamon Press.

Miller, W. R. (1989). Matching individuals with interventions. In R. K. Hester & W. R. Miller (Eds.), *Handbook of alcoholism treatment approaches* (pp. 261–271). New York: Pergamon Press.

Mills, C. W. (1959). *The sociological imagination.* New York: Oxford University Press.

Nelsen, J. C. (1975). Social work's fields of practice, methods, and models: The choice to act. *Social Service Review, 49,* 264–270.

Patterson, G. R. (1976). The aggressive child: Victim and architect of a coercive system. In E. J. Mash, L. A. Hamerlynck, & L. C. Handy (Eds.), *Behavior modification and families* (pp. 267–316). New York: Brunner/Mazel.

Peile, C. (1993). Determinism versus creativity: Which way for social work? *Social Work, 38,* 127–134.

Perlman, H. H. (1979). *Relationship, the heart of helping people.* Chicago: University of Chicago Press.

Reid, W. J. (1977). Social work for social problems. *Social Work, 22,* 374–381.

Reid, W. J. (1992). *Task strategies.* New York: Columbia University Press.

Richmond, M. (1917). *Social diagnosis.* New York: Russell Sage Foundation.

Rogers, C. (1957). The necessary and sufficient conditions of therapeutic personality change. *Journal of Consulting Psychology, 22,* 95–103.

Schwartz, A. (1983). Behavioral principles and approaches. In A. Rosenblatt & D. Waldfogel (Eds.), *Handbook of clinical social work* (pp. 202–228). San Francisco: Jossey-Bass.

Sisson, R., & Azrin, N. (1989). The community reinforcement approach. In R. K. Hester & W. R. Miller (Eds.), *Handbook of alcoholism treatment approaches* (pp. 242–258). New York: Pergamon Press.

Social casework: Generic and specific (report of the Milford Conference). (1974). Washington, DC: National Association of Social Workers. (Original work published 1929)

Sue, S., & Zane, N. (1987). The role of culture and cultural techniques in psychotherapy. *American Psychologist, 42*(1), 37–45.

Thyer, B. A. (1994). Social learning theory: Empirical applications to culturally diverse practice. In R. R. Greene (Ed.), *Human behavior theory: Diversity applications.* New York: Aldine de Gruyter.

2

The Ecosystems Perspective: Implications for Practice

Carol H. Meyer

The term "ecosystems" appears at first glance to be abstract and unnecessarily complicated, but some understanding of why it was invented will help explain why it is used in modern social work practice. Since the beginning of the profession, practice has focused on the person *and* the environment, also called the inner and outer aspects of the case. This psychosocial focus is so important as a distinguishing feature of social work that it has become its identified purpose: to address the psychosocial aspects of individuals, families, groups, and communities. Although the person-in-environment concept has governed practice since 1917 (Richmond, 1917) and has been defined and redefined (Hamilton, 1951; Hollis, 1972) over the years, its hyphenated construction has contributed to the continuing imbalance in emphasis on the person *or* the environment. The term itself suggests that the person and the environment are independent of each other, so a practitioner could readily choose to see problems in one or the other aspect of a case. Among the consequences of attending to only the person or the environment have been that cases were frequently misunderstood. For example, a child who refused to attend school might have been treated for depression, with no attention paid to the role of his school or his family (his environment) in his behavior. Conversely, attention only to serious dysfunction in a school or a family might have led to ignoring the plight of a child's response. Often, practitioners would select a focus that was compatible with their preferences, assigning peripheral status to either the person or the environment.

Another consequence of the perceived separation of the person-in-environment construct has been the tendency of practitioners to avoid environmental interventions in favor of changing people in isolation from their life situations because the environment is so intractable and so difficult to affect. This emphasis has been encouraged by the development of knowledge of human development and a less well-developed, cohesive knowledge of the environment. Clinical social workers' choice to focus on the person to the exclusion of the environment may also have had something to do with the view that their professional status was dependent on their engaging in

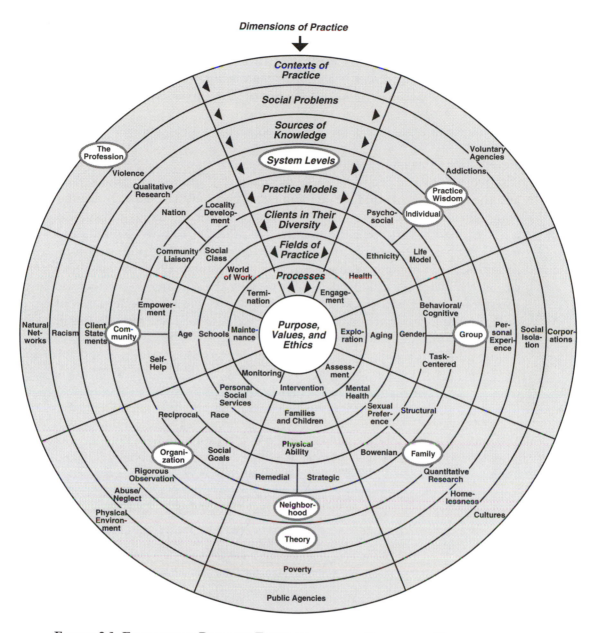

Dimensions of Practice

FIGURE 2-1. ELEMENTS OF PRACTICE EMPHASIZED IN THE ECOSYSTEMS PERSPECTIVE

practice that was like that of psychiatrists and psychotherapists. Thus, the psychosocial purposes of social work were being eroded, and the person-in-environment construct did not appear to be helping.

Beyond clinical consequences such as these, during the 1960s and 1970s the severe social upheaval brought to the fore awakened populations who were calling for social services. Previously noticed mainly in public services, poor people, ethnic and racial minority group members, women, people with severe social problems, and those with new lifestyles demanded help from social workers in the voluntary sector. Problems such as child abuse, family violence, acquired immune deficiency syndrome (AIDS), and homelessness caused all professions to redefine their approaches to account for the evident psychosocial features of these problems. By 1970 it was time to review and rethink the person-in-environment construct so that social workers would find it possible to intervene in a more *transactional* fashion in cases that were clearly (nonhyphenated) psychosocial events. The "invented" construct was called the "ecosystems perspective."

Ecosystems Perspective

The ecosystems perspective is a way of seeing case phenomena (the person and the environment) that are interconnected and multilayered to order and comprehend complexity and avoid oversimplification and reductionism. It is a way of placing conceptual boundaries around cases to provide limits and define the parameters of practice with individuals, families, groups, and communities. It can be pictorialized as an ecomap (Hartman 1978; Meyer, 1970) or a circle, which is a graphic device for viewing the relevant, connected case variables together, within a boundary that will offer the practitioner a unit of attention, or a case system as the focus of work. A typical ecomap of a case in social work practice may look like this:

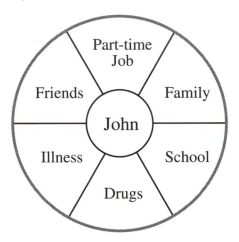

A fundamental purpose of all professional practice, including social work, is to individualize people. In the case of social work, this individualizing process applies to individuals, families, groups, and communities. Because no person can be understood apart from his or her defining social context, the ecomap presents a *field* of elements in which a person is embedded. The use of the ecomap makes it virtually impossible to separate the person and his or her environment in one's perception of the phenomena of a case. The ecomap represents a holistic picture of the case, and it changes the viewpoint of the one who is looking at it. It guides one to see connectedness and thus to eliminate the hyphen between the person and his or her environment. This idea is important because the way one presents and works with case data depends on one's habits of thought.

The term "ecosystems" (Auerswald, 1968; Meyer, 1976) encompasses two sets of ideas: *ecology* (DuBos, 1972) and *general systems theory* (GST) (von Bertalanffy, 1967). Ecology is the science that is concerned with the adaptive fit of organisms and their environments and the means by which they achieve a dynamic equilibrium and maturity. Drawn from biology, ecological ideas denote the transactional processes that exist in nature and thus serve as a metaphor for human relatedness through mutual adaptation. GST is a general science of wholeness that describes sets of elements standing in interaction, or the systemic interconnectedness of variables, such as people and their environments. It is an organizing conceptual framework in which many otherwise disparate elements are integrated into a synthetic view and fall into place. As GST explains, when the variables of a case are enclosed within a boundary (as in an ecomap) and exhibit certain systemic properties, they demonstrate reciprocal responses. That is, if one factor in the case is touched by an action or an event, another factor responds because the two factors are systemically connected. For example, in John's ecomap, if he cannot withdraw from drugs, then his schoolwork will be affected, as will all the other aspects of his life that are depicted within the circle of the case. If an intervention *in any part* of John's life is successful, it is theoretically possible that his drug use will be affected. When one intervenes in a system, such as in John's case, in which the components are interconnected, an intervention can take place directly or indirectly and affect something that is distant from the object of intervention, yet result in the same desired outcome. For example, one may intervene in the school so that a teacher pays special attention to John, which will affect his self-esteem and lessen his interest in pursuing the drug culture. In GST this process is called "equifinality," which means that one may enter a case through multiple avenues, any one of which will lead to a comparable result.

The psychosocial focus, in which all processes are addressed to the person in the environment, distinguishes social work from other professional disciplines such as psychiatry or psychology. It implies that individuals and their environments are always actually or potentially adaptive to each other and that interventions can be carried out in either sphere of the case and can be expected to affect other spheres. The ecosystems perspective has enabled social workers to enhance this psychosocial focus through the use of a systemic lens that does not separate the person from the environment, but requires that they be seen in interaction with each other. The use of the ecomap as the graphic depiction of a case allows both the practitioner and the client literally to see things concretely. The reader will note that terms like "see" and "lens" have been used to indicate that the ecosystems idea is a *perspective*, or a way of looking. It is not a practice model and hence does not tell one what to do. It only directs one's vision toward the complex variables in cases, permitting one to connect them and recognize their interaction. Once a practitioner has done so, his or her choice of interventions will be guided by the practice theories, knowledge, and values the practitioner has.

SYSTEMIC THINKING VS. LINEAR THINKING

The idea of *systemic thinking*, rather than *linear thinking*, is important in social work practice. Systemic thinking (used in the ecosystems perspective) allows the practitioner to recognize, understand, and intervene in the environmental context of cases while maintaining a focus on the individuals in the case. Once a case is defined as a system, all its components are interconnected, and thus interventions to affect the client can be made anywhere in the case. Linear thinking, on the other hand, implies a one- or two-way connection from point A to B, or say, only from the social worker to John, creating a more narrow perspective that may diminish the practitioner's attention to the other significant variables in the case.

The shift from linear thinking to systemic thinking in all disciplines is a consequence of the findings of modern physics, which, in the age of atomic fusion, considers phenomena "explosive," spontaneous, or even unpredictable. In contrast, according to the old Newtonian physics, an apple falling from a tree, straight down in a linear fashion, could go in only one direction. This has been an epistemological change in that the *way of seeing or knowing* has changed. Systems thinking is not ontological, which is about how things *are*, as, for example, in theories of social systems; it is not about essential characteristics, but about the way elements interact with each other. Thus, theorists talk about "systems thinking," rather than about "social systems," and are concerned not with the nature of things, but with the construction of reality, the *processes* that bind people, events, and, yes, social systems together. Modern views of reality are more open to individual interpretation than ever in history; it is difficult to claim that a person's "reality" is positively this or that, by one's own criteria. For example, a child in an inner-city school and a child in a suburban school will have diverse views of the educational establishment, a feminist individual and a fundamentalist individual will recognize biases in the political process differently, a welfare commissioner will evaluate the worth of public services from a perspective that is foreign to a welfare client. Therefore, it is always useful to reflect on how one views phenomena because one's standpoint will make a great difference in the reality one accepts. (This is a good reason to have clients draw their own ecomaps.) Systems thinking is useful because it describes interactive processes and lays no claim to the *nature* of the variables that are interactive. The features of people and the environment that are knowable are best described according to their relevant theories.

Linear thinking leads to a greater certainty, even to asserting causal connections, such as "If *x* happens first, *y* will follow." In John's case, linear thinking would assume that John had turned to drugs because his father rejected him. In systems thinking, consequences (such as *y*) may be ascribed to multiple causes. In John's case, systems thinking would note that as a consequence of his father's rejection, John relied more heavily on his peers, particularly an older boy who was a drug dealer. This new social environment enticed John to play hooky from school, which brought him to the attention of the social worker. (One can see several entry points to this case through the use of systems thinking.) Linear thinking can generate greater predictability, whereas systems thinking may well lead to a contrary outcome. For example, if a person tosses one marble in the air, one can pretty much predict where it can be caught. However, if the person tosses five marbles in the air, it is not possible to predict where all the marbles will land. Systems thinking is intended to accommodate multiplicity, complexity, and uncertainty. In exchange for this lack of certainty and predictability, one gains a palette of options to think about and to choose for interventions. Besides, the environment affects clients in multiple ways, which creates uncertainty and unpredictability, and systems thinking brings one closer to the true reality of these influences.

THE STRUCTURE OF SYSTEMS: IMPLICATIONS FOR PRACTICE

Systems in GST have certain distinguishing properties that will be briefly considered here, for they can illuminate the usefulness of the ecosystems perspective in social work practice. John's ecomap, when taken as a whole, is a case system that can illustrate the application of the structure of systems. Recall that GST is about "wholeness," the search for the integration of parts, and the processes of interaction. The following are some of its salient features (for a more detailed discussion, see Greif & Lynch, 1983):

1. Systems have *boundaries,* which is how they can be identified. These boundaries can be drawn in physical space, as in a classroom in which the class is a system. Or they can be viewed conceptually, as in John's case, when one brings together the salient variables and creates a boundary (a circle) around them. (Systems have *patterned relationships*—students meet regularly in classrooms, for example. On the other hand, if an accident occurs on a street, the people who gather to watch it are not a system, but a random event.) A physical boundary is usually self-evident; a classroom or a school building, for instance, has walls. When it comes to conceptual boundaries, however, the social worker's judgment is involved in creating the ecomap. Do John's family members belong inside the ecomap if they do not live in the same city as John? Should John's friend in prison be included because John considers him a role model? There is some power in the creation of this case system because the picture that is finally drawn will shape the understanding of the case.

2. All organic, or living, systems are *open,* in that their boundaries are permeable and they can exchange energy (interact) with their environments. This exchange enables the system to grow and permits its elements to differentiate and develop. Closed systems, on the other hand, are self-contained and will not thrive because they do not exchange energy with their environments. In John's case, if he were to become isolated and afraid to leave home, he would sooner or later wind down like an unattended clock. In GST this phenomenon is called *entropy.* It is a universal law of nature that all forms of organizations

move toward disorganization or death (entropy) without the importation of energy. When systems are open, they import more energy from the environment than they expend (negative entropy); then they grow and become more adaptable. John's isolation implies that he is "closing down," and any number of social work interventions could help him maintain his connections with people and places in his environment so he could "import" energy, information, and life.

3. Systems tend to preserve their structures and characteristics, even when the relatedness of their elements shifts. For example, in family therapy the parental roles do not change, but the parents may behave differently. Perhaps because of this need to preserve their structure, systems tend to resist change and attempt to maintain a steady state or equilibrium. This is a *dynamic* homeostasis, not paralysis. A see-saw is in perfect balance, but organic systems, like people, cannot be mechanically perfect. They respond to the world and can easily become imbalanced when the environment overwhelms them or when they receive too little nutriment from the environment. A functioning system seeks to maintain its equilibrium through negotiations with the environment. In viewing John's case as a (systemic) ecomap, one sees that John's equilibrium may be "tipped" if he becomes self-reliant in his isolation. Yet, one can recognize multiple sources of energy—relationships, events, programs, ideas—that can be tapped so John can regain his balance. Helping him to find his way back to school or to get a job or bringing his family members back into his life, as well as talking with him, are all possible options. Conversely, systems can be overwhelmed if too much energy is introduced precipitously, so John does not have the time or tools to cope with this input and still maintain his equilibrium. For example, if John was slowly emerging from his isolation the social worker would have to be sensitive about pushing him too quickly to join a group or find a girlfriend. If John was feeling overwhelmed, his self-balancing mechanisms would take over, and he might have to pull back from the onrush of interventions.

4. The elements of systems are potentially *reciprocal*, in that they act on each other. Thus, if John's family members were brought back into his life, they would have an impact on him, just as he would have an impact on them. But John and his family are not all that is reciprocal in this case. John's use of drugs, school, friends, and illness are reciprocally connected as well because they all exist within the boundary of the system (ecomap). Thus, as was noted earlier, change in one part of the system generates change in all its parts and thus interventions in one or another aspect of the case *always* have a reciprocal effect on all

the elements of the case. This notion of *equifinality* has great practical implications because it means that a social worker can have an impact in "distant" parts of the case by intervening in a more proximate (available or yielding) area. So, removing John from his drug culture may have a reciprocal effect on the way John's mother responds to him, even if the social worker does not have direct contact with her.

5. In closed systems, the final state is determined by the initial conditions. For instance, the planetary system follows its course on the basis of its original structure. In personality theory, an example of a final state's dependence on its initial conditions might be the idea that after suffering an emotional trauma, a child is fixated at a certain age, and his or her personality is forever shaped by the original trauma. On the other hand, in viewing child development as an open system of thought, one would factor in broadening experiences as the child matures, which would allow for the assumption that good teachers, friends, parents, and successful life experiences could counteract the effect of the original trauma and result in the child's development. Thus, the child's life course can be viewed as independent of the child's initial condition. This is the meaning of equifinality—that change can be introduced in many "locations," each of which can contribute to the same end point, because the systemic properties of the case are independent of the initial, anchored state (or trauma). The converse of equifinality is *multifinality*, which means that a single event, such as the birth of a baby or a carefully pointed therapeutic intervention, can be introduced into a case, and it will have multiple effects, changing the way a person views his or her problems. The fact that the initial state does not determine the outcome offers an optimistic view of systemically oriented practice.

The ecological metaphor and the principles of GST have contributed to the ecosystems perspective and the ecomap, which represents a *case system*. Thus, it is possible to use GST to understand the functions of case boundaries, the properties of open systems, the ways in which case variables are related and interactive (reciprocal), and the uses of the concepts of equifinality and multifinality. Once one views cases systemically, or as a field of connected events, institutions, and people, it is difficult to return to linear views of isolated case variables and not to notice the transactional potential among adjacent parts of the field or to ignore the reverberating effects taking place in more remote parts of the field.

The foregoing discussion commented on a few of the structures and processes that are characteristic of GST using John's individual case as an illustration. Imagine now that a community is "the case," for systems thinking applies to systems of all sizes (see chapter 8 for an elaboration of systems thinking). In the community under consideration (which was a real case), there is a neighborhood social services center that young people and their families use. The immediate neighborhood is bordered by a commercial area that includes three small stores, a restaurant, and a movie theater. A nearby park, a primary school, a police station, a health care center, and two churches constitute the rest of the community. This is the ecomap of the community:

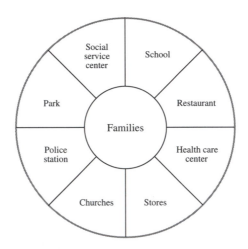

The problem brought to the attention of the neighborhood services center was that a group of about a dozen 11-year-old boys had been harassing the storekeepers by menacing customers and drawing graffiti. The police could not catch them, their parents felt helpless to stop them, they resisted the pleas of their pastor and priest, they would not attend group sessions at the social services center, and the school provided no after-school programs. Thinking systemically, the social worker at the social services center assessed the situation of the aggressive boys and the lack of neighborhood resources and developed a plan. She approached the store owners and, after a heated exchange with them, helped them consider alternative ways of dealing with the boys. Chasing and scolding them were not working. The store owners (enabled by the social worker) called the boys together for lunch at the neighborhood restaurant and created a neighborhood baseball team, bought the boys uniforms (with the names of the stores on them) and equipment, and took turns managing the team when it played other teams in the park. Needless to say, all the people in the neighborhood who had felt the impact of the boys' destructive behavior were relieved.

As in John's case, there were many options for intervention, including clinical treatment of the boys and their families. The social worker chose what appeared to be both a parsimonious and a powerful intervention. One can only speculate about the later well-being of the neighborhood; the increase in the boys' self-esteem; and the relief of the parents, the police, the pastor and priest, and the teachers, as well as the store owners and their customers. The reader should be able to recognize the GST principles demonstrated in this example.

THE ECOMAP AND CHOICES IN PRACTICE

Drawing an ecomap to include the significant variables of a case and to provide a boundary around them offers the practitioner (and the client) the opportunity to explore and assess the dynamic relationships among the variables. Furthermore, although neither systems thinking nor an ecomap prescribes actions, the laying out of the case as a field of forces enables the practitioner to choose from a selection of possible interventions. Instead of a predefined template that is determined by the dominant discipline or methodology, an ecomap presents options, and its use can recast traditional modes of helping. This recasting means that the practitioner may use any or all of the social work modalities (individual, family, group, and community) and one or many methodological approaches (Meyer, 1983). This flexibility is possible because the principles of reciprocity, equifinality, and multifinality are in operation. Thus, the social work practice repertoire, as well as the ecomap, is intended to be an open system.

The following are some examples of the ways in which systemic principles can contribute to the recasting of case situations. The foregoing example of the neighborhood boys turning from a gang into a baseball team reflects the systemic thinking of the practitioner, who chose the simplest intervention that would have the broadest effect (an example of multifinality).

Another example is the case of a boy with "school phobia," classically treated by either psychodynamic or behavioral psychotherapy. An ecomap of the boy's situation of being afraid to go to school might depict his mother who has just had a baby, a teacher who is excessively demanding, and a tough neighborhood through which the boy must walk to school. Interventions in any or all of these arenas have the potential of improving the mutual adaptations of the boy and his family, his school, and his neighborhood. Again, one notes the opening up of interventive choices because the ecomap has displayed the field of forces from which a focus can be chosen. This approach allows the practitioner to enter cases that appear to have some capacity for change.

Now that people's environments can be depicted as part of their lives, not only as background, one can better understand the emergence of family therapy. Once, the family was thought to be the background of a person's life. Today it is recognized as the dynamic part of every family member. Thinking systemically, a practitioner would not treat a young child without directly engaging the child's parents. In the case of a group of tenants who are dissatisfied with their housing manager, the systems-oriented practitioner might be apt to mediate a meeting between tenants and manager, rather than to assume the total responsibility of advocating on the tenants' behalf. Systems thinking has also affected the way social workers view organizational processes. In medicine, although the authority of physicians still prevails, practitioners of other significant disciplines that are important in hospitals are no longer viewed as secondary; rather, the approach to patients is interdisciplinary. In systems terms, a hospital contains interrelated "parts" that are dependent on each other, and interdisciplinary teams are more reflective of that reality than are hierarchical levels of decision making.

The ecomap lays out all the significant complex dimensions of a case and thus allows the social worker to think about different ways to connect the variables in the case, to gain newer and deeper insights into its dynamics. The ecomap describes an open system in which the social worker can contemplate multiple points of entry into the case. In keeping with the range of roles that social workers enact, the ecosystems perspective helps the practitioner envision the possibility of engaging in many different kinds of professional activities. In John's case, one may see the potential for advocacy with the school, therapy with his family, group work with John and others in his situation, a drug program, or community action in the neighborhood. The use of this perspective helps one to conceptualize phenomena in their realistic complexity, and it creates the opportunity to choose from a range of interventions. The use of the ecomap also allows the social worker to evaluate his or her progress in practice by placing a transparency of an ecomap at Time 2 over an ecomap at Time 1 and hence to note changes in the configuration of stress. As was noted earlier, the ecosystems perspective does not tell the practitioner what to do; it generates the presentation of case phenomena in such a way that the practitioner's attention is drawn to the possibilities of what may be done. As such, it is an important tool for assessment, which is the process by which all cases are individualized. The ecosystems perspective provides the broadest possible canvas on which the social work practitioner can, with the client, draw a plan for intervention.

SUMMARY

This chapter introduced the ecosystems perspective, a conceptual framework that allows the social work practitioner to organize the complexity that exists in a client's world. The ecological metaphor of mutual adaptation between the person and the environment is the context for the principles of GST. These principles explain the way case variables interrelate and reverberate and the way the structures and functions of open systems can serve as a model for social work cases. The ecomap is a concrete depiction of the elements in a case, enabling the practitioner and the client literally to draw its components.

The ecomap has many uses in social work practice. It can help make order out of chaos, illustrate the ways in which the case system functions, serve as a communication tool between the practitioner and the client or between professionals, and chart the progress in a case. One of its most important functions is its use as a tool in assessment, for the ecomap can show the client's assets and liabilities, adaptations, and dysfunctions. Finally, the ecomap can widen the perspective of the practitioner who is seeking points of intervention and allow the practitioner to entertain the use of multiple modalities, methods, and roles with any or all of the actors and conditions in the case.

This open view of social work practice reverberates throughout this book. Although reading a book is a linear experience, the reader will discover that each chapter that follows contributes to a systemic perspective on practice. Furthermore, in keeping with the idea of equifinality in systems theory, it will not matter which chapter is read first because all the chapters resonate this view and so will help the reader to reach the same end state.

REFERENCES

Auerswald, E. H. (1968). Interdisciplinary versus ecological approach. *Family Process, 7,* 202–215.

DuBos, R. (1972). *The god within.* New York: Charles Scribner's Sons.

Greif, G., & Lynch, A. (1983). The ecosystems perspective. In C. H. Meyer (Ed.), *Clinical social work in the ecosystems perspective* (pp. 35–71). New York: Columbia University Press.

Hamilton, G. (1951). *Theory and practice of social casework.* New York: Columbia University Press.

Hartman, A. (1978). Diagrammatic assessment of family relationships. *Social Casework, 59,* 465–476.

Hollis, F. H. (1972). *Casework: A psychosocial therapy* (2nd ed.). New York: Random House.

Meyer, C. H. (1970). *Social work practice: A response to the urban crisis.* New York: Free Press.

Meyer, C. H. (1976). *Social work practice: The changing landscape* (2nd ed.). New York: Free Press.

Meyer, C. H. (Ed.). (1983). *Clinical social work in the ecosystems perspective.* New York: Columbia University Press.

Richmond, M. E. (1917). *Social diagnosis.* New York: Russell Sage Foundation.

von Bertalanffy, L. (1967). General systems theory. In N. Demerath & R. A. Peterson (Eds.), *Systems change and conflict* (pp. 119–129). New York: Free Press.

3

Values and Ethics

Brenda G. McGowan

P rofessional social work education emphasizes the acquisition of the knowledge and skills required for effective practice. Yet practitioners' choice of values is always the primary determinant of what they actually do with clients. Therefore, it seems essential for a textbook on the foundations of practice to present an overview of social work values and ethical issues before it addresses the specifics of different modalities and methods of practice. This chapter examines the ways in which values shape professional decision making; reviews historical shifts in professional ethical concerns; identifies the core social work values, ethics, and legal responsibilities; examines the ways in which social workers address ethical issues; and explores alternative frameworks for analyzing ethical dilemmas.

ROLE OF VALUES IN DECISION MAKING

The primacy of professional values in practitioners' decision making and actions is derived from four sources. First, the social services programs and other institutions in which social workers are employed were all established to serve specific populations and to achieve definite purposes. Decisions about who to serve and to what end always reflect choices among values. Beginning students need only to review the mission statements of different field placement settings to realize how these choices differ from one organization to another and how value-laden the settings are. Even apparently neutral goals, such as "promoting independence," "preventing delinquency," or "enhancing family life," reflect decisions about which social issues should be given priority.

Second, as Reamer (1982) demonstrated, decisions by individual practitioners about the objectives of service and priorities in different cases reflect value choices about which are the most desirable. Take, for example, the case of a substance-abusing single mother who had been in recovery but has started drinking again, beaten her teenage son, and threatened her younger children. The social worker must decide what to do first: protect the children by filing

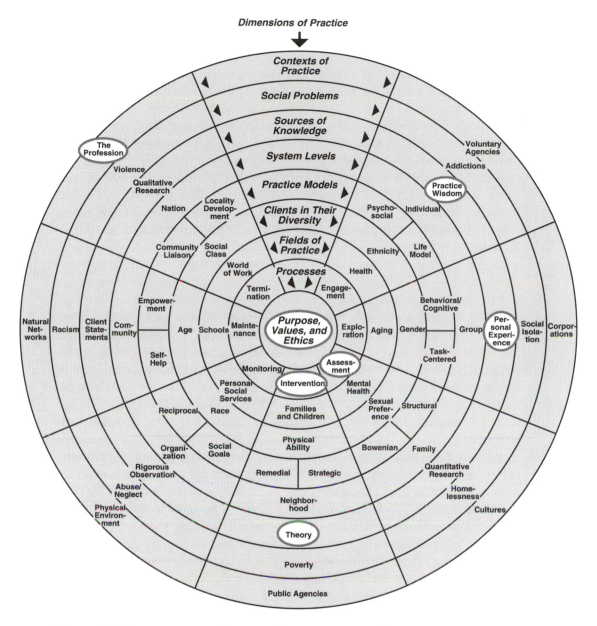

FIGURE 3-1. DIMENSIONS OF PRACTICE HIGHLIGHTED IN VALUES AND ETHICS

a complaint of child abuse, help the mother reenroll in an alcohol treatment program, or work on reducing stress and improving family relationships. All three strategies may ultimately be necessary, but the initial focus of attention is determined, in part, by the social worker's value preferences.

Third, because time and resources are always scarce in human services agencies, social workers must frequently make choices about the amount of time they will devote to different activities with different clients and which clients will be granted access to supplementary benefits like children's attendance at summer camps, food vouchers, or psychiatric consultation. Lewis (1972) convincingly argued that such decisions reflect value choices about which clients are the most worthy or deserving of help and which types of problems deserve the greatest attention.

Finally, as Loewenberg (1984) discussed, because of limitations in empirically based social work knowledge and the absence of middle-range theories required to guide practice, social workers often resort to personal value preferences when deciding which theoretical approach or modality to apply to a specific case. For example, in cases of wife abuse, practitioners have no hard evidence to help them decide what they should try to accomplish and whether they should rely on feminist, family systems, or behavioral theory to help these families. Consequently, they are likely to choose the approach that best fits their agencies' or their own values regarding marital and family relationships and the primacy of different family members' interests.

SHIFTS IN PROFESSIONAL ETHICS

Despite the primacy of values in professional decision making, social workers' value preferences and ethical concerns have shifted dramatically since the late 19th century. In the 1880s and 1890s the friendly visitors (the forebears of social workers), who worked in such agencies as the Charity Organization Society and the Association for Improving the Condition of the Poor, focused primarily on the morality of their clients. The writings of this period referred frequently to the shortcomings of the destitute and distinguished repeatedly between "worthy" and "unworthy" poor people. The consistent emphasis of these early workers was on helping poor people reform themselves by overcoming their alleged "character defects" of thriftlessness, laziness, intemperance, and immorality.

This attitude began to shift around the turn of the 20th century, with the development of the settlement house movement. Some of the leading figures in this movement raised persistent questions about the morality of social and economic institutions that denied poor people the opportunity to care properly for themselves and their children. Although these early social reformers advocated vigorously for changed societal values, they paid little explicit attention to defining their own professional values.

It was only in the 1920s that social workers began to examine the morality of the profession and to discuss how best to define professional ethics. Despite several efforts to draft a professional code of ethics during that decade, no formal code of ethics for social workers was established until the American Association of Social Workers adopted one in 1951. The National Association of Social Workers (NASW), established in 1955 in a merger of seven professional social work organizations, adopted its first code of professional ethics in 1960 (Loewenberg & Dolgoff, 1992).

One reason for the delay in promulgating a code of professional ethics is that the efforts to do so in the 1920s were initiated in the context of a broader movement to obtain full professional status for the field of social work.

Consequently, primacy was given to identifying common professional knowledge and skills, rather than values, and this emphasis continued throughout the next few decades.

Reamer (1983) suggested that another reason for the inattention to professional ethics from the 1930s to the 1950s (Pumphrey's 1959 classic text was an exception) was that the "early years of the profession also happened to coincide with an era in which science and the scientific method were in the academic limelight" (p. 31). Consequently, social work, like other professions in this period, focused on issues that could be addressed empirically, not on ethical concerns and values.

Since the 1970s social workers, like many other professional groups, have paid increased attention to value questions and ethical dilemmas in practice. This shift has been demonstrated in the increasing number of articles and texts on social work ethics (see, for example, Levy, 1976; Lewis, 1972; Loewenberg & Dolgoff, 1992; Reamer, 1982, 1983; Reamer & Abramson, 1982; Rhodes, 1991). The following are among the many reasons for this renewed interest in ethical issues:

- rapid social and technological changes that have posed new value dilemmas for the profession
- increased attention to ethical issues by other human services professionals, evidenced, for example, by the development of bioethics committees in hospitals and required courses on ethics for medical students
- consumers' challenges to the assumed authority of all professionals
- more stringent regulation of social work and other human services professions by public funding agencies and the courts
- more widespread publicity in the mass media of egregious violations of clients' rights by members of different professions
- greater political sophistication about the inherent conflict of interests between human services bureaucracies and the people they are designed to serve
- growing recognition of the ways in which even the development and use of different types of knowledge reflect professional value choices.

DISTINGUISHING VALUES, ETHICS, AND LEGAL RESPONSIBILITIES

Values and Ethics

Although the terms "values" and "ethics" are often used interchangeably, they refer to different concepts. As Loewenberg and Dolgoff (1992) noted, "values are concerned with what is *good* and *desirable,* while ethics deal with what is *right* and *correct*" (p. 21). Although professional values are often defined as one of the core distinguishing characteristics of the social work profession, these values reflect larger societal values and express general preferences, rather than specific directives for action. Consequently, there is widespread consensus among social workers, as among members of other professions, about core professional values.

Professional ethics, in contrast, are guidelines about how members of the profession can translate their values into action. In other words, they provide direction about how people *ought* to act. Therefore, they are more specific, demanding, and potentially controversial.

Although there have been repeated debates throughout the history of the profession about how social work values are best implemented, there is relative agreement about the values themselves and which should be emphasized in the training of new social workers. Discussions of social work values frequently highlight such concepts as upholding the dignity and worth of each individual, facilitating clients' self-determination, respecting clients' diversity, providing opportunities and resources that people need to achieve self-actualization, fostering the empowerment of clients, promoting social justice, safeguarding clients' confidentiality, respecting colleagues, and accepting responsibility for one's professional conduct.

The importance attached to values in professional education is demonstrated by the requirements of the Council on Social Work Education (CSWE), the

Programs of social work education must provide specific knowledge about social work values and their ethical implications, and must provide opportunities for students to demonstrate their application in professional practice. Students must be assisted to develop an awareness of their personal values and to clarify conflicting values and ethical dilemmas. Among the values and principles that must be infused throughout every social work curriculum are the following:

1. Social workers' professional relationships are built on regard for individual worth and dignity and are furthered by mutual participation, acceptance, confidentiality, honesty, and responsible handling of conflict.
2. Social workers respect people's right to make independent decisions and to participate in the helping process.
3. Social workers are committed to assisting client systems to obtain needed resources.
4. Social workers strive to make social institutions more humane and responsive to human needs.
5. Social workers demonstrate respect for and acceptance of the unique characteristics of diverse populations.
6. Social workers are responsible for their own ethical conduct, the quality of their practice, and seeking continuous growth in the knowledge and skills of their profession.

FIGURE 3-2. SOCIAL WORK VALUES AND ETHICS
Reprinted with permission from Council on Social Work Education. (1992). Curriculum policy statement for master's degree programs in social work education (Sec. M6.5). Alexandria, VA: Author.

accreditation body for all schools of social work in the United States and Canada. Figure 3-2 summarizes the responsibilities of all schools of social work to include content on social work values in their curricula, as specified in CSWE's 1992 policy statement.

Social work ethics are embodied in the *NASW Code of Ethics* (presented in Appendix A), which was adopted in 1979 and revised in 1990 and 1994. This code is designed "to serve as a guide to the everyday conduct of members of the social work profession and as a basis for the adjudication of issues in ethics when the conduct of social workers is alleged to deviate from the standards expressed or implied in this code" (NASW, 1994, p. v). Based on the fundamental values of the profession, the code specifies principles of behavior in six broad areas: the social worker's (1) conduct and comportment, (2) responsibility to clients, (3) responsibility to colleagues, (4) responsibility to employers, (5) responsibility to the profession, and (6) responsibility to society.

Technically, only NASW members can be held responsible for abiding by the provisions of the code; however, many schools of social work mandate that their students follow the code, and state regulatory agencies and courts often rely on provisions of the code to determine whether social workers who are charged with violations have acted in accordance with accepted professional principles. Therefore, it is important for all professional social workers and social work students to be informed about the ethical provisions of the code and to behave accordingly.

Legal Responsibilities

Although social work values and ethics reflect collective voluntary preferences and decisions about what professionals should believe and how they should act, many of these values and ethical standards are embodied in state laws and regulations and court decisions promulgated to regulate the behavior of social workers. In the early days of social work, there were few, if any, laws governing professional performance. Since the 1970s, however, there has been a rapid expansion of regulatory mechanisms designed to govern the behavior of social workers and other human services professionals. Consequently, social workers must now be knowledgeable about their legal duties, as well as their ethical responsibilities and the ways in which the two may converge or diverge.

Social work is a socially mandated profession that has been given the authority to perform certain functions for the community and has been prohibited from performing other activities that are delegated to different professions. With the authority to perform certain social functions comes legal responsibility to perform these tasks in an acceptable manner and a set of legal obligations to the clients one is serving. These legal duties are perhaps best understood as an essential component of the fiduciary relationship that social workers develop with clients.

As Kutchins (1991) discussed in his seminal article on this topic, the fiduciary relationship with clients is derived from the fact that social workers, like other professionals, have specialized knowledge and skills that their clients do not possess. Therefore, when clients consult with a social worker (or a physician or a lawyer), they essentially grant the professional the authority to influence them in unforeseen ways and trust that the professional will act in their best interests. This arrangement is different from a business contract in which it is assumed that the two parties are equal and that they each must protect their own interests.

The concept of fiduciary responsibility is usually applied to relationships in which the professional or trustee assumes some financial obligation for a client and makes economic decisions on behalf of this person. But a number of recent court cases have used the concept to describe the obligations that human services professionals have to their clients. Although legal theory and case law in this area are still evolving, Kutchins (1991) identified three key areas in which the fiduciary responsibilities of the social worker seem clear: confidentiality, duty to tell the truth, and loyalty to clients.

The right to confidentiality is protected legally as the result of a series of case decisions and by the statutes of many states that grant clients of licensed or certified social workers privileged-information status. This status means that the information that clients divulge to social workers cannot be revealed without their consent unless there is a significant, legally recognized reason, such as a mandated report of the suspected maltreatment of a client or the threat of imminent danger to the client or another person.

The duty to tell the truth encompasses not only the social worker's responsibility to deal honestly with clients and to report honestly on his or her practice, but the fiduciary obligation to ensure that clients give informed consent to any proposed social work intervention and to the release of any information about them. That is, clients must be fully informed about the nature and intent of any proposed service or release of information, possible risks and benefits, potential effects on them and others who are significant to them, available alternatives, and projected costs (Reamer, 1987). The potential ramifications of this obligation are enormous and have not been fully examined by the profession. For example, social workers are often encouraged to exaggerate or modify diagnoses to make clients eligible for specific services or insurance reimbursements. Yet, as Kutchins (1991) pointed out, "deliberate misdiagnoses place practitioners in great jeopardy of being sued by clients, insurance companies, and others. Practitioners also risk [the] loss of their licenses and criminal prosecution" (p. 111).

The concept of loyalty to clients means that the professional has a fiduciary responsibility to place a client's interests first when there is any conflict of duty to the client, the employer, or another interested party. Unfortunately, although this concept seems simple, it is not. The *NASW Code of Ethics* also spells out social workers' responsibilities to colleagues, employers, the profession, and society at large, and social workers often feel torn among these potentially competing loyalties. And the profession has provided relatively little guidance to social workers in the past about how best to resolve such conflicts. However, since the mid-1980s an increase in the number of malpractice suits has led to the "growing recognition of the fiduciary relationship and legal obligations that result from the trust that clients place in professionals" (Kutchins, 1991, p. 112). Thus, one may expect clearer standards for professional performance in the future.

ADDRESSING ETHICAL DILEMMAS

It is easy for professionals to agree on the social work values that they should try to uphold in their practice. Dilemmas arise, however, when they are confronted by situations that pose two conflicting values, that is, when they are forced to choose between two apparent goods or to avoid two equally undesirable courses of action. For example, social work's commitment to the dignity and worth of each individual suggests that every clinical or programmatic decision should advance the welfare of the individual client; yet the professional commitment to promoting social justice means that the social worker must also consider whether a particular practice decision will further the interests of the larger community. Thus, a social worker can feel ambivalent about advocating to obtain a room in a residential treatment program for a mentally ill homeless man who is disruptive and violent and is likely to cause real tension among the other residents. The social worker knows that if this difficult client is placed in a shelter for homeless people, he is unlikely to receive the treatment he needs. On the other hand, the worker realizes that the safety of the other residents could be jeopardized if the client is placed in the treatment program that would be best for him.

Similarly, social work's commitment to the well-being of clients can conflict with the obligation to promote clients' self-determination. Hospital social workers, for example, are often torn between trying to arrange safe discharge plans for frail older patients who cannot care for themselves safely at home and respecting the patients' right to decide where they want to live and whether they want any support from family members or providers of home health care.

The other primary source of ethical conflict for social workers is their frequently competing loyalties (Loewenberg & Dolgoff, 1992). Unlike attorneys, who define their responsibilities to their clients as absolute, social workers are expected to consider the impact of their actions on others in their clients' environment and to remember their responsibility to their employing agencies and to the society at large. Consequently, they are often forced to choose between doing what is best for their clients and what is best for other members of the clients' families, as, for instance, when they debate whether to report a suspicion of child abuse against parents who have requested marital treatment. Similarly, social workers must often decide whether to follow their agencies' policies or to do what is in their clients' best interests. For example, they may be expected to terminate services abruptly to a client who appears intoxicated for an interview or to refuse to make a home visit to a client who is immobilized by a temporary crisis because an agency's policy prohibits this action.

It is sometimes not easy to resolve ethical dilemmas. The code may not contain precisely relevant principles that should be used to analyze ethical problems. The *NASW Code of Ethics* should, of course, be the first resource for social workers who are trying to resolve ethical dilemmas. But the code presents a set of ethical principles without offering any underlying rationale or philosophical framework (Rhodes, 1991). A social worker is expected to accept these guidelines simply because they have been approved by the professional association and embody generally accepted professional values, not because they represent any coherent ethical theory. Moreover, the code does not address many of the specific conflicts that social workers confront in practice; instead, it presents what can often be conflicting obligations to clients and to other interested parties. For these reasons, many professionals do not find the code as helpful as it could be.

To illustrate, in a study of ethical dilemmas facing hospital social workers in St. Louis, Proctor, Morrow-Howell, and Lott (1993) discovered that 85 percent of the conflicts that the social workers mentioned reflected a conflict among principles listed in the *NASW Code of Ethics.* Furthermore, over half the 342 NASW members in New York State in Mattison's (1994) study reported that they were not familiar with the *NASW Code of Ethics,* and over 70 percent said "they had never consulted the Code in relation to decision-making in practice" (p. 122).

Unfortunately, there have been few systematic studies of the ethical dilemmas that social workers confront or how these dilemmas are resolved. As Holland and Kilpatrick (1991) noted: "Little is known about how practitioners respond to moral and ethical issues, how they understand and cope with these aspects of their work, or what resources are used or needed for improving performance in this area" (p. 138). The few studies that have been done have raised troubling questions about social workers' apparent inattention to ethical concerns.

One of the earliest studies to address this aspect of practice was conducted by Billingsley (1964) in Boston in the early 1960s. Billingsley discovered that when child welfare workers and supervisors were confronted with conflicts between their agency's policy and their own professional values, they were likely to make decisions consistent with the agency's policy. Similarly, in a more recent study of 59 fieldwork instructors in New York City, Congress (1986) discovered that these social workers were unlikely to challenge their agencies' policies when these policies conflicted with the clients' right to self-determination. Finally, in a qualitative study of how practitioners resolve ethical issues, Holland and Kilpatrick (1991) discovered that practitioners tend to rely on intrapersonal and interpersonal factors, rather than ethical reasoning, to resolve dilemmas. The three variables they identified as being associated with social workers' ethical decision making were the focus of decisions (means versus ends), interpersonal orientation (individual autonomy, mutual responsibility, or social control), and locus of decision-making authority (external versus internal).

Walden, Wolock, and Demone's (1990) study was the only one that reported somewhat different findings. When social work students, child protective services workers and supervisors, and hospital social workers and supervisors in New Jersey were asked to respond to a series of vignettes posing conflicts between clients' wishes and needs, organizational policies, and professional and societal norms, they tended to make choices that avoided an extreme position in favor of either the client or the organization. However, they rarely selected a nonintervention option, such as seeking consultation or delaying action. On the basis of this finding, Walden et al. concluded that the "participants have internalized a code of ethics that governs their behavior and that is congruent with the expectation of autonomous professional decision-making" (p. 73). What is not clear from their discussion was which ethical principles the participants used to resolve the ethical conflicts that were posed.

The research findings regarding social workers' relative ignorance of ethical principles and inattention to ethical issues in practice are perhaps not surprising when one considers the complexity and intensity of historical debates on the proper criteria for resolving moral dilemmas. As Reamer (1983) noted: "The challenge of resolving difficult ethical dilemmas is an ancient one involving many schools of philosophical thought and principles of ethics regarding what constitutes right and wrong conduct and action" (p. 34). Such abstract debates are often of little interest to the doers and activists who tend to become social workers. But all social workers have a responsibility to assess the ethical implications of their decisions and to develop a framework for addressing the value dilemmas that inevitably arise in practice. Furthermore, some may wish to assume a more active role in debates about professional ethics by serving on hospital bioethics committees, agency ethics committees, or NASW's local and national Committees on Inquiry.

FRAMEWORKS FOR ANALYZING ETHICAL DILEMMAS

Two major schools of thought in ethical theory have influenced ethical analysis in social work: deontology and utilitarianism. Deontologists believe that certain actions are inherently good or right and emphasize the importance of fixed ethical rules, such as the client's right to self-determination. Utilitarians, in contrast, argue that actions are good or right because of their consequences and define an act as morally correct if it promotes the greatest good. Therefore, in this view, the client's right to self-determination can be limited if the exercise of this right would threaten the well-being of others.

Although these philosophical arguments are often used to justify different types of professional actions, social work ethicists generally agree that neither approach provides a sufficient ethical guide for decision making about practice. Consequently, they have proposed several alternative frameworks for the ethical analysis of dilemmas in social work practice.

Reamer (1982), who is perhaps the leading ethicist in social work today, proposed a set of moral principles that he claimed can be justified on the basis of the principle of generic consistency, proposed by Gewirth (1978). This principle states that any responsible person will hold that he or she has a right to freedom and well-being; hence, to be consistent, one must assume that other people have equal rights to freedom and well-being. And if other people have these same rights, the ethical person must refrain from interfering with the freedom and well-being of others.

On the basis of this principle, Reamer suggested six rules or guidelines that can be used to resolve ethical dilemmas in social work (see Figure 3-3). These guidelines suggest a clear hierarchy of values and thus help practitioners make their value assumptions more explicit and think more systematically about the ethical conflicts they confront. Unfortunately, because these rules are abstract and general, they do not provide the specific guidance that social workers often need in complex, real-world situations.

In the fourth edition of their now classic text on social work ethics, Loewenberg and Dolgoff (1992) suggested a lexical ordering of principles that is similar to Reamer's. However, they argued that Reamer, as well as a number of other writers on this topic, "have not taken into sufficient consideration how social workers make decisions" (p. 59). Pointing out that practitioners rarely consider philosophical principles in their daily practice, Loewenberg and Dolgoff proposed a set of ethical principles that parallel the practice principles that social workers must use as they make ongoing decisions about practice. They presented these principles in what they termed two "ethical screens."

1. Rules against basic harms to the necessary preconditions of action (such as life, health, food, shelter, mental equilibrium) take precedence over rules against harms, such as lying or revealing confidential information, or threats to additive goods, such as recreation, education, and wealth.

·····

2. An individual's right to basic well-being (the necessary preconditions of action) takes precedence over another individual's right to freedom.

·····

3. An individual's right to freedom takes precedence over his or her own right to basic well-being.

·····

4. The obligation to obey laws, rules, and regulations to which one has voluntarily and freely consented ordinarily overrides one's right to engage voluntarily and freely in a manner which conflicts with these laws, rules, and regulations.

·····

5. Individuals' rights to well-being may override laws, rules, regulations, and arrangements of voluntary associations in cases of conflict.

·····

6. The obligation to prevent basic harms, such as starvation, and to promote public goods, such as housing, education, and public assistance, overrides the right to retain one's property.

FIGURE 3-3. ETHICAL GUIDELINES PROPOSED BY FREDERIC REAMER
Reprinted with permission from Reamer, F. G. (1982). Ethical dilemmas in social services (pp. 76–79). New York: Columbia University Press.

Ethical Principle 1: Principle of the protection of life
Ethical Principle 2: Principle of equality and inequality
Ethical Principle 3: Principle of autonomy and freedom
Ethical Principle 4: Principle of least harm
Ethical Principle 5: Principle of quality of life
Ethical Principle 6: Principle of privacy and confidentiality
Ethical Principle 7: Principle of truthfulness and full disclosure

FIGURE 3-4. ETHICAL PRINCIPLES SCREEN
Source: Reprinted by permission of the publisher from Loewenberg, F. M., & Dolgoff, R. (1992).
Ethical decisions for social work practice *(4th ed., p. 60). Itasca, IL: F. E. Peacock.*

The first proposed "ethical rules screen" suggests that in any case of ethical conflict, a social worker should first consult the *NASW Code of Ethics* to determine whether any of its rules are relevant. If so, the practitioner should follow those rules. If not, or if the rules seem to conflict, the social worker should consult the "ethical principles screen." This screen identifies a series of straightforward principles that serve as a guide to ethical decision making in practice (see Figure 3-4).

The rank ordering of values proposed by Reamer, Loewenberg and Dolgoff, and others is appealing because it can help clarify social workers' thinking about ethical issues and simplify decision making. Yet as Rhodes (1991) pointed out, "the central question, 'how ought we to act in relation to others?' suggests the primacy of relationships in understanding ethics" (p. 43). And relationships inevitably involve complexities that cannot be reduced to rules. Thus, Rhodes suggested that ethical decision making should begin with a consideration of what one's relationships ought to be with all the significant people with whom one interacts. And because ethical belief systems are inevitably tied to the circumstances of the time and the social situation in which one lives, Rhodes argued that one must also consider "the political and social beliefs that form an integral part of any vision of how we should live in relation to others" (p. 45).

On the basis of this analysis, Rhodes stated that what is most important for practitioners is not a set of ethical guidelines, but an approach to ethical analysis that focuses on the questions to be posed in any dilemma to arrive at the best possible decision. The specific questions she proposed are as follows:

1. What is the client's point of view?
   • • • • •
2. What is my perspective as a worker?
   • • • • •
3. How should I, as a worker, handle differences between my client's and my own views?
   • • • • •
4. What choice is required?
   • • • • •

5. What are the alternative courses of action?

· · · · ·

6. What positions do these different alternatives represent and what arguments can be made for each?

· · · · ·

7. Is the solution I reach consistent with my goals as a human service worker? (pp. 51–53)

Rhodes concluded with a plea for increased dialogue and debate, not only about specific ethical dilemmas, but about the values, philosophical systems, and social and agency contexts that shape social workers' ethical analysis.

CONCLUSION

This chapter has argued that values are a primary determinant of social workers' decision making and that social workers confront frequent ethical dilemmas in their practice. Yet, the profession has not developed useful frameworks for ethical assessment, and there have been few systematic studies of the types of dilemmas that social workers confront daily in practice or how such dilemmas are resolved.

The *NASW Code of Ethics* is a baseline guide to which all workers can be held accountable. However, there is widespread discomfort with some of the conflicting obligations that the current code presents that reflect its lack of a coherent ethical philosophy. A few of the profession's leading experts in ethics have proposed alternative ethical frameworks for analyzing some of the apparently unresolvable conflicts that workers occasionally confront, but none of the proposals has gained widespread professional approval.

In recognition of the necessity to address emerging practice issues, NASW appointed a committee in 1994 to propose a revised code for review by the association's Delegate Assembly. Therefore, social workers may be able to look forward in a few years to adoption of a more functional professional code of ethics.

In the interim social workers have a responsibility not only to follow the current code as closely as possible but to identify and debate openly the profession's ethical assumptions and dilemmas, to make their personal criteria for ethical decision making explicit, and to develop a set of questions they can use to examine equitably the specific conflicts they confront in their daily practice.

REFERENCES

Billingsley, A. (1964). Bureaucratic and professional orientation patterns in social casework. *Social Service Review, 38,* 400–407.

Congress, E. P. (1986). *Analysis of ethical practice among field instructors in social work.* Unpublished doctoral dissertation, City University of New York Graduate Center, New York.

Council on Social Work Education. (1992). *Curriculum policy statement for master's degree programs in social work education* (Sec. M6.5). Alexandria, VA: Author.

Gewirth, A. (1978). *Reason and morality*. Chicago: University of Chicago Press.

Holland, T., & Kilpatrick, A. (1991). Ethical issues in social work: Toward a grounded theory of professional ethics. *Social Work, 36,* 138–144.

Kutchins, H. (1991). The fiduciary relationship: The legal basis for social workers' responsibilities to clients. *Social Work, 36,* 106–113.

Levy, C. S. (1976). *Social work ethics.* New York: Human Sciences Press.

Lewis, H. (1972). Morality and the politics of practice. *Social Casework, 53,* 404–417.

Loewenberg, F. M. (1984). Professional ideology, middle range theories and knowledge building for social work practice. *British Journal of Social Work, 14,* 309–322.

Loewenberg, F. M., & Dolgoff, R. (1992). *Ethical decisions for social work practice* (4th ed.). Itasca, IL: F. E. Peacock.

Mattison, M. (1994). *Ethical decision making in social work practice*. Unpublished doctoral dissertation, Columbia University, New York.

National Association of Social Workers. (1994). *NASW code of ethics*. Washington, DC: Author.

Proctor, E., Morrow-Howell, N., & Lott, C. (1993). Classification and correlates of ethical dilemmas in hospital social work. *Social Work, 38,* 166–177.

Pumphrey, M. W. (1959). *The teaching of values and ethics and social work* (Vol. 13). New York: Council on Social Work Education.

Reamer, F. G. (1982). *Ethical dilemmas in social service*. New York: Columbia University Press.

Reamer, F. G. (1983). Ethical dilemmas in social work practice. *Social Work, 28,* 31–35.

Reamer, F. G. (1987). Informed consent in social work. *Social Work, 32,* 425–429.

Reamer, F. G., & Abramson, M. (1982). *The teaching of social work ethics*. New York: Hastings Center.

Rhodes, M. L. (1991). *Ethical dilemmas in social work practice*. Milwaukee: Family Service America.

Walden, T., Wolock, I., & Demone, H. W., Jr. (1990). Ethical decision making in human services: A comparative study. *Families in Society, 71,* 67–75.

4

Diversity and Oppression

Aurora P. Jackson

Race, ethnicity, gender, sexuality, and class are important social categories that influence the quality of family life, individual identities, and the choices and opportunities that people have (Walker, 1993). Although it is politically correct to acknowledge and appreciate diversity, at least intellectually, working with people from diverse American minority groups presents special challenges. The life experiences and well-being of minority populations in the United States are complicated by issues that those in the majority do not face. Political, economic, cultural, and social factors interact with such developmental concerns as self-esteem, increased autonomy, access to resources and networks of support, relations with significant others, achievement in school, employment opportunities, and the attainment of valued goals.

This chapter considers these issues in relation to the historical, social, and cultural characteristics of specific American racial and ethnic minority groups—African Americans, Asian Americans, Latino Americans, and Native Americans—as well as gay men and lesbians. Concerning the latter, although gay men and lesbians span all racial, ethnic, and socioeconomic groups, Lukes and Land (1990) stated that they "often are rejected by, and may reject, those holding the norms, values, and ideologies of their native culture" and that this rejection, in turn, may result in a greater identification with the "sexual minority group" (p. 156). This chapter presents an overview of professional knowledge about multicultural social work practice and discusses how multiculturally competent practice is grounded in knowledge and skills that are relevant to phases of the helping process.

OVERVIEW

It has been predicted that by 2050, racial and ethnic minority groups will approach a statistical majority in the United States (D. W. Sue, Arrendondo, & McDavis, 1992; U.S. Bureau of the Census, 1991). This projection has aroused substantial interest in developing approaches to social work education (see,

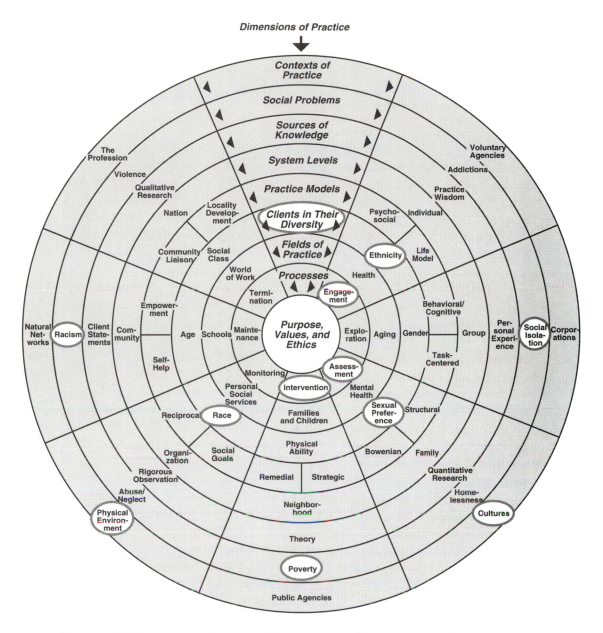

Dimensions of Practice

Contexts of Practice

Social Problems

Sources of Knowledge

System Levels

Practice Models

Clients in Their Diversity

Fields of Practice

Processes

Purpose, Values, and Ethics

Engagement

Assessment

Intervention

Monitoring

Termination

Maintenance

Exploration

The Profession

Violence

Qualitative Research

Nation

Locality Development

Community Liaison

Social Class

World of Work

Empowerment

Natural Networks

Racism

Client Statements

Community

Age

Schools

Self-Help

Reciprocal

Race

Personal Social Services

Families and Children

Physical Ability

Social Goals

Organization

Rigorous Observation

Abuse/ Neglect

Physical Environment

Remedial

Strategic

Neighborhood

Theory

Poverty

Public Agencies

Voluntary Agencies

Addictions

Practice Wisdom

Psycho- social

Individual

Ethnicity

Life Model

Health

Behavioral/ Cognitive

Aging

Gender

Group

Personal Experience

Social Isolation

Corporations

Task-Centered

Mental Health

Sexual Preference

Structural

Bowenian

Family

Quantitative Research

Homelessness

Cultures

FIGURE 4-1. ELEMENTS OF PRACTICE EMPHASIZED IN DIVERSITY AND OPPRESSION

for example, Chestang, 1993; Greene, 1993; Walker, 1993) and practice (see, for example, Gutierrez, 1990; Ho, 1991; Longres, 1991; McGoldrick, 1982; D. W. Sue & D. Sue, 1990; S. Sue & Zane, 1987) that address the diverse traditions, worldviews, and needs of clients.

Although multicultural practice is frequently defined as professional activity that involves individuals from different racial and ethnic minority groups, it can be argued that all social work practice is multicultural in that the beliefs, worldviews, and behavioral patterns of all practitioners and clients reflect their socioeconomic status, race, sexuality, and culture. Nevertheless, to avoid the cultural biases and "cultural encapsulation" (Wrenn, 1985) that can emanate from an uncritical acceptance of the assumptions of the majority culture, scholars and practitioners seem to concur on a set of common professional beliefs and practices.

Common Professional Beliefs and Practices

Appreciation of clients' identities and worldviews

It is widely noted that cultures are characterized by distinctive sets of beliefs, values, and worldviews that shape clients' experiences and are important components of racial and ethnic identity (Helms, 1990; Norton, 1993; D. W. Sue & D. Sue, 1990). Because the majority culture often disparages and undervalues minority worldviews, social work scholars and practitioners are especially concerned with clients' approbation and empowerment (Gutierrez, 1990; Pinderhughes, 1983; Simon, 1990). Efficacious work with racial and ethnic minorities demands knowledge and understanding of cultural differences, as well as skills in assessing, contracting, and intervening that are based on appropriate combinations of biological, psychological, historical, and sociocultural influences.

Attention to contextual factors that influence clients' needs, concerns, and problems

Members of minority groups experience disproportionate poverty and social injustice (Pearson, 1993). Hence, understanding clients who are members of a minority group requires an examination of the contexts within which they struggle to attain a satisfactory level of social functioning. Frequently, when problems arise, the lack of person–environment fit is a result of deficiencies in the environment, rather than of deficits in individuals. Often, moreover, noxious, as well as salutary, transactions among people and their social, cultural, and physical environments are reciprocal (Bronfenbrenner, 1986). For these reasons, multiculturally competent social workers frequently take a broad ecological approach, functioning within the parameters of an ecosystems perspective (see, for example, Meyer, 1976, 1993). In so doing, they address contextual needs and deficiencies, as well as individual exigencies and predicaments (see, for example, Germain & Gitterman, 1980). In short, they view people within the context of their specific situations.

Anticipation of clients' initial suspicion or lack of trust

There is evidence that minority group clients are more difficult to engage and sustain in individual, family, and group services than are their majority group counterparts (McGoldrick, 1982; D. W. Sue & D. Sue, 1990; S. Sue & Zane, 1987). Davis and Proctor (1989) noted that individuals who vary on important attributes are likely to assume that they experience and view the world differently; moreover, such perceptions of difference are likely to affect the client–worker relationship adversely. Situations of racial or class differences, however, cannot be avoided, given that most professional social workers are middle class and white and their clients frequently are not. That minority group clients of color, in particular, have endured and perceive that they have endured historical and contemporary hardships at the hands of middle-class white Americans increases the likelihood that trust will be a significant issue during early contacts.

Thus, an important skill in professional work with oppressed minority group members is the ability to anticipate and handle three central concerns that are likely to be expressed, either overtly or covertly (Davis & Proctor, 1989):

1. Is the worker a person of goodwill? The issue is the extent to which the client will initially trust the worker to be a person who values the client, wants to help, and will pursue the client's best interests.
2. Does the worker have professional expertise or mastery of skills that can resolve my problems? The issue is the worker's *competence,* or capacity to be helpful.
3. Does the worker have sufficient understanding of my social reality or my worldview? The issue is the extent to which the worker is seen as *credible,* and the extent to which advice and suggestions can be accepted as valid and meaningful. (p. ix)

Davis and Proctor (1989) have asserted that while minority group clients of color are likely to distrust the goodwill of white social workers, they may question the competence of social workers who are themselves members of a minority group. The ability to handle these issues of distrust nondefensively is imperative for successful work with racial and ethnic minority groups (Pedersen, 1988). Moreover, skillful workers develop a repertoire of helping responses that demonstrate their professional competence, their empathy, and their knowledge of specific minority groups. Toward the latter purposes, a brief synopsis of the historical, social, and cultural characteristics of the four principal American minority groups, as well as of gay men and lesbians, is presented in the following sections. Because an exhaustive discussion of these issues is beyond the scope of this chapter, the reader is urged to read relevant works, including research on significant demographic and societal processes that mediate individual, family, and social functioning within and across racial and ethnic groups.

MINORITY GROUPS: HISTORICAL AND SOCIOCULTURAL INFLUENCES

Minority groups differ in their history and in their immediate sociocultural condition; they are not homogeneous. For example, although Puerto Rican, Mexican, and Cuban immigrants are all Latino, they came to this country for different reasons, experienced diverse socioeconomic circumstances in their native countries, and attain different rates and types of employment and education in the United States (Moore & Pachon, 1985; Szapocnik & Kurstnes, 1980; Vega, 1990). Likewise, considerable variation exists among African Americans and Asian Americans, based on such factors as geographic origin, social class background, economic status, mobility patterns, and area of residence (McAdoo, 1993; Wilkinson, 1987). Native Americans are also heterogeneous; although they live in all parts of the country (with high concentrations in

California, New Mexico, and South Dakota), there are many tribal affiliations with disparate languages and traditions (LaFromboise, 1988; Wilkinson, 1987). Despite the particular challenges and opportunities that different groups encounter in the majority culture, these groups are all separated from the majority culture by their differential access to the sources of economic and political power (Wilkinson, 1987).

African American People

African American people, now the largest racial minority in the United States, have a high proportion of families headed by single women. These single-parent families are disproportionately poor and suffer a range of problems associated with economic hardship (Garfinkel & McLanahan, 1986; McLoyd, 1990; Wilson, 1987), particularly when the mothers have young children, have low educational levels, and are not employed (Jackson, 1992, 1993; Kamerman & Kahn, 1988).

Numerous studies (see, for example, Wilson, 1987) have found a relationship between income and African American family structure; that is, the proportion of female-headed families decreases as family income increases. Furthermore, socioeconomic factors are related not only to family formation but to the processes of family interaction, child rearing, and individual adaptation.

According to Wilkinson (1987; see also Blackwell, 1985; Wilkinson & Taylor, 1977), the obliteration of class distinctions under slavery and the powerlessness of African American men to support and protect their families for more than two centuries have had a detrimental and enduring impact on African American family relations. In the inner cities, young African American men continue to face an uncertain employment opportunity structure and have high rates of unemployment, in part because of the scarcity of blue-collar jobs (Bowman, 1991a; Kasarda, 1983; Wilson, 1987), but also because of discrimination (Bowman, 1991b; Jencks, 1992; Kirschenman & Neckerman, 1989).

Moreover, as Wilson (1987) has contended, increased social isolation in areas of concentrated urban poverty and limited interaction with individuals in the mainstream (including middle- and upper-income African Americans) affect the worldviews and life chances of African American inner-city youths and the persistence of social problems. Others have concurred, noting that the combination of economic dislocation; discrimination in housing; inadequate social, occupational, and educational resources; and the exodus of middle-class African Americans from inner-city communities have resulted in desolate and turbulent social environments (Bell-Scott & Taylor, 1989) and individuals who, if they do not entirely lack hope, frequently do not have the means to attain their goals (Spencer, 1990).

Among other works that shed further light on the diversity among African Americans are West's (1993) discussion of the increasing gulf between lower-, middle-, and upper-income African Americans; Cose's (1993) consideration of the problems of the African American "privileged class"; and Gaiter's (1994) provocative discourse on what he termed "the revolt of the black bourgeoisie."

Latino American People

Even though Latino Americans are a highly diverse population, only Puerto Ricans and Mexican Americans are highlighted in this section because they are the largest Latino groups in this country. Latinos of Puerto Rican ancestry are concentrated mainly in New York City, although a significant number also live in parts of New Jersey and Pennsylvania. Mexican Americans live principally in California and the Southwest, but also in some parts of the Midwest (Wilkinson, 1987).

In the late 1970s the majority of Latino families were headed by married couples. However, since then there has been a considerable increase in female-headed families among Puerto Ricans (Wilkinson, 1987, 1993), who, like their African American counterparts, are disproportionately poor. Moreover, Puerto Rican men experience greater discrimination in the job market and longer periods of unemployment than do other Latino men, in part because those with dark skin encounter more racial prejudice (Chilman, 1993; Mann & Salvo, 1985).

Many Puerto Ricans migrate to the continental United States because of the widespread poverty in Puerto Rico. Although there have been virtually no empirical studies on Puerto Rican family life in this country (Chilman, 1993), clinical observations have suggested that Puerto Rican families place a high value on family unity and honor, the precedence of the group over the individual, the dignity of the individual and respect for each person regardless of social status, and obligations to and from the extended family (Garcia-Preto, 1982). Although a belief in defined sex roles has been prevalent, this view is changing as more and more women enter the paid workforce (Chilman, 1993).

Mexican Americans, like Puerto Ricans, have been socialized to a set of cultural norms rooted in the tradition of male authority. In addition, Wilkinson (1987) noted that Mexican American families assign importance to the following beliefs: the integral nature of the family in daily living; the functional dominance of men, complemented by a positive and traditional role for women; the reinforcement of sex-role distinctions through child-rearing practices; strong kinship bonds; the centrality of children in the family; the repression of feminine attributes in men; and a precedent for the men to be heads of households.

Studies of the nexus between women's employment and family processes in Latino families have indicated that employment, especially among highly educated women, has had an impact on family life. For example, both Ybarra (1982) and Baca Zinn (1980) reported that in Mexican American families with employed mothers, the husbands shared more nontraditional responsibilities in the home than did husbands in families in which the wives were not employed. Cooney, Rogler, Hurrer, and Ortiz's (1982) study of Puerto Rican couples in New York City obtained similar results. In her review of this research, Chilman (1993) concluded that these role shifts, although generally beneficial to women's emotional well-being, are frequently associated with considerable stress in Latino families.

Asian American People

Like Latinos, Asian Americans are a widely diverse population. In the United States, the largest group is the Chinese, followed by the Japanese, the Filipinos, and the Koreans (Wilkinson, 1987). A majority of these families are concentrated in California (specifically, Los Angeles and San Francisco), and many live in New York City. In addition, a large proportion of Filipinos and Pacific Islanders live in Hawaii, and numerous Vietnamese live in Texas.

Although there is much variation within and among these groups, some scholars, such as Wilkinson (1993), have described the traditional Asian American family as patriarchal, extended, and stable. Marriage is integral to family cohesion and the socialization of children. Family life is pivotal, and filial obligation and duty to elders are accepted practices (Filmore & Cheong, 1980). The strength of these traditional beliefs and practices is conditioned by the degree to which each group has been assimilated into the majority, or Western, culture. Regardless of the extent of assimilation, however, Asian Americans are likely to share certain values, including a strong belief in the importance of the family over the individual, an appreciation of one's ancestral and cultural lineage, and self-control to accomplish social goals (Staples & Mirande, 1980; S. Sue & Kitano, 1973).

When compared with other racial and ethnic minorities, Asian Americans are generally less poor and better educated. Indeed, some researchers have found that native-born Asian Americans are significantly better educated than their white counterparts and that their occupations and earnings equal or are slightly higher than those of the majority population (Hirschman & Wong, 1981; Wong & Hirschman, 1983). Others have concluded that this income parity is largely a result of the higher educational attainment of Asian Americans than of other minority groups (see, for example, Walker, 1993). However, although the average educational attainment of Asian Americans is considerably greater than that of white Americans (Walker, 1993; Yoshiwara, 1983), their average earnings are not, so that, in effect, Asian Americans actually earn less than do comparably educated white Americans. Racial bias is probably a factor. In addition, the education and income of different Asian American groups vary widely. Thus, whereas Asian Indian Americans and Japanese Americans, on average, tend to be well educated and often relatively prosperous, Cambodian refugees and more recent waves of Vietnamese immigrants, for example, often are not.

When Wong and Hirschman (1983) compared the labor force participation and socioeconomic attainment of Asian American and white women, they found that Asian American women were better educated, had higher employment rates, worked longer hours, and earned higher incomes (perhaps because of their longer working hours) than their white counterparts.

However, because minority women have been largely excluded from research on the impact of maternal employment on family processes, it is not known how well Asian American women combine multiple work and family roles in families with young children. In previous publications, this author (Jackson, 1992, 1993, 1994) noted that the subjects of most of these studies have been middle-class white married women. This line of inquiry must be extended to include poor, single-parent, and minority families.

Native American People

Native Americans are greatly heterogeneous and broadly dispersed: There are approximately 500 Native American tribes, and over 200 tribal languages are spoken (LaFromboise, 1988). Although an exhaustive discussion of this diversity is beyond the scope of this chapter, it is important to note that tribal identities are consequential because they are associated with diverse languages, family structures, traditions, rituals, patterns of lineage, and kinship relations (D. W. Sue & D. Sue, 1990; Wilkinson, 1987).

Native Americans share a similar history of subordination with African Americans. As a group, they have been subjected to "conquest, dislocation, cultural disintegration, and spatial segregation" (Wilkinson, 1993, p. 32), and their personal estrangement and continued isolation are associated with family problems and high rates of alcoholism, suicide, and crime on reservations.

In general, extended family relations are highly valued and instrumentally important. Networks of relatives frequently live in close proximity. Women play a pivotal role in extended family processes, which include collective problem solving, sharing resources, and equal responsibility for the socialization of young children (Red Horse, Lewis, Feit, & Decker, 1978; Wilkinson, 1993). Red Horse et al. suggested that transactions within and among family networks take place in a "community context," and Wilkinson (1987) described a "village-type" organization of related households.

Although education is important to Native Americans, and many who leave reservations for training return to use their skills in the service of their tribes, American Indians as a group have low educational levels. For example, nearly half those who reside in rural communities have only an elementary school education (Wilkinson, 1993), and overall, only one in five has a high school education (LaFromboise, 1988).

In addition to the prevalence of poverty and high unemployment, as well as alcoholism and suicide, economic hardship and minority status are significant risk factors for poor mental health, especially depression (see, for example, Kessler & Neighbors, 1986). Indeed, Rhodes et al. (1980) found that Native Americans scored high on indicators of depression. Moreover, because many Native Americans equate mental illness with human weakness (LaFromboise, 1988), they view the need for mental health services as an indication of personal weakness.

This view of mental illness presents special challenges to mental health providers. In addition, the probable links among depression, suicide, alcoholism, and environmental factors in this population are poorly understood.

Therefore, a better understanding of the strategies used by Native Americans who cope successfully with demanding life circumstances (LaFromboise, 1988) is needed to devise programs and craft interventions that will efficaciously address the needs of those who are at the greatest risk.

Gay Men and Lesbians

Gay men and lesbians span all racial, ethnic, and socioeconomic groups. Nevertheless, elements of an identifiable culture can be derived from the literature. For example, Lukes and Land (1990) stated that many gay men and lesbians—especially those who live in large urban centers—seem to have recurring cultural experiences that are distinct from those embedded in their majority or ethnic minority culture. These experiences include pairing behavior; definitions of the family; the time, place, and reasons for celebrations; religious observances; and institutions and communities with purposes and boundaries that are defined by the sexual minority group.

The number of gay and lesbian people in the United States is uncertain, depending on the question being asked. An approximate rate of 10 percent of the population with a primarily same-gender sexual preference is often given (Dulaney & Kelly, 1982), but a more recent study (Billy, Tanfer, Grady, & Klepinger, 1993) suggested that some 2 percent of sexually active men age 20 to 39 have engaged in same-gender sexual activity during the past 10 years. A study by researchers at the Harvard University School of Public Health and the Center for Health Policy Studies ("Homosexual Attraction," 1994) reported rates of same-gender sexual behavior of about 6 percent for men and 3 percent for women over a five-year period, but indicated that about one person in five has reported being attracted to someone of the same sex at some time since age 15. Reported rates of same-gender sexual preference and behavior are clearly related to the extent of homophobia that is present at a given time and to changing societal values. It has been well documented that the oppression of and discrimination against these groups, especially gay men, have a long history (DiNitto & McNeece, 1990; Gramick, 1983; Kelly, 1990).

The homosexual experience is variable, and the population is highly diverse, owing to such factors as gender, socioeconomic status, race, geographic domicile, and the decision to be or not to be open about one's sexual preference. Nevertheless, although numerous lesbians and gay men develop long-lasting relationships, homosexual attachments, especially among gay men, are likely to change more often than are heterosexual ones (Kelly, 1990).

Cohabitant gay and lesbian couples, in comparison with their heterosexual counterparts, frequently have fewer or no children living at home and fewer shared legal commitments (marriage, for example) that tie them together. Children and binding or "fiat" obligations make it more difficult to end relationships; in short, emotional (as opposed to legal) bonds can be more variable.

In addition, much has been written about the socialization, affiliation, and intimacy functions of "gay bars," especially for men (DiNitto & McNeece, 1990; Kelly, 1990). DiNitto and McNeece observed, however, that gay bars often are unhealthy environments, particularly because they foster substance abuse and sexual risks.

Regarding group identification, individual identity formation, and decisions about openness, some theorists have contended that the construction of a homosexual identity may begin at various developmental points. For example, Coleman (1982) stated that most gay men and lesbians are aware of their sexual orientation during adolescence. However, for many, inhibition or repression may prevent them from identifying themselves as gay or lesbian until later in life (MacDonald, 1982). In fact, several researchers have found that one in five gay men and more than one in three lesbians married a heterosexual person before they identified themselves as homosexual (Bell & Wienberg, 1978; Hammersmith, 1987; Lukes & Land, 1990; Saghir & Robins, 1973).

When, if, and how lesbians and gay men decide to disclose their homosexuality are complex issues because gay men and lesbians are not easily distinguishable to each other or to their heterosexual counterparts. Furthermore, these decisions may result in either social support or social isolation, both from those in the sexual minority group and from those in the larger society. Of particular concern are the potentially negative consequences of social isolation because validating social supports can have a moderating influence on adverse psychological effects (see, for example, Lukes & Land, 1990).

Finally, it is important to note that homosexuality is no longer considered a disease (for a discussion of this and related historical influences, see Hyde, 1990), and should not be treated as such when person–environment mismatches culminate in clients' distress.

CULTURAL SENSITIVITY IN SOCIAL WORK PRACTICE

Cultural sensitivity in social work practice means the ability to interweave cultural awareness and an appreciation of the sociocultural forces that influence people's experiences into all phases of the helping process. However, no single specific activity or set of activities performed with or on behalf of particular clients provides a complete answer to what culturally sensitive practice is.

In general, practice is made culturally sensitive through a series of adaptations that connect the process of helping with the sociocultural characteristics of the particular persons, the specifics of their particular situations (presenting complaints or needs and expectations), and the ecological contexts (neighborhoods, relationships, families, communities, opportunity structures) within which these people and situations are embedded. Furthermore, because political correctness frequently masks the biased attitudes of helping professionals in the majority group, the attainment of cultural sensitivity is an ongoing, open-ended process.

Thus, an exhaustive account of all the ways in which practice can be made culturally sensitive is neither possible nor desirable. Rather, this author proposes that multiculturally competent practice is grounded in the differential application of knowledge and skills that are relevant to each phase of the helping process. The first, or engagement, phase is particularly important, given that poor and minority clients are more likely to drop out of treatment during this phase (McGoldrick, 1982; D. W. Sue & D. Sue, 1990; S. Sue & Zane, 1987; Tolson, 1988).

Minority clients may drop out of treatment during the first phase because they often feel disaffected and undervalued by the majority culture and are frequently distrustful, owing to past experiences with prejudice and oppression (Davis & Proctor, 1989; D. W. Sue & D. Sue, 1990). Thus, during early contacts, skillful social workers should anticipate manifestations of wariness and suspicion and be prepared to respond both empathically and nondefensively. This manner of response demonstrates not only their competence and credibility, but an appreciation of the validity of the clients' concerns and a willingness to address them.

Moreover, multicultural competence demands the active engagement of the larger contexts within which clients are embedded. For example, in an inner-city school-based program in which services are delivered by a child welfare agency located at a different site, the social worker must establish a clear and visible presence in the school community by, for example, participating in organizations, committees, and extracurricular activities. In so doing, the social worker is able to stay in touch with the needs and concerns of the school and to create an atmosphere in which he or she can address needs at the individual, group, and institutional levels.

To return to the beginning phase of the helping process, it is common to begin an assessment of the strengths and weaknesses of a client. The multiculturally competent social worker will extend this process to include an appraisal of the strengths and shortcomings of the contexts as well. Such a procedure ultimately leads to the formulation of an intervention plan.

The ecosystems perspective is uniquely suited to the attainment of culturally sensitive social work with minority clients because it emphasizes the ecological contexts within which people's needs and concerns are understood (see, for example, Meyer, 1993). Bronfenbrenner (1988) stated that a basic tenet of the ecological perspective is the fit between the characteristics of living organisms and their surroundings. He also noted that because people are limited in the kinds of ecologies in which they can survive and develop, it is important "to identify the nature of this finite set of ecological conditions and to assess their . . . potential for sustaining and fostering human growth" (p. 47).

The preceding discussion points the way to the exigency that early assessment activities, particularly with minority clients, should focus on the person–environment fit (see also Germain & Gitterman, 1980; Meyer, 1976). No presumptions are made about whether presenting problems are a result of individual deficiencies, detrimental physical and sociocultural contexts, or some interaction of the two. Rather, the social worker explores the specific situations associated with a client's needs and concerns, attempting to determine the unique strengths and shortcomings in both the person and his or her environment.

Data gathered during the assessment process typically provide both the social worker and the client with plausible notions—or hypotheses—about the nature of the person–environment fit and mismatches. Although it may not be easy to integrate this information and make a full assessment of persons in context, for minority clients, whose social functioning may be intertwined with issues of immigration, acculturation, poverty, and discrimination, this approach is particularly appropriate.

The processes and outcomes of engagement and assessment are even more significant for planning and implementing interventions. Specifically, the social worker and the client collaborate to determine the desired outcomes, the strategies to achieve them, and the duration of the work that will make up the middle phase of the helping process. This plan—or contract—guides the subsequent work and provides a standard for evaluating practice effectiveness at predetermined intervals. Furthermore, client empowerment, an important objective of multiculturally competent practice, is maximized from the outset by the collaborative nature of the assessment, contracting, and ongoing intervention processes (Gutierrez, 1990).

The literature on specific interventions that are used in the middle phase is vast and variable and this is not detailed here (see, for example, Tolson, 1988). In the context of multiculturally competent practice, it is important to note, however, that the middle phase of practice, regardless of the theories, models, and modalities used, includes approaches and strategies that address the enhancement of personal and environmental resources (Herr, 1991). For example, interventions may include facilitating new experiences through the development and handling of the social worker–client relationship; facilitating the client's attainment of competencies, skills, and support networks that increase his or her efficacy and personal empowerment; and working with the client on initiatives that define policies, practices, and priorities at the societal and institutional levels. Such work becomes multicultural and multicontextual when the social worker and the client collaborate to generate strategies for strengthening individual and environmental resources.

Persons and contexts continue to be immersed in patterns of inequity and discrimination for racial, cultural, and sexual minorities. Despite progress in many areas, the opportunities and choices of certain groups are still constrained. The ultimate goal of social work practice is to facilitate experiences of equity, justice, validity, and empowerment for people and their environments. The ideas presented here are offered in support of the latter effort. If this discussion contributes to the achievement of a portion of this goal, it will have served its foremost ambition.

References

Baca Zinn, M. (1980). Employment and education of Mexican-American women: The interplay of modernity and ethnicity in eight families. *Harvard Educational Review, 50*, 47–62.

Bell, A. P., & Wienberg, M. S. (1978). *Homosexuality: A study of diversity among men and women.* New York: Simon & Schuster.

Bell-Scott, P., & Taylor, R. L. (1989). Introduction: The multiple ecologies of black development. In P. Bell-Scott & R. L. Taylor (Eds.), *Journal of Adolescent Research* [Special issue on black adolescents], *30*, 119–124.

Billy, J.O.G., Tanfer, K., Grady, W. R., & Klepinger, D. H. (1993). The sexual behavior of men in the United States. *Family Planning Perspectives, 25,* 52–60.

Blackwell, J. E. (1985). *The Black community: Diversity and unity.* New York: Dodd, Mead.

Bowman, P. J. (1991a). Worklife. In J. S. Jackson (Ed.), *Life in Black America* (pp. 124–155). Newbury Park, CA: Sage Publications.

Bowman, P. J. (1991b). Joblessness. In J. S. Jackson (Ed.), *Life in Black America* (pp. 156–178). Newbury Park, CA: Sage Publications.

Bronfenbrenner, U. (1986). Ecology of the family as a context for human development: Research perspectives. *Developmental Psychology, 22,* 723–742.

Bronfenbrenner, U. (1988). Interacting systems in human development. Research paradigms: Present and future. In N. Bolger, A. Caspi, G. Downey, & M. Moorehouse (Eds.), *Persons in context: Developmental processes* (pp. 25–49). Cambridge, England: Cambridge University Press.

Chestang, L. W. (1993). Infusion of minority content in the curriculum. In D. M. Pearson (Ed.), *Perspectives on equity and justice in social work* (pp. 1–14). Alexandria, VA: Council on Social Work Education.

Chilman, C. S. (1993). Hispanic families in the United States: Research perspectives. In H. P. McAdoo (Ed.), *Family ethnicity: Strength in diversity* (pp. 141–163). Newbury Park, CA: Sage Publications.

Coleman, E. (1982). Developmental stages of the coming-out process. *Journal of Homosexuality, 7,* 31–43.

Cooney, R. S., Rogler, L. H., Hurrer, R., & Ortiz, V. (1982). Decision making in Puerto Rican families. *Journal of Marriage and the Family, 44,* 621–631.

Cose, E. (1993). *The rage of a privileged class.* New York: HarperCollins.

Davis, L. E., & Proctor, E. K. (1989). *Race, gender and class.* Englewood Cliffs, NJ: Prentice Hall.

DiNitto, D. M., & McNeece, C. A. (1990). *Social work: Issues and opportunities in a challenging profession.* Englewood Cliffs, NJ: Prentice Hall.

Dulaney, D., & Kelly, J. (1982). Improving services to gay and lesbian clients. *Social Work, 27,* 178–183.

Filmore, L. W., & Cheong, J. (1980). The early socialization of Asian-American female children. In *Conference on the Educational and Occupational Needs of Asian-Pacific-American Women.* Washington, DC: U.S. Department of Education, National Institute of Education.

Gaiter, L. (1994, June 26). The revolt of the black bourgeoisie. *New York Times Magazine,* pp. 42–43.

Garcia-Preto, N. (1982). Puerto Rican families. In M. McGoldrick, J. K. Pearce, & J. Giordano (Eds.), *Ethnicity and family therapy* (pp. 164–186). New York: Guilford Press.

Garfinkel, I., & McLanahan, S. (1986). *Single mothers and their children: A new American dilemma*. Washington, DC: Urban Institute Press.

Germain, C., & Gitterman, A. (1980). *The life model of social work practice*. New York: Columbia University Press.

Gramick, J. (1983). Homophobia: A new challenge. *Social Work, 28*, 137–141.

Greene, M. (1993). Diversity and inclusion: Toward a curriculum for human beings. *Teachers College Record, 95*, 211–221.

Gutierrez, L. M. (1990). Working with women of color: An empowerment perspective. *Social Work, 35*, 149–153.

Hammersmith, S. K. (1987). A sociological approach to counseling homosexual clients and their families. In E. Coleman (Ed.), *Integrated identity for gay men and lesbians* (pp. 173–190). New York: Harrington Park Press.

Helms, J. E. (1990). *Black and white racial identity: Theory, research and practice*. Westport, CT: Greenwood Press.

Herr, E. L. (1991). Ecological challenges to counseling in a world of cultural and racial diversity. In E. L. Herr & J. A. McFadden (Eds.), *Challenges of cultural and racial diversity to counseling* (pp. 9–20). Alexandria, VA: American Association for Counseling and Development.

Hirschman, C., & Wong, M. (1981). Trends in socioeconomic achievement among immigrant and native born Asian Americans, 1960-1976. *Sociological Quarterly, 22*, 495–513.

Ho, M. K. (1991). Use of Ethnic-Sensitive Inventory (ESI) to enhance practitioner skills with minorities. *Journal of Multicultural Social Work, 1*, 57–67.

Homosexual attraction is found in 1 of 5. (1994, September 6). *New York Times*, p. A14.

Hyde, J. (1990). *Understanding human sexuality*. New York: McGraw-Hill.

Jackson, A. P. (1992). Well-being among single, black employed mothers. *Social Service Review, 66*, 399–409.

Jackson, A. P. (1993). Black single working mothers in poverty: Preferences for employment, well-being, and perceptions of preschool-aged children. *Social Work, 38*, 26–34.

Jackson, A. P. (1994). The effects of role strain on single, working, black mothers' perceptions of their young children. *Social Work Research, 18*, 36–39.

Jencks, C. (1992). *Rethinking social policy: Race, poverty, and the underclass*. Cambridge, MA: Harvard University Press.

Kamerman, S. B., & Kahn, A. J. (1988). *Mothers alone: Strategies for a time of change*. Dover, MA: Auburn House.

Kasarda, J. (1983). Caught in the web of change. *Society, 21,* 4–7.

Kelly, G. (1990). *Sexuality today: The human perspective.* Guilford, CT: Duskin.

Kessler, R. C., & Neighbors, H. W. (1986). A new perspective on the relationships among race, social class, and psychological distress. *Journal of Health and Social Behavior, 27,* 107–115.

Kirschenman, J., & Neckerman, K. M. (1989, September). *We'd love to hire them, but. . . .* Paper presented at the Social Science Research Council's Conference on the Truly Disadvantaged, Chicago.

LaFromboise, T. D. (1988). American Indian mental health policy. *American Psychologist, 43,* 388–397.

Longres, J. F. (1991). Toward a status model of ethnic-sensitive practice. *Journal of Multicultural Social Work, 1,* 41–56.

Lukes, C. A., & Land, H. (1990). Biculturality and homosexuality. *Social Work, 35,* 155–161.

MacDonald, G. (1982). Individual differences in the coming-out process for gay men: Implications for theoretical models. *Journal of Homosexuality, 80,* 47–60.

Mann, E. S., & Salvo, J. J. (1985). Characteristics of new Hispanic immigrants to New York City: A comparison of Puerto Rican and non-Puerto Rican Hispanics. *Research Bulletin* (Hispanic Research Center), *8,* 1–8.

McAdoo, H. P. (Ed.) (1993). *Family ethnicity: Strength in diversity.* Newbury Park, CA: Sage Publications.

McGoldrick, M. (1982). Ethnicity and family therapy: An overview. In M. McGoldrick, J. K. Pearce, & J. Giordano (Eds.), *Ethnicity and family therapy* (pp. 3–30). New York: Guilford Press.

McLoyd, V. C. (1990). The impact of economic hardship on black families and children: Psychological distress, parenting, and socioemotional development. *Child Development, 61,* 311–346.

Meyer, C. H. (1976). *Social work practice: The changing landscape.* New York: Free Press.

Meyer, C. H. (1993). *Assessment in social work practice.* New York: Columbia University Press.

Moore, J., & Pachon, H. (1985). *Hispanics in the United States.* Englewood Cliffs, NJ: Prentice Hall.

Norton, D. G. (1993). Diversity, early socialization, and temporal development: The dual perspective revisited. In D. M. Pearson (Ed.), *Perspectives on equity and justice in social work* (pp. 17–33). Alexandria, VA: Council on Social Work Education.

Pearson, D. M. (Ed.) (1993). *Perspectives on equity and justice in social work.* Alexandria, VA: Council on Social Work Education.

Pedersen, P. B. (1988). *A handbook for developing multicultural awareness.* Alexandria, VA: American Association for Counseling and Development.

Pinderhughes, E. (1983). Empowerment for our clients and for ourselves. *Social Casework, 64,* 331–338.

Red Horse, J. G., Lewis, R., Feit, M., & Decker, J. (1978). Family behavior of urban American Indians. *Social Casework, 59*, 67–72.

Rhodes, E. R., Marshall, M., Attneave, D., Echohawk, M., Bjork, J., & Beiser, M. (1980). Mental health problems of American Indians seen in outpatient facilities of the Indian Health Service, 1975. *Public Health Reports, 96*, 329–335.

Saghir, M. R., & Robins, E. (1973). *Male and female homosexuality: A comprehensive investigation.* Baltimore: Williams & Wilkins.

Simon, B. L. (1990). Rethinking empowerment. *Journal of Progressive Human Services, 1*, 27–39.

Spencer, M. B. (1990). Development of minority children: An introduction. *Child Development, 61*, 267–269.

Staples, R., & Mirande, A. (1980). Racial and cultural variations among American families: A decennial review of the literature on minority families. *Journal of Marriage and the Family, 42*, 142–168.

Sue, D. W., Arrendondo, P., & McDavis, R. J. (1992). Multicultural counseling competencies and standards: A call to the profession. *Journal of Multicultural Counseling & Development, 70*, 64–88.

Sue, D. W., & Sue, D. (1990). *Counseling the culturally different: Theory and practice* (2nd ed.). New York: John Wiley & Sons.

Sue, S., & Kitano, H. (1973). Asian American stereotypes. *Journal of Social Issues, 29*, 83–98.

Sue, S., & Zane, N. (1987). The role of culture and cultural techniques and psychotherapy: A critique and reformulation. *American Psychologist, 42*, 37–45.

Szapocnik, J., & Kurstnes, W. (1980). Acculturation, biculturalism, and adjustment among Cuban-Americans. In A. M. Padilla (Ed.), *Acculturation: Theory, models and some new findings* (pp. 85–109). Boulder, CO: Westview Press.

Tolson, E. R. (1988). *The metamodel and clinical social work.* New York: Columbia University Press.

U.S. Bureau of the Census. (1991). *Statistical abstract of the United States, 1991* (111th ed., Table 17). Washington, DC: U.S. Government Printing Office.

Vega, W. A. (1990). Hispanic families in the 1980s: A decade of research. *Journal of Marriage and the Family, 52*, 1015–1024.

Walker, A. J. (1993). Teaching about race, gender, and class diversity in United States families. *Family Relations, 42*, 342–350.

West, C. (1993). *Race matters.* Boston: Beacon Press.

Wilkinson, D. (1987). *Ethnicity.* In S. Steinmertz & M. B. Sussman (Eds.), *Handbook of marriage and the family* (pp. 345–405). New York: Plenum Press.

Wilkinson, D. (1993). Family ethnicity in America. In H. P. McAdoo (Ed.), *Family ethnicity: Strength in diversity* (pp. 15–59). Newbury Park, CA: Sage Publications.

Wilkinson, D., & Taylor, R. (Eds.) (1977). *The Black male in America: Perspectives on his status in contemporary society.* Chicago: Nelson Hall.

Wilson, W. J. (1987). *The truly disadvantaged: The inner city, the underclass, and public policy.* Chicago: University of Chicago Press.

Wong, M. D., & Hirschman, C. (1983). Labor force participation and socioeconomic attainment of Asian American women. *Sociological Perspectives, 26,* 523–546.

Wrenn, C. G. (1985). The culturally encapsulated counselor revisited. In P. Pedersen (Ed.), *Handbook of cross-cultural counseling and therapy* (pp. 323–330). Westport, CT: Greenwood Press.

Ybarra, L. (1982). When wives work. *Journal of Marriage and the Family, 44,* 169–177.

Yoshiwara, F. M. (1983). Shattering myths: Japanese American educational issues. In D. T. Nakanishi & M. Hirano-Nakanishi (Eds.), *The education of Asian and Pacific Americans: Historical perspectives and prescriptions for the future* (pp. 15–37). Phoenix: Oryx Press.

5

Knowledge for Practice

Mark A. Mattaini

Bartlett (1970) suggested that "mature professions rest on strong bodies of knowledge and values" (p. 63). A case can be made that professionals and nonprofessionals may share similar values (discussed in chapter 3) (although holding them *in common* is crucial for a profession) and therefore that knowledge is the most distinctive aspect of professional practice. This chapter discusses the difficulties in defining and sharing knowledge and explores a variety of strategies for discovering and testing knowledge that have proved valuable to social workers.

KNOWLEDGE

The nature of knowledge is not straightforward. Among the definitions of knowledge listed in The New Shorter Oxford English Dictionary (1993) are the following:

(a) the fact of knowing a thing, state, person, etc.; acquaintance, familiarity gained by experience;

(b) intellectual perception of fact or truth; clear and certain understanding or awareness, esp. as opposed to opinion; and

(c) theoretical or practical understanding of an art, science, industry, etc. (p. 1503).

"Knowledge propositions," Bartlett (1970) suggested, "refer to verifiable experience and appear in the form of rigorous statements that are made as objective as possible" (p. 63). Even without immersing oneself and becoming enmeshed in the current "crisis in philosophy" (Smith, 1988, p. 51), one can see that the potential difficulties are clear: What counts as "practical understanding," "intellectual perception," "fact or truth," or "clear and certain awareness," for example?

Theoreticians of social work also engage in conflicts regarding the nature of evidence, the possibility of objectivity, and appropriate strategies for observing, making sense of, and transforming reality (see, for example, Pieper &

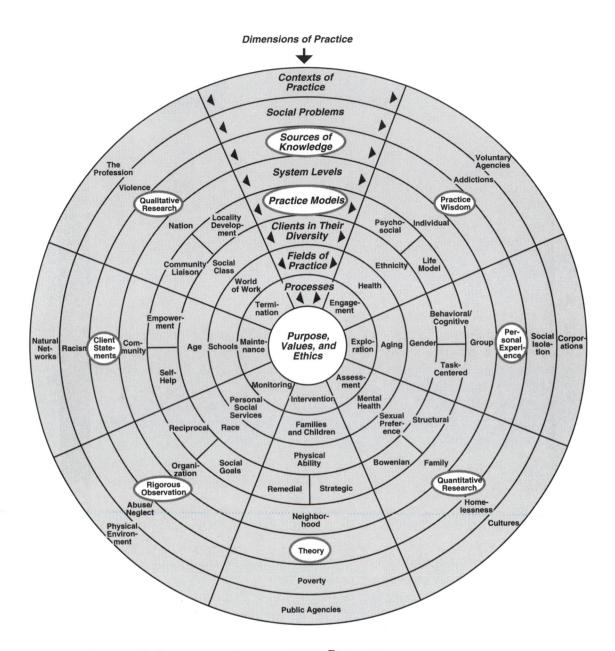

Dimensions of Practice

FIGURE 5-1. SOURCES OF KNOWLEDGE FOR PRACTICE

Pieper, 1993; Wakefield, 1993). Scientists and philosophers long ago recognized people's almost limitless potential for self-deception, especially when particular beliefs lead to actions that are likely to be rewarded in various ways. The scientific method may be seen as a system of rules to control impulses to believe what one wishes to believe, whether or not it is based on facts (Ainslie, 1993).

Misperceptions of causal relationships are another danger. Actions that are followed by positive events or conditions tend to be repeated. Note, however, that the relationship is essentially temporal: Whatever comes before a positive outcome is likely to be repeated, *whether or not there is a genuine causal connection*. For example, particular rituals, if repeated often enough, are likely to be followed eventually by rain or bountiful harvests and are then likely to be repeated whenever that outcome is desired. Even pigeons readily develop superstitions: If a pigeon happens to be scratching or turning when it receives a food pellet delivered randomly, its scratching or turning increases (Skinner, 1948). Thus, although a client may improve after a social worker provides an emotionally supportive environment for several sessions, a connection between the two is possible, but by no means certain. The cause of the change may be something else, such as an increase in hours of daylight that ameliorates seasonal affective disorder or the concurrent resolution of an ongoing interpersonal conflict.

Rules to limit such misperceptions are clearly important. At the same time, "social constructionists" have pointed out that "belief is . . . a form of behavior and subject to the needs and wishes of the individual, with or without the mediation of culture" (Ainslie, 1993, p. 72). In other words, it is difficult to see clearly through lenses clouded by experiences, theoretical stances, and incentives to believe one of several possible alternatives. In the method that is used to understand this subjective reality, often called "deconstruction," one attempts to discern the meaning for the speaker or author of a narrative or text. (The language used in this area is not yet entirely stable; one reads of "social constructionists" or "social constructivists" [emphasizing the way realities are constructed] and of "deconstructionists" and "deconstructionism" [emphasizing the way social constructions can be dissected]. I am using Ainslie's language here.)

It is possible to "marry" empiricism and constructionism, as long as the possibility of connecting—to some extent—with reality is acknowledged (Gould, 1993). Radical constructionists, however, suggest that reality is altogether unknowable, that no attempt to develop knowledge corresponding to objective fact is possible, and that the scientific method is just another set of beliefs with no special claim to validity. This stance is taken seriously in some areas of the humanities, social sciences, and philosophy of science, although generally not in the natural sciences (Searle, 1993).

Radical constructionism is not a serious alternative for social work practice any more than it is for engineering. Bridges stand or fall, and a hungry child, a battered spouse, or an alcoholic person racked by despair is real enough to be accepted as genuine by most practitioners, even though they recognize that their observations may include some distortion. Most people accept that external reality exists and that they can observe and affect it to some extent. At the same time, there are multiple ways to examine and understand that reality, each of which has limitations. These approaches are the subject of this chapter.

Although the distinctions may be artificial, the sources of knowledge that are considered here include practice wisdom gleaned from narrated experiences of the profession and professional colleagues, the personal experience of the practitioner, literature, history and current events, descriptive research (qualitative and quantitative), experimental research, information provided by the case itself, and theoretical and conceptual analyses. With regard to the last source, there is substantial variation among theoretical schools within the profession, and it will be necessary to think about that area in some depth.

The social worker may draw explicitly on some of these sources of knowledge in making a specific practice decision (which may be as apparently simple as whether to say, "I wonder how that affected you?" or "What happened next?"— to go deeper or to move on), whereas others may remain unarticulated background, but still shape practice in crucial ways.

SOURCES OF KNOWLEDGE

Practice Wisdom

Although it is often mentioned in discussions of social work practice, "practice wisdom" is seldom defined or explored in depth in textbooks on practice. Practice wisdom is a slippery concept, yet there can be little doubt that much of what happens in practice is based on something like it. In this chapter, the term "practice wisdom" is used to refer to two separate but related phenomena: (1) explicit rules that are handed down by experienced practitioners to others that appear to "work"—heuristic rules of thumb that are "good enough" to guide much of practice—and (2) patterns of professional behavior, which may or may not be articulated, that have been shaped and refined over years of practice and serve as models for other workers. These two forms of knowledge are passed on from generation to generation of social workers, sometimes as a form of oral tradition.

Examples of the first type of practice wisdom include general maxims like "Start where the client is," as well as more specific rules, such as, "With this client population, it is important to meet concrete needs before trying to explore emotional issues." Although such suggestions could be examined empirically, social workers do not have time to test everything, and a common core of generally accepted knowledge of this kind probably guides much of practice. Experienced social workers often have learned a tremendous amount that can be of value to others, so the importance of this type of knowledge should not be minimized.

There are risks associated with a reliance on such rules, however. First and most important, the rules may be inaccurate (having been passed on persuasively by those who strongly believe in the erroneous rules) and therefore result in less-than-adequate services to clients. For example, social workers in the field of substance abuse often apply codependency theory, which "assert[s] that a woman married to an alcoholic contribute[s] to her husband's addiction because of her own disturbed personality needs" (Collins, 1993, p. 471). Though this concept is commonly presented as a fact and many social workers now operate according to this framework, there is substantial reason to doubt its accuracy (Collins). Personal values may also obscure accurate perceptions.

Another risk is that accepted rules sometimes grow more from what works for the practitioner than what works for the client. For instance, it is common to hear practitioners say that some clients, or even whole classes of clients, are "not ready," "not motivated," or "resistant" to intervention and therefore to concentrate on other less troublesome clients. There are reasons for resistance, however, and it is often possible to work effectively with clients who initially seem resistant (Gitterman, 1983).

The second type of practice wisdom, patterns of professional behavior shaped by practice experience, is also essential, although it is more difficult to capture. Sometimes workers know what they are doing and why they are doing it and can pass this information on verbally. At other times, effective practitioners cannot explain exactly what they do or why, but by observing their timing or the inflection of their voices during clinical sessions, for example, others can learn to do much the same thing. This is one reason why video- or audiotaped sample sessions and real or simulated clinical presentations are valuable. Not only can those observing notice the principles that are the focus of a session or demonstration, but they may be able to observe and learn, consciously or not, from the many subtle behavioral events that occur simultaneously.

These behaviors are often described as part of the "art" of practice, which has been shaped, often outside the social worker's awareness, by practice events over years of experience. Some researchers have tried to develop methods to extract principles from such unarticulated practice (for example, Schön, 1983) with some success. "Knowledge engineering" in the development of computerized expert systems is a related approach, in which an expert is interviewed in a structured way in an attempt to extract the rules on which the expert bases his or her professional decisions. The expert does not always recognize the factors that shape his or her behavior, however, and there is some risk that the explanation presented may be plausible, but inaccurate.

Despite its essential role, practice wisdom should be applied cautiously. Because of the possibility of distortion, it is important for the social worker to constantly monitor whether approaches rooted in this body of knowledge (or any other) contribute to meeting a client's goals. If they do not, other options should be examined. Second, knowledge that has been hardened by support from multiple sources (practice wisdom and empirical testing, for example, or common rules suggested by multiple experienced practitioners) should ordinarily be preferred to knowledge that lacks such support. Interventive strategies that are experimental should be presented as such to a client and should be monitored closely to avoid iatrogenic outcomes.

Personal Experience

In addition to learning from the experiences of other practitioners, social workers base their work on their own life experiences (personal and professional). It is crucial for them to do so, in effect, to develop their own personal practice wisdom, so they do not need to begin again with every client. The basic interpersonal and problem-solving skills that social workers have developed throughout their lives also inform their practice.

It is important to recognize explicitly the influence of personal history because one may overgeneralize from one's experiences, transforming a potential resource into an obstacle. For example, a success or failure with one client may lead the social worker to select or avoid using particular interventive strategies again, and that is as it should be. Nevertheless, an intervention that works or does not work in one case may produce different results in other cases in which a different configuration is present. Therefore, the ability to individualize a case and to be open to learning new state-of-the-art approaches is crucial to both effectiveness and ethical requirements.

Personal life experiences can inform or impede practice in other ways. Personal values that are learned early in life often guide a practitioner's professional activities. These values can be beneficial when they are congruent with professional values, as is the case with acceptance and caring. However, when personal values conflict with professional values, they create a dilemma for practitioners—witness the struggle of some social workers who believe that abortion is wrong, but are required by professional values to support a client's right to choose whether or not to have an abortion (self-determination).

There is no simple answer to such dilemmas, but the profession holds that conduct that is consistent with professional values is ordinarily required. Self-determination is among those professional values, but even it is not as simple as it may appear to be. In many cultures, the good of the group, rather than self-interest, is seen as a core value, which suggests the need for a sophisticated reexamination of this concept within a multicultural context (Ewalt, 1994). The issue of the extent to which clients freely choose among courses of action—either because of limited personal capacity or because many theories of behavior suggest that much of human action is determined by factors outside the awareness or control of the individual—also requires careful thought. And, of course, when self-determination and safety conflict, social workers must make difficult decisions.

A situation in which a client is struggling with issues that the social worker dealt with in the past presents both advantages and disadvantages. Although such common experiences may increase the practitioner's empathy for the client, they may also lead the practitioner to push the client toward alternatives that worked for the practitioner, but that may not be helpful to the client. For example, a social worker who has benefited (as many have) from a 12-step program for substance abuse may consider those programs to be the most effective available (although studies have suggested that the situation is far more complex) and refer clients to those programs to the exclusion of others that may be a better fit for the clients (Miller, 1989). Each case is different; each person is different and may have different needs.

Likewise, issues of self-disclosure become significant when the social worker has had personal experiences similar to the client's. For example, a practitioner who has been treated for cancer may find it helpful to share that fact with a client who has been recently diagnosed with cancer, but in other cases, the disclosure of personal information may inhibit the client from sharing genuine feelings. The research on self-disclosure has not yet clarified specifically how and in what situations it should be used, so social workers must decide what information to disclose and when to disclose it on a case-by-case basis. A moderate level of self-disclosure, consciously used to benefit the client (rather than to meet the needs of the social worker) can often be valuable for communicating empathy and demonstrating authenticity. That practitioners are using self-disclosure more than they did in the past (S. Anderson & Mandell,

1989) suggests that the value of appropriate self-disclosure has become part of the profession's body of practice wisdom.

A potential dilemma occurs when a client is struggling with an issue that the worker is also currently facing. This is usually a serious problem; although self-disclosure is generally not appropriate under those circumstances, the issues go well beyond that. For example, a practitioner who is going through a divorce may find it difficult to work effectively with couples (because of countertransference—a form of overgeneralization). Similarly, a social worker with a substance abuse problem may minimize, deny, or project such problems onto clients. And a practitioner who continues to be deeply disturbed by images of abuse in her childhood is unlikely to be able to deal with either a victim or a perpetrator of abuse.

In such circumstances, social workers need, at a minimum, close supervision and consultation, but because the welfare of the clients is the primary consideration, such cases may have to be transferred to other practitioners. A social worker who is significantly impaired (emotionally or by substance abuse) has an ethical responsibility to get help, and his or her colleagues who are aware of the problem have an ethical responsibility to assist the practitioner to get help and to protect his or her clients.

Clearly, such situations illustrate the need for personal self-awareness by practitioners. Social workers must be in touch with their own constantly shifting thoughts and emotions in practice, recognize that their needs and experiences may color what they see and do—and that possible distortions introduced by such thoughts and emotions may interfere with the quality of service given to the client. When social workers notice strong emotions in themselves, they should reflect on the roots of these feelings and be willing to talk with a supervisor, a respected colleague, or a therapist who can help them make sense of what is happening. Putting these struggles into words and sharing them is a primary way of clarifying and sorting them out. The client, however, is not an appropriate audience for such reflections. Practitioners should also take time to think about how their life experiences and values may affect their work in the future and prepare to deal with the probable conflicts that may arise from them.

History and Current Events

Because practice is embedded in the broader social context, knowledge of social policy (both current policy and its historical roots) and of shifting social forces is important for social workers at all levels. Although this domain is treated primarily in social policy courses, its integral interconnections with practice must be recognized. Both the technical policy literature and the mass media are sources of this information; however, social workers must view data from any source critically in the context of their full knowledge base because each source observes and reports events according to its own value base and political position.

It is common, of course, for news stories in the mass media to be reported in less than fully objective ways, and with some inaccuracies, but the same is true even of the more technical literature. Even relatively objective "facts," such as the number of people living below the poverty line, tend to be reported and interpreted differently by those of varying political bents. The differences are even more profound in discussions of the causes of and potential solutions to social problems. Although this situation can be frustrating, and one may be tempted simply to avoid the issues, they must be engaged because they are important to the well-being of clients. The only defensible solution is to read widely—to avoid slipping blindly into one's own selective bias—and to think critically in the context of professional values.

Defining Art and Literature

Professional social work practice is grounded in a broad knowledge of the liberal arts, including history, science (considered later), and art and literature, which capture cultural values and wisdom differently than anything else does. Art and literature provide both context and content for decision making and action in practice. For example, the Ashcan school of painting in the early 20th century captured the realities of urban life in new ways, whereas Japanese sumi-e ink paintings and Zen art use symbols and simplicity to express eternal truths (see, for example, Figure 5-2).

Or consider poetry. How better to remind oneself of the dignity and value of every person, of genuine acceptance and respect, than with the words of Walt Whitman (1892/1992):

drinking
a bowl of green tea
I stopped the war

FIGURE 5-2. A "ZEN TELEGRAM"
Reprinted with permission from Rep, P. (1959). bowl of tea. In Zen telegrams *(p. 47). Rutland, VT: Charles E. Tuttle.*

None has understood you, but I understand you,

None has done justice to you, you have not done justice to yourself,

None but has found you imperfect, I only find no imperfection in you,

None but would subordinate you, I only am he who will never consent to subordinate you,

I only am he who places over you no master, owner, better, God, beyond what waits intrinsically in yourself. (p. 177)

Drama, novels, and other classical and contemporary literature help define the cultures within which clients and social workers live out their lives and can immeasurably enrich practice. From authors like William Shakespeare, Toni Morrison, Herman Melville, and Joseph Heller come many of the words and shared experiences that inspire and guide practice, either explicitly or implicitly.

Naturalistic Research

Naturalistic research is the rigorous observation of phenomena that are important to social work practice (as opposed to experimental research, in which the investigator makes changes in some variables and observes the outcome). Just as many natural events can be studied only through observation (as in astronomy or some branches of ecology), many social phenomena with which social workers are concerned can be understood best when examined in their natural state.

There is a wide variety of approaches to naturalistic research. The social worker may use existing epidemiological or agency data or gather new data using interviews and questionnaires, for example, using quantitative or qualitative methods or a combination of the two. The research questions may relate to who clients (or potential clients) are; the extent and patterns of problems that clients experience; other factors that may cause, be the result of, or otherwise be associated with the problems; or the way that practice is conducted and what its outcomes are. If knowledge is the basis of professional practice, social workers need to know a great deal about such issues.

For example, the January 1994 issue of *Social Work* included reports of naturalistic studies of contacts between incarcerated mothers and foster care workers, the disengagement of divorced fathers, the effects of social values on support for public assistance for poor people, the causes and trends of homelessness in rural areas, and a number of other topics of concern to social work practice at various levels—from work with individuals to community and policy practice.

Knowing what is happening and to whom, as well as when, where, and why is obviously essential. Why, then, is the importance of such research sometimes controversial in the profession? There seem to be several reasons. The least defensible reason is that research is not always easy to understand. For example, in his article, "Ideological influences on public support for assistance to poor families," Groskind (1994) reported the results of techniques such as factor analysis and multiple regression, including statistics, significance levels, and other information that is important in quantitative research. For those who understand these things, the results are meaningful, but for those who do not, they may seem like an unknown language. The phenomena with which social workers deal are, by their very nature, complex. Therefore, analytic techniques adequate to capture the issues will also be complex, and social workers must rise to the challenge of understanding those techniques. Although research of this kind is not always informative for practice, some of it is, and the only way to know the difference is to be able to judge for oneself.

Quantitative vs. Qualitative Research

Another issue that complicates the use of research is the controversy in some professional circles over the relative values of quantitative and qualitative research. Quantitative research, which uses methods that have been developed over the past several centuries in the natural sciences, emphasizes objectivity, measures that remain constant over time and often across studies, and efforts to quantify a phenomenon (to determine "how much" of a phenomenon exists) by counting frequencies of events (such as how many children died from child abuse in the past year) or using standardized ratings and scales (to determine, for instance, how depressed a client is, using the Beck Depression Inventory). (Quantitative research also often places particular value on experimental results.)

Qualitative research, on the other hand, emphasizes efforts to understand phenomena holistically, including their subjective aspects. Qualitative researchers often use the data as a guide for developing their categories and concepts and sometimes view themselves as the "instruments" of the research (Lincoln & Guba, 1985). The methodology tends to focus on techniques such as participant observation, semistructured interviews, and hermeneutic analyses of "texts." Qualitative studies like Rycraft's (1994), which traced the reasons why social workers remain in positions in public child welfare, can produce findings that are rich in detail and accessible in ways that other approaches cannot equal.

Resolution of the split between quantitative and qualitative methods is difficult (for more details, see Reid & Smith, 1989, pp. 86-91), although some researchers have been able to combine the two approaches coherently (Miles & Huberman, 1994). To the extent that the epistemologies within which the approaches are based are incommensurate, the issue cannot be resolved by logical argument. However, some principles may help practitioners through this philosophical minefield. One such principle is that rigor is important; if the research is to guide practice with people facing difficult or painful problems, there should be persuasive evidence that the data presented reflect more than the researchers' personal bias. The literature is littered with case studies that describe the amazing effectiveness of every imaginable technique, including many that have ultimately been found to be dangerous, so there is reason to maintain a healthy skepticism about all results that do not present persuasive evidence.

In quantitative studies, "controls," statistics, and measures of reliability and validity provide such evidence. In qualitative studies, techniques such as presenting extensive direct quotations so readers can make their own judgments and having several other researchers examine the raw data to ensure that the findings do not reflect a single researcher's biases are critical. The increasing use of matrices and networks that explicitly indicate and model connections extracted from qualitative data is an important development in qualitative analysis (Miles & Huberman, 1994). And, of course, no one study can be regarded as definitive; thus, it is essential that important findings be replicated by other researchers.

There is much to learn from a variety of types of research. The rich detail provided by qualitative methods can be especially valuable for suggesting hypotheses (structured observation has proven crucial, especially in the discovery stage, in many sciences), and patterns that seem to be present can later be tested in other ways. For example, a network of causal connections among variables discovered by qualitative methods could be tested for accuracy and the magnitude of direct and indirect effects using path analysis, a quantitative method rooted in multiple regression. At the same time, the precision and generality offered by quantitative approaches can be critical for understanding large-scale social problems, as well as for testing the results of interventive strategies. Qualitative research may identify important factors and relationships in a single case or in the examination of a service system that would otherwise be missed. Quantitative research can be helpful in specifying patterns among the data to determine how important and reliable those factors and relationships are.

Experimental Research

"To experiment, to try it, seems to me the natural impulse, inhibited and replaced in our education by subservience to authority, acceptance of dogma, from our parents or our leaders" (Bates, 1950/1990, p. 274). Experimentation is valuable precisely because it allows social workers to test accepted wisdom and to try new approaches that may result in better outcomes for clients.

Group designs

There are two major subtypes of experimental research, and many variations of each. One general approach is the group design, in which (in its standard form), one group of clients receives an intervention, and the other group, the control, does not, and each is measured before and after the intervention. In the purest designs, clients are randomly assigned to these groups, and the researcher then looks to see if there is a statistically—and socially—significant difference in the outcomes for the two groups. Because there are ethical problems in withholding treatment from one group in many cases, common variations include giving one group the "standard intervention" and giving the other group the proposed innovative treatment or comparing the efficacy of two different interventive packages. An example of a group experimental study with immediate practice implications is Brunk, Henggeler, and Whelan's

(1987), which compared the outcomes of a structured parent training program with multisystemic family therapy for abusive and neglectful parents. By using a creative design and a variety of measures, the authors found that different approaches seemed to work best for different types of families. Some of the findings were surprising; for example, the parent training group proved to be particularly helpful with system problems, probably, according to the authors, because of the level of sharing that occurred among group members.

Although such group designs clearly have many benefits, they also have limitations (Johnston, 1988), some of which are particularly significant. A major limitation is that the results of group designs are averages and usually reflect some people who did very well, some who did marginally well or for whom the intervention had no effect, and some who actually did worse. Group designs do not allow one to disaggregate these results or to trace the possible causes of the differences. It is not possible to vary the intervention in response to the characteristics of individual clients in a group experiment without loosing rigor, although different factors and interventions may be relevant to each. And practically speaking, an individual social worker usually cannot muster the level of financial and human resources necessary to implement a group design. For these and other reasons, a number of researchers in social work and other helping fields have increasingly turned to single-case experimental designs (also called "single-subject" or "single-system" designs).

Single-case designs
Single-case designs reflect an effort to test the value of interventions with single client systems (which may be individuals, families, groups, or communities or other systems) in as rigorous a way as possible. Simple descriptive case studies have been a staple of the social work literature since the earliest days of the profession and were the first approximation of a single-case design. Unfortunately, all the issues discussed earlier with regard to subjective bias can come into play in such descriptions. As Wakefield (1993) noted, "Every one of the therapeutic theories . . . is supported by case evidence . . . including dramatic cures" (p. 675), so a substantial measure of caution is required in using such descriptions.

Some targets of practice (such as tantrums) can actually be counted and therefore relatively easy to assess, but others (say, depression) are inherently more difficult to capture objectively. Social workers are increasingly turning to observational counts, standardized instruments, and "self-anchored" and other rating scales to try to measure outcomes as precisely as possible. Although rating scales have generally worked fairly well (Nugent, 1992), they can be somewhat subjective; one way to "harden" them is to use behaviorally anchored rating scales (see Figure 5-3 for an example).

Single-case designs also have limitations. Measuring complex clinical issues is always challenging. In addition, demonstrating that an intervention works with one client does not mean that it will work with others, so multiple replications with different clients in different contextual situations, by different workers, and in different settings are necessary to

Goal: To teach a child to comply with parental requests

Behaviors: The parent clearly requests appropriate behavior from the child.
The parent reinforces the child's appropriate behavior.

1	2	3	4	5	6	7	8	9	10
Does not clearly request appropriate behavior, does not reinforce it when it occurs.		Requests appropriate behavior and reinforces it with prompting from the social worker.		Requests appropriate behavior at least 10 times per day and reinforces 50% of the correct responses		Requests appropriate behavior at least 15 times per day and reinforces 70% of the correct responses		Requests appropriate behavior at least 20 times per day and reinforces 85% of the correct responses	Requests appropriate behavior at least 20 times per day and reinforces 95% of the correct responses

FIGURE 5-3. **BEHAVIORALLY ANCHORED RATING SCALES**

Note: In many cases, only a single behavior should be rated on one scale because performance may be high on one dimension and low on another. However, in other situations, like that shown here, two or more actions must be combined to make progress toward the goal. The scale is constructed with "1" defined as the worst level of performance that may occur and "10" as the ideal. As many other points as necessary to make ratings clear are then defined in observable terms. Overt events are the easiest to scale precisely, but it is also possible to rate, for example, number or percentage of particular types of self-talk, scores on a rapid assessment instrument, the extent of social support, or satisfaction with employment (in which case points would be defined on the basis of a client's verbalizations about the job, for example, "I can't stand being here one more minute" or "I would strongly prefer doing something else"; note the potential to individually tailor the scale to the clinical situation).

Source: Adapted from Daniels, A. C. (1994). Bringing out the best in people (p. 95). New York: McGraw-Hill.

begin to establish the generalizability of such findings. (For further information on such designs, see Bloom, Fischer, & Orme, 1995; Mattaini, 1993b; Reid & Smith, 1989.)

Most of the naturalistic observations and experiments that inform practice have been done by others, and the social worker learns about them by becoming immersed in the professional literature. The social worker also compiles a collection of more or less rigorous observations and experimental data from the cases—on whatever systemic level—that he or she handles. In other words, some of the knowledge that informs practice comes directly from the case itself.

Knowledge from the Case

The client (an individual, family, or other system) and the environmental context within which the client is embedded provide a good deal of particularized information that is specific to the case, is more or less objective, and can guide collaborative assessment and intervention. Because many things that the client experiences and knows need to be part of the shared worker–client knowledge base for intervention to be maximally effective, a social worker usually asks a number of questions, both during the initial engagement and throughout the intervention process. The client may not know or understand everything that is relevant, but it would be a mistake to dismiss information—even partial, distorted, and relatively subjective information—that the client provides.

Clients often can describe their situations, behavior, and feelings relatively accurately. A sophisticated understanding of human behavior can be helpful in sorting out the circumstances under which such descriptions may not be accurate. These circumstances tend to be of two types: when clients have a reason for not providing an accurate description (for example, when there are incentives that encourage falsification) and when they lack the capacity for accurate description because their reality testing is impaired by severe mental illness or because they have simply never learned to recognize and describe their feelings, for example. In most cases, however, including these, it is important to hear and understand the clients' perceptions as being important case data.

Observation of the client can also provide crucial information. For example, the combination of observations of repetitive patterns of exchange—positive or negative—in a couple or a family with research about the importance of such patterns (see, for example, Burman, John, & Margolin, 1992) can provide a great deal of direction to the family clinician. When such observations are placed in the context of environmental transactions (Mattaini, Grellong, & Abramovitz, 1992)—information about which often comes from the family and segments of their social networks—the potential for broadly based family-centered practice that transcends the limitations of family therapy alone is enhanced.

Frequently, there are substantial advantages to rigorous observations of clients, family members, and group or community members, either by the clients themselves or by the social worker. With regard to parenting issues, the actual counting, and often charting, of a child's behavior is valuable not just for case-monitoring purposes, but for motivational ones (Sloane, 1976/

1988). Gradual improvements, for example, can be graphically evident when parents chart them, but may not otherwise be noticed. Self-observation and self-monitoring may also be empowering for clients because they involve the clients directly in the assessment and increase their involvement and control throughout the interventive process (Kopp, 1993). The data presented can also be useful to the social worker because they lend precision to what may otherwise often be a somewhat unstructured and subjective process.

Finally, every case is, in some respect, a single-case experiment. Although the social worker may be confident of the efficacy of the interventive strategy and tactics that he or she and the client have agreed to adopt, the final test is the way the case evolves over time. Thus, monitoring cases is important, not because it is increasingly required by funders and bureaucratic structures, but because it is crucial for social workers to know what they are trying to accomplish with their cases and whether they are succeeding. Any intervention should be regarded as experimental, and therefore to be monitored, until its efficacy for a particular case has been established. One way to do so is to use a "clinical analytic" single-case design, which permits the intervention to evolve over time as guided by the case (see Figure 5-4 for an example).

Luckily, the social worker does not need to start from scratch with each case. In addition to information from the case and knowledge from the other sources discussed thus far, the graduate social worker should also be immersed in the findings of contemporary scientific disciplines that study the phenomena with which social workers are involved, especially the biological and behavioral sciences.

Biological and Behavioral Sciences

Social workers work with people (who are biological, emotional, behavioral, and social beings); with families, groups, communities, and organizations (which are sociocultural entities); and with the relationships among and between people, social entities, and the physical world. Because these are the "raw materials" of practice, it is important to understand as much as possible about them. Thus, social workers need to know not only about practice and social issues, but about the basic sciences that underlie them, including biology and genetics, ecology, and the disciplines that examine larger systems, such as social psychology, sociology, and anthropology.

Biology, genetics, and behavior

Much of the behavior of "lower" animals is genetically determined. Sociobiologists suggest that the same is true for human beings, but critical examination of the data suggest that only very limited areas of human behavior (primarily some of what is common among people but not how they differ) can be understood in this way (Harris, 1979). For example, behavior such as facial expressions and the specifics of some forms of sexual behavior appear to have substantial biological roots (Fisher, 1992; Harris, 1979), but many of them can be overridden by learning. Some conditions that social workers deal with also have clear physiological dimensions; for instance, although the

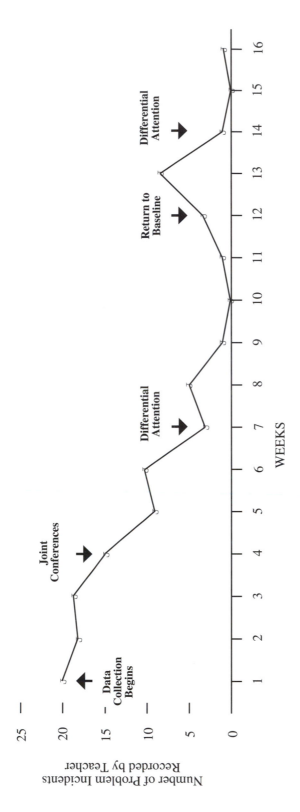

FIGURE 5-4. AN EXAMPLE OF A CLINICAL ANALYTIC DESIGN

Note: In this hypothetical case of a child displaying behavioral problems in a classroom, the social worker begins by gathering baseline data. After three weeks, she might begin twice-weekly conferences among the student, the teacher, and herself to improve student and teacher communication and to help clarify expectations and needs. In this figure, note that although the problems abated somewhat with this intervention, they continued at a distressing level. As a result, the worker might introduce an alternative procedure (designing a program to ensure high levels of the teacher's and peers' attention to appropriate behavior and extinction of inappropriate behavior). If this program resolved the problem, as seems to be the case here, the social worker and the teacher might withdraw the procedure to see whether it is still required. Note that in this case, withdrawal led to a resurgence of the classroom problems, which again remitted after the differential attention procedure was reintroduced. The graph suggests both that the problems have been brought under control and that the intervention was responsible for the improvement.

Source: Reprinted from Mattaini, M. A. (1993b). More than a thousand words: Graphics for clinical practice (p. 190). Washington, DC: NASW Press.

effects of the environment appear to be important determinants of the course and severity of schizophrenia, it is clear that the illness has a biological basis (C. M. Anderson, Reiss, & Hogarty, 1986). Similarly, severe depression is thought to be associated with changes in the levels and actions of neurotransmitters in the brain (Maxmen, 1986).

Feelings and behavior are physiological phenomena. That "psychological" interventions are valuable for many cases of depression (Elkin et al., 1989) again demonstrates the essential unity of the organism. Appropriate medication is essential for stabilizing or ameliorating many psychotic and affective disorders. It is also known that children of some types of alcoholic parents have a substantially increased risk of becoming alcoholics themselves (even when they are reared apart from their parents) and that there are many psychophysiological connections in substance abuse (Donovan, 1988; Secretary of Health and Human Services, 1987a, 1987b). Therefore, knowledge of biological and medical information in whatever area the social worker is practicing is essential.

Ecological science

Wilson (1992) noted that

> humanity is part of nature, a species that evolved among other species. The more closely we identify ourselves with the rest of life, the more quickly we will be able to discover the sources of human sensibility and acquire the knowledge on which an enduring ethic, a sense of preferred direction, can be built. (p. 348)

Since the 1960s social workers have recognized that ecological science has much to offer them for understanding practice in a complex, interconnected world. First, human beings are literally part of the natural world and, like many other animals, must be able to obtain certain resources, including food, shelter, and social interaction, from their environments to survive effectively. (Tragically, many homeless and poor people lack even these basic resources.)

Ecological science has also been applied on a more abstract level. It is one of the theoretical roots of the ecosystems perspective, for example (see chapter 2), and is the primary metaphor in the life model (Germain & Gitterman, 1980, 1986) of social work practice. There is much for the practitioner to learn and apply, directly or indirectly, from ecological science and natural history.

Behavioral and social sciences

There is no way to summarize or even suggest the wealth of information that social workers draw on from the behavioral and social sciences; most graduate programs include several courses on human behavior in the social environment. Knowledge from psychology, social psychology, sociology, anthropology, economics, and political science, as well as such disciplines as medicine, psychiatry, and family therapy, is critical for effective practice. At the same time, social workers do not practice social psychology, anthropology, or medicine; information from these sources greatly informs practice, but must be incorporated into practice models and approaches. Thus, the real challenge for social workers is not so much to know the information as to determine how it applies in the messy world of practice.

A few thoughts about evaluating such knowledge may be useful. Much of behavioral science is based on—and involves the testing of—theory. To a significant extent this situation also applies to the social sciences at higher system levels. Theory is discussed in the next section, but it is important to note here that adequate science depends on adequate theory, and vice versa. One way of evaluating the extent to which findings from the sciences are applicable to practice is to determine whether the findings fit coherently within (or, just as valuable, conflict with) an overall conceptual framework for looking at cases.

In some cases social workers have had to do their own research precisely because the questions for which they needed the answers had not been asked. In other cases social workers have sometimes ignored important findings because the language the findings were couched in or the way the statistical data were presented were daunting. This is clearly unacceptable.

Science does not produce just a random collection of facts, however. To be meaningful, the findings of science must be organized into coherent conceptual frameworks that seek to model phenomena in their organic complexity, which is the realm of theory. In simple cases, one can sometimes decide how to intervene based simply on data from other similar cases; in any complex case, however, the configuration is different from that of any other case, so one needs a theoretical framework to make sense of the patterns one finds. Likewise, information from the biological, behavioral, and social sciences does not simply map onto the case; the social worker requires a theoretical base to make sense of the events of the case. Theory, then, is not so much a discrete source of knowledge as it is an essential way of organizing and integrating knowledge from all the sources discussed thus far.

Theoretical and Conceptual Analyses

"There is nothing so practical as a good theory" (Lewin, 1976, p. 169). Observations and facts are valuable, but, by themselves, provide only limited guidance for practice; theory explicates the connections among them, leading to potentially greater generality. Although theory can be seen as the "basic aim of science" (Kerlinger, 1986, p. 8), it is not the basic aim of social work practice; rather, it is a primary tool for that practice and is crucial for drawing out the connections among discrete pieces of information that guide practice. Understanding the underlying causes of personal and social problems, the factors that maintain them, and what it will take to resolve them requires theoretical and conceptual analyses.

Theories are available at all practice levels, although their breadth and the extent to which they are well explicated and tested varies considerably. There are a tremendous range of theories that attempt to explain individual behavior, there is substantial theory available at the family and group levels, and some explaining organizational phenomena, but only quite limited theory has emerged to guide community practice. Although each of the behavioral and social sciences has theoretical frameworks, only some of these theories have been rigorously tested against reality. Hence, it is important for social workers to know how solidly established and supported the various theoretical approaches and models are.

The selection of theories

The philosophy of science provides some guidance about how to select theoretical frameworks (although philosophers are currently engaged in their own struggles, and scientists do what makes sense to them, seldom turning to the philosophy of science for direction). Along with the extent to which a theory has been supported by experiment and observation, other important considerations include its breadth and simplicity. All else being equal, a higher-level theory that explains a broader range of phenomena is preferable to a lower-level theory that explains only a few events. For example, a theory of human behavior that partially explains why people become anxious in particular situations or events is useful, a theory that explains the connections between anxiety and relationship issues is more useful, and a theory that explains the connections between a wide range of emotional and behavioral issues and external events over the life course is the most useful.

Simple explanations are generally preferred to more complicated ones. The Copernican revolution occurred when it became clear that if one assumed that the Earth (and other planets) revolve around the sun, rather than the other way around, it was much easier to trace the paths that each planet takes. Science generally relies on Occam's razor, a rule that suggests that parsimonious theory is to be preferred. If, for example, it is possible to explain and predict the rate of a particular behavior (say, a child's tantrums) on the basis of social and environmental events, little is to be gained by hypothesizing that an unobservable cognitive "tantrum schema" becomes activated, is filtered through a mental representation of the external world, and then causes the tantrum. Note that this is not to say that intervening variables should not be included in theoretical models when they appear, empirically, to make a difference. Simpler theoretical elaborations also allow the field to codify what has been learned and to move on to new issues and questions that the model suggests.

Acceptable theories also predict events and connections among them that can be tested. If a theory suggested that the primary reason for depression is anger produced by inadequate parenting in childhood, but also indicated that such (unconscious) anger can be inferred only from the level of depression, the argument is at risk of becoming circular. Testing theory of this type requires either some other evidence for the hypothesized unobservable factors (anger, in this case) or theoretically rooted predictions (for example, one might treat the client for anger and see if the level of depression changed). Things that cannot be seen are sometimes real, but, of course, they can be useful for practice only if they can be contacted in some way.

For the purposes of practice, theory must be able to guide intervention with the types of cases the social worker is treating. For example, it is clear that cognitive and behavioral theories (Beck, Rush, Shaw, & Emery, 1978; Rush, 1982; Yankura & Dryden, 1990) provide guidance for effective treatment in many cases of severe depression (Elkin et al., 1989). (Note that interpersonal therapy, which has psychodynamic roots, also often produces excellent outcomes.) There are limitations to the use of cognitive approaches for some client–situation configurations, however (Poppen, 1989). Some environments in which clients are embedded are extremely aversive, and helping clients to accept these circumstances cognitively may not be a responsible or effective approach.

Types of theory

It may already be clear from this discussion that "theory" actually refers to several different types of integrated understanding. In particular, there are underlying theories that help explain why people and larger systems function as they do (generally emerging from basic research in the behavioral and social sciences, although social workers have made substantial contributions as well) and practice theories (usually developed by social workers) that explain and predict what will happen when particular interventive strategies and techniques are used with particular types of cases in social work practice. Psychodynamic theories (including contributions from modern ego psychology, self psychology, and object relations theory) may help the social worker to understand case events, but one does not "do" object relations, for example. The practitioner who operates from this basic framework is likely to apply a psychosocial (or psychodynamic) practice approach, using one of the multiple theoretical paradigms or practice models in current use (Dorfman, 1988).

A schematic depicting the connections among important theoretical and conceptual paradigms and some common practice approaches is shown in Figure 5-5. This figure was developed from published descriptions of the approaches and reflects the author's interpretation of their content. Note that some approaches are linked to a number of bodies of theory, whereas others rely on fewer. Although it is possible, for example, to use nearly any practice approach within an ecosystems perspective, published accounts and actual practice vary in the extent to which it is done. Contemporary psychosocial, ecological, task-centered, and ecobehavioral models often explicitly identify their ecosystemic nature, and descriptions of practice based on them tend to include interventions that focus on environmental, family, and personal issues and their interconnections. Some other models, like Wright's (1988) elaboration of cognitive therapy or Krill's (1988) elaboration of existential practice, do not emphasize those links, and to some extent, this selective attention probably reflects the realities of day-to-day practice. The models with more extensive linkages in the figure may be applicable to a broader range of practice situations.

Some practice models have been developed for and applied in work with individuals, families, groups, communities, and organizations, whereas others focus on fewer systemic levels. The task-centered model, developed by Reid and his collaborators (1989), has been elaborated primarily for work with

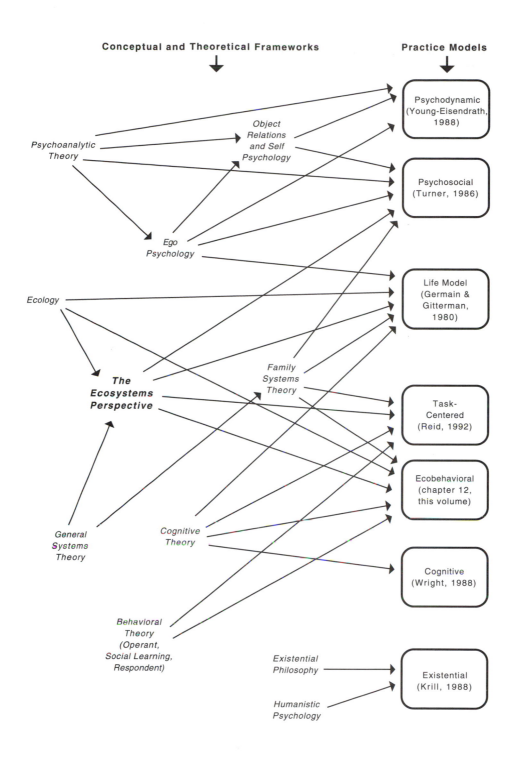

Conceptual and Theoretical Frameworks

Practice Models

Psychoanalytic Theory

Object Relations and Self Psychology

Ego Psychology

Ecology

The Ecosystems Perspective

Family Systems Theory

General Systems Theory

Cognitive Theory

Behavioral Theory (Operant, Social Learning, Respondent)

Existential Philosophy

Humanistic Psychology

Psychodynamic (Young-Eisendrath, 1988)

Psychosocial (Turner, 1986)

Life Model (Germain & Gitterman, 1980)

Task-Centered (Reid, 1992)

Ecobehavioral (chapter 12, this volume)

Cognitive (Wright, 1988)

Existential (Krill, 1988)

FIGURE 5-5. CONNECTIONS AMONG THEORETICAL FRAMEWORKS AND PRACTICE MODELS

individuals, families, and groups, for example, whereas the life model focuses particularly on work with individuals and families, but has close links with the mutual aid model of group work (see chapter 9) and some forms of organizational practice. Ecobehavioral or sociobehavioral approaches have been presented for each systemic level, but some have been more thoroughly developed than have others (see chapter 12). Cognitive approaches have been used primarily with individuals and groups; even marital treatment is commonly conducted in individual sessions in cognitive work (see, for example, Ellis, Sichel, Yeager, DiMattia, & DiGiuseppe, 1989).

Practice models and their connections with bodies of theory and knowledge have evolved over time. For example, the task-centered model was initially tied more closely to ego psychology than it tends to be now, and it may currently be more closely linked to behavioral and cognitive theory. Most contemporary models evolved from earlier approaches; for an extensive discussion of this history and figures that trace it, see Germain (1983).

Use of theory

Sophisticated practitioners must be familiar, for at least two reasons, with all the major theoretical frameworks that are commonly applied in practice. First, they must be able to communicate with other professionals who may be operating from a different conceptual framework than their own. Second, because no theory is adequate to explain all phenomena at all levels of practice, social workers may sometimes need to turn to theories other than the ones from which they usually operate. For example, if those whose primary base is psychodynamic and ego psychological are dealing with severe child behavior problems, it is likely that they will need to turn, in some cases, to behavioral methods (see Sloane, 1976/1988). It is not enough, however, to apply such techniques blindly; practitioners must understand the theoretical frameworks well enough to select which to use and to tailor the approach to the specifics of a case. Doing so requires an understanding of the underlying theory.

At the same time, each social worker must have a relatively coherent, integrated theoretical base from which he or she ordinarily works. Drawing techniques randomly from psychodynamic, behavioral, ecological, and humanistic-existential approaches when working with individuals without having reasons for doing so creates confusion because each theory often suggests doing something different. This way of operating will certainly confuse, and probably alienate, the client as well. Similarly, a clinical social worker seeing a family may operate for a few sessions from a behaviorally oriented task-centered approach (emphasizing collaboration with the client in specifying goals and developing interventive tasks). If the worker then suddenly switches to a strategic approach that emphasizes paradoxical assignments that the client is expected to defy, the family will certainly struggle with the process and may think that their collaborative contract has been violated.

A far better approach is to select a basic theoretical paradigm, based on the criteria identified earlier (empirical support, breadth, simplicity, and coherence), and to "push" it as far as possible. For example, behavior analytic theory (which emphasizes relations between environmental events and behavior, see Mattaini, 1993b) has generally been applied at the individual, group, and family levels, but as the theory has become increasingly broad and transactional, it is also being used to understand phenomena at the organizational (Daniels, 1994) and community (Mattaini, 1993a) levels. Social workers often report that the more difficult and confusing the case they are dealing with, the more they need to turn to their basic theoretical understanding of the issues for guidance.

The foregoing discussion also hints at the importance of recognizing that phenomena must be understood theoretically and conceptually at the appropriate systemic levels. Although everything that occurs in a family interaction could be described in terms of biological processes that occur within the individuals in the context of environmental objects and events, this reductionistic description would not help the social worker (or the family) understand the processes that are occurring very well. Family systems theories, on the other hand, may be much more helpful because they attempt to explain what happens within families at a more appropriate systemic level.

Not all social workers see practice at any systemic level through the same theoretical lenses. The ecosystems perspective, if properly applied, can provide some assurance that all social workers are seeing the basic facts and events in cases—one crucial link among different theoretical approaches. Although different theories occasionally suggest similar interventions, they sometimes suggest different strategies. And some of these strategies will result in better outcomes for clients than will others. Because there is no general agreement in the field about which approaches generally produce the best outcomes for which kinds of cases, the need to monitor practice, to find ways to track whether a case is moving in the desired direction, is an ethical responsibility. Blind faith in any theory cannot be justified.

Finally, because social work cases are complex, social workers must achieve a high level of theoretical sophistication in their chosen areas. If, for example, one adopts ecological theory as the core of one's practice and the life model (Germain & Gitterman, 1980, 1986) as the primary practice approach, it is not enough simply to know that from this perspective clients' issues are seen as problems in life transitions, environmental problems, or maladaptive patterns of interpersonal relationships and communication. Responsible professionals must also strive to stay current with emerging findings in ecological science (see Wilson, 1992), in the evolutionary biology and natural history in which ecology is based (see Gould, 1993), and in the social sciences that are closely tied to both of them (see Harris, 1989). Not only should they be familiar with popular treatments of these areas, but they should achieve the sophistication needed to understand the original sources.

Integrating Sources of Knowledge in a Case
It may seem overwhelming to think about integrating science, theory, practice wisdom, information specific to a case, and all the other material

discussed here when dealing with a case, and it can be. For students, important resources include field instructors, who can draw out each area as appropriate and hence ensure that all areas are considered evenly. Other professionals, instructors, required and recommended readings assigned in courses, and other literature are also valuable sources. Ultimately, students and eventually autonomous professionals are responsible for ensuring that they expose themselves to the necessary sources of knowledge, but courses, supervision, and peer consultation can be helpful in making the links among sources of knowledge that result in excellence in practice. Staying current with developments in the field by reading, attending continuing education programs, and interacting with colleagues is an ethical imperative because it can substantively affect the well-being of clients.

Approaching cases analytically (that is, thoughtfully and with an eye to understanding what is happening) is crucial to professional practice. During the course of this work, practitioners will often face questions for which they have no good answers. This is a clear signal that it is time to stop and think about the case theoretically or conceptually, to pull a book off the shelf, to do a literature review, or to consult with others. Given the complexity of the phenomena with which social workers practice, this effort is never ending.

REFERENCES

Ainslie, G. (1993). A picoeconomic rationale for social constructionism. *Behavior and Philosophy, 21*(2), 63–75.

Anderson, C. M., Reiss, D. J., & Hogarty, G. E. (1986). *Schizophrenia and the family: A practitioner's guide to psychoeducation and management.* New York: Guilford Press.

Anderson, S., & Mandell, D. (1989). The use of self-disclosure by professional social workers. *Social Casework, 70,* 259–267.

Bartlett, H. M. (1970). *The common base of social work practice.* New York: National Association of Social Workers.

Bates, M. (1990). *The nature of natural history.* Princeton, NJ: Princeton University Press. (Original work published 1950)

Beck, A. T., Rush, A. J., Shaw, B. F., & Emery, G. (1978). *Cognitive therapy of depression.* New York: Guilford Press.

Bloom, M., Fischer, J., & Orme, J. G. (1995). *Evaluating practice: Guidelines for the accountable professional* (2nd ed.). Boston: Allyn & Bacon.

Brunk, M., Henggeler, S. W., & Whelan, J. P. (1987). Comparison of multisystemic therapy and parent training in the brief treatment of child abuse and neglect. *Journal of Consulting and Clinical Psychology, 55,* 171–178.

Burman, B., John, R. S., & Margolin, G. (1992). Observed patterns of conflict in violent, nonviolent, and nondistressed couples. *Behavioral Assessment, 14,* 15–37.

Collins, B. G. (1993). Reconstruing codependency using self-in-relation theory: A feminist perspective. *Social Work, 38,* 470–476.

Daniels, A. C. (1994). *Bringing out the best in people.* New York: McGraw-Hill.

Donovan, D. M. (1988). Assessment of addictive behaviors: Implications of an emerging biopsychosocial model. In D. M. Donovan & G. A. Marlatt (Eds.), *Assessment of addictive behaviors* (pp. 3–48). New York: Guilford Press.

Dorfman, R. A. (1988). *Paradigms of clinical social work.* New York: Brunner/Mazel.

Elkin, I., Shea, M. T., Watkins, J. T., Imber, S. D., Sotsky, S. M., Collins, J. F., Glass, D. R., Pilkonis, P. A., Leber, W. R., Docherty, J. P., Fiester, S. J., & Parloff, M. B. (1989). National Institute of Mental Health treatment of depression collaborative research program: General effectiveness of treatments. *Archives of General Psychiatry, 46,* 971–982.

Ellis, A., Sichel, J. L., Yeager, R. J., DiMattia, D. J., & DiGiuseppe, R. (1989). *Rational-emotive couples therapy.* New York: Pergamon Press.

Ewalt, P. L. (1994). Visions of ourselves. *Social Work, 39,* 5–7.

Fisher, H. E. (1992). *Anatomy of love: The natural history of monogamy, adultery, and divorce.* New York: W. W. Norton.

Germain, C. B. (1983). Technological advances. In A. Rosenblatt & D. Waldfogel (Eds.), *Handbook of clinical social work* (pp. 26–57). San Francisco: Jossey-Bass.

Germain, C. B., & Gitterman, A. (1980). *The life model of social work practice.* New York: Columbia University Press.

Germain, C. B., & Gitterman, A. (1987). Ecological perspective. In A. Minahan (Ed.-in-Chief), *Encyclopedia of social work* (18th ed., Vol. 1, pp. 488–499). Silver Spring, MD: National Association of Social Workers.

Gitterman, A. (1983). Uses of resistance: A transactional view. *Social Work, 28,* 127–130.

Gould, S. J. (1993). *Eight little piggies: Reflections in natural history.* New York: W. W. Norton.

Groskind, F. (1994). Ideological influences on public support for assistance to poor families. *Social Work, 39,* 81–89.

Harris, M. (1979). *Cultural materialism: The struggle for a science of culture.* New York: Vintage.

Harris, M. (1989). *Our kind.* New York: HarperCollins.

Johnston, J. M. (1988). Strategic and tactical limits of comparison studies. *Behavior Analyst, 11,* 1–9.

Kerlinger, F. N. (1986). *Foundations of behavioral research* (3rd ed.). New York: Holt, Rinehart & Winston.

Kopp, J. (1993). Self-observation: An empowerment strategy in assessment. In J. B. Rauch (Ed.), *Assessment: A sourcebook for social work practice* (pp. 255–268). Milwaukee: Families International.

Krill, D. F. (1988). Existential social work. In R. A. Dorfman (Ed.), *Paradigms of clinical social work* (pp. 295–316). New York: Brunner/Mazel.

Lewin, K. (1976). Problems of research in social psychology (1943–1944). In D. Cartwright (Ed.), *Field theory in social psychology: Selected theoretical papers* (pp. 155–169). Chicago: University of Chicago Press.

Lincoln, Y. S., & Guba, E. G. (1985). *Naturalistic inquiry.* Beverly Hills, CA: Sage Publications.

Mattaini, M. A. (1993a). Behavior analysis in community practice. *Research on Social Work Practice, 3,* 420–447.

Mattaini, M. A. (1993b). *More than a thousand words: Graphics for clinical practice.* Washington, DC: NASW Press.

Mattaini, M. A., Grellong, B. A., & Abramovitz, R. (1992). The clientele of a child and family mental health agency: Empirically-derived household clusters and implications for practice. *Research on Social Work Practice, 2,* 380–404.

Maxmen, J. S. (1986). *Essential psychopathology.* New York: W. W. Norton.

Miles, M. B., & Huberman, A. M. (1994). *Qualitative data analysis: An expanded sourcebook.* Thousand Oaks, CA: Sage Publications.

Miller, W. R. (1989). Matching individuals with interventions. In R. K. Hester & W. R. Miller (Eds.), *Handbook of alcoholism treatment approaches* (pp. 261–271). New York: Pergamon Press.

The New Shorter Oxford English Dictionary. (1993). Oxford, England: Clarendon Press.

Nugent, W. R. (1992). Psychometric characteristics of self-anchored scales in clinical application. *Journal of Social Service Research, 15*(3–4), 137–152.

Pieper, M. H., & Pieper, W. J. (1993). Response to "Psychoanalytic fallacies: Reflections on Martha Heineman Pieper and William Joseph Pieper's Intrapsychic Humanism." *Social Service Review, 67,* 651–654. (Comment on J. C. Wakefield)

Poppen, R. L. (1989). Some clinical implications of rule-governed behavior. In S. C. Hayes (Ed.), *Rule-governed behavior: Cognition, contingencies, and instructional control* (pp. 325–357). New York: Plenum Press.

Reid, W. J. (1992). *Task strategies.* New York: Columbia University Press.

Reid, W. J., & Smith, A. D. (1989). *Research in social work* (2nd ed.). New York: Columbia University Press.

Rep, P. (1959). bowl of tea. In *Zen telegrams.* Rutland, VT: Charles E. Tuttle.

Rush, A. J. (Ed.). (1982). *Short-term psychotherapies for depression.* New York: Guilford Press.

Rycraft, J. R. (1994). The party isn't over: The agency role in the retention of public child welfare caseworkers. *Social Work, 39,* 75–80.

Schön, D. A. (1983). *The reflective practitioner: How professionals think in action.* London: Temple Smith.

Searle, J. R. (1993). Rationality and realism, what is at stake? *Daedalus, 122*(4), 55–83.

Secretary of Health and Human Services. (1987a). *Alcohol and health.* Washington, DC: U.S. Department of Health and Human Services.

Secretary of Health and Human Services. (1987b). *Drug abuse and drug abuse research* (Second Triennial Report to Congress). Washington, DC: U.S. Government Printing Office.

Skinner, B. F. (1948). "Superstition" in the pigeon. *Journal of Experimental Psychology, 38,* 168–172.

Sloane, H. N. (1988). *The good kid book.* Champaign, IL: Research Press. (Original work published 1976)

Smith, H. (1988). The crisis in philosophy. *Behaviorism, 16,* 51–56.

Turner, F. J. (1986). *Social work treatment* (3rd ed.). New York: Free Press.

Wakefield, J. C. (1993). Following the Piepers: Replies to Tyson, Steinberg, and Miller. *Social Service Review, 67,* 673–682.

Whitman, W. (1992). *Leaves of grass* (Deathbed edition). New York: Quality Paperback Book Club. (Original work published 1892)

Wilson, E. O. (1992). *The diversity of life.* Cambridge, MA: Harvard University Press.

Wright, F. D. (1988). Cognitive therapy. In R. A. Dorfman (Ed.), *Paradigms of clinical social work* (pp. 179–195). New York: Brunner/Mazel.

Yankura, J., & Dryden, W. (1990). *Doing RET: Albert Ellis in action.* New York: Springer.

Young-Eisendrath, P. (1988). Mental structures and personal relations: Psychodynamic theory in clinical social work. In R. A. Dorfman (Ed.), *Paradigms of clinical social work* (pp. 43–73). New York: Brunner/Mazel.

6

Fields of Practice

Sheila B. Kamerman

What goes around comes around. Graduate social work education began with a focus on specialized fields of practice because there was no holistic concept of social work practice. Over time, the profession developed a comprehensive concept of a shared core of knowledge, values, and skills, beginning with a common core for casework and moving to include other social work methods: group work; community organizing; administration; and, much later, policy practice. So strong was the emphasis on the common core that the context of practice was given limited attention. In the 1970s, social workers recognized that the overall field of social welfare had expanded and diversified greatly, and as a consequence, other professions and disciplines were entering the field and carving out pieces that were relevant to their expertise. Adequate professional social work performance increasingly required some specialization in addition to the core of common knowledge. As a result, social work curricula now increasingly reflect a concentration in a field of practice in addition to a social work method.

In this context, "fields of practice" refers to the distinctive settings, population groups, or social problem areas in which social workers practice and to which social workers adapt their practice. What is meant by fields of practice, how these fields relate to the overall social welfare domain, what the most salient fields are for today's social work professional, how the concept of field of practice relates to social work methods and fits in a social work curriculum, and how different fields can be assessed are the focuses of this chapter; but first, some history.

BACKGROUND AND CONTEXT

The debate about the balance between an emphasis on social work methods and fields of practice has been long-standing in social work education and still is not fully resolved. The two major professional organizations, the National Association of Social Workers (NASW) and the Council on Social Work Education (CSWE), have played an important role in advancing the concept

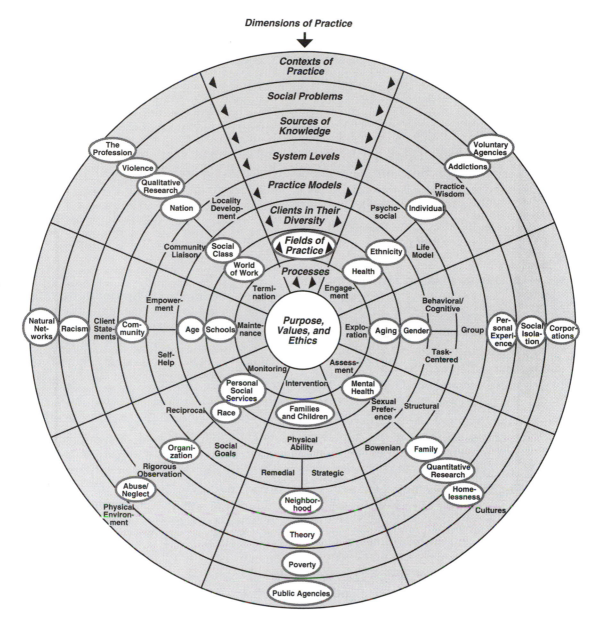

FIGURE 6-1. FIELDS OF PRACTICE

of fields of practice, but their ambivalence continues to be reflected in various publications. Thus, a brief review of historical development of the concept also offers some insight into the important role that these organizations have played—and can continue to play—in the development of social work knowledge and skills.

The preface to the 18th edition of the *Encyclopedia of Social Work* (Minahan, 1987) stated that its purpose was "to provide an objective overview of social work in the United States—and its history, its current concerns and interests, the state of its art, and its view of the future" (p. v). However, although the

15th and 16th editions of the encyclopedia (Lurie, 1965; Morris, 1971) contained entries on fields of practice, neither the 17th edition (Turner, 1977) nor the 18th edition did so. Why there was an almost 25-year hiatus in the coverage of this topic is not yet clear.

Even the concept of specialization received little, if any, attention in the 18th edition. But when entries referred to this concept, fields of practice seemed to be the focus. Thus, for example, Briar (1987) stated that

> the trend toward specialization continues in social work. . . . Specializations continue to be defined according to (1) the population served, as in the cases of child welfare and aging; (2) the focal problem, such as substance abuse; (3) the practice setting as in corrections or health; or (4) some combination of the above. (pp. 396–397)

CSWE Attends to Fields of Practice

Perhaps even more significant than the lack of attention to fields of practice for more than two decades in the definitive sourcebook of social work knowledge was the reverse pattern in social work education, in which there was a dramatic increase in attention to fields of practice in the social work curricula. Thus, for example, CSWE's 1983 *Curriculum Policy for the Master's Degree and Baccalaureate Programs in Social Work Education* (Minahan, 1987) stated that the curriculum for the master of social work (MSW) "is to require a concentration of specialized knowledge and practice skills in one or more areas relevant to social work. . . . Each graduate program will determine which concentrations it will make available to students and the framework it will use to organize them" (p. 963). The four concentrations listed were field of practice, population groups, problem areas, and methods, and a combination of method and one other concentration was urged. The statement offered no explanation of why field of practice was separated from population groups and problem areas, even though they were all treated as fields of practice in earlier NASW and CSWE publications.

Even more revealing was Vinton's 1989 survey of 98 accredited MSW programs designed to assess trends in social work education concentrations and specializations that reported that between 1974 and 1989 the major trend was a move from specialization by *method only* to a specialization by *method and field of practice* (Vinton, in press). Although Vinton understated this development by following the earlier CSWE conceptualization, separating fields of practice from social problems and population groups, she pointed out that ever since a 1979 survey, specialization by fields of practice had dramatically increased and that health and mental health, family and children's services, and aging were the dominant fields in both 1979 and 1988. Among the other fields represented in the social work curricula in this survey were corrections, school social services, mental retardation and developmental disabilities, substance abuse, industrial social work, and social services for women. Vinton characterized this development as a "boutique" effect, but most social work scholars would label it for what it is—an increase in the number of fields of practice. Whether this growth makes for dysfunctional fragmentation or greater opportunities for needed expertise is addressed later.

First Field, then Common Core

How, then, did the concern with fields of practice emerge, and what are the implications for education in social work today? Kahn (1965) pointed out that social work began to mature as a profession only when several different streams of service interventions and reform came together. The symbol of this unification and the climax of a long process toward "conceptual, methodological, ideological and organizational unity" (Kahn, 1965, p. 750) was the creation of NASW in 1955. In effect, from the establishment of the Conference of Boards of Public Charities in 1874 (which became the National Conference of Charities and Corrections in 1879 and later the National Conference on Social Welfare) to the mid-1940s, when the various streams began to move toward comprehensiveness, coherence, and integration, the social work profession focused its attention on the development of individual fields of practice. The five "major" fields, identified as far back as the 1920s and the Milford Conference of 1923–1928 (*Social Casework,* 1929/1974) were family welfare, child welfare, medical social work, psychiatric social work, and school social work. Later, NASW added the field of corrections to this listing and combined child and family welfare. (In current terms, these fields are child and family welfare, health and mental health, school social work, and corrections.) Little, if any, attempt was made in those years to identify a common core of social work practice.

The key element in social work professional developments following World War II was the recognition of a core of knowledge, values, and skills shared by all social workers. It is this core that permitted interfield mobility and the notion that one's identification with a particular method of intervention (casework, group work, community organization, or administration) was more important than the setting in which one practiced.

Returning to Fields

For the next 15 years social work responded to the earlier problem of fragmentation and to the dynamics of professionalization by suggesting that there was a generic core of social work practice and that whatever variations existed were linked more to method than to field (in so far as "field" was limited to specific settings). But with further growth and maturation, the search for greater refinement of practice theory and skills resumed.

CSWE began exploring the field-of-practice concept in 1959, identifying nine fields as salient (Bartlett, 1961): public assistance, family welfare, child welfare, corrections, psychiatric social work, medical social work services and public health, school social work, group services, and community planning. Note that from the outset, population groups, social problems, and settings were all included as the basis for the different fields of practice. Moreover, Bartlett (1961) also stressed the need to distinguish between "the operations of professional social workers and a consistently defined area of practice within which social workers operate" (p. 16).

Even more important than this CSWE initiative was NASW's establishment of its first Commission on Social Work Practice in 1955. This commission, which functioned until 1963, began to explore the definitional issues related to social work practice soon after its establishment. The commission's Subcommittee on Fields of Practice reported its recommendations to NASW in 1962 (NASW Commission, 1962). The subcommittee's members, who represented the intellectual leadership of the profession at that time, rediscovered the value of specialization with regard to settings, problems and tasks, and client or population groups and determined why specialization by fields of practice should be reestablished, in addition to specialization by method.

Stressing the value of a two-dimensional model, one based on method and the other based on field of practice, the subcommittee's report confirmed that fields of practice were a "characteristic feature of social work" (Bartlett, 1965, p. 758) and strongly supported the concept as an organizing principle to be applied to social work knowledge, values, and skills and to supplement the existing conceptualization of social work practice by method. It further stressed that within any given field of practice, all methods (casework; group work; community organization; and, in current terms, administration and policy development and analysis) should be represented; that the particular cluster of interventions used might also vary by field of practice; and, perhaps even more important, that the patterns of fields of practice would vary from time to time in response to social change.

Bartlett (1965) also urged the development of criteria for defining emerging fields of practice. Earlier, she had presented her framework for analyzing a field of practice (Bartlett, 1961):

1. the problem (condition, phenomenon, task) of central concern, which is the starting point
2. the system of organized services (policies and programs) established to respond to the problem
3. the client population served
4. knowledge, values, and skills (or interventions) used in the field.

Bartlett concluded:

> As analysis proceeds from field to field, these components may well be redefined and new elements may be identified. It should be noted that a field of practice, as defined, has a distinct identity. There are certain problems and activities that run all through social welfare. These are important, but we do not think of them as representing fields. *Those areas that have developed a relatively stable constellation of organized services, theory, methods, and other characteristics . . . can be recognized as fields* [italics added]. (1961, p. 41)

Bartlett's Refinements
In the last edition of the *Encyclopedia of Social Work* to have an article on the topic (Morris, 1971), Bartlett reminded the profession that the

original concept was based on the different types of practice that emerged in the various settings (programs and social services) and the ways in which these settings shaped social work practice. With the development of a concept of a core of social work knowledge, defining fields of practice in terms of settings, programs, and services alone was not sufficient. The definition should now include practice in relation to different problems and population groups as well.

Bartlett pointed out that fields of practice have been a feature of social work since the profession emerged. She argued that efforts to develop a more coherent and internally consistent definition had not been successful because most fields "developed largely through historical accident and do not lend themselves to logical definition" (Bartlett, 1965, p. 1477). Thus, there was a need to include practice in relation to different social problems and with different population groups, as well as in different settings, all under fields of practice. Bartlett also stated that criteria for determining what is a field of practice must reflect the specific types of practice adaptations that arise in connection with the development of new forms of social services.

"One characteristic of fields that has created difficulty in defining criteria," Bartlett (1965) observed, "is the changing nature of settings, programs, and social services within which social work is practiced. . . . Societal problems and programs come and go, assuming a multiplicity of forms as they emerge, combine, and sometimes fade away" (p. 1478). She noted that some fields will disappear, other fields will be combined (and subsequently recombined), and still other fields will emerge. For example, she suggested that the health and psychiatric fields might combine and that child and family welfare would probably be integrated. In effect, she suggested that over time the profession might find certain fields of practice were no longer relevant or no longer distinctive and that new fields would arise.

Drawing on the work of the subcommittee and the original formulations of the NASW Commission on Social Work Practice, Bartlett (1965) presented specific criteria for identifying a field of practice:

1. A major human need or social problem and the services organized to meet the need or problem.
2. A distinctive social work contribution to the overall program and to the population served (those who have the need or problem).
3. Social work practice in the field that demonstrates the common and essential elements of all social work practice (knowledge, values, and intervention techniques), including administration, research, and policy.
4. Specialized competence required to practice effectively in the particular field.
5. Criteria for fields that are flexible and not held to a standard of covering practice completely in a logical manner. As social change occurs, new fields will emerge and old ones may disappear or merge with others. (p. 1480)

Bartlett concluded by stressing that the notion of social problem should be combined with that of field of practice as an extension of the concept, not as a separate concept.

To round out the picture, the report of the NASW Commission (1962) called attention to three other important aspects of fields of practice:

1. Private Practice of social work is not a field of practice in the sense under discussion. Theoretically, there might be private practice in any or all fields. Like certain other dimensions (public/voluntary, sectarian/nonsectarian, urban/rural) it is independent of the fields of practice notion.

2. Not every social worker is working at a given moment in a professionally recognized field of practice. Some inevitably will be working in newly emerging fields of practice, not yet fully recognized or established. Schools and professional organizations need to take account of this.

3. A large complex agency such as a settlement house or a community center may be identified with more than one field of practice. (p. 14)

FIELDS OF PRACTICE TODAY

Defining the Concept

Drawing on the work of Bartlett, Kahn, and Briar, I offer the following definition of social work fields of practice: the context for practice that is shaped and developed in response to the *settings* in which social workers practice (for example, public or private social agencies; government or nongovernment organizations; distinctive organizations, such as the workplace, hospitals, and military bases), the social *problems* in which social workers intervene (including child, elder, or spouse abuse; substance abuse; homelessness; chronic mental illness; and poverty), and the client *populations* whom social workers help (children, youths, families, older people, racial and ethnic groups, and refugees).

The assumption of the concept of field of practice is that there is a core foundation of social work knowledge, values, and skills that applies to all social work practice but that the arena in which social workers practice is so large and diversified that there are distinctive variations in practice within the fields of social work and social welfare. These variations provide the basis for significant practice specializations that have implications for all social work methods (work with individuals, families, and groups; community organization and development; administration and management; and policy formation and analysis).

Salient Fields

"Social welfare"—a term used interchangeably in the United States with "social sector" and "social policy" and internationally with "social services" and "the social protection system"—is an institution that comprises all the policies and programs by which a government guarantees or affirms a defined minimum level of income, consumption rights, and an overall standard of living. The term "human services," used in the United States, is still another variation on this lexicon. Governments achieve this overall goal through the use of distributive principals and mechanisms based on other than market criteria. For example, financial or social need, vulnerability, social risk, and age may all be criteria for the receipt of government-provided, -funded, or -regulated social benefits and services.

Kahn (1979) conceptualized six components of the social sector following the model developed earlier in Britain (Townsend et al., 1970): health care, education, housing, income transfers, employment, and personal social services. (The British did not include employment services, but Kahn did, following the practice of several other countries.) One could add a seventh system: the justice system.

Although social workers may—and indeed do—practice in all six (or seven) "social services," they are the dominant profession only in the personal social services. Nonetheless, the various fields of social work practice include those in which social work plays an ancillary role (which may be a major one), as well as those in which it is the host profession. The fields of practice based in settings in which social work plays an adjunctive role today include

- health and mental health (earlier termed medical and psychiatric social services but excluding public health, which now has its own established professional base)
- education (school-based social services but not the formal educational component, which clearly has its own professional base)
- housing (social services, including services for homeless people)
- employment (social services at or linked to work and the workplace, a relatively new field of practice)
- justice (corrections)
- income transfers (not the delivery of cash assistance, which is no longer an individualized service, but social services linked to welfare and the social insurance programs, which also have largely disappeared in recent years, but may yet reemerge).

In addition, however, there is the field of personal social services. This field has expanded and become increasingly diversified since the War on Poverty programs for poor people and the expanded social service programs linked to public assistance in the 1960s, the enactment of Title XX of the Social Security Act of 1974 and its transformation of the social services field in the 1970s (Gilbert, 1977), and the explosion in the establishment of categorical service programs in the 1970s and 1980s.

In this context, personal social services is the field that encompasses the totality of publicly subsidized and publicly and privately delivered individualized services that are designed to meet both the ordinary and special needs of individuals and families (Kahn, 1979; Kamerman & Kahn, 1976):

- information, referral, advocacy, and advice
- therapy, counseling, help, and rehabilitation
- life cycle development and socialization
- protection, practical help, and care
- self-help and mutual aid.

Historically, the personal social services emerged as services for people who were poor, troubled, or deviant (for example, juvenile delinquents, vagrants, and people who abuse substances), but they have expanded since the 1970s in response to the demands and needs of broader population groups, including frail older people, people with chronic illness or developmental disabilities, young parents, and working parents.

Although they are not necessarily delivered through any one system (public or private, for profit or nonprofit, religious or secular, integrated or categorical), these services have been recognized in the United States and many other advanced industrialized countries as sharing common functions, regardless of the setting in which they are provided (residential facility, community center, workplace, school, home, family and children's service agency, senior center), the age group served (children, youths, adults, or older individuals), or the presenting problem (alcoholism, parent–child or marital conflict, social isolation, and so forth). However, here, too, subfields are emerging as separate fields of practice.

It has been the spate of federal legislation on social services enacted since the 1960s that has led to the emergence and growth of new fields of practice within the personal social services. For example, the passage of Title XX of the Social Security Act of 1974 (now the Social Services Block Grant [SSBG]) permitted the states to use federal funds flexibly for whichever services they viewed as worthwhile. As a result, in 1993, 29 different services were funded under this law for children, youths, families, and older individuals, with significant variations among the states (U.S. House of Representatives, 1993). In addition to the general social services funding provided by the SSBG, many categorical programs were established by federal legislation, each (or perhaps each cluster) contributing to the development of yet another field of practice. Thus, for example, among the numerous categorical initiatives that were enacted between 1965 and 1994 were the Older Americans Act of 1965, providing funds for social services and meal services for older people; the various child welfare amendments to the Social Security Act, providing funds for foster care; adoption assistance; preventive, protective, and supportive services for troubled children and their families; support for living arrangements for youths who are too old to be in foster care; the developmental disabilities program; the Americans with Disabilities Act of 1990; the Runaway and Homeless Youth Act of 1974; family planning services; child care services; and services for homeless people, people who abuse drugs or alcohol, and refugees.

The U.S. House of Representatives' 1992 report *Federal Programs Affecting Children and Families* listed 36 federal social services programs for children and families (along with 15 income transfer programs, 29 education-related programs, 19 health-related programs, nine child nutrition programs, and more than 10 housing-related programs). Certainly, if students are to practice social work with children and their families, they should be familiar with these programs. And knowing something about these programs (and a lot about some of them) clearly has implications for the nature of practice and the kinds of interventions that can be used, as well as for whom help can be provided.

Thus, in addition to the fields of practice that are derived from the major non–social work components of the social sector (health and mental health, school-based social services, corrections, and employment-related social services), within the personal social services domain, one can identify at least two major fields of practice (child and family welfare and services for older people) and several smaller fields (services for adolescents, services for people who abuse alcohol or drugs, military social services, services to refugees and immigrants, services for people with physical disabilities, and services to people who have developmental disabilities). And some would add the emerging field of international social welfare.

There is no way that a social worker can develop expertise in all these fields, let alone in a two-year period. Clearly, just knowing the relevant federal policies and programs and the relevant state and local policies and their various requirements regarding who can be served and what services can be provided points to the need to set some parameters. And the natural parameters are what constitute a field of practice. Moreover, although today emphasis is placed on community-based services in each field, the prevalence of service delivery models varies from field to field, with some stressing home-based services and others stressing neighborhood-based, rather than home-based, services, and some inherently focused on an authoritative model and others on a voluntary model. Furthermore, there are variations in the use and emphasis on the practice modes that are field specific. Finally, whether one uses the overarching concept of personal social services, the concept of field of practice has its own internal validity and clearly is a central component of social work education and practice.

No school can support training in all the fields (and all social work methods), but all schools should provide training at least in the major fields. And all should aim to include one or two smaller fields that have particular salience for their own institution or community. For example, graduate schools of social work in large urban communities with high proportions of immigrants and refugees should include courses and practice experience in this field.

Most important, even if schools cannot mount the expertise for in-depth training, all should try to identify and monitor the emergence of new fields so they can respond to new professional practice and educational needs. New fields are likely to emerge as a consequence of new categorical legislation (the Stewart B. McKinney Homeless Assistance Act of 1987 and the development of social services for homeless people, for example). They are also likely to emerge when a new problem arises and efforts are made to cluster relevant interventions (such as social services to people infected with the human immunodeficiency virus [HIV] and their families) or when fields disappear (for instance, public assistance, when the program became an entitlement and social services were separated from the delivery of cash benefits). Curricula must be adapted or modified to take account of these developments. Moreover, all schools should teach students how to conceptualize and identify a field of practice and how to analyze or assess the field in which they are practicing or intend to practice. This framework for assessing a field of practice is presented next.

ASSESSING A FIELD OF PRACTICE

This framework is applicable whether social work is the host profession or plays an adjunctive role in relation to another profession and whether one uses the overarching concept of personal social services or assesses only the discrete, categorical social services fields (although this author believes that an understanding and use of the former is essential for understanding how the several fields relate to each other). Applying the framework to an emerging field and comparing the results across fields can help clarify whether a new field is emerging or an established one is phasing out. An outline of the generic framework, which can be applied to any field, is presented in Table 6-1. In this section, the major components are described and illustrations from different fields are given.

Major Components of the Framework

There are seven major components of the framework:
  1. the target or focal point (population, problem, setting)
  2. earlier historical responses
  3. relevant legislation and policies
  4. program models and the delivery system
  5. modes of practice (interventions) and staffing patterns
  6. research, evaluation, and outcomes
  7. issues, trends, and current debates

The target

Fields of practice are organized around specific population groups, such as children (and their families), adolescents, older people, or women; or around specific problems, such as substance abuse, homelessness, the acquired immune deficiency syndrome (AIDS), delinquency, or domestic violence; or around distinctive settings, such as hospitals, schools, military bases, rural or urban communities, or the workplace. These targets become the takeoff points for identifying the specific laws, programs, and practice interventions that are designed to respond to the needs of each group, problem, or setting.

Earlier historical responses

Although the major fields of practice have existed for a long time, many of the most significant developments date from the 1960s and 1970s—the years when federal social services policy really took shape, with the dramatic expansion of federal social protection policies. Thus, although many social programs (for example, orphanages and homes for aged individuals) were originally funded by private philanthropies, they emerged in the 1960s in the form of public services, funded largely by the federal government and attached to public assistance. Counseling services and child care services, for instance, were viewed in these years as ways to help recipients of Aid to Families with Dependent Children to move off the welfare rolls and into employment or to cope better with the difficulties of daily life on their meager incomes. Only in the 1970s, when the delivery of social services was separated from the delivery of cash

Table 6-1. A Framework for Assessing a Field of Practice

   I. The target population (such as children, youths, older people, or women), the problem addressed in the field (for example, substance abuse, homelessness, AIDS, or immigrants and refugees), or the specialized settings (including schools, the workplace, hospitals and clinics, or prisons)

  II. Earlier historical responses to the problem, population, or setting

III. Framework for provision

    A. Laws and regulations

    B. Explicit and implicit policies (manifest and latent goals, objectives, and purposes)

    C. Funding

    D. Policy-making agency and distribution of responsibility among the levels of government: federal, state, and local

    E. Criteria for eligibility

    F. Coverage (the proportion of the population with the problem or need that is eligible for the service) and take-up (the proportion of eligible persons who receive the service)

    G. Comparative perspectives (optional, as relevant)

IV. Program models and delivery systems

    A. Program function: access, entry, or liaison service, case or treatment service, social utility or developmental service, or a combination (specify which)

    B. Community service (neighborhood or home based), residential facility, or both

    C. Formal or informal service (self-help or mutual aid)

    D. Administrative auspice (public or private nonprofit or private for profit, sectarian or nonsectarian, autonomous-freestanding or part of a system other than personal social services

    E. Funding

    F. Mission

    G. Access (how clients find out about and obtain the service)

    H. Channeling (how clients get processed through the organization or agency)

continued

Table 6-1. continued

  I. Characteristics of the clientele: criteria for eligibility and the number and types of clients served

  J. Links with other services in the same field or in different fields

  V. Practice modes and staffing patterns

    A. Types of services provided and interventions used

    B. Innovative practice modes

    C. Staffing patterns

      1. Professional and paraprofessional roles

      2. Specialist, generalist, case manager roles

      3. Individual or team roles

      4. Unidisciplinary or multidisciplinary staff

  VI. Research, evaluation, outcomes

    A. Theoretical knowledge base employed or not

    B. Knowledge of effects, effectiveness, impact, costs, and so forth

    C. Program innovations

    D. Critiques

  VII. An overview of issues, trends, and debates, including positions taken by interest groups and professional associations, new legislative proposals, quantitative and qualitative adequacy of service provisions

---

Note: This framework builds on an earlier formulation developed during the 1970s by a committee at the Columbia University School of Social Work.

---

benefits, did these services develop a distinctive, independent identity, valued for the help they could provide, not just as supplements to financial assistance.

Services in the workplace date from 19th-century employers' paternalistic provision of benefits, but also blossomed in the 1970s and 1980s as the workplace became more diverse and a higher proportion of the population (almost two-thirds of the nonaged adults) were in the workforce. This change, along with the increase of women in the workforce, made the workplace a more accessible point of entry for many types of help.

Identifying how help was provided for a particular population or problem in the past permits those who make assessments to discern whether a specific field of practice is well established, with a long history of attention, such as services to children and their families, or a newly emerging field, such as services to people with HIV or AIDS. It also helps to understand current developments in programs and practice.

Legislation and policies

A key component in learning about a field of practice is identifying the relevant legislation. Laws, whether federal or state, define the parameters of practice—what type of help can be offered, how much can be offered, and to whom. Thus, for example, if the target population is older people, it would be essential to know something about Old Age and Survivors Insurance (OASI) and Medicare, the two most important universal entitlement programs for older people; Supplemental Security Income (SSI) and Medicaid, the two most important means-tested entitlements for poor older people; and the Older Americans Act of 1965 and SSBG, the two most important personal social services programs for older people.

The Older Americans Act established the general philosophy in this field of practice, which emphasizes the planning, coordination, and delivery of personal social services for older people. Moreover, it provides funds specifically for senior centers, congregate meal services, home-delivered meals (Meals-on-Wheels), and a variety of services for frail older people. It is not an entitlement program, but it is a universal program; the services may be provided to any older person in need, regardless of income. About $1 billion was appropriated by Congress for these services in 1994.

The SSBG provides funds for a wide range of services for individuals and families with low or moderate incomes. Typically, half the resources (about $1.5 billion) go to older people for such services as home help, foster care, counseling, and information and referral services. In contrast to the programs funded under the Older Americans Act, eligibility for these services is limited to those who qualify on the basis of low income, not just need. Thus, despite the seemingly significant funds that are expended, many needy older people may still not qualify for Title XX (SSBG) social services. Nonetheless, these social services and the Older Americans Act services are essential to the operation of any social services agency that serves older people, and all these benefits and services are central to the knowledge and skills of the social workers who practice with this population.

If the field of practice is organized around a problem or setting, the relevant legislation is equally important. Thus, for example, if the problem is homelessness, the most important federal legislation is the Stewart B. McKinney Homeless Assistance Act of 1987, which provides funds for shelters and soup kitchens, some counseling and referral services, and a miscellany of other services for homeless people. If practice is based in a medical setting, such as a clinic or hospital, Medicare and Medicaid (Titles XVIII and XIX, respectively, of the Social Security Act) would be the key laws for social workers to know, in addition to Title XX.

Program models and delivery system

Once the first three components are identified, it is necessary to explore the range of program models and where a particular agency fits in the larger social services delivery system. Thus, for example, one would want to know whether an agency is public or private, religious or sectarian, and part of a large organization or a small and specialized program. All this information has immediate implications for the kinds of help that can be offered, the client population that can be served, and the skills and knowledge needed to provide help.

Today, most fields of practice emphasize the provision of help to individuals in their own homes or communities. Thus, even though child and family service agencies may offer a variety of service programs, including residential care and treatment and foster family care, the emphasis is on providing treatment and supportive services to children and their families while they are living at home; this is often the case for emotionally troubled children, for children who have developmental or physical disabilities, and for children of parents who have been neglectful or otherwise inadequate. Similarly, agencies that serve older people also concentrate on providing services that sustain older people in their own homes.

With regard to alternative program models, social services for adolescents may be used as an illustration. Among the possible service options for adolescents, in addition to residential treatment facilities and group homes, are school-based services, both medical clinics and peer support groups; community-based services for pregnant teenagers and teenage mothers that offer counseling, family planning services, parenting classes, child care services, and tutoring; multiservice programs that facilitate adolescents' transition from school to work and provide various other health and mental health, education, employment, and personal social services; and programs for delinquent or predelinquent youths. Some of these programs are for teenage girls, others are for teenage boys, still others are for adolescent parents, and some serve a mixed population of adolescents. Social workers who practice with adolescents must be familiar with these alternatives, be able to assess which are appropriate for a particular teenager who requests or needs help, and know how to help an adolescent qualify for the needed help.

Similarly, programs that deal with substance abuse include residential treatment programs; outpatient programs; and self-help groups, such as Alcoholics Anonymous. Knowing what each program provides and what type of person and problem can be best treated in each can help social workers achieve more effective practice.

In addition, social workers must know who is eligible for help in different programs. For example, are services limited to those who live in a particular neighborhood? Are they means-tested and thus limited to poor people, or are they universal and available to all, perhaps with income-related fees? Unfortunately, regardless of the field of practice, the supply of services (except for the entitlement programs) is not adequate to meet even the needs of those who qualify for help. Nevertheless, knowing the criteria for eligibility often enables social workers to find an appropriate "fit" for their clients.

Social workers also must know how people find and gain access to different kinds of help, that is, whether they do so on their own or with the help of professionals. For some groups and some types of problems, there are special services just for this purpose. Thus, for example, for older people, for parents in need of child care, for women, and for people who abuse drugs or alcohol, various types of information and referral services, hot lines, and crisis services provide information about the kinds of help available and where to go for help. Some people are able to take the information provided and proceed on their own, but others require more assistance.

Modes of practice and staffing patterns
In some fields, the core help involves personal social services provided by social workers. Thus, in agencies serving children and their families, the core staff are often those with master's or bachelor's degrees in social work, depending on the knowledge and level of skill that the tasks require. These social workers must be prepared to assess the severity of the problem and the type of help needed; to provide short- or long-term, more intensive or less intensive, individual, group, or family counseling and other practical helping services; to ensure that multiple types of help are provided, if needed; and to establish appropriate linkages with other agencies.

In other fields, especially in multidisciplinary settings, social work practice may involve teamwork with other professionals, such as physicians and nurses in a hospital or clinic or lawyers in the courts. In some settings, such as schools or large corporations, even if the actual practice is carried out by social workers, effective intervention requires knowledge of the host institution, the constraints that the institution imposes, and other specialized staff.

Sometimes new modes of practice may develop in a particular field, such as the emergence in the 1980s of comprehensive, short-term, intensive, and goal-oriented interventions ("family preservation") in child and family services whose objective is to avoid the placement of neglected or abused children in foster care. Social workers in other fields gradually began to test this mode of intervention, for example, when the objective was to avoid the institutionalization of delinquent or emotionally disturbed adolescents and to help families through particular crises. In short, interventive methods may be specific to a field of practice or may be used or adapted by many fields. In either case, one needs specialized knowledge to choose which modes are appropriate for which clients.

Research, evaluation, and outcomes
One question that is frequently raised is, Is social work intervention effective? Two types of research are especially relevant for answering the question: one for the evaluation of programs and the other for the evaluation of individual practice interventions. Thus, for example, in the innovative practice mode just described, the central issue is whether it is effective in reducing the rate of placement and resolving crises. Studies have found that this mode can be helpful when it is used along with a variety of other services, but that it may not, by itself, achieve all that it was initially thought to. On the one hand, recognizing the limitations of a particular intervention can be important for developing a new program or changing an existing one. On the other hand, it is equally as important to know when a program is successful. For example, good-quality child care services have been shown to have important

positive consequences for young children from poor families. Thus, facilitating access to such programs can be beneficial for young children from dysfunctional families (as well as for those from well-functioning families, of course). From another perspective, the knowledge that certain types of self-help groups have proved effective in dealing with certain problems, such as alcoholism and domestic violence, can help social workers recommend particular treatment modes for clients.

Current issues, trends, and debates
Finally, it is important to know what the major current developments are in one's chosen field of practice, which issues are being debated, and who is taking the different stances. Obviously, how the problem is defined has major implications for policy, program, and practice. Thus, for example, in the field of homelessness, a major issue is whether the problem is one of individual dysfunction (mental illness or substance abuse) or the lack of affordable housing, or some combination of the two. Similarly, there is a debate about whether child abuse is a problem of family pathology or inadequate social policy or both. And those who work in the field of services to adolescents differ on how much attention should be given to young fathers compared with young mothers and whether providing free, readily available contraceptives would be more effective in reducing teenage pregnancy than would the use of peer support groups, counseling, or a more punitive approach. Some of these issues can be resolved through research, but others may reflect differences in ideologies or values about the role that the government should play in family matters. Such issues vary not only across fields of practice but within fields and over time.

CONCLUSION

Graduate social work education began with a focus on specialized fields of practice, and there was no holistic concept of social work method. Over time, it was recognized that there was a core body of social work knowledge that stressed the distinctiveness of social work intervention methods in relation to this core. Since the 1960s leading practitioners and theoreticians have advocated a two-dimensional model that organizes graduate social work education along two axes: interventive method and field of practice. With the explosion in the size and diversity of the U.S. social sector since the 1960s and the recognition that personal social services has been a distinctive domain within the social sector since the 1970s, the need to organize professional education around both axes, including the different fields of practice, has become more urgent.

The delineation is not meant to suggest that fields of practice is a static concept. These fields are more fluid than the social work methods because they emerge, disappear, combine, and recombine in response to social change, new social problems, changing values, and new legislation. For professional social workers to begin to practice with appropriate expertise, so they are competitive with professionals from other disciplines who work in the same or related fields, they must have expertise in a particular field of practice. Only a practitioner who has been exposed to and become conscious of the field-of-practice dimension can make an optimum contribution to practice.

This chapter has traced the development of the field-of-practice concept, demonstrated its relevance to social work practice today, provided a framework for analyzing the various fields, and illustrated how this framework can be used in several fields. The challenge is for both social work researchers and educators to be vigilant in monitoring the fields as they change and in adapting and refining the relevant knowledge base for students.

REFERENCES

Americans with Disabilities Act of 1990. P.L. 101-336, 104 Stat. 327.

Bartlett, H. M. (1961). *Analyzing social work practice by fields.* New York: National Association of Social Workers.

Bartlett, H. M. (1965). Social work practice. In H. L. Lurie (Ed.-in-Chief), *Encyclopedia of social work* (15th ed., pp. 755–763). New York: National Association of Social Workers.

Bartlett, H. M. (1971). Social work fields of practice. In R. Morris (Ed.-in-Chief), *Encyclopedia of social work* (16th ed., Vol. 2, pp. 1477–1481). New York: National Association of Social Workers.

Briar, S. (1987). Direct practice: Trends and issues. In A. Minahan (Ed.-in-Chief), *Encyclopedia of social work* (18th ed., Vol. 1, pp. 393–398). Silver Spring, MD: National Association of Social Workers.

Gilbert, N. (1977). The transformation of the social services. *Social Service Review, 51,* 624–641.

Kahn, A. J. (1965). Social work fields of practice. In H. L. Lurie (Ed.-in-Chief), *Encyclopedia of social work* (15th ed., pp. 750–754). New York: National Association of Social Workers.

Kahn, A. J. (1979). *Social policy and social services* (2nd ed.). New York: Random House.

Kamerman, S. B., & Kahn, A. J. (1976). *Social services in the United States.* Philadelphia: Temple University Press.

Lurie, H. L. (Ed.-in-Chief). (1965). *Encyclopedia of social work* (15th ed.). New York: National Association of Social Workers.

Minahan, A. (Ed.-in-Chief). (1987). Encyclopedia of social work (18th ed.). Silver Spring, MD: National Association of Social Workers.

Morris, R. (Ed.-in-Chief). (1971). *Encyclopedia of social work* (16th ed.). New York: National Association of Social Workers.

NASW Commission on Social Work Practice, Subcommittee on Fields of Practice. (1962). Identifying fields of practice in social work. *Social Work, 7*(2), 7–14.

lder Americans Act of 1965. P.L. 89-73, 79 Stat. 218.

Runaway and Homeless Youth Act of 1974. P.L. 93-415, 88 Stat. 1129.

Social casework: Generic and specific (report of the Milford Conference). (1974). Washington, DC: National Association of Social Workers. (Original work published 1929)

Social Security Act of 1974. P.L. 93-647, 88 Stat. 2337.

Stewart B. McKinney Homeless Assistance Act of 1987. P.L. 100-77, 101 Stat. 482.

Townsend, P., Sinfield, A., Kahan, B., Mittler, P., Rose, H., Meacher, M., Agate, J., Lynes, T., Bull, D. (1970). *The fifth social service.* London: Fabian Society.

Turner, J. (Ed.-in-Chief). (1977). *Encyclopedia of social work* (17th ed.). Washington, DC: National Association of Social Workers.

U.S. House of Representatives, Committee on Ways and Means. (1993). *Overview of entitlement programs: The 1993 green book.* Washington, DC: U.S. Government Printing Office.

U.S. House of Representatives, Subcommittee on Children, Youth and Families. (1992). *Federal programs affecting children and their families, 1992.* Washington, DC: U.S. Government Printing Office.

Vinton, L. (in press). The "boutique effect": Trends in MSW curriculum patterns. *Journal of Teaching in Social Work.*

7

Social Work Practice with Individuals

Carol H. Meyer and Josie Palleja

In the Reform Era, when social workers practiced in settlement houses and as friendly visitors through the Charity Organization Societies, they offered their helping services to people as individuals, families, groups, and communities. This was long before the professionalization of social work, and the helpers of the late 19th and early 20th centuries simply did what seemed to be necessary in case situations using common sense. When Richmond (1917) codified a casework approach to helping people, she devised the first methodology in social work, making it possible to replicate and teach casework practice. This methodology contributed to the ensuing professionalization of social work because it defined a mode of helping that was to justify (more than could common sense) the purposes and processes of the new profession. Thus, casework, or practice with individuals, was the first *professionally defined* modality in social work. Practices with families (1950s), groups (1940s), and communities (1960s) were similarly developed and, in turn, contributed to the diversified practice repertoire of social workers. As each modality was devised, its practitioners called themselves by the title of the modality. Thus, they were caseworkers, family workers (later, family therapists), group workers, and community workers (later, community organizers). Modern social workers, having evolved from identifying themselves by the method they practice to achieving a professional identity (including a commitment to social work values and ethics, reliance on a knowledge base, and a contextual connection to social policy and service structures), now call themselves social work practitioners, who work with individuals, families, groups, and communities through theoretically defined modalities.

The ecosystems perspective has helped to conceptualize the social work practitioner's multiple roles (using the diverse modalities) by laying out the "picture" of a case and enabling the practitioner to determine which modality is most appropriate to use—where and when—in the case. The typical social worker today has some facility in moving from one modality to another, although many tend to use one or two with which they feel most comfortable

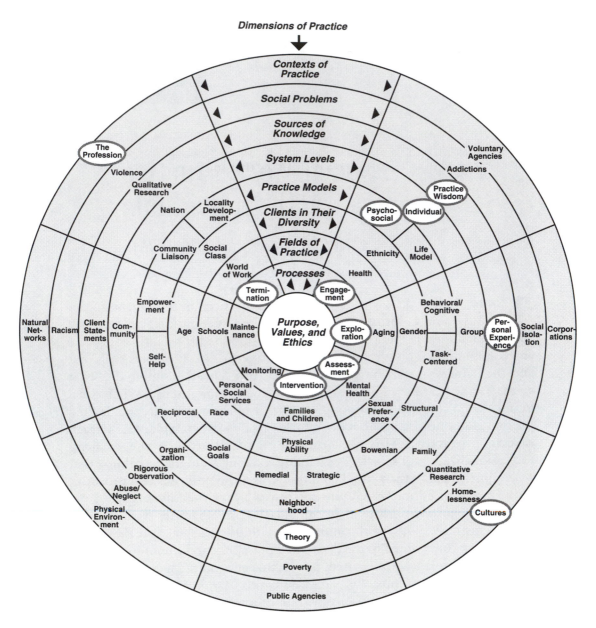

Dimensions of Practice

Contexts of Practice
Social Problems
Sources of Knowledge
System Levels
Practice Models
Clients in Their Diversity
Fields of Practice
Processes

Purpose, Values, and Ethics

The Profession

Violence
Qualitative Research
Nation
Locality Development
Community Liaison
Social Class
World of Work
Empowerment
Termination
Engagement
Natural Networks
Racism
Client Statements
Community
Age
Schools
Maintenance
Exploration
Aging
Gender
Group
Personal Experience
Social Isolation
Corporations
Self-Help
Monitoring
Intervention
Assessment
Mental Health
Personal Social Services
Reciprocal
Race
Families and Children
Sexual Preference
Structural
Organization
Social Goals
Physical Ability
Bowenian
Family
Rigorous Observation
Remedial
Strategic
Quantitative Research
Abuse/Neglect
Physical Environment
Neighborhood
Homelessness
Cultures
Theory
Poverty
Public Agencies

Voluntary Agencies
Addictions
Practice Wisdom
Psychosocial
Individual
Ethnicity
Life Model
Health
Behavioral/Cognitive
Task-Centered

FIGURE 7-1. DIMENSIONS OF PRACTICE EMPHASIZED IN WORK WITH INDIVIDUALS

or most skilled. The chief indicator of the progress that has been made from the earliest days of identification solely with a method is that modern social workers first attempt to assess what is needed and is possible to achieve in a case and *then* choose a modality that is appropriate to the circumstances. This is a more logical and sophisticated response than the former one, in which caseworkers, family workers, group workers, or community organizers practiced their methods simply because that was what they knew, not necessarily what the case needed.

This chapter is about practice with individuals, which is also still called casework or clinical practice. In an active and evolving profession such as social work, it is to be expected that, over time, many approaches to practice with individuals would have been developed. It is beyond the scope of this chapter to describe all of the more than two dozen approaches. In general, most of these practice "models" derive from three identifiable theoretical bases: the psychosocial, the sociobehavioral, and the human ecology approaches. In addition, there are evolving practice approaches that are empirically derived, based on experimental research that indicates which interventions are effective in particular circumstances.

The *psychosocial approach* (Hamilton, 1951; Hollis, 1964), the oldest model in continuous use, evolved from Richmond's (1917) *Social Diagnosis.* In the 75 years or so since its development, this approach has relied on psychodynamic theory, which developed from psychoanalytic theory in the 1920s, as well as the modern approaches of ego psychology and object relations theory. Two themes distinguish this approach: the psychological and social components in people's lives (an "inner-outer," person-in-environment focus) and the requirement of assessment (or, in Richmond's terms, "social diagnosis") as the key to understanding the psychosocial dynamics of the case.

The *sociobehavioral* approach was integrated into social work practice in the 1960s by Thomas (1967). Originally derived from behavioral psychology (Skinner, 1969), today this approach also relies on cognitive and learning theories. The distinctive feature of this approach is its focus on clients' overt behaviors (in contrast to the psychodynamics of the psychosocial approach). Current contextual behavioral approaches (Mattaini, 1990) contain a person-in-environment focus that is similar to the psychosocial approach, and assessment is central to this practice. (Assessment as an interpretive process is generic in social work practice, although each theoretical approach obviously assigns different factors to be assessed.)

The *human ecology approach,* including the life model approach (Germain & Gitterman, 1980), was developed in 1980 and is based on ecological theories that account for the mutual adaptation of the person and the environment. This approach emphasizes the processes of exchange between the person and environment; the temporal phases of practice, called the beginning, the middle, and the end; and the centrality of the worker–client relationship to effect this mutual adaptation. It differs from the psychosocial and sociobehavioral approaches in its focus on *processes,* rather than on assessment, as a tool to understand the *content* of cases.

Although no practice approach is pure in its application and some social workers occasionally blend the ideas of all the approaches, it is helpful to practitioners to recognize the distinctions among these approaches so they will recognize the distinctive languages, methodologies, and expectations of outcomes. Furthermore, as practitioners seek to deepen their knowledge, it is important for them to know that they are reading about psychodynamic, behavioral, or ecological theory and that the roots of dozens of current practice approaches, all with different titles, can often be identified as being derived from these three approaches. The proponents of each approach claim that their approach is "better" than the others, but it has not been impartially determined which approach is more (or less) successful in some or all case situations. Given the diversity of the client population and the openness of social work thought, it is all to the good that practitioners are free to experiment, to mix and match if they will, or to stay with the approach that works for them.

Social workers do not practice personality or behavioral theory directly; rather, their practice is strained through the available social work–defined approaches that rest on professional purposes, values and ethical contexts, and service structures. This is one of the ways in which social workers can distinguish themselves from practitioners in other disciplines, who may use the same personality, behavioral, and ecological theories for their own unique professional purposes.

This chapter discusses practice with individuals, highlighting methodological principles. In light of the foregoing discussion of distinctive practice approaches, it was necessary to choose one for the purposes of discussion. The authors chose the psychosocial approach, but when possible will identify the differences, as well as the similarities, of this and other approaches.

The primary distinction between practice with individuals and practice with families, groups, and communities is, of course, that the practice takes place one-on-one between the practitioner and a single client. Despite this small unit of attention, every client is recognized as being part of a family and community, even though these units of attention may not enter the interviewing situation. Thus, facing a single client always means seeking to understand the family and community to which that client belongs and whose personal transactions can be traced through the client's intimate and environmental relationships.

DEFINING THE CASE

The ecosystems perspective allows the practitioner to "view" the components of a case to determine where the adaptations and dysfunctions are occurring between the client and his or her "ecological surround." A good conceptual grasp of the case in this way helps the practitioner develop an understanding of the client's unique situation. The case of Ms. R illustrates this "pictorialization."

Case Example

> Ms. R, age 26, is a divorced parent of a four-year-old girl who attends a neighborhood day care center. Ms. R attends church, where she experiences her most gratifying relationships. She belongs to a singles club sponsored by the church, whose members often baby-sit for each other as well as provide emotional support. Ms. R works as a computer programmer, but her job is an

hour's commute from her home. The rent of Ms. R's modest three-room apartment is a little too high for her income.

Ms. R came to this country from the Dominican Republic five years ago with her husband and has no relatives here. When she divorced her husband two years ago, she was left with no social supports but she managed to find them through the church, and she had created a generally stable, though lonely, life for herself.

Ms. R came to the neighborhood mental health center because her rent was raised, and she could no longer afford the fee for day care. This was a crisis for her, and she was anxious about whether she might have to move or even quit her job.

An ecomap is useful for both Ms. R and the social worker to examine this situation visually, to seek entry sites in both Ms. R's coping repertoire and in her ecological surround. This ecomap shows Ms. R's resources and lack of resources. As her story unfolds, the social worker can determine where the

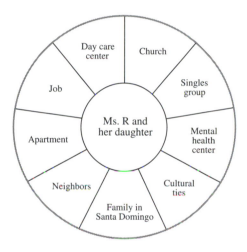

psychosocial features of Ms. R's case can be strengthened or realigned. The unique person and her particular environment can be understood only by individualizing the case—understanding her connections with her ecological surround and her lifestyle and historical profile.

CHOOSING THE THEORETICAL FRAMEWORK

Professional practice requires a theoretical framework that will make sense of the case data. Whichever theory or practice approach is used to explain the dynamics of this case, it will direct the practitioner to the kinds of knowledge necessary to understand what is observed and will offer certain interventive principles. Each approach "sees" the case data in a slightly different way, emphasizes different features of the case, and may focus on different interventive points. As was mentioned, this chapter uses the psychosocial approach, although the case could, of course, be treated with the sociobehavioral-cognitive approach or the life model approach.

Psychosocial practice, reflecting its person-in-environment focus, draws from a broad base of knowledge. This knowledge has to account for understanding the individual's personality and coping capacity; the nature of particular psychosocial problems; and the transactions developed (or that need to be developed) between the person and other people, events, institutions, and physical spaces in his or her environment. Given the multiple influences in a person's life, the social worker must have some knowledge and appreciation of contentious issues regarding genetics, class, gender, culture, family, ethnicity, religion, and personality development. Also, given the inequities of this modern society, people suffer from economic deprivation, racial oppression, gender discrimination, and social criticism of their lifestyles. Social workers have to be sensitive to and aware of the many ways in which these factors affect individual clients. Finally, clients are subject to all types of physical and mental illnesses, and practitioners whose clients are ill must be familiar with the course and treatment of these illnesses.

Even given the difficult lives that social work clients live, the psychosocial approach is fairly optimistic in that the person's adaptation is stressed and achieved when optimal conditions of growth and change are developed in the person's environment. As one of its theoreticians, Hollis (1977), stated, this approach is "an attempt to mobilize the strengths of the personality and the resources of the environment at strategic points to improve the opportunities available to the individual, and to develop more effective personal and interpersonal functioning" (p. 1308). The optimistic view stems from the recognition of the individual's potential to thrive despite adverse situations, such as economic deprivation, oppression, or abuse and neglect, and that the person's endowment, development, and life history play a role. Despite a destructive and deprived childhood, for example, a person can overcome (or at least come to terms with) severe past psychological and social assaults and be helped to tap into his or her latent and unrealized potential. Thus, this approach is committed to the expectation that a person can grow and change.

Furthermore, this approach shares with all other practice approaches an appreciation of the uniqueness of each person. Even though all people may share common attributes and environmental influences, each person is affected and responds in his or her own way. Like thumbprints or facial characteristics, which are never repeated, an individual's biopsychosocial makeup is uniquely shaped by his or her endowment and experiences. Thus, social workers must individualize their attention to people with problems. However, both clients and social workers live in the real world, and thus it is never possible to view professional help outside the social-political-economic context in which it is always embedded. Today, the constraints on the autonomous and need-meeting practices of all helping professionals (social workers, psychologists, psychiatrists, physicians, nurses, and teachers) are severe. The obligation to individualize interventions with clients is now limited by reduced funding and managed care, for example, and "ideal" practice approaches have had to respond by adapting their processes to these real-world demands. Therefore, before the actual practice processes are discussed, it is necessary to comment on some of the constraints that challenge them.

Constraints on Practice

Impact of Managed Care and Reduced Funding

The present political, economic, and social forces in the United States are all directed to saving money by reducing services, downsizing organizations, and doing things more efficiently with less labor and in a shorter time. In managed care in the field of health and mental health, insurance companies have the authority to make decisions about the type, length, focus, and outcomes of treatment. This situation has, of course, had a major impact on professional practice, not the least of which have been the limitations placed on professional decision making in case practice. Individualizing has given way to prescriptions and formulas; goals of feelings of well-being have given way to specific, measurable behavioral changes; and open-ended contacts between clinicians and clients have given way to a predetermined number of short-term contacts. In other fields, such as family and child welfare, in which managed care is not an influence, restricted funding has caused social agencies to seek similar goals of speed and efficiency.

Although one can easily bemoan these constraints and all social workers should advocate to change them, it should be noted that social work has survived other tough times for over a century because it has remained open to new ways of working. In the spirit of adaptiveness, social workers have developed tools to evaluate effectiveness, to "prove" the helpfulness of professional interventions. Furthermore, practitioners of all approaches, including the psychosocial, have learned how to shift their practice goals to more immediate outcomes and to develop short-term approaches. Ironically, it has been discovered that planned short-term treatment approaches can be more effective than open-ended approaches because of the necessity to focus on and remain aware that the case will soon end.

Impact of Organizations

Just as social workers cannot practice without reference to the social-political-economic environment, they must be continually aware of the organizational context in which their practice is embedded. Social agencies, clinics, hospitals, drug treatment centers, children's institutions, and so forth have structures, purposes, histories, and cultures, and people who staff them. That is, these organizations are dynamic entities, some of which are more open to change, more client centered, and more adept at enhancing professional roles than are others. The central feature of organizationally based practice, whether in medicine or social work, is that organizations are sanctioned and paid (publicly or privately) by communities, taxpayers, and philanthropists to conduct specific programs. Thus, the organizationally based social worker must continually find a balance between the organization's policies and his or her professional autonomy. This abstraction becomes more concrete when it comes to clinical decision making that includes such issues as timing, focus, and content of the helping process. Again, the "ideal" process may be enhanced or chipped away, depending on a host of factors in a particular organization.

The setting also affects the way a problem is focused. For example, a case of child abuse may be seen in its acute phase in a hospital emergency room, where the physical and emotional trauma would be treated as a crisis. When the case is referred to a child welfare agency, decisions about long-term planning have to be made. Although the client's story and the assessment of the dynamics involved would be similarly understood in both settings, the focus on the problem would be different. Each setting defines for itself the services it will offer and the problems it will address; thus, if a client goes to a mental health clinic, he or she will be viewed as having a mental health problem, whereas if the same client goes to a family service agency, he or she will be viewed as having a family problem. The social worker must be alert to protecting the client's integral difficulties, so the service program does not predefine the problems in the case. If the client's need and the agency's services do not fit properly, then a referral to a different type of agency may be indicated.

Impact of Involuntary Clients

Social work clients may come voluntarily to the helping process because of a perceived need, such as feelings of anxiety or depression, or because they want something fixed, such as a job, school, or a family relationship problem. However, a large proportion of social work clients come involuntarily because they are forced by their circumstances, behavior, or intimates to seek help or because some other service has been made contingent on their going for help. Clients who are mandated by the courts to seek help are often the most involuntary clients (Rooney, 1988). When people go for help because someone else has defined their behavior as a problem, but they do not acknowledge that they have a problem, they may be difficult to engage in treatment and thus the involuntariness itself will have an impact on the processes of practice, particularly in the beginning. An applicant is not a client until he or she has negotiated a helping contract with the social worker (Alcabes & Jones, 1985). Once again, the "ideal" approach must accommodate to the less-than-ideal reality. Even so-called voluntary clients are normally hesitant about seeking help, for who really wants to change? Whether voluntary or involuntary, clients (like all people) want bad situations to be better, but they do not necessarily want to assume the burden of changing their attitudes, feelings, or behavior. For this reason, among others, social work practice relies on its processes to move a client along from the beginning to the end of the clinical encounter. Leading a client through the helping process is more effective than confronting the client with the demand to change.

Impact of Time

Time is a dynamic in all areas of life (Germain, 1976), and all people have to make adaptations to it, but in professional practice there is little leeway for avoiding its continuing pressures. Time is a factor in determining when, how often, and how long a social worker will see a client. One way to conceptualize time frames (Meyer, 1993) is as planned short-term, episodic, and open-ended practice.

Short-term approaches

Short-term approaches are commonplace today, for the reasons discussed earlier. But even "short" has different meanings, depending on the nature of the problem and the organizational setting. For example, a patient in a hospital may be discharged within a few days, so the social worker will have a clear end point that is known from the outset and must adapt the helping process to the time that is available. Another example is a woman in a rape crisis center, whose experience with rape must be treated as a crisis for her to move on to resolve its consequences. Crises are, by definition, time limited (Parad & Parad, 1990), so the beginning, middle, and end of the process are compressed, perhaps into a single interview.

A final example is a child who has been physically abused and must have protection at once. Although the discovery of the abuse may create a family crisis, "sufficient" time has to be allowed for exploration of the circumstances of the abuse and assessment of the potential family supports for the child, so the child is not removed precipitously. Such a case, which requires both speed and thoughtfulness, has to be resolved in a "short" time, but with enough latitude to allow for well-thought-out interventions. In addition to crisis intervention, task-centered practice (Reid & Epstein, 1977) is an exemplar of short-term, empirically based interventions.

Planned short-term interventions mean that these are not accidental accommodations to time pressures, but that there is always a clear focus on the purposes of the client's contact with the agency. Generally, the idea of planned short-term interventions has more to do with striving toward an end point or keeping a specific outcome in the forefront of the work between the client and practitioner. Thus, such interventions require a greater degree of concentration and activity by practitioners than do open-ended interventions, and there is always less time to consider clients' associative content; therefore, practitioners must always help clients to keep to the major threads of their stories. The current interest in using short-term approaches may require social workers to review potential long-term cases and to revise ambitious outcomes or to achieve a stricter interviewing focus. The great advantage to planned short-term intervention is that clients are more apt to have their immediate needs met. Practicing more expediently does not necessarily mean practicing less effectively.

Episodic interventions

Episodic interventions are different from either short-term or open-ended interventions. In a sense, they may be defined as short-term "bits" of practice within an open-ended framework. This approach is appropriate in cases of chronic physical or mental illness or when people require intermittent supports or supervision for an indeterminate period. A client may be known for many years in an agency, but may need professional services only at times of transition, as when he or she is about to get married, attend a new school, or start a new job. Or some clients who have fragile ego structures and are often overwhelmed by pressures in life may need occasional supportive interventions. Each type of case will define the moments when episodic contacts are necessary, such as when financial aid has to be recertified, when medical appointments are scheduled, or when the client and practitioner decide that contacts would be appropriate.

Open-ended treatment

Open-ended treatment was once the typical time frame in practice with individuals, perhaps because in the 1920s, when psychoanalytic theory was new, social workers, along with psychiatrists and psychologists, experimented with it and were attracted to the idea of probing people's innermost thoughts and motives and seeking the root causes (in childhood) of people's current problems. This approach is now part of the history of the development of the social work profession, but it is no longer the preferred mode of practice. Rather, psychosocial theorists and practitioners may seek to understand people's deepest problems, but only as they are manifest and significant in the here and now. Modern ego psychology has provided knowledge of people's functioning (their coping and mastery) that does not require the probing that was so popular over 70 years ago. Another reason for the retreat of open-ended treatment modes in social work is that social workers have learned new skills that effectively help clients by focusing on their functioning in their particular environments and more about interventions in the environment that will enhance individual functioning.

In open-ended interventions, the practitioner is a more passive participant in the helping process than he or she is in short-term approaches. This passivity allows a case to unfold in an indeterminate time frame; the practice is like a discovery process, and the client works at his or her own pace, raising new material and taking new directions. Clearly, open-ended interventions have great appeal for practitioners in all disciplines, just as they do for some clients who need to unfold their stories slowly and in their full complexity. However, they are not only a luxury in these days of managed care, they are also impractical in terms of time and financial cost and are rarely funded by funding sources. Professional help today means dealing with a client's problems in as efficacious a way as possible; it no longer means helping clients live their lives over again within the helping relationship. Despite these constraints, no limit is placed on *thinking* about the complexities of a client's story. The challenge is to translate what is known and inferred into a "doable" problem that can be a reasonable focus for intervention.

PROFESSIONAL RELATIONSHIP

Social work practice always entails person-to-person encounters between both the practitioner and the client. Therefore, the professional relationship is an important theme that flows through every phase of the practice process (Perlman, 1979) and is discussed before the practice process is explicated. This relationship is different from ordinary relationships in several ways. The primary difference is that it is *client centered;* that is, whatever is expressed by the practitioner is guided by who the client is and what he or she is ready and able to hear. Because a client who comes for help usually has troubles and feels upset, it is likely that the client will be in a state of anxiety, anger, or even suspicion. Although the practitioner may feel normal human emotions in response to expressions of anger, affection, sadness, and so on, relating professionally means that he or she has to control these feelings and respond in ways that will be helpful to the client. The professional discipline does not require that these emotions should not be felt, but that they should not be expressed openly without considering the client's need or ability to experience them. What, then, do practitioners do about these suppressed emotions? Ordinarily, they share them with their supervisors and colleagues or with friends and family members or seek other outlets.

The professional relationship imposes these restraints so that the work with clients remains client centered, serving both the purposes of intervention and the values and ethics of social work. Generally, social workers use their professional relationships to enable clients to explain their situations; to support their self-determination; to empower them, when possible, to assume responsibility for their own lives; and to help them contemplate alternative actions.

The relationship with a client is the engine that moves the process forward; it is not, in itself, the primary treatment tool that will solve the client's problems. In some situations, the relationship (used professionally) may assume greater significance, such as when a teenager needs the social worker to act as a behavioral model, when a desolate client needs an extra display of empathy, or when a young child in a crisis needs a hug. But even in such situations, it is the client's need and the purposes of intervention, not the social worker's impulses, that should guide the behavior. Usually, the social worker offers a supportive relationship, so the client will find an understanding ear and a sustaining environment in which the work can be done.

The ways in which the client relates to the social worker offer the opportunity to observe habitual behavioral responses that can then be used as case data. Just as one can understand a female client better by observing her behavior in her mothering role with her child, so one can learn more by observing how she manages stress or relates in an interview. The repetition of behavioral responses is common, and noting them can contribute to the social worker's understanding of the client's affective, behavioral, and cognitive styles. On the other hand, the way in which the practitioner relates to a client is an aspect of intervention; therefore, the use of the professional self in that context demands a discipline that is not expected of the client. A central principle involved in that discipline is that the helping relationship is, in a sense, a "one-way street."

Students often wonder if they have to become "cold" to maintain a professional relationship. The answer is that each practitioner has his or her unique personal style of relating, which is the style that the practitioner should use. The important thing is that the practitioner must understand what the *client* needs. If a client needs support through a difficult time, one practitioner may say, "This must be hard for you," whereas another may say "Gee, that's tough," and it doesn't much matter which style is used, as long as the goal of empathic support is attained. Being "professional" does not mean being distant or passive in the relationship. On the contrary, it means being always attentive, active in listening and responding, and sincerely concerned about a client's welfare (Kadushin, 1972).

PRACTICE PROCESS

Process means action or movement. It is a way of expressing what happens next, and all practice approaches account for process, albeit with different terminology, different emphases, and different purposes. In the psychosocial approach, the phases of the process are called exploration, assessment, intervention, and termination. In a way, one can recognize that one phase follows another; the social worker explores the case data (as with an ecomap), assesses or interprets the meaning or implications of the data, and then intervenes (does something helpful) on the basis of the first two processes. (The life model approach uses the terms "beginning," "middle," and "end" as a temporal framework, indicating that activities are shaped by the timing of their entrance into the case.)

Exploration

The exploration phase is the crucial time in a case when the client and the social worker meet and come to a mutual agreement about whether there will be a case and, if so, what the terms of work will be. Thus, during this phase, such important processes as engagement and contracting, as well as collecting case data and organizing it in some coherent way, occur. Even though there is a beginning, or introductory, phase in all practice, there is also a blurring of phases in that each phase folds into the preceding one.

Engagement

The first phase of practice is dependent on the agency context in which the encounter takes place and on whether the client has come voluntarily or has been mandated to be there. It is in this phase that the social worker creates a supportive ambience, so the client can tell his or her story. Almost immediately, an oral or written *contract* is negotiated (Seabury, 1976), so the client understands the conditions of work, including the purpose, focus, time, place, fees, and who will be involved. It is through contracting that the practitioner and client come to a mutual understanding of the purpose and general focus of their ongoing work together. (This contract is particularly important in light of the earlier discussion of the constraints of managed care and limited funding.) In this beginning phase, the client should be helped to understand that their work together will remain *confidential* and that if a legal or dangerous situation arises, the client will be informed if the practitioner must report it.

Learning the client's story

Data collection is, of course, the central purpose of the exploratory phase of the practice process. It is in this phase that the content of the ecomap is derived. The timing, depth, and direction of the social worker's inquiry must depend on the reason the client is there, the agency's purposes, and the client's motivation and capacities. The principles of *relevance* and *salience* (Germain, 1968) are useful to consider here. Are the exploratory areas relevant and sensible, or are they extraneous? Are they salient and significant to the client's presenting problem, or are they of only academic interest? Social workers are as curious as anyone, and clients are often glad to find a listening ear. Yet, the professional encounter must lead to a helping goal; it cannot be an open-ended, aimless exchange. One can listen to a client's story in "free form," as it were and use even apparently disparate data to fill in the picture. But in professional practice, in contrast to writing a novel, for example, information about the case has to be siphoned into practical action.

History taking is part of the exploratory process and learning the client's story, but it must be seen in the context of the focus just mentioned. Exploration means gaining an understanding about the person and his or her connections to the "ecological surround," not about everything that has happened in the client's life. Every event has a history—people are born and mature through the life process, and their school, work, family, and community experiences all have histories—so the social worker has to use his or her judgment and common sense to determine the relevance and salience of the history that must be learned to help the client. For example, a parent–child conflict may have been developing over a long time, an adolescent using crack may have had a history of alienation since the first grade, a homeless person may have a lifelong history of social isolation, and a community group may complain of their history of police harassment. These historical narratives are important to know to understand the current problem, but even though the past illuminates the present, it is the current situation to which the practitioner and the client must attend because only that situation can be changed.

History taking is rarely a linear process in which the client tells his or her story coherently, thematically, logically, or sequentially. First, clients are often troubled and may distort information, perhaps as a way of avoiding painful recollections. Second, facts that are remembered and colored by emotions are not always "accurate," but to the client, they are the true version of events and must be accepted as such before they can be clarified. The most effective way of learning about a client is by understanding his or her narrative (however it is related), helping to organize it, and hence making sense of past events that are affecting the presenting problem. This process allows the client to gain cognitive mastery of his or her experiences and perhaps to rethink them with greater reasonableness. Although it is valuable to learn the history of events, one must keep in mind the pressures of time and agency purposes, as well as the interests of the client and the nature of the problem to be resolved. These factors will serve as ready reminders of the necessity to take a client's history only for the purpose of throwing light on the current situation. Luckily, it is known that people's life histories are always expressed in their current lives, so it is usually more effective to explore case data in the present or to go back in time only when it will help to explain some current issue. The past cannot be changed, but people have the capacity to move on with their lives in spite of, as well as because of, the way things were.

Other sources of information
All people are dependent on public institutions such as schools, the police, the health care system, and community services, but social work clients are often people who are poor and have few personal resources and are totally reliant on these services. When such problems as substance abuse, child abuse and neglect, spouse battering, or street crime, for example, are observable outside the family home, both the perpetrators and the victims are likely to be referred to social workers in a variety of agencies. In such a referral, it is often necessary (if not legally required) for the social worker to gain information about a client from other sources. The need to do so places an ethical responsibility on the practitioner to remain open with the client about the source and content of the information that is received or sought. The client is always the primary source of information, and when it is necessary to seek information from others, the reasons and implications must be discussed frankly with the client.

However the practitioner views the client's story, at the end of the exploratory phase it is necessary to have at least a tentative focus for action. Recall that the phases of the practice process are conceptually discrete, but tend to blur in actuality. For example, one may move through the process and discover the need for further exploration in a later phase. Nevertheless, the time comes (sooner, rather than later) when a determination must be made about which problems are to be addressed, a time when the client and the practitioner together get "a fix" on what is wrong and what may be done about it. It is at this point that the case data (organized and focused) are put to use as the basis for understanding the case. The story itself will not reveal this understanding; some meaning has to be made of the story before the problems are defined.

Assessment
Assessment means interpreting the data of the case to arrive at a decision about what to do in it. This part of the practice process differs from the exploratory phase in the same way as painting a scene differs from taking a photograph of it. The exploration process should be as objective as possible in the collection of case data; the assessment process must include the practitioner's reasoning and translating of the raw data into meaning. In the exploratory phase, the data are generated from the client as he or she narrates the story of the case. Even though the social worker enables the client to tell

the story, the data are embedded in the story, not the worker. In the assessment phase, the practitioner uses his or her knowledge and judgment to interpret or make sense of the story, so in this phase, the social worker intrudes (at least intellectually) (Meyer, 1993). Assessment is a search for meaning. When the client describes an occurrence, such as having been beaten by her partner, the social worker can draw on the literature of theory and research to learn what is known about wife beating in general. This knowledge will help the practitioner to understand better the specific instance of wife beating in that case and will indicate what is known to work or not work in such cases. It is true that every case presents a unique set of features, but it is also true that an accumulated body of knowledge is available about groups of similar unique cases.

The outcome of assessment should be a definition of the problem or problems to be worked on, and again, this decision will be guided by the social worker's theoretical commitments; theory shapes the practitioner's view of what is significant in a case. In addition, the same adaptations to real-world constraints have to be made in defining problems as were made during the exploratory phase. For example, the practitioner may assess that a family's central difficulty is the need for housing, but there well may be no housing available, and even if the social worker advocated for housing on behalf of the family, he or she might not succeed. The lack of available housing would not mean that one would change the assessment, but it would mean that the "problem to be worked on" would be (unhappily) to help the family find creative adaptations to their situation. This is a common process in cases of chronic mental illness, for example, in which the assessment of schizophrenia will not bring forth a cure for the illness. Thus, mental health practitioners will adjust the definition of the problem to what is possible to accomplish. In the case of schizophrenia, it will mean the assurance of medication and possibly a protected living situation with a job scaled to the client's capacities.

It is in the assessment phase that a social worker determines what is "workable" in the case. Having learned the client's story and (at least tentatively) having understood the nature of the presenting problems and the client's resources in the exploratory phase, the social worker will also have observed the client's strengths in coping and dysfunctional behaviors. That is when decisions must be made (and shared with the client) about what exactly can be done to help. The client's preference always plays a vital role in defining the problem to be worked on.

Although the client may agree with the practitioner's assessment of the situation, he or she may choose not to focus on the practitioner's definition of the problem. For example, a battered woman who has related her horrendous story of abuse may well feel that she cannot or will not decide to take action to move away from her partner. If this is the case, the definition of the problem cannot be the need to relocate; rather, it would have to focus on the woman feeling stuck in her abusive relationship. Of course, with involuntary clients, it may be difficult to help them agree to any definition of a problem. If a man was forced by the court to see a social worker about his nonpayment of child support as an alternative to going to jail, it is likely that he would be reluctant to agree to working out a payment plan; thus, a more useful problem focus might be the need for him to confront his limited alternatives. Similarly, a group of adolescents who were referred for violent behavior in school probably would not at first choose to confront that problem; rather, they might prefer to work on their discontent with various aspects of their lives that were brought out during the assessment process.

The client's culture (language and customs) also will have a bearing on how problems are defined. In this society, in which new immigrants continue to replenish the population, dealing with diversity is a requisite in social work practice. Practitioners have to keep in mind that the theories of human development and the practice approaches they use are shaded by Western culture and North American values. Some people who have grown up in conservative, non–Western or non–North American cultures may find notions of competition, empowerment, or self-actualization, as well as the kind of sexual freedom, alternative lifestyles, and social mobility that are available in this society, to be incomprehensible. For instance, people from some cultures that use chaperones for young people may consider the freedom allowed American adolescents to be alienating. Thus, it is possible that immigrants would not understand the definition of problems that were alien to their own life experiences. Therefore, problems must always be defined within the language and cultural parameters of the client.

The intervention phase is dependent on the assessment phase, which is an anchoring step in the total process. However, just as exploration may take place further on in the process, assessments can be changed as more information throws new light on the situation, but the step must be taken, even if it is not final. This part of the process is probably the most difficult for any practitioner because it requires the risk of stating what is wrong and how it can be fixed. This phase requires the practitioner to assume responsibility for significant professional decisions. And what are these decisions?

Intervention

Choice of modality
The first important decision is to choose the interventive modality. Should it be individual, couples, family, group, or community work? The problem itself will play a part in this decision. For example, is this a person who is isolated from others and needs the opportunity to experience relationships in a controlled small group? Or is this a depressed person who is not up to relating to others, but needs to talk to someone about his or her life? Or is this a family in which the children have been in trouble in school and have told their teachers about the pervasive conflict at home? Or is this a group of people who want to join together to combat violence among the youths in their neighborhood?

Ideally, the choice should be dependent on the client's preference, the perceived needs of the case, and what research has determined works best in similar situations. However, once again "real-world" constraints enter the decision-making process. An agency's resources, a practitioner's best skills, the time that is available, and the client's willingness to be involved generally have the greatest influence on the choice of modality. Increasingly, social workers are sensitized to the client's ethnic/cultural inclinations. Perhaps a close-knit extended family would find it more in line with their experience to be seen as a family, rather than to have one of their members considered the client. In relation to the influence of managed care and decreased funding on the time available for therapeutic encounters, shifting from an individual to a group focus may speed up the helping process, partly because group members participate with the practitioner in inducing changes among the members. When a client's problem is identified as being connected with a community problem, the practitioner may move the focus to a neighborhood group or a supportive network of some kind. When problems are not so clearly defined and it is not evident which modality should be used, the practitioner may search the research literature for suggestions about which modalities work for certain types of problems. This section focuses only on the individual modality.

Who to include
Another decision that is related to the choice of modality is the selection of the person or persons to be included in the intervention. The concern here is with people's motivation and capacity for becoming engaged in a professional intervention. It is always necessary to adapt one's interventive techniques to the client's developmental level and intellectual and emotional capacities. As for motivation, this is a complicated issue in that people often come to social work agencies involuntarily because someone in authority has sent them, because they are failing in some aspect of their lives, or because they are unhappy or in painful conflict about something. The presence of such difficulties is not always equated with being motivated to get help. Frequently, people want things to be better in their lives, but few feel expressly motivated to participate in the work of changing their own behavior. They may place responsibility for their troubles on others or on external conditions, and it takes some skill to help them to assume responsibility for their own lives and thus be motivated to change.

Available resources
Intervention planning must take into account the resources that are available in the community and in the client's life. Again, it is unrealistic to plan interventions that do not take into account realistic possibilities. For example, despite one's view of an ideal family life, poverty, the availability of drugs and guns, the presence of oppression, and unemployment wreak havoc on families, and it is difficult for them to sustain even marginal family life. These are significant social problems that may not be fixable through direct social work practice, so interventive plans must find their way around them to make smaller changes in the lives of families. When social services, health care, child care, housing, and well-functioning schools are lacking, then ideal interventive planning is unrealistic.

Nevertheless, there are infinite environmental interventions that can be effective in all social work cases. Each client is connected to some sector of the larger institutions of society, and it is those smaller sectors that serve as the arena for social work practice. Is a school providing the right program for a child? Can a teacher be helped to understand a child's worries about his home life? Is advocacy necessary to help a client receive her public assistance check? Does a landlord need reminding about a tenant's rights? Does a person who is abusing drugs or alcohol need a support group developed? Does a physician need help in understanding a patient's noncompliance with a medical protocol? Every case has a psychosocial aspect, and the social worker always acts on this dual focus. The planning of interventions accounts for the person-in-environment, and when an ecomap is drawn, the boundaries of the configuration of a case are displayed.

Termination

This final phase in the helping process, ending, is perhaps the most universal experience individuals share. Endings are an everyday occurrence. All people lose intimate relationships through separations and death; leave school, friends, and family members; and end a class, a day's work, or just the day. Most endings (especially those connected with people whom one has loved) arouse emotional reactions that one often feels again when one experiences new endings. When endings are felt as losses, these losses may be reactivated when the helping process ends. If a client experiences these feelings during the termination phase, the practitioner must be sensitive to their presence and recognize the difficulty the client (and perhaps he or she) is experiencing. How the practitioner terminates the helping process can have an impact on the client's perceptions of the help received, as well as his or her future help-seeking behavior.

Given the significance of the time frame in social work practice, it should be evident that increasingly, the conclusion of a case is being foretold at the time of planning. During this ending phase, one can recognize all the themes in a case (Fortune, 1985; Fox, Nelson, & Bolman, 1969; Mayadas & Glasser, 1981; Siebold, 1991). It is a time of review: Was the original contract observed? Has the presenting problem been resolved? Was this a learning and growth experience? It is a time for a critique of the experience: Is there unfinished business? Did the client feel respected and empowered? It is a time to look forward: What can the client do by himself or herself? What referrals are necessary? Can the outcomes of the intervention be sustained? Termination should never come as a surprise to a client, particularly in planned short-term treatment when the focus is on specific outcomes and intervention is not expected to be unending. Yet, when a client has experienced a helpful relationship with a social worker, there are often emotional ties to be resolved, and the termination phase provides the opportunity to do so. The inevitability of termination in all social work cases (for whatever reason) makes it important for the end to be kept in mind from the beginning so that both the practitioner and the client can focus on the outcome of their work together.

NECESSARY SKILLS AND TECHNIQUES

The foregoing outline of the method used in social work practice describes the basis of all professional action in cases. If one were to observe an experienced social worker interviewing a client, treating a family, or leading a small group, one would notice only the techniques used, and the process might not look complicated. However, when one realizes that the selection of words, the timing, the words not expressed, and the choice of clarifying questions all derive from what was understood in the exploration, assessment, and interventive planning phases of the case, then one would recognize the *disciplined* use of techniques. Practice techniques themselves are not scientific, as is the method in which they are embedded; even though techniques can be classified and learned, their use often expresses the practitioner's personal style. Given this freedom to choose from a broad repertoire of techniques, it is important that each professional practitioner has a rationale for the technique he or she uses. Theoretical approaches to practice normally provide this rationale along with their recommended techniques.

The use of words is paramount in all the modalities of social work practice, as it is in all human encounters. Words, of course, are representational or symbolic and therefore what they imply can have a greater import than what they actually mean. For example, asking a friend in a social situation how he is getting along with his wife may be an innocuous question, but asking the same question of a man accused of battering his wife takes on a more significant meaning. Words are shortcut ways of communicating complex ideas, so it is always best for the practitioner to select the words that a client can comprehend and that the practitioner feels comfortable using. Supportive measures in social work practice require that the client understand that the practitioner recognizes his or her suffering. Of all of the words most useful in encouraging a person to tell his or her story, the words "oh?" and "go on" are both parsimonious and powerful. Because it is the purpose of social work practice to enable people to cope with their lives, it is more important for a client to come to his or her own realizations than for the practitioner to lecture or to inundate the client with words. Words are tools in practice, and, like tools, they must be used sparingly and suitably.

Activities of various kinds are certainly within the repertoire of social work practice techniques. Young children express themselves through play as well as words, and a great deal is known about the use of age-related toys and games that help practitioners communicate with children (Schaefer & O'Conner, 1983). Often older children are mistrustful of the helping experience and may choose games through which they express themselves, although one must be careful to keep in mind that problems are not resolved through play alone and that the ever-present need for focus ultimately requires the use of words for communicating serious thoughts and feelings. In family work, role-playing and "acting out" family conflicts often can move the helping process forward. In groups, particularly with young people, games can elucidate issues and can relieve tensions. As with the use of words, activities are tools to be used judiciously in accordance with the requirements of planning a case.

Interventive techniques may generate support of the client's behavior ("That was a good thing to do") or they may challenge the client to reflect on his or her choices ("Are you sure that is what you want to do?"). Some techniques are useful in enabling the client to tell his or her story ("That's interesting; please go on"), whereas others help the client review something already said ("Can we go back to what you said before?"). It is not possible in the abstract to cite the repertoire of techniques because what the practitioner says or does always depends on the type of case with which one is working. Students will find through their direct practice with clients that they will develop their own skills base as they gain experience with a range of cases. Obviously, students want to know immediately what to do, but the hard truth is that all professional actions derive from understanding the case; doing is an expression of knowing. The purpose of professional education is for student social workers to gain knowledge so that, in the end, they will know exactly what to do.

SUMMARY

Practice with individuals in social work is one of the modalities used to help people who have difficulties in their lives. As this chapter has shown, this modality has a method—exploration, assessment, intervention, and termination—and uses the professional relationship as the medium for interaction between the client and the practitioner. Furthermore, practice is never ideal; it is always constrained by real-world factors—organizational settings and the imperatives of social policy; therefore, the institutional context from which social workers gain sanction and direction must be kept in mind.

Social work practice is defined in various ways, in accordance with the several practice approaches that are available. Yet, diverse as these approaches are, there is much that all practitioners (and social workers who have social policy and administrative tasks) hold in common. First, of course, is the purpose of social work, which is to work toward the mutual adaptation of people in their environments—the psychosocial focus. Second, social workers have a common attachment to professional values and ethical behavior, as well as a commitment to knowledge-based practice. The most important areas of knowledge, and the most fruitful for practitioners to pursue, are the social problems and human development that are the substance of their work. Third, all social work practitioners share a view of the challenges and gratifications of living and working in a multicultural society, in which ethnic and cultural differences must shape the nature and direction of practice. Given the continuing social change in this country, social workers have come to appreciate the need to avoid fixed notions and expectations of family life, lifestyles, and gender roles. This sensitivity to differences has allowed them to maintain their relevance in the world they share with their clients.

REFERENCES

Alcabes, A., & Jones, J. (1985). Structural determinants of clienthood. *Social Work, 30,* 49–53.

Fortune, A. E. (1985). Planning duration and termination of treatment. *Social Service Review, 59,* 647–661.

Fox, E., Nelson, M., & Bolman, W. (1969). The termination process: A neglected dimension in social work. *Social Work, 14,* 59–68.

Germain, C. B. (1968). Social study: Past and future. *Social Casework, 49,* 403–409.

Germain, C. B. (1976). Time as an ecological variable in social work practice. *Social Casework, 57,* 419–442.

Germain, C. B., & Gitterman, A. (1980). *The life model of social work practice.* New York: Columbia University Press.

Hamilton, G. (1951). *Theory and practice of social casework.* New York: Columbia University Press.

Hollis, F. M. (1964). *Casework: A psychosocial process.* New York: Random House.

Hollis, F. M. (1977). Social casework: The psychosocial approach. In J. Turner (Ed.-in-Chief), *Encyclopedia of social work* (17th ed., Vol. 2, pp. 1300–1308). Washington, DC: National Association of Social Workers.

Kadushin, A. (1972). *The social work interview.* New York: Columbia University Press.

Mattaini, M. A. (1990). Contextual behavioral analysis in the assessment process. *Families in Society, 71,* 236–245.

Mayadas, N., & Glasser, P. (1981). Termination: A neglected aspect of social group work. *Social Work with Groups, 4,* 193–204.

Meyer, C. H. (1993). *Assessment in social work practice.* New York: Columbia University Press.

Parad, H., & Parad, L. (1990). *Crisis intervention book 2: The practitioner's source book for brief therapy.* Milwaukee: Family Service America.

Perlman, H. H. (1979). *Relationship: The heart of helping people.* Chicago: University of Chicago Press.

Reid, W. J., & Epstein, L. (Eds.). (1977). *Task-centered practice.* New York: Columbia University Press.

Richmond, M. E. (1917). *Social diagnosis.* New York: Russell Sage Foundation.

Rooney, R. H. (1988). Socialization strategies for involuntary clients. *Social Casework, 69,* 131–140.

Seabury, B. (1976). The contract: Uses, abuses, and limitations. *Social Work, 21,* 16–21.

Schaefer, C. E., & O'Conner, K. J. (1983). *Handbook of play therapy.* New York: John Wiley & Sons.

Siebold, C. (1991). Termination: When the therapist leaves. *Clinical Social Work, 19,* 191–204.

Skinner, B. F. (1969). *Contingencies of reinforcement.* Englewood Cliffs, NJ: Prentice Hall.

Thomas, B. J. (Ed.). (1967). *The sociobehavioral approach and applications to social work.* New York: Council on Social Work Education.

Practice with and on Behalf of Families

Peg McCartt Hess and Helene Jackson

The perceptions and expectations of the American family have changed dramatically since the 1970s because of rapid demographic, social, and economic changes in this country. In response to these changes, choices among individual and family lifestyles have become both broader and more available. Driven by disenchantment with the traditional patriarchal family and empowered by the availability of contraception, the feminist movement has encouraged greater opportunities for women in the home and the workplace. At the same time, however, unrelieved poverty and family and environmental violence have increased the stress on and challenges to many families.

Two-career, blended, and single- and same-gender parent families have proliferated, altering and extending the acceptable configurations of family life (Carter & McGoldrick, 1989; Walsh, 1993). As the nuclear family has become "less and less the American norm" (Goldenberg & Goldenberg, 1990, p. 3), definitions of the family have become more flexible, and notions of normality have become increasingly ambiguous (Walsh, 1993).

Competent social work practice with families—whether with families as the clients, with individual clients with family as context, or with organizations and communities on behalf of families—draws on a remarkably wide and diverse body of knowledge. The nature of practice knowledge is complex. Since the 1960s there has been an unparalleled expansion in knowledge relevant to practice with families—knowledge that social workers continue to integrate into their practice. However, the availability of practice-relevant theories and conceptual frameworks, especially with regard to practice with families, is necessarily limited by both individual and collective discoveries and comprehension. This chapter represents an overview of the theories, concepts, and models that are most commonly used to inform and guide social work practice with families and examines practice with and within organizations and communities on behalf of families, with client family systems, and with individual family members.

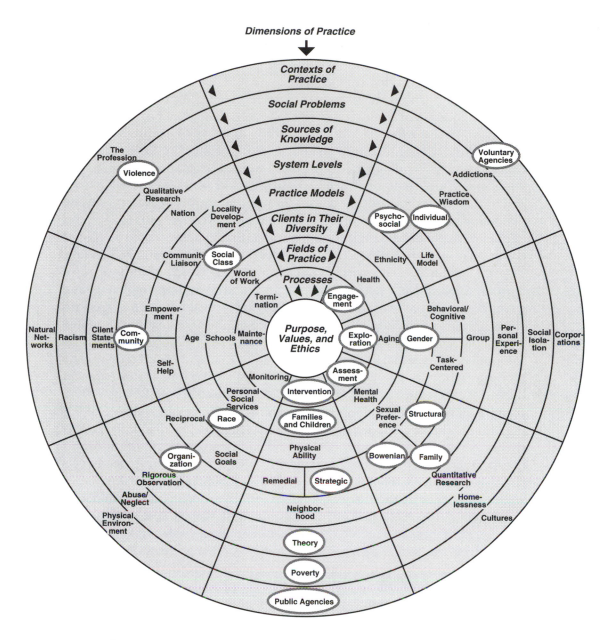

Dimensions of Practice

Contexts of Practice

Social Problems

Sources of Knowledge

System Levels

Practice Models

Clients in Their Diversity

Fields of Practice

Processes

Purpose, Values, and Ethics

FIGURE 8-1. DIMENSIONS OF PRACTICE IN WORK WITH FAMILIES

THEORIES AND CONCEPTS

Particular substantive knowledge supports practice with families in various fields, such as health, corrections, aging, mental health, child and family welfare, and the workplace. Practice with families who are confronting specific tasks and traumas draws on knowledge about human needs, responses, and coping that is specific to these situations. Regardless of the settings in which services are delivered and the clients' presenting problems, social work practice with and on behalf of families draws on a number of theoretical and conceptual frameworks, including knowledge about human development and relatedness, the internal functioning of families as systems, and the ecosystemic relationships between families and their environments.

Human Development and Relatedness

By definition, a family includes two or more people. Hartman and Laird's (1983) explication of family emphasizes the coming together of family members in ways that meet the individual needs of each: "A family becomes a family when two or more individuals have decided they are a family, that in the intimate, here-and-now environment in which they gather, there is a sharing of emotional needs for closeness, of living space which is deemed 'home,' and of those roles and tasks necessary for meeting the biological, social, and psychological requirements of the individuals involved" (p. 30).

Theories of individual human development have emphasized the role of family relationships (Erikson, 1959; Mahler, Pine, & Bergman, 1975; White, 1963). Therefore, practice with families requires knowledge of the individual biological, cognitive, emotional, moral, and social developmental tasks and issues across the life span and the strategies that individuals use to cope with stress (Coelho, Hamburg, & Adams, 1974). Social workers must also understand how family members promote or present obstacles to each other's development. Some social workers have conceptualized and explicated the complex interactions of family members' individual and reciprocal development (Carter & McGoldrick, 1989; O'Connell, 1972; Pollack, 1960; Rhodes, 1977; Rhodes & Wilson, 1981). For example, in the tradition of Erikson's (1959) individual life cycle, Rhodes's (1977) seven-stage model of change in families over time begins when two people join and ends with the death of the founding members. Except for the first stage, in which the major struggle involves the partners' development of a realistic and intimate relationship, these stages are shaped by the entry of children into the family and the children's movement through the tasks of childhood, adolescence, and young adulthood. The stages are generated by a convergence of biological, sociological, and psychological processes that require "change from everyone in the family—in each stage the family faces a major turning point" (Rhodes & Wilson, 1981, p. 16).

Although Rhodes's model provides one way of understanding the parallel development of children and adults in families, it does not address diversity in family forms and cultures, the influence of individual family members' unique needs or characteristics on other family members, or the effects of social context and unexpected events on a family's development. Germain (1991) proposed, as an alternative, a life-course model, of which she wrote that

> a conception of family development based on the various common and unique *life issues* confronting a family over its life course is more dynamic and closer to contemporary families' experience than constructions based on universal sequential stages. Life issues may be generated by internal pressures arising from members' biological maturational changes; nondevelopmental status

transitions; idiosyncratic troubles; external pressures arising from cultural imperatives and the societal context of racism and sexism and other abuses of power; or from other exchanges between the environment and the family or individual members. In order to cope effectively with such life issues as they come along, the family must modify its form or structure of roles and tasks. (p. 140)

Germain's discussion of the tandem development of family members in their environment provides a detailed examination of individual and family development and functioning using the life-course model in place of the life-cycle models.

The strengths of the family as an institution lie in its capacity to change. To work effectively with families, social workers must understand and be prepared to apply concepts of the development of individual family members and of the ongoing interaction of normative and unique developmental issues within a family, of the effects of unexpected events and stressors on the functioning of the family and of its members, and of the opportunities and obstacles presented to individual and family development and functioning by the constantly changing socioeconomic and cultural environment.

Social workers draw on attachment theory to understand family relationships and family members' reactions to separation and loss. Formulated by Bowlby (1958), attachment theory has contributed significantly to social workers' understanding of the distress of children (Ainsworth, 1982; Ainsworth, Blehar, Waters, & Wall, 1978; Karen, 1994) and adults (Golan, 1981; Parkes, Stevenson-Hinde, & Marris, 1991; Weiss, 1982) caused by the threatened, impending, or actual separation from or loss of an attachment figure, usually a family member. Crisis theorists (Golan, 1978; Parad, 1965; Rapoport, 1965) have generalized Bowlby's observations (1969, 1973, 1980) of the phases of the trauma of separation (protest, despair, and detachment) that young children experience.

According to the attachment theorists, humans, like other primates, are instinctively concerned with maintaining contact and proximity to attachment figures because their survival as individuals and as a species depends on their receiving not only food, water, and shelter, but affection and protection. Empirical research has found attachment behavior in infants and young children, as well as among adult male and female caregivers, and stable interactional patterns between infants and their parents, children's responses to separation from persons to whom they are attached, and a relationship between each of these factors and children's cognitive and socioemotive development (Ainsworth, 1982; Ainsworth et al., 1978; Greenberg, Cicchetti, & Cummings, 1990; Karen, 1994; Lamb, 1977; Main & Weston, 1981; Parke, 1981; Vaughn, Egeland, Sroufe, & Waters, 1979; Weiss, 1982). Attachment theory highlights the importance of policies, programs, and practices that value, support, and enhance secure attachments between children and parents, protect attachments that are at risk, and address the serious and often long-lasting effects of separation and loss on family members (Borgman, 1985; Gitterman & Germain, 1976; Hartman, 1990; Hegar, 1993; Hess, 1982, 1986).

Internal Functioning of Families as Systems

The theoretical understanding of the internal functioning of families as systems is a prerequisite to social work practice with families. As was discussed in chapter 2, general systems theory provides a framework for conceptualizing families as dynamic systems. This section describes selected concepts that are essential to understanding the internal functioning of family systems (for detailed discussions of family theory, see Germain, 1991, pp. 122–146; Hartman & Laird, 1983, pp. 59–107).

Boundaries

As systems, families comprise interrelated and interdependent units—family members. A family's boundary is the metaphorical parameter that defines who is in and who is outside the family at a given time. To maintain themselves as systems, families must have boundaries that are sufficiently permeable to allow for the exchange of information and energy with their environments, yet are sufficiently defined to permit families to function as discrete entities (Minuchin, 1974). Boundaries also delineate subsystems within families, including those shaped by generational differences (the parental and sibling subsystems), role relationships (parent–child subsystems and adult–adult spousal–partnership subsystems), and gender (mothers–daughters, fathers–sons). Within immigrant families, subsystems may be shaped by languages spoken by family members and by the nature and degree of family members' acculturation and cultural duality (McGoldrick, Pearce, & Giordano, 1982).

It is important to recognize that a family's boundary is defined by the family itself and may not be immediately evident to others. Thus, for example, the boundaries of families with same-sex partners and co-parents may or may not be openly identified to the partners' families of origin and to others with whom family members interact (Dahlheimer & Feigal, 1991; Roth, 1991; Woolley, 1991). In addition, family boundaries may be strongly shaped and may vary by ethnicity. For instance, Hispanic American, Asian American, African American, and Native American families may include persons other than "nuclear" family members, such as extended family members, close friends, and godparents (Attneave, 1982; Boyd-Franklin, 1989; Garcia-Preto, 1982; McAdoo, 1978; Redhorse, Lewis, & Decker, 1978; Shon & Ja, 1982; Vidal, 1988). As Meyer (1993) stated, "The assessment of the presence or absence of those external and internal boundaries is a first task in determining the viability of the family as a functioning system" (p. 82).

Hartman and Laird (1983) identified *separateness and connectedness* as the concept "probably most valuable of all in understanding and helping families" (p. 82). A family system in which members are unable either to be close or to tolerate separateness jeopardizes the development and functioning of all its members.

Organization and structure

A family system's internal functioning is also understood by examining its organizational structure, which is discernible in family roles, rules, and rituals. These components of family structure are interrelated and typically reflect family members' ethnic, cultural, and religious heritages, as well as their intentional responses to life transitions, individual members' needs, and the family's environment. Family assessment and intervention require an understanding of these factors and the ability to identify them.

Perlman (1968) defined *role* as "some recognized social position carried by a person into action. Because it is recognized and regulated it offers some firm footing, some ground rules for what and how and with whom the person claiming that status is supposed to act . . . no roles are carried solo; all are carried in transaction with one or more other persons. Therein lies the greater part of their meaningfulness" (pp. 41–42).

Family roles are always defined in the context of relationship. They may be clearly and formally designated (such as mother–daughter or co-mother–daughter, stepmother–stepdaughter, or mother-in-law–daughter-in-law) or more ambiguously and informally determined (for example, family gatekeeper, scapegoat, peacemaker, or historian). Family roles may be gender related and enacted intergenerationally. For example, over many family generations, the eldest daughter may play the role of caregiver initially to younger siblings and subsequently to aging parents.

Family *rules* regulate the patterns of family members' roles and behaviors, the family's use of time and space, accepted and taboo topics for family discussion, expression of feelings, and the nature of the relationships within and outside the family. "They also direct the flow and the nature of family boundaries and family communication . . . [and] confer status and power, define family rituals, and express meaning and value systems" (Hartman & Laird, 1983, p. 297). Families' rules about rules (metarules) determine whether rules can be talked about openly, both within and outside the family, and whether and in what way rules can be changed and by whom. Rules regarding intergenerational relationships, particularly intergenerational dependence and sharing between aging parents and their adult children, vary considerably across cultures (Hines, Garcia-Preto, McGoldrick, Almeida, & Weltman, 1992).

Family *rituals* further structure members' shared experience across generations and in the present. Germain (1991) noted that "family rituals are part of the family's own unique culture derived, in part, from the partners' families of origin . . . ., the larger cultural group and, in part, from the family's own experience. Rituals help shape themes and transactional patterns in family life and may contribute to constancy in the family" (pp. 134–135). Rituals mark individual and family transitions and holidays and give meaning to a family's shared experiences. Social workers may encourage families to use traditional rituals as a source of family sustenance and continuity; to develop rituals that reflect and therefore honor the blending of family members' ethnicities, culture, and religions; or to adapt or discontinue rituals that undermine the family's development and functioning or no longer serve a purpose.

Families' internal functioning at any point in time reflects the patterns of earlier generations' family boundaries, experiences of connectedness and separateness, and organizational structure, as well as other family characteristics. For the purposes of assessment, these intergenerational patterns and influences can be explored and understood through the visual depiction of a genogram (see Figure 8-2).

Ecosystemic Relationships between Families and Their Environments
All families live within and continually interact with a physical, social, and cultural environment. The conceptualization of families as dynamic systems recognizes the necessarily reciprocal nature of these interactions. The science that examines the relationships between living systems and their environments, ecology, has provided a metaphor for the ecosystems perspective (Germain, 1991; Hartman & Laird, 1983; Meyer, 1983).

The application of the ecosystems perspective to social work practice with families requires an understanding of transactions on multiple levels—between individual family members, between family subsystems, within the family as a system, and between the family and the numerous systems in the family's environment with which individual family members, family subsystems, and the family system transact. To maintain the family as a functional system, family members interact with the environment to obtain resources to meet their individual and collective biological, cognitive, emotional, moral, and social needs; to support and enhance individual and family development; to cope with life events and stressors; and to respond to environmental demands and opportunities. For any family, the environment necessarily includes systems that relate to family members' housing; sources of economic support; caregiving and supervision; physical and mental health; education; spiritual, relational, and recreational needs; safety and security; and services to supplement the members' resources.

From an ecosystems perspective, a family's relationship with its environment requires frequent, ongoing transactions with multiple, complex systems—transactions through which both the family and the other systems are changed with consequences for both. When the consequences for the family undermine family functioning or integrity, increase stress for family members, or deplete the family's resources, social work intervention may be focused on the family, on the environmental system or systems, or on the transactions between them. As is discussed in chapter 2, an ecomap can be used to depict graphically both the presence and the nature of the transactions between families and their environments at a given time.

Social work practice with families focuses on the interaction between the family's internal needs and its resources. It consists of purposeful intervention to improve the reciprocity in the exchange between the family and its environment. Depending on their position and role, social workers' practice may emphasize interventions within their own or other organizations and communities on behalf of clients or with family systems as clients, or both. The following sections further clarify the relevance of the selected theories and concepts identified earlier, as well as the range of approaches that are relevant to practice that focuses on the needs of families.

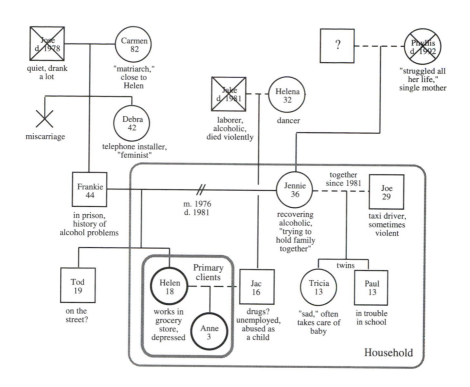

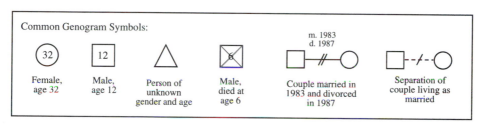

FIGURE 8-2. A SAMPLE GENOGRAM DEPICTING A FAMILY SYSTEM OVER FOUR
GENERATIONS.

PRACTICE WITH AND WITHIN ORGANIZATIONS AND COMMUNITIES ON BEHALF OF FAMILIES

Direct practitioners, supervisors, consultants, program developers, administrators, policy developers, and community organizers all potentially practice
with organizations and communities on behalf of families. Social workers
assist individual families in their transactions with organizations and with
their communities. They are obligated to promote the development of an
environment within their own and other organizations that is user-friendly
to families. Social workers also attempt to enhance the community's commitment and capacity to support the well-being and development of families.

Assisting Families in Transactions with Organizations

Historically, professional social workers have actively facilitated transactions between families and the formal and informal organizations in their neighborhoods

and communities—a task that is a fundamental component of direct practice. For many families, "engagement with larger systems becomes problematic and remains problematic for long periods of time, taking a toll on normative development, potential, and problem solving while supporting symptomatic behavior and a narrowed sense of choice and creative capacity" (Imber-Black, 1988, p. 14). In recognition of the serious difficulties that many families face in transactions with larger systems, services have been developed in which social workers focus primarily on facilitating these transactions, such as in public defenders' offices (Ashford, Macht, & Mylym, 1987), victim-offender mediation programs (Umbreit, 1993), and community hot lines (Loring & Wimberley, 1993).

For example, families who are coping with the chronic physical or mental illness of a family member realistically anticipate that they will negotiate relationships with multiple social services, health care, educational, occupational, and legal professionals and institutions throughout their ill members' lifetimes. Social workers often develop specialized knowledge and expertise in a particular area to assist such families and may collaborate or affiliate with local, national, and international networks that provide families with information, referrals, mutual support and self-help groups, and advocacy.

The social work roles of *broker, mediator, advocate,* and *case* or *care manager* are typically identified as central in assisting families in their transactions with organizations and communities (Compton & Galaway, 1994; Germain & Gitterman, 1980; Grinnell, Kyte, & Bostwick, 1981; Hartman & Laird, 1983; Manser, 1973; Middleman & Goldberg, 1974; Vosler, 1990). As brokers, social workers help families identify and make connections with needed resources in their communities. As mediators, they work with families to resolve disputes with individuals and organizations in their communities. With the families' knowledge and consent, they act as advocates, representing the families' cause to others, typically individuals or organizations (both theirs and others) that have failed to provide services to which the family members are entitled. In the case or care manager role, social workers typically broker, mediate, and advocate as they coordinate and facilitate the provision of multiple, diverse, and often complex services to families and individual family members.

Considerable knowledge and skills are required to carry out these roles successfully. Assisting families with needs and problems related to environments requires an understanding of their needs and choices to ensure that interventions support the families' adaptive fit with environmental resources. Practitioners must have current information about community resources, including family support and advocacy groups, and skill in identifying the most efficient pathways to obtain resources. They must also understand the complex relational, organizational, legal, and political variables that may undermine or facilitate families' relationships with their environments.

Promoting "Family-Friendly" Organizational Environments
Paralleling the technological concept "user friendly," the concept "family friendly" describes a human services environment that purposefully eases families'

transactions with organizations, particularly in the initial interaction of families and the staff. Family-friendly organizations are intentionally inclusive; they are physically, socially, and culturally accessible. Such organizations develop policies, programs, and practices that demonstrate their valuing of families and their theoretical understanding of the multiple and powerful forces within and outside family boundaries that shape families' complicated needs for services.

Inclusiveness and accessibility

An agency communicates its commitment to serve diverse races, ethnic groups, and family forms through its brochures and advertisements, responsiveness to telephone inquiries, freedom from stereotypical and discriminatory wording and categories in written and verbal communication, and in the nature of initial face-to-face transactions between families and agency staff. For example, the questions that families are asked directly and on intake forms either encourage clients to acknowledge openly their families' unique membership and set of relationships, roles, and needs or convey the assumption that client families must be traditionally constituted. Questions should anticipate that children may be biological, step-, adopted, or foster children or members of the extended family (nieces or nephews) and that they may have one caregiver (a single mother or father, a grandmother, an aunt, or a godparent), two caregivers (such as a mother and a father, a mother and a mother, a father and a father, a mother and an aunt, or a grandmother and a grandfather), or two or more parents in separate households who share joint custody. Social workers must be mindful that simple questions about family membership can be posed in ways that shame or alienate the client or encourage deception.

An organization demonstrates respect for client families through the arrangement and design of its physical space (Germain, 1981) and its willingness to locate services in community settings, such as churches, that families are comfortable entering (Solomon, 1985), or in clients' homes, where clients may feel more empowered to play an active role (Gutheil, 1992). The provision of office space for meetings with large families or with families with a member in a wheelchair conveys the belief that all family members have something to offer and something to gain from participating in a service. Play materials to occupy restless children and the routine scheduling of services during hours that do not require children to miss school or parents to miss work communicate respect for family members' responsibilities and commitments. Ironically, organizations often must struggle to achieve a balance in their respect for client families' needs for evening and weekend services with their respect for employees' family commitments.

Organizational mission and theoretical orientation

Human services organizations clearly convey their commitment to the enhancement of the well-being of families through the recruitment and retention of professional staff who are prepared to serve client families competently and to contribute to the ongoing development of an organizational mission and theoretical orientation that are responsive to families' needs. This commitment is operationalized to a greater or lesser degree in organizations' policies, programs, and practice approaches.

In many settings in which social workers practice, such as hospitals and schools, the organizational mission gives priority to serving individuals. Individuals' needs and responsibilities as family members and the needs of their families are often viewed as secondary at best. In such instances, social workers must provide leadership in the development and implementation of innovative family-focused programs that shape and expand the organizational mission. For example, members of the Social Work Department at Memorial Sloan-Kettering Cancer Center in New York City developed an orientation program and support groups for families of newly admitted cancer patients. This innovation not only helps to lessen family members' anxiety and to increase their coping during the crisis of hospital admission, but according to Parsonnet and O'Hare (1990) it acknowledges that "as family involvement in home care and discharge planning increases, families' needs must be recognized and addressed as distinct from patients' needs" (p. 40).

The theoretical orientation of some agencies continues to support practice with family members as a collection of individuals, rather than as a family system. As Janzen and Harris (1980) emphasized: "A family systems approach is not merely the addition of a treatment technique such as conjoint family interviewing (though that technique may be utilized) to another conceptual base and set of skills. It is a different way of thinking about presenting problems. . . . Where agencies have continued to define problems as problems of individuals rather than of families, the tendency to divide families up among agencies has persisted" (pp. 294–295). In such agencies, social workers must be willing to explore and articulate the consequences for both individual clients and their family members of engaging with clients in processes and decisions that do not take into account the needs and reactions of and consequences for family members. An agency's inability or unwillingness to operate from a family systems perspective may reflect the need for staff development, the influence of funding mechanisms, or other factors. Social work staff, however, can play a pivotal role in identifying and implementing steps that will facilitate the shift in an agency's theoretical orientation to incorporate family systems concepts.

Responsive to families' changing service needs
Social workers must also help their own agencies and other community organizations to anticipate and respond to the increased family stressors and service needs associated with natural disasters; local and national socioeconomic changes; changes in local, state, or federal policies; and events in the community, such as increased violence, the closing of a factory, or a school strike. For example, in many communities, social workers have provided leadership in identifying and responding to the need for psychosocial, legal, and economic supports for parents who have the human immunodeficiency virus (HIV) or acquired immune deficiency syndrome (AIDS), their children, and

other family members. In communities with growing immigrant populations, social services organizations have recognized that the provision of courses in English as a second language not only supports immigrant parents in their roles as wage earners, but improves their ability to communicate with their children and their children's friends. The timely development of programs that are responsive to families requires social workers in their multiple roles continually to anticipate and assess their clients' changing needs.

ENHANCING COMMUNITIES' COMMITMENT AND CAPACITY TO SUPPORT FAMILY FUNCTIONING

Communities have been understood as both geographic entities and as entities that represent broader and more fluid interests (Kettner, Daley, & Nichols, 1985). As is discussed in chapter 10, families may be members not only of a geographic community, but of racial, ethnic, and religious communities and communities that are defined by a family member's vocation and association with a specific institution, such as a school or labor union. In partnership with families, social workers must assess the roles that various communities play in facilitating or undermining families' achievement of their goals. In many instances, social workers cannot effectively serve an individual family without intervening in the community within which the family lives and the informal and organized communities with which the family identifies.

Social workers are also members of geographic, informal, and organized communities, including professional networks and organizations. As noted in chapter 10, the knowledge and skills that are essential for practice with communities are powerful tools for change. The perspectives that social workers can bring to bear on local, state, and national decisions that may affect the well-being of families are uniquely grounded in their daily interactions with families. On behalf not only of families who are their clients, but of all families, social workers must share those perspectives with the communities in which they practice.

PRACTICE WITH CLIENT FAMILY SYSTEMS

Social work practice with families has been significantly shaped by recent interdisciplinary developments in family theory and therapy. Although the pioneers of family theory and therapy came from different theoretical backgrounds, they had a common goal—to challenge the power and domination of psychoanalytic theory and technique and to find more effective strategies for treating individuals with severe mental illnesses (Anderson & Goolishian, 1988; Piercy, Sprenkle, & Associates, 1986). In developments parallel to those in social work, they adapted concepts from the physical sciences, stimulated primarily by cybernetics, general systems, and communications theories. Furthermore, they shared certain assumptions: that "the family is the context of human problems" (Nichols & Schwartz, 1991, p. 69), that the family is greater than the sum of its in dividual members, that all families demonstrate structure and process, and that human problems can and should be treated within a family context.

With the exception of Virginia Satir (a social worker), the early family therapists were middle-class white men, primarily psychiatrists, whose theories and practices were consistent with the political conservatism of the 1950s (Goldner, 1988). They demonstrated little awareness of possible definitional variations of the family and of the impact of the social context on behavior and had a limited interest in the differences in power that are inherent in race, ethnicity, gender, or socioeconomic class (Nichols & Schwartz, 1991).

Until the 1950s the family unit was typically viewed either as outside the domain of therapeutic interest or as an obstruction to the client's treatment (Nichols & Schwartz, 1991). Impressions about families were obtained from individual clients' perceptions, rather than from direct observation and assessment (Bowen, 1971). As the focus shifted from the individual to the view of "family behavior with the individual as carrier" (Auerswald, 1985, p. 4), the seminal works of anthropologist Gregory Bateson and family theorists and therapists, such as Salvador Minuchin, Carl Whitaker, Virginia Satir, Murray Bowen, Jay Haley and others, led to the proliferation of different approaches (Nichols & Schwartz, 1991).

Although social work has historically demonstrated an abiding concern for families (Hartman & Laird, 1983; Hollis, 1932; Overton & Tinker, 1959; Reid, 1985; Richmond, 1930; Satir, 1967, 1971; Scherz, 1954), the field of family therapy has rarely acknowledged the profession's influence on the development of family theory and therapy. The roots of family systems theory and therapy can be found in the early works of Charlotte Towle, Jane Addams, and Lillian Wald (Luepnitz, 1988; Nichols & Schwartz, 1991).

In most settings, social workers are able to work directly with families. In addition, either because of family members' inaccessibility or on the basis of assessment, social workers work with many clients as individuals whose needs and problems can neither be understood nor resolved without explicit attention to the family context. Consequently, current clinical social work practice with families and with individuals draws heavily on developments in the family therapy field.

The following sections discuss the major theories of family treatment, which, although they are different in many ways, share some basic assumptions. All the theories are based on a systems approach and view symptoms in an individual as a function of problems in the entire family. Most contemporary family therapists use a variety of methods and techniques borrowed from different theoretical frameworks. Students may find some of this material fairly advanced, but it is important to know what is available in this field, to recognize some of the themes to follow in work with families, and to make direct work with families as a unit a comfortable part of the social work practice repertoire.

Using a case illustration, the authors present and compare each model's theoretical assumptions and concepts, goals, emphases in assessment, and methods for effecting change and conclude by commenting on the past and future directions of family therapy. The aim is to support practitioners in identifying those aspects of each school of thought that would be most effective for the particular problems presented by their clients and that are compatible with the purposes and values of social work practice.

CASE EXAMPLE

> Mrs. Gutierrez and her two children, Maria, aged 14, and José, aged 9, arrived in the United States from the Dominican Republic one year ago. They immediately moved in with Mrs. Gutierrez's mother, an aunt, and the aunt's daughter Carla, aged 14, in a small and already overcrowded apartment. Left behind in the Dominican Republic were Mrs. Gutierrez's ex-husband, and her father, from whom she and her mother are alienated. Mrs. Gutierrez is unemployed and speaks no English. Maria and José have a limited ability to communicate in English.
>
> The family came to the attention of the social worker at Maria's school when Maria began speaking out impulsively and getting into fights with other children. She was absent frequently and had difficulty concentrating and sitting still; her clothes were often dirty, smelly, and torn.
>
> During her first meeting with the social worker, Maria appeared sad. She described herself as an outsider at school and at home. She admitted to having recently attempted suicide by taking 25 of her grandmother's pain pills. She felt "ganged up on" and "blamed for everything" by her grandmother, mother, aunt, and cousin. She described her grandmother as punitive, always yelling, and unfair. She expressed hatred for her cousin, who she said "thinks she's my mother, always telling me what to do, and siding with my grandmother and mother against me."
>
> In the first family meeting, Mrs. Gutierrez described her family as "very close," except for Maria, and complained that she had no control over her daughter. According to Mrs. Gutierrez, Maria was disrespectful; stole money from her; ran away for a week at a time; was sexually promiscuous; and was physically abusive to her younger brother, whom Mrs. Gutierrez described as a "good boy, an angel." Maria's grandmother threatened to send them all back to the Dominican Republic if they continued to meet with the social worker.

Bowenian Theory and Therapy

One of the earliest pioneers of family theory and therapy, Murray Bowen was initially absorbed with the intrapsychic life of his patients (Nichols & Schwartz, 1991). Bowen's experience with middle-class families with a psychotic member led him to conceptualize the family as a system that is dependent on the larger system and subsystems of which it is a part. In his work with schizophrenics, Bowen (1971) found it "impossible to see a single person without seeing his [or her] total family sitting like phantoms alongside him [or her]" (p. 164). This observation led him to formulate schizophrenia in the context of a multigenerational process of psychopathology (Luepnitz, 1988) and family dynamics (Piercy et al., 1986).

Among the concepts that form the basis for Bowenian therapy are boundaries, triangles, the multigenerational transmission process, and emotional cutoff. Like the definition given earlier in this chapter, *boundaries* refer to unobservable family structures that can be either rigid or permeable and can be found horizontally within the present family or vertically across generations (Minuchin & Fishman, 1981). The *undifferentiated family ego mass* refers to "the emotional tensions [that] shift about [the family] in an orderly series of emotional alliances and rejections" (Bowen, 1971, p. 172). On a spectrum of differentiation, the family ego mass can range from being overly intense (symbiosis) to having a well-defined sense of self as separate. A *triangle* refers to an affective, two-person structure in which a vulnerable third person (often a child) has been drawn into a subsystem (such as the parental subsystem) to side with one person against the other (Bowen, 1971; Hoffman, 1981; Piercy et al., 1986; Walsh, 1993). The *multigenerational transmission process* refers to the often unconscious transmission of family patterns passed down through multiple generations (Boyd-Franklin, 1989). *Emotional cutoff* refers to the rejection or isolation of a family member (Walsh, 1993).

Working with the Gutierrez family: A Bowenian perspective
According to Bowenian theory, the degree to which a family is differentiated from its family of origin determines its level of functioning (Piercy et al., 1986). Working with the Gutierrez family, the social worker may speculate that the conflicted relationships among family members demonstrate Mrs. Gutierrez's lack of psychological independence from her mother, which is reflected in her inability to respond positively to Maria's attempt to gain autonomy and separateness. The social worker would consider Maria's symptoms to be a manifestation of the family's historical difficulty with the psychological separation of individual family members, and the emotional cutoffs that have isolated the current generation from their family of origin (Nichols & Schwartz, 1991). According to this view, the family re-creates and passes on to its children the problems of previous generations (Piercy et al., 1986; Walsh, 1993).

The goal of Bowenian treatment goes beyond the alleviation of symptoms to a complete restructuring of the family. To achieve the therapeutic goal, the social worker would avoid focusing on the emotional conflicts and relationships evident in the contemporary Gutierrez family (Piercy et al., 1986; Walsh, 1993). Rather, he or she would seek to understand current themes and events as part of an intergenerational pattern (Nichols & Schwartz, 1991). Using a genogram, the social worker and the family would begin to identify and gain insight into past significant events and relationships that have been re-created in the present (Hartman & Laird, 1983; Walsh, 1993). Consistent with systems theory, the social worker would expect that meaningful changes would spontaneously occur in the family as the two women achieved differentiation from their own families of origin (Piercy et al., 1986).

Relying more on what the family says than on observation, the social worker would identify triangles and attempt to "detriangulate" them (Nichols & Schwartz, 1991). Accordingly, he or she would try to strengthen the sibling subsystem by distancing Maria's brother and cousin from their intense emotional relationship with Mrs. Gutierrez and their grandmother (Walsh, 1993). At the same time she would encourage the family members to develop a clear sense of who they are and what they believe in (Nichols & Schwartz, 1991).

In the role as a teacher of family systems theory (Nichols & Schwartz, 1991), the social worker would "coach" Mrs. Gutierrez and her mother to reconnect and renegotiate with Mrs. Gutierrez's husband and father, both of whom had been geographically and emotionally cut off from the family. For example, the two women would be directed to contact the men, either by telephone or by mail, to gain any information about the family that might contribute to understanding the current problems (Piercy et al., 1986; Walsh, 1993). The transgenerational patterns of emotional cutoffs and conflicted mother–daughter relationships would probably be attenuated as Mrs. Gutierrez and her mother approached their estranged family members in more effective ways (Madanes, 1981). As Mrs. Gutierrez became aware of the repetitive patterns across generations, she would be encouraged to think about her relationship with her own mother and to imagine how she would have liked it to be different. As a result, Mrs. Gutierrez would become more attuned to Maria's emotional needs and would understand that Maria's defiance and acting-out behavior were reflections of Maria's need to complete age-appropriate developmental tasks.

Working with the Gutierrez family, the social worker would minimize the chances of being pulled into the family system by maintaining a posture of objectivity and detachment. Assuming that a proper balance of thinking and feeling are necessary for healthy functioning, the social worker would attempt to ease the family's intense emotionality; toward this end, the worker would direct the family to avoid any emotional interchanges (Madanes, 1981). Using a didactic style, the social worker would educate the Gutierrezes about family systems to prepare them to continue their efforts to change after the termination of family therapy (Nichols & Schwartz, 1991).

Application to social work practice

This approach provides therapeutic tools with which to explore complicated family structure and organization. According to Boyd-Franklin (1989), the Bowenian model can be particularly effective when working with families from diverse racial and ethnic groups. Although the focus on the family of origin and the use of genograms may instill anxiety during the early stages of treatment, these techniques can be helpful in the middle phases once trust has been established.

Feminists argue, however, that the core concept of differentiation perpetuates the notion that the predominantly male attributes of psychological separateness are ideal and devalues the predominantly female attributes of maintaining connections and building relationships (Gilligan, 1982; Luepnitz, 1988). From a pragmatic point of view, the long-term nature of Bowenian treatment presents problems in the current climate of decreasing resources and managed care. From a research point of view, the goals of differentiation, insight, and renegotiation of interpersonal relationships are difficult to observe or measure (Piercy et al., 1986). Thus, the model presents problems for the evaluation of practice outcomes.

Structural Family Theory and Therapy
The structural school is the best known of the family theories and therapies. Developed initially by Salvador Minuchin, this approach is an extension of Minuchin's work with underprivileged boys and their families (Boyd-Franklin, 1989; Lappin, 1988). (For other influences on structural theory and techniques see Haley, 1978, 1987; and Speck & Attneave, 1973.)

As a researcher and therapist, Minuchin observed the relative ineffectiveness and irrelevance to his clients of the traditional "talk" therapies (Aponte, 1976a; Aponte & VanDeusen, 1981; Piercy et al., 1986). Applying a structural framework, Minuchin (1974) began to use a more active, problem-solving approach. He introduced the notion of "co-responsibility—the idea that all parties in a social system contribute to a shared reality" (Lappin, 1988, p. 221). Starting "where the client is," he shifted his focus to the individual in the context of family organization and to family structure and the variety of social contexts in which the individual acts, interacts, and transacts (Minuchin, 1974; Minuchin & Fishman, 1981).

The concepts of boundaries and triangles are also used by structural family practitioners. In addition, however, there are concepts that are particularly associated with this approach: structure, disengagement, enmeshment, parental child, and underorganization. Structure refers to the implicit or explicit rules that determine family transactions (Aponte & VanDeusen, 1981; Minuchin, 1974, 1992; Minuchin & Fishman, 1981; Piercy et al., 1986). Boundary problems may be manifest in *disengagement* (extreme separateness and isolation among family members) or *enmeshment* (extreme closeness that precludes the possibility of individual members' independence and autonomy) (Piercy et al., 1986). A *parental child* is one who has been designated by his or her parents (parental subsystem) to assume the power, authority, and functioning of the parental role (Minuchin, 1974). *Underorganization* refers to a structure with dysfunctional boundaries and power issues (Aponte, 1976b).

Working with the Gutierrez family: A structural perspective
The aim of structural family treatment would be to alter the current family organization and its ecosystem (Auerswald, 1985), so that Maria's symptoms would no longer be necessary (Madanes, 1981). Unlike the practitioner applying Bowenian concepts, the social worker would "not . . . explore and

interpret the past" (Minuchin, 1974, p. 14). Rather, he or she would attempt to change the repetitive, stereotypical, and destructive ways in which the Gutierrez family members relate to each other (Madanes, 1981; Madanes & Haley, 1977; Minuchin, 1974).

Together, the family and social worker would agree about the definition of the problem and the goals for change. A major goal would be to expand the family's definition of its difficulties from its narrow focus on Maria to a broader focus on the family system (Minuchin, 1974). Although the ultimate aim would be similar to that of Bowenian treatment—to enable the Gutierrez family to take charge and maintain itself in the absence of the social worker—the duration of treatment would be brief.

Structural theory provides a particular way to organize information that informs and guides the therapeutic process over time. At the core of this approach is the "concept of a system of interconnected people who influence each other" (Minuchin, 1974, p. 132). Thus, the goodness of fit between the Gutierrez family and the particular demands that have been made of it will determine the degree to which it is viewed as well functioning.

While the social worker was considering cultural differences (Minuchin, 1974; Minuchin & Fishman, 1981), he or she would view Maria's symptoms as an indicator of the family's inability to adapt its structure to the shifting events that occurred in their transition from the Dominican Republic to the United States (Madanes, 1981; Minuchin & Fishman, 1981; Nichols & Schwartz, 1991) and to "balance the respective demands of the family and each other" (Minuchin, 1974, p. 315). Thus, the focus would be on the family's structural dysfunction, rather than the presenting problem. Every intervention would depend on the social worker "joining" with the Gutierrez family, becoming a part of their family structure (Madanes, 1981; Madanes & Haley, 1977; Minuchin, 1974; Minuchin & Fishman, 1981) and getting to know them intimately.

The use of family mapping (Minuchin, 1974; Minuchin & Fishman, 1981) (like a genogram) would give the social worker and the Gutierrez family a picture of the family organization, its boundaries, and interactive patterns (Piercy et al., 1986). Attempts to open the boundaries between the Gutierrez family and potential support networks and to strengthen the boundaries between the parental and child subsystems would be active, directive, and aggressive (Nichols & Schwartz, 1991).

To reinforce Mrs. Gutierrez's parental role, the social worker would focus initially on the relationship between Maria's grandmother and mother to alter the imbalance in power in which Mrs. Gutierrez perceives herself as powerless and unable to function effectively. Meeting with the family, the social worker might assign a scenario or enactment that would be designed to get the two women or the children to demonstrate in the session the way they usually interact and then suggest different ways of relating. He or she might ally or affiliate him- or herself with Mrs. Gutierrez in an effort to shift the hierarchical structure between her and her mother.

A variety of restructuring techniques in the session, such as altering seating arrangements, would be used to facilitate change in the family system

(Minuchin, 1974; Minuchin & Fishman, 1981). Hypotheses would be developed about the multiple functions of the family's transactional patterns (Aponte & VanDeusen, 1981). For example, Maria's symptoms might be viewed as a way to shift attention away from the conflicts between Maria's mother and grandmother and to help the family avoid the painful feelings of separation and loss experienced in their immigration to a foreign country.

To address the family's ecological context, the social worker would evaluate the emotional and concrete resources available to the Gutierrez family to determine whether they could be used to bring about change. Thus, the social worker would meet with various members of the school system, for example, to identify ways in which they might become more responsive to Maria's and her family's needs (Aponte & VanDeusen, 1981). Depending on the need to increase or decrease the power of any particular subsystem, different configurations of the Gutierrez family (such as Maria and her mother or Maria and her cousin) could be seen (Minuchin, 1974). As structural changes occurred, alternative structures that would be more sensitive to the developmental, social, educational, and economic needs of its members would be identified (Piercy et al., 1986)

Application to social work
Minuchin was among the first in the field of family therapy to acknowledge the importance of culture and to involve the extended family, particularly grandmothers in minority families, in treatment (Boyd-Franklin, 1989). He was also the first to recognize the therapeutic problems inherent in cultural differences between practitioners and their clients (Nichols & Schwartz, 1991).

Despite the approach's sensitivity to the importance of a family's culture and ecological surround, feminists have argued that the focus on hierarchy and power reinforces the familial status quo while ignoring the developmental, social, psychological, and economic needs of women and children (Luepnitz, 1988). Further, they have found that the assumption that the family is growth producing and curative denies its potential for "violence and exploitation" (Luepnitz).

From a research point of view, the structural approach is the most completely developed of the family theories. Yet, the ease with which techniques from other theoretical perspectives, such as behavioral and strategic theories, can be incorporated into its broad perspective may interfere with testing its validity and the effectiveness of its techniques (Gurman & Kniskern, 1981).

Strategic Family Theory and Therapy
This approach grew out of the seminal research of anthropologist Gregory Bateson in the early 1950s. With Jay Haley, John Weakland, and Don Jackson, Bateson concluded that schizophrenia was a product of dysfunctional family patterns of communication, rather than, as was believed at the time, of childhood traumas. Basic to a strategic understanding of families is the assumption that all people have a need to assert power and control over one another (Madanes, 1981; Nichols & Schwartz, 1991).

Strategic family therapists focus on the message and the relationship (Madanes, 1981; Nichols & Schwartz, 1991). According to them, all communication is contextual; messages occur at different levels and have multiple meanings that may be either congruent or incongruent (Haley, 1990). Because "behavior and communication are synonymous" (Nichols & Schwartz, 1991, p. 40), change is achieved through their modification, rather than through self-awareness. Strategic therapists hold that "the family is a self-regulating system which controls itself according to rules formed over a period of time through a process of trial and error" (Palazzoli, Boscolo, Cecchin, & Prata, 1978, p. 3). The sign of a well-functioning family is the capacity to change and solve problems in stressful and unfamiliar situations (Nichols & Schwartz, 1991).

Strategic family therapists share with their colleagues from the Bowenian and structural schools the concepts of boundaries and triangles. However, some of the concepts that are particularly associated with the strategic school are power, hierarchies, and the double bind. *Power* refers to how and why people relate to one another. Its use can be innocent, malevolent, exploitive, or helpful, and allocations of power may be equal or unequal or may shift, depending on the situation or task involved (Madanes, 1981). The *double bind* is the communication of simultaneously conflicting messages that confuse the recipient, leaving him or her in a "no-win" situation (Madanes, 1981). *Hierarchy* refers to the power to influence or determine events that affect another person. Some hierarchical organizations are more democratic than others (Haley, 1990) and may shift according to the situation or task involved (Madanes, 1981).

Working with the Gutierrez family: A strategic perspective
As is structural family therapy, strategic family therapy is oriented toward change and problem solving and is brief (Madanes, 1981; Madanes & Haley, 1977). Similarly, the social worker would attempt to expand the family's perception of the problem beyond Maria (Minuchin & Fishman, 1981). From the strategic perspective, Maria's symptoms would be viewed as an alternative "to living in a world of social relationships in which [she has] little or no control" (Haley, 1990, p. 15). Thus, the social worker would aim to change the family's communication patterns, so that Maria's symptoms would no longer be critical to the stability of the family (Madanes, 1981).

The social worker would be active, directive, and challenging. Focusing on the present (Nichols & Schwartz, 1991), he or she would "take charge" (Haley, 1990; Minuchin & Fishman, 1981) and remain "emotionally distant" (Nichols & Schwartz, 1991). The social worker would interrupt those communications identified as contributing to or maintaining the family's difficulties and would confine interventions to the structural problems that he or she had identified (Madanes, 1981; Minuchin & Fishman, 1981; Piercy et al., 1986).

To stimulate change, the social worker would engage in tactics that would address the dysfunctional hierarchies evident in the overpowering control of Mrs. Gutierrez's mother (Haley, 1990; Madanes, 1981; Nichols & Schwartz,

1991). Techniques, drawn from Milton Erikson, could be direct or indirect, overt or covert, clear or paradoxical (Luepnitz, 1988; Minuchin & Fishman, 1981; Nichols & Schwartz, 1991).

The introduction of paradoxical communication would be intended to "disrupt the [family] ecology . . . reflected [in Maria's] symptomatic behavior and interrupt the feedback cycles that maintain it" (Freud, 1988, p. 376). For example, the social worker might direct Mrs. Gutierrez to forbid Maria to do her homework or direct Maria not to take a bath or wash for a week. Such communications are designed to be experienced as absurd; they are therapeutic only if they encourage the family to defy the social worker and rebel against the directives (Madanes, 1981). Using the technique of reframing, the social worker might present Maria's problem in ways that would make her symptoms seem less pathological (Luepnitz, 1988) and allow her family to respond to her differently. For example, she could redefine Maria's self-destructive behavior as an attempt to be closer to her mother. Then she could direct Mrs. Gutierrez to engage in an activity in which she and Maria could spend time together.

Application to social work
According to Boyd-Franklin (1989), the use of paradoxical interventions and reframing can be helpful when extended family members who hold power are reluctant to being included in family treatment. They "can often tap a well-spring of love and concern" (Boyd-Franklin, p. 129). Luepnitz (1988), however, criticized this model for its authoritarian posture; tendency to look for short-term solutions; "emphasis on behavior change . . . without critical reflection" (p. 84); and lack of interest in domestic violence, incest, or the imbalance in the allocation of labor and power. From a feminist perspective, inequalities in the therapist–client relationship that reinforce patriarchal values and the status quo are deemed unacceptable.

Self-Reflection and Self-Understanding
The need for self-reflection and self-awareness transcends any particular theoretical or practice model (Jackson & Nuttall, 1994). Working with families, social workers draw not only on professional knowledge, skills, and values, but on their experiences as family members. Current and previous family experiences may shape workers' definitions of the family, perceptions of client families' needs and problems, and expectations of and preferences for the outcomes of services. In many instances, social workers' personal experiences in various family roles serve as a resource for empathy. However, they may also undermine social workers' capacity to perceive accurately the feelings, needs, or hopes of family members and may bias their attempts to understand families who are either very similar to or very different from their own. The potential effects of social workers' own family experiences on their practice depend, in part, on their capacity for self-reflection, self-understanding, and the competent management of reactions that potentially interfere with services to clients.

The lens through which a social worker "sees" the client family's situation requires careful focusing to ensure that there emerges a family picture that is of the client family, not of the worker's family. Therefore, social workers must monitor their personal reactions, especially when clients are in family crises or in situations that they themselves have experienced. They must also be alert to personal reactions prompted by their current family roles and developmental phase. For example, a family who is seeking an agency's help with the resolution of a parent–child conflict might be served by one of the following first-year social work interns placed in the agency: a young adult living independently for the first time, a first-time parent struggling to balance family responsibilities and professional education, or a grandparent making a career change. In such situations, unless the social workers are aware of the potential influence of their current family developmental phase on their assumptions, observations, and conclusions, they may inadvertently selectively attend to family members' frustrations and identify with either the parents' or the children's point of view.

Identifying the essential skills and qualities necessary for effective social work practice, Cournoyer (1991) asserted that a well-developed understanding of self is vital. He recommended that social work students prepare both a multigenerational genogram and an ecomap of their current social situation to facilitate their exploration of the ways in which their family and social contexts shape their beliefs, feelings, and actions. Cournoyer noted that "sometimes it is entirely proper for a social worker to use a part of his family-based self in social work practice. However, the professional social worker should be aware that he is doing so" (p. 11). Systematic self-scrutiny occurs privately, as an aspect of professional training, in consultation and supervision with colleagues, and through practitioners' personal therapeutic work. It is a necessary component of competent practice with families.

FUTURE OF FAMILY THERAPY

Traditional approaches to family therapy are being challenged on both theoretical and pragmatic grounds (Carter & McGoldrick, 1989; Goldner, 1988; Hoffman, 1990; Luepnitz, 1988) and are seen as particularly noxious in cases of family violence and abusive relationships (Hoffman, 1990; Nelson-Gardell, 1994).

This disenchantment has led to the development of alternative ways of understanding systems and their problems and of intervening with families. These efforts are reflected in approaches that draw on constructionist theory, such as solution-focused, psychoeducational, externalization, and internal family systems theories (for excellent overviews, see Nichols & Schwartz, 1991; Schwartz, 1987). They represent a radical shift from a focus on structure, patterns of family interaction, and functions to a focus on "understanding and changing the sets of assumptions that all the people involved with a problem have about the problem" (Nichols & Schwartz, 1991, p. 142). From this perspective, "reality is not discovered through objective means but is agreed upon consensually through social interaction, through conversation" (Real, 1990, p. 258). Because reality is socially constructed (Baber & Allen, 1992), one reality is as valid as another (Hoffman, 1990; Nichols & Schwartz, 1991).

Unlike the models reviewed earlier, these schools of therapy reject the notion of the family as an autonomous organism with boundaries, internal structures, and a need to perpetuate itself. They discard the adversarial metaphors of combat, strategy, and war in favor of the benign metaphors of narratives, histories, conversations, and flows (Chubb, 1990; Hoffman, 1990; Minuchin, 1991; Real, 1990).

From this perspective, families who seek help are seen as a group of burdened, overwhelmed individuals who are motivated to change. The therapeutic emphasis is on the negative impact of the family's problems, rather than on their cause (Minuchin & Fishman, 1981). The practitioner's charge is to create a psychologically safe climate in which there are few preconceived notions and everyone is encouraged to engage in conversation (Anderson & Goolishian, 1988). Problems are no longer viewed as residing in any particular family system. Rather, they are seen as a product of the subjective reality of those who are involved with the problem. The therapeutic goal is to foster the emergence of a new, more optimistic and empowering story about the presenting problem that will, in turn, generate positive change (Nichols & Schwartz, 1991).

Some view the recent attempts to develop more collaborative, reflective, nonjudgmental therapies as an indication that the field of family therapy has taken note of feminist concerns and has abandoned the notion that "finding the right technique" will solve a family's problems (Goldner, 1988, p. 30). Others are fearful that challenging the authority and objectivity of the therapist, although "seductive" and "politically correct," neglects the fundamental issue of power, permitting it "to remain safely invisible and unexamined" (Minuchin, 1991, p. 48).

According to Anderson and Goolishian (1988), the field of family therapy is moving in two seemingly different directions, each of which reflects a particular view of human behavior and how to go about changing it. One, based on the social sciences, focuses on authority and action; the other, based on linguistics, focuses on collaboration and meaning. Because empirical evidence for the effectiveness of either of these models is equivocal (Gurman & Kniskern, 1981; Nichols & Schwartz, 1991), the choice of approach depends on social workers' training, the agencies in which they work, the needs of their clients, their ability to integrate a variety of concepts and techniques with which they feel comfortable, and their personalities and worldviews (Nichols & Schwartz, 1991).

CONCLUSION

As the authors have emphasized throughout this chapter, the body of knowledge that is relevant to practice with and on behalf of families is wide, diverse, and continually expanding. From an ecosystems perspective, social work intervention may be focused on the family, on the family's environment, or on the transactions between them. Serving families also requires promoting family-friendly organizational environments and communities' responsiveness to families' needs. In addition, knowledge about families supports practice with individuals. A social worker who attempts to help an individual client without attending to the inevitable presence of family context is likely to be shallow in his or her assessment and unnecessarily limited in intervention options.

Competent social work practice with and on behalf of families requires thorough and ongoing preparation, creativity, tenacity, and self-awareness. Therefore, practitioners who are effective in assisting families rely on supervision, consultation, and continuing education opportunities to ensure that they are applying current relevant knowledge and are appropriately monitoring their use of self in their professional work. Increasingly, family work is found across all fields of social work practice, including child welfare, health and mental health, and substance abuse. Although practice with families may be demanding, the opportunities to make a difference in families' lives are limitless.

REFERENCES

Ainsworth, M. (1982). Attachment: Retrospect and prospect. In C. Parker & J. Stevenson-Hinde (Eds.), *The place of attachment in human behavior* (pp. 3–30). New York: Basic Books.

Ainsworth, M., Blehar, M., Waters, E., & Wall, S. (1978). *Patterns of attachment: A psychological study of the strange situation*. Hillsdale, NJ: Lawrence Erlbaum.

Anderson, H., & Goolishian, H. (1988). Human systems as linguistic systems: Preliminary and evolving ideas about the implications for clinical theory. *Family Process, 27,* 371–393.

Aponte, H. (1976a). The family-school interview: An eco-structural approach. *Family Process, 15,* 303–310.

Aponte, H. (1976b). Underorganization in the poor family. In P. Guerin (Ed.), *Family therapy: Theory and practice* (pp. 432–448). New York: Gardner Press.

Aponte, H., & VanDeusen, J. (1981). Structural family therapy. In A. Gurman & D. Knisken (Eds.), *Handbook of family therapy* (pp. 310–360). New York: Brunner/Mazel.

Ashford, J., Macht, M., & Mylym, M. (1987). Advocacy by social workers in the public defender's office. *Social Work, 32,* 199–204.

Attneave, C. (1982). American Indians and Alaska Native families: Emigrants in their own homeland. In M. McGoldrick, J. Pearce, & J. Giordano (Eds.), *Ethnicity and family therapy* (pp. 55–83). New York: Guilford Press.

Auerswald, E. (1985). Thinking about thinking in family therapy. *Family Process, 24,* 1–12.

Baber, K., & Allen, K. (1992). *Women and families: Feminist reconstructions*. New York: Guilford Press.

Borgman, R. (1985). The influence of family visiting upon boys' behavior in a juvenile correctional institution. *Child Welfare, 64,* 629–638.

Bowen, M. (1971). The use of family theory in clinical practice. In J. Haley (Ed.), *Changing families* (pp. 159–192). New York: Grune & Stratton.

Bowlby, J. (1958). The nature of a child's tie to his mother. *International Journal of Psychoanalysis, 39,* 350–373.

Bowlby, J. (1969). *Attachment and loss: Vol. 1. Attachment.* New York: Basic Books.

Bowlby, J. (1973). *Attachment and loss: Vol. 2. Separation: Anxiety and anger.* New York: Basic Books.

Bowlby, J. (1980). *Attachment and loss: Vol. 3. Loss: Sadness and depression.* New York: Basic Books.

Boyd-Franklin, N. (1989). *Black families in therapy: A multisystems approach.* New York: Guilford Press.

Carter, B., & McGoldrick, M. (Eds.). (1989). *The changing family life cycle: A framework for family therapy* (2nd ed.). Boston: Allyn & Bacon.

Chubb, H. (1990). Looking at systems as process. *Family Process, 29,* 169–175.

Coelho, G., Hamburg, D., & Adams, J. (Eds.) (1974). *Coping and adaptation.* New York: Basic Books.

Compton, B., & Galaway, B. (1994). *Social work processes* (5th ed.). Belmont, CA: Wadsworth.

Cournoyer, B. (1991). *The social work skills workbook.* Belmont, CA: Wadsworth.

Dahlheimer, D., & Feigal, J. (1991). Bridging the gap. *Family Therapy Networker, 15,* 44–53.

Erikson, E. (1959). *Identity and the life cycle.* New York: International Universities Press.

Freud, S. (1988). Cybernetic epistemology. In R. Dorfman (Ed.), *Paradigms of clinical social work* (pp. 356–387). New York: Brunner/Mazel.

Garcia-Preto, N. (1982). Puerto Rican families. In M. McGoldrick, J. Pearce, & J. Giordano (Eds.), *Ethnicity and family therapy* (pp. 164–186). New York: Guilford Press.

Germain, C. B. (1981). The physical environment and social work practice. In A. Maluccio (Ed.), *Promoting competence in clients* (pp. 103–124). New York: Free Press.

Germain, C. B. (1991). *Human behavior in the social environment: An ecological view.* New York: Columbia University Press.

Germain, C. B., & Gitterman, A. (1980). *The life model of social work practice.* New York: Columbia University Press.

Gilligan, C. (1982). *In a different voice: Psychological theory and women's development.* Cambridge, MA: Harvard University Press.

Gitterman, A., & Germain, C. B. (1976). Social work practice: A life model. *Social Service Review, 46,* 601–609.

Golan, N. (1978). *Treatment in crisis situations*. New York: Free Press.

Golan, N. (1981). *Passing through transitions: A guide for practitioners*. New York: Free Press.

Goldenberg, H., & Goldenberg, I. (1990). *Counseling today's families*. Pacific Grove, CA: Brooks/Cole.

Goldner, V. (1988). Generation and gender: Normative and covert hierarchies. *Family Process*, *27*, 17–31.

Greenberg, M., Cicchetti, D., & Cummings, E. (Eds.). (1990). *Attachment in the preschool years*. Chicago: University of Chicago Press.

Grinnell, R., Kyte, N., & Bostwick, G. (1981). Environmental modification. In A. Maluccio (Ed.), *Promoting competence in clients* (pp. 152–184). New York: Free Press.

Gurman, A., & Kniskern, D. (1981). *Handbook of family therapy*. New York: Brunner/Mazel.

Gutheil, I. (1992). Considering the physical environment: An essential component of good practice. *Social Work*, *37*, 391–396.

Haley, J. (1978). *Problem-solving therapy: New strategies for effective family therapy*. San Francisco: Jossey-Bass.

Haley, J. (1987). *Problem-solving therapy: New strategies for effective family therapy* (2nd ed.). San Francisco: Jossey-Bass.

Haley, J. (1990). *Strategies of psychotherapy* (2nd ed.). Rockville, MD: Triangle Press.

Hartman, A. (1990). Family ties. *Social Work*, *35*, 195–196.

Hartman, A., & Laird, J. (1983). *Family-centered social work practice*. New York: Free Press.

Hegar, R. (1993). Assessing attachment, permanence, and kinship in choosing permanent homes. *Child Welfare*, *72*, 367–378.

Hess, P. (1982). Parent-child attachment concept: Crucial for permanency planning. *Social Casework*, *63*, 46–53.

Hess, P. (1986). Promoting access to access with divorcing parents. *Social Casework*, *67*, 594–604.

Hines, P., Garcia-Preto, N., McGoldrick, M., Almeida, R., & Weltman, S. (1992). Intergenerational relationships across cultures. *Families in Society: Journal of Contemporary Human Services*, *73*, 323–338.

Hoffman, L. (1981). *Foundations of family therapy: A conceptual framework for systems change*. New York: Basic Books.

Hoffman, L. (1990). Constructing realities: An art of lenses. *Family Process*, *29*, 1–12.

Hollis, F. (1932). The function of a family society. *Family*, *13*, 280–283.

Imber-Black, E. (1988). *Families and larger systems*. New York: Guilford Press.

Jackson, H., & Nuttall, R. (1994). Effects of gender, age, and a history of abuse on social workers' judgments of sexual abuse allegations. *Social Work Research, 18,* 105–113.

Janzen, C., & Harris, O. (1980). *Family treatment in social work practice*. Itasca, IL: F. E. Peacock.

Karen, R. (1994). *Becoming attached*. New York: Warner Books.

Kettner, P., Daley, J., & Nichols, A. (1985). *Initiating change in organizations and communities*. Monterey, CA: Brooks/Cole.

Lamb, M. (1977). Father-infant and mother-infant interaction in the first year of life. *Child Development, 48,* 167–181.

Lappin, J. (1988). Family therapy: A structural approach. In R. Dorfman (Ed.), *Paradigms of clinical social work* (pp. 220–252). New York: Brunner/Mazel.

Loring, M., & Wimberley, E. (1993). The time-limited hot line. *Social Work, 38,* 344–346.

Luepnitz, D. A. (1988). *The family interpreted: Psychoanalysis, feminism, and family therapy*. New York: Basic Books.

Madanes, C. (1981). *Strategic family therapy*. San Francisco: Jossey-Bass.

Madanes, C., & Haley, J. (1977). Dimensions of family therapy. *Journal of Nervous and Mental Disease, 165,* 88–98.

Mahler, M., Pine, F., & Bergman, A. (1975). *The psychological birth of the human infant*. New York: Basic Books.

Main, M., & Weston, D. (1981). The quality of the toddler's relationship to mother and father: Related to conflict behavior and readiness to establish new relationships. *Child Development, 52,* 932–940.

Manser, E. (Ed). (1973). *Family advocacy: A manual for action*. New York: Family Service Association of America.

McAdoo, H. (1978). Factors related to stability in upwardly mobile Black families. *Journal of Marriage and the Family, 40,* 761–776.

McGoldrick, M., Pearce, J., & Giordano, J. (Eds.). (1982). *Ethnicity and family therapy*. New York: Guilford Press.

Meyer, C. (1983). The search for coherence. In C. Meyer (Ed.), *Clinical social work in the ecosystems perspective* (pp. 6–34). New York: Columbia University Press.

Meyer, C. (1993). *Assessment in social work practice*. New York: Columbia University Press.

Middleman, R., & Goldberg, G. (1974). The interactional way of presenting generic social work concepts. *Journal of Education for Social Work, 8,* 48–57.

Minuchin, S. (1974). *Families and family therapy*. Cambridge, MA: Harvard University.

Minuchin, S. (1991). The seductions of constructivism. *Family Therapy Networker, 15*, 47–50.

Minuchin, S. (1992). *Family healing*. New York: Macmillan.

Minuchin, S., & Fishman, H. (1981). *Family therapy techniques*. Cambridge, MA: Harvard University Press.

Nelson-Gardell, D. (1994). Feminism and family social work. *Journal of Family Social Work, 1*, 77–95.

Nichols, M., & Schwartz, R. (1991). *Family therapy concepts and methods*. Needham Heights, MA: Allyn & Bacon.

O'Connell, P. (1972). Developmental tasks of the family. *Smith College Studies in Social Work, 42*, 203–210.

Overton, A., & Tinker, K. (1959). *Casework notebook*. St. Paul, MN: Greater St. Paul United Fund and Council.

Palazzoli, M. S., Boscolo, L., Cecchin, G., & Prata, G. (1978). *Paradox and counterparadox: A new model in the therapy of the family in schizophrenic transaction*. New York: Jason Aronson.

Parad, H. (Ed.). (1965). *Crisis intervention: Selected readings*. New York: Family Service Association of America.

Parke, R. (1981). *Fathers*. Cambridge, MA: Harvard University Press.

Parkes, C., Stevenson-Hinde, J., & Marris, P. (Eds.). (1991). *Attachment across the life cycle*. New York: Tavistock/Routledge.

Parsonnet, L., & O'Hare, J. (1990). A group orientation program for families of newly admitted cancer patients. *Social Work, 35*, 37–45.

Perlman, H. (1968). *Persona*. Chicago: University of Chicago Press.

Piercy, F., Sprenkle, D., & Associates. (1986). *Family therapy sourcebook*. New York: Guilford Press.

Pollack, O. (1960). A family diagnosis model. *Social Service Review, 34*, 1–50.

Rapoport, L. (1965). The state of crisis: Some theoretical considerations. In H. Parad (Ed.), *Crisis intervention: Selected readings* (pp. 22–31). New York: Family Service Association of America.

Real, T. (1990). The therapeutic use of self in constructionist/systemic therapy. *Family Process, 29*, 255–272.

Redhorse, J., Lewis, R., & Decker, J. (1978). Family behavior of urban American Indians. *Social Casework, 59*, 67–72.

Reid, W. (1985). *Family problem solving*. New York: Columbia University Press.

Rhodes, S. (1977). A developmental approach to the life cycle of the family. *Social Casework*, *58*, 301–311.

Rhodes, S., & Wilson, J. (1981). *Surviving family life: The seven crises of living together*. New York: G. P. Putnam's Sons.

Richmond, M. (1930). *The long view*. New York: Russell Sage Foundation.

Roth, S. (1991). Psychotherapy with lesbian couples: Individual issues, female socialization, and the social context. In M. McGoldrick, C. Anderson, & F. Walsh (Eds.), *Women in families* (pp. 286–307). New York: W. W. Norton.

Satir, V. (1967). *Conjoint family therapy* (rev. ed.). Palo Alto, CA: Science & Behavior Books.

Satir, V. (1971). The family as a treatment unit. In J. Haley (Ed.), *Changing families* (pp. 127–132). New York: Grune & Stratton.

Scherz, F. (1954). What is family centered casework? *Social Casework*, *34*, 343–348.

Schwartz, R. (1987). Our multiple selves: Applying systems thinking to the inner family. *Family Networker*, *11*, 25–31, 80–83.

Shon, S., & Ja, D. (1982). Asian families. In M. McGoldrick, J. Pearce, & J. Giordano (Eds.), *Ethnicity and family therapy* (pp. 208–228). New York: Guilford Press.

Solomon, B. (1985). Seminar presentation. In S. Gray, A. Hartman, & E. Saalberg (Eds.), *Empowering the black family: A roundtable discussion with Ann Hartman, James Leigh, Jacquelynn Moffett, Elaine Pinderhughes, Barbara Solomon, and Carol Stack*. Ann Arbor: National Child Welfare Training Center, University of Michigan School of Social Work.

Speck, R., & Attneave, C. (1973). *Family networks*. New York: Vintage Books.

Umbreit, M. (1993). Crime victims and offenders in mediation: An emerging area of social work practice. *Social Work*, *38*, 69–73.

Vaughn, B., Egeland, B., Sroufe, A., & Waters, E. (1979). Individual differences in infant-mother attachment at twelve and eighteen months: Stability and change in families under stress. *Child Development*, *50*, 971–975.

Vidal, C. (1988). Godparenting among Hispanic Americans. *Child Welfare*, *67*, 453–459.

Vosler, N. (1990). Assessing family access to basic resources: An essential component of social work practice. *Social Work*, *35*, 434–441.

Walsh, F. (1993). Conceptualization of normal family processes. In F. Walsh (Ed.), *Normal family processes* (2nd ed., pp. 3–69). New York: Guilford Press.

Weiss, R. (1982). Attachment in adult life. In C. Parkes & J. Stevenson-Hinde (Eds.), *The place of attachment in human behavior* (pp. 171–184). New York: Basic Books.

White, R. (1963). *Ego and reality in psychoanalytic theory*. New York: International Universities Press.

Woolley, G. (1991). Beware the well-intentioned therapist. *Family Therapy Networker, 15,* 30–35.

The authors gratefully acknowledge the comments and suggestions of Professor Martha Dore on a previous draft of this chapter.

9

Practice with Groups

Randy H. Magen

The Progressive Era, which spawned the early caseworkers, also produced the first group workers. The ancestors of caseworkers and group workers were mindful of democratic values, critical of the political-economic system, concerned with the needs of individuals, and inspired by religiously based notions of humanity (Schwartz, 1986). Unlike casework, however, the roots of group work can also be found in the recreation movement and the progressive education movement (Germain, 1983).

At the beginning of the 20th century, groups were used for two purposes: to instill democratic values and to socialize individuals. In settlement houses, groups were established for people to learn the skills necessary to participate in their neighborhoods and communities. John Dewey, one of the fathers of the progressive education movement, was influential in the settlement houses' development of the democratic purpose of groups. For a short time, he lived and worked at Hull House under the leadership of Jane Addams. Dewey (1922) wrote that groups provided experience in democratic action through participation in activities in which there was shared decision making and a focus on common social problems. This is what Addams (1910/1960, p. 97) referred to as groups serving as a "building block of democracy."

Addams, the founder of Hull House, was also one of the founding officers of what eventually became known as the National Recreation Association (Reid, 1991). From the recreation movement came the use of groups to socialize individuals. In organized associations, such as the Young Men's and Young Women's Christian Associations, the Boy Scouts, and the Girl Scouts, and to a lesser extent in the settlement houses, a variety of small groups were established in which children could play, develop friendships, and participate in recreational activities (Reid, 1991; Schwartz, 1986). Children's participation in groups was believed to promote healthy development through character building—what is now called the acquisition of social skills.

In comparing early casework to early group work, Toseland and Rivas (1995) listed five differences between the methods.

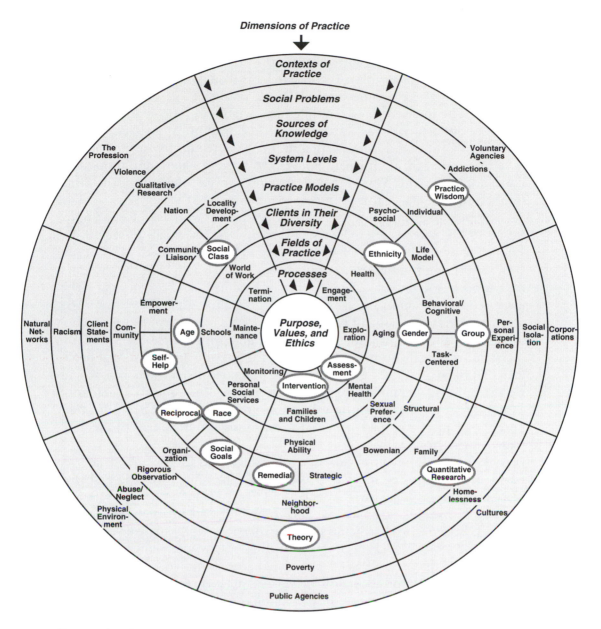

Dimensions of Practice

Contexts of Practice
Social Problems
Sources of Knowledge
System Levels
Practice Models
Clients in Their Diversity
Fields of Practice
Processes

Purpose, Values, and Ethics

FIGURE 9-1. DIMENSIONS OF PRACTICE IN WORK WITH GROUPS

1. In casework clients changed as a result of the development of insight and through concrete assistance, whereas in group work, their change was a function of participating in group activities.
2. Whereas casework focused primarily on problem solving, group work focused on both recreation and problem solving.
3. Caseworkers worked with clients, whereas group workers were involved with group members. This was more than a difference in terminology; it also resulted in a difference in the

quality of the relationship between the social worker and the person being helped.

4. As a result of the differences in their relationship with clients, group workers placed more emphasis than did caseworkers on shared decision making and shared power.

5. The interaction of multiple members in a group required a different set of skills than those developed by caseworkers.

Before World War II, there were some limited attempts to use group work in settings other than settlement houses and recreational organizations, but it was not until World War II that group work moved solidly into rehabilitation settings. Several factors propelled group work into the new settings. The development of group work practice theory in social work (see, for example, Coyle, 1937), as well as research on small groups by social scientists (see Lewin, Lippitt, & White, 1939; Sherif, 1936) helped to "clarify the method" (Garvin, 1987). At the same time, group work was increasingly taught in the curricula of schools of social work. The influence of Freudian psychoanalysis and the increased collaboration among psychiatrists, psychologists, and social workers as members of treatment teams also led to the use of groups for psychotherapy. Finally, the push for group work came from the thousands of soldiers and veterans who needed assistance for physical and emotional problems. Thus, by the 1950s, groups could be found in such settings as psychiatric institutions, veterans' hospitals, correctional facilities, and child guidance clinics. From the movement of groups into these new settings a third purpose for groups developed, namely, the diagnosis and treatment of the individual in the group.

In 1952 the Council on Social Work Education (CSWE) published its first curriculum policy statement. This document, which was the basis for accrediting professional social work education programs, defined social work practice as casework, group work, and community organizing. These three methods became the organizing structure for social work curricula for many years. In 1969 CSWE changed its curriculum policy statement (Council on Social Work Education, 1969) to promote the integration of methods and to encourage training for generalist social work practice. One of the effects of this change in policy has been the precipitous decline in the institutionalization of group work in social work curricula. In 1963, 76 percent of social work graduate programs had concentrations in the group work method. With the growth of generalist and advanced generalist curricula by 1974, only 22 percent of the programs had this concentration, and by 1981 only nine schools did (Rubin, 1982). After 1982, *Statistics on Social Work Education* no longer reported the number of schools with group work concentrations (Rubin, 1983). A survey conducted in 1991 (Birnbaum & Auerbach, 1992) of 89 of the 97 graduate schools of social work accredited by CSWE revealed that only 6 programs (7 percent) offered a concentration in group work.

At the same time, there appears to be a resurgence of interest in group work. In this era of cost containment and managed care, it is generally recognized that group services are more cost-efficient than are individual interventions

(Toseland & Siporin, 1986), and there has been an explosion of self-help and 12-step-style groups. If social workers are to continue to stay true to their professional roots and to be responsive to clients' needs, they must have knowledge and skills in social work group work. This chapter provides a basic foundation in social work group work for the beginning social worker, but it is no substitute for the specialized knowledge and training that are necessary to be a competent social work group worker.

APPROACHES TO GROUP WORK PRACTICE

Social work group work has been defined as a "goal-directed activity with small groups of people aimed at meeting socioemotional needs and accomplishing tasks. This activity is directed to individual members of a group and to the group as a whole" (Toseland & Rivas, 1995, p. 12). With this definition, it is clear that throughout the life span, people belong to a variety of groups, starting with the family and progressing through, for example, play groups, educational groups, work groups, and task groups or committees (Northen, 1982). Although groups are a natural and constant force in people's lives, social workers need a system for organizing and understanding the various types of "goal-directed activities" that take place in small groups. Presumably, a differential application of professional knowledge and skills is required in distinct types of small groups.

In examining various types of groups, one may logically distinguish between natural and formed groups. A family is a natural group, membership in which is gained through birth and adoption. In other natural groups— peer groups and social networks—membership may come about serendipitously. In formed groups, membership is dependent on the fit between the purpose of the group and the needs or skills of the potential members. This distinction may be logical, but the concept of a formed group is so inclusive that it provides little guidance. Furthermore, the unique history of natural groups requires a different approach by social workers, as is evident by the voluminous literature on social work with families.

One of the first useful systems for distinguishing types of group work approaches was developed by Papell and Rothman (1966), who differentiated group work approaches by function. The differences in function, or group purpose, lead to differences in the focus of the group's activities and the role of the group worker. The three approaches to group work practice identified by Papell and Rothman were the social goals model, the reciprocal model, and the remedial model. Although Papell and Rothman referred to these types of groups as models, it is more accurate to adopt the nomenclature of Germain (1983) and hence to conceive of them as approaches. According to Germain, "the term *approach* is preferred over the more common *model*, because of the confusion between a theoretical model in science, useful for its predictive value, and a practice model—so called—that merely sets forth the several dimensions of a coherent consistent approach to social work practice but has no predictive value" (p. 31).

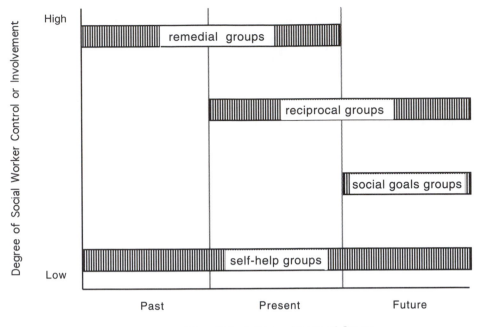

FIGURE 9-2. GROUP WORK APPROACHES

From Middleman, R. R. (1981). The pursuit of competence through involvement in structured groups. In A. N. Maluccio (Ed.), Promoting competence in clients: A new/old approach to social work practice *(p. 187). Copyright © 1981 by The Free Press, A Division of Simon & Schuster, Inc. Adapted with permission of the publisher.*

Models Approaches

The interaction among group function, role of the worker, and focus of the group for the four most common types of groups can be seen in Figure 9-2. These four common models of groups are now examined in greater detail.

Social goals model

The core function of the social goals model is the translation of "private troubles into public issues" (Schwartz, 1969, p. 22). The target for this model of group work is the social order, often defined as a neighborhood or community. The group's work is directed toward action and primary prevention with a focus on the future. To achieve its purpose, the social goals group requires its members, as one of their first tasks, to increase their "social consciousness" and "social responsibility" (Papell & Rothman, 1966). The group worker in such a group may be a consultant or a convener, whose role is to promote the democratic functioning of the group. Clearly, the social goals model of group work has its roots in the group work of the settlement houses. Today, groups that function within this approach can be found in public housing complexes where tenants organize themselves to fight crime.

Reciprocal model

What Papell and Rothman (1966) labeled the reciprocal model of group work has today become known as the mutual aid model. The focus of activity in this model of group work is the reciprocal or "symbiotic" relationship between individual clients and the group. The social worker is an enabler or mediator who seeks to prevent imbalances in the relationship or boundaries between the individual and the group and to help the group release its power to change—to learn how to be a mutual aid system. Schwartz (1986) referred to the social worker's role as "the two clients conception, in which the worker's function is to help both the individual and the group, the one to meet his needs within the system, the other to pursue its collective tasks" (pp. 17–18). The reciprocal or mutual-aid model requires the social worker to share power and control over the group with its members. Gitterman and Shulman (1994) give many examples of mutual aid groups, for example, a group of people with acquired immune deficiency syndrome (AIDS) in which they receive support and reassurance and are mobilized to take control of their lives. Groups that are commonly referred to as support groups fall within this conceptualization of the reciprocal model. Schopler and Galinsky (1993) suggested that support groups "lie midway between" remedial groups and self-help groups in terms of their leaders' behavior and the control that members have.

Remedial model

The focus of the remedial model is on the treatment of the individual through the use of a group method. In this model, the group is the means or context for achieving individual goals, and changes in group structure and group process are means to an end, rather than an end in themselves. One of the characteristics of the remedial group is that the social worker exerts a great deal of power and influence over the formation and operation of the group. Group members are selected by the social worker, who is guided in composing the group by the purpose of the group; members are often selected because of similarities in presenting problems or target complaints. In fact, the most critical issue in the effectiveness of remedial groups may be group composition. A group that fits the definition of a remedial group would be a skills-training relapse-prevention group for people who are recovering from alcohol abuse.

Mainstream model

The broadening of social work practice and knowledge in the 1970s and 1980s resulted in some types of group work falling outside Papell and Rothman's (1966) original typology. Several group work theorists (Lang, 1979; Middleman & Wood, 1990) recognized this fact when they suggested that the practice of group work could be conceptualized with one model: the mainstream model. Papell and Rothman (1980) distinguished the mainstream model from group psychotherapy by the latter's focus on changing the individual through the use of a group context. Group work approaches that fall within the mainstream model are all concerned with developing a mutual aid system within the group, an interest in moving the group through developmental phases, and members' shared goals. The leader role in the mainstream model gradually shifts from the social worker to the group members as the group develops over time.

Although the mainstream model is an eclectic approach to group work that is consistent with the movement within social work to identify a nucleus of practice concepts, this author agrees with Garvin (1987), who suggested that it is "premature" if not impossible to encompass all group work approaches in one model. For example, the mainstream model does not accurately conceptualize one of the most common types of groups that social workers are likely to encounter: the self-help group. Therefore, the mainstream model has not been included in Figure 9-2.

Self-help groups

The most well-known and the oldest self-help group is Alcoholics Anonymous (AA). Founded in 1935, AA had over 87,000 chapters worldwide as of 1990 (Miller & McCrady, 1993). Many different self-help groups that exist for specific life problems, like AA, are typically sponsored by international, national, or regional organizations. These sponsoring organizations often prescribe the format and procedures used in group meetings. However, leadership and control of the self-help group lie with the group members. Studies of self-help groups indicate that members of these groups not only have clear goals about how they want to end up, but clear ideas of how they want to move toward their goals (what the process should be) (Lieberman & Borman, 1979). The primary difference between self-help groups and the reciprocal model of group work is that in self-help groups the social worker serves as a consultant, resource person, or referral source *outside* the group (Schopler & Galinsky, 1993). Self-help groups can also be distinguished from informal helping networks by the existence of a group structure and boundaries.

Other conceptualizations abound in the social work literature as means for organizing knowledge and skills for group work (see, for example, Garvin, 1987; Toseland & Rivas, 1995). The importance of any typology is in helping the social worker develop a schema for categorizing small groups that allows him or her not only to generalize from group to group, but to begin to understand how to work with specific types of groups.

Group Purpose and Structure

Purpose
Given the definition of a group presented earlier, in theory there should be no such thing as a group without a purpose. However, the failure of many groups can be attributed to the lack of a consensus on the purpose of the group. The purpose of any group should be a clear and specific statement pertaining to how the group will address an unmet need of clients. The statement of the group's purpose sets parameters for issues of structure (selection of members, group composition, and orientation), time (duration,

frequency and length, and group development), and leadership (characteristics and number). Thus, in group work, "structure follows function." Of course, other systems and forces, such as an agency's policy, affect the composition and structure of a group, but the most important factor is the group's purpose.

Structure

Selection of members

A great deal has been written in the group work literature about the importance of the selection of members (Dies & Teleska, 1985; Ormont, 1969; Papell & Rothman, 1966). Members must feel that they fit in and belong to the group (Beck, 1983). The selection of members is the process that affects the goodness of fit between members and the group. Although Shulman (1994) argued that guidelines for the selection of group members are "myths" because leaders take what they can get, this statement does not mean that every applicant is appropriate to be a group member.

The guiding principle in the selection of members is that extremes are a problem. Obviously, when there are too many members, the group members lose the ability to interact with each other; when there are too few members, the advantages of conducting a group are lost. At the risk of being redundant, the size of the group is dependent on the purpose of the group. In general, the group work literature contains examples of groups that have four to 10 members. Social goals groups may be able to tolerate more clients, whereas in remedial groups with clients who are experiencing severe problems, the groups are usually kept small. As the size of the group gets larger, the ability of each member to participate fully in the group decreases.

Groups with extremely heterogeneous or homogeneous members are also problematic (this includes individual characteristics such as age as well as presenting problems). For example, in groups of parents who met for support and parent training, mixing parents of teenagers with parents of preschoolers resulted in the failure of the members to identify with each other's problems, whereas a group composed of parents with preschoolers successfully mixed single and married mothers (Magen, 1991). Similarly, one can imagine how slow and silent a group with all severely depressed individuals would be.

The best rule for avoiding extremes in a group is never to have only one of anything in a group. Yalom (1985) referred to this rule as the Noah's Ark principle. There is some evidence that clients from dominant groups (such as white people and men) prefer groups that mirror the racial and gender composition of society. For black people, however, one study indicated a preference for groups that are composed of equal numbers of white people and black people (Davis, 1979). The literature on women's membership in mixed-gender groups indicates that women prefer large groups, but also suggests that they are less expressive in these groups (Davis & Proctor, 1989).

Although groups that are homogeneous in terms of race or gender are often discouraged, in some instances the purpose of the group dictates that the group should be homogeneous. For example, a group to enhance racial, ethnic, or gender identity—often referred to as a consciousness-raising group—would be the most effective with a homogeneous membership. At the other extreme, a group that is designed to decrease racial tensions (or to increase interracial understanding) would be most effective with members of different racial groups.

The social worker must assess whether there is some common ground between the unmet needs of the client and the purpose of the group. This mutuality of interests is essential for the client to be able to connect with the work of others in the group. Clients must also have the interpersonal skills necessary to participate in a group of five to 10 other members (Rose, 1989) because it is only through interpersonal interaction that the work of the group takes place. Finally, clients must have the cognitive skills to participate in the group at a level similar to that of other group members. For some groups, such skills may be the ability to read and write, whereas for others, the skills may be the ability to help problem solve at a developmentally compatible level. Thus, group workers must examine and assess the fit of clients' characteristics, needs, interpersonal skills, and cognitive abilities with other group members, as well as with the group's purpose.

Composition

Group composition refers to whether the group can continually accept members (an open group) or whether the membership is fixed (closed) at some point. Burlingame and Fuhriman (1990) reported that 60 percent of the groups they examined were open, and the remaining 40 percent were closed. An agency's mission affects this aspect of the group as well; for example, an acute care psychiatric inpatient unit has a fairly high turnover rate of patients and thus, any group that it operates must either be of short duration (such as one session) or maintain some form of open membership. A support group for survivors of child sexual abuse might maintain a fixed membership to minimize difficulties in relation to trust and self-disclosure.

Fixed membership and flexible membership can be thought of as two poles on a continuum. Some groups have a fixed membership but allow members to drop in and out according to their needs. Other groups may start as flexible membership groups but become fixed membership groups at a predetermined point. For example, a large agency in New York City that operates support groups for individuals with cancer has flexible membership in the first two group sessions. After the second session, though, the group has "formed," and the remaining 10 sessions are held with a fixed membership.

Orientation

Orientation to the group, or what some may call "socialization to the client role" is a crucial task of the group worker. Orientation is the shaping of members in their role as group members. It involves both the establishment of ground rules (Tuckman, 1965) and the differentiation of roles (Garvin, 1985). Brower (1988) argued that group members enter the group with their own perceptions—their unique cognitive schemata of the group. The task of the group worker, then, is to help members develop a shared cognitive schema of the group—a capacity to work toward mutual aid and purpose (Glassman & Kates, 1990) and common "perceptions and expectations for how each [member] will behave" (Garvin, 1985, p. 205).

Dies and Teleska (1985) cited evidence that one of the factors involved in negative group experience is unrealistically high expectations. Flowers (1987) reported that members who did not improve were those who did not agree with others on a rank ordering of curative factors. He suggested that these group members may have come to the group with different expectations than did other group members; another explanation may be that the group did not initially induce the same expectations in these members as it did in the other members. Thus, one of the central tasks for the group worker and the group in the forming phase is to help members develop appropriate expectations for the group. Kaul and Bednar (1986) noted that structure, especially in early sessions, helps to induce appropriate expectations and to socialize members in their roles. Perhaps the most direct method for inducing expectations in a structured manner is through contracting. Shulman (1994) discussed three areas for which contracts can be made in group work: the role of the worker, the mutual needs of the members, and the mutual obligations of the members and leaders.

TIME

There are three ways to examine time in group work: the duration of the group, the frequency and length of group sessions, and group development.

Duration

Descriptions of groups that have lasted a single session to several years can be found in the literature. Open-ended groups have no fixed ending point, whereas closed-ended (or time-limited) groups have a set termination date. The duration of a group may be constrained by the clients' circumstances, by the agency environment, or by the group's purposes. For example, an inner-city hospital used single-session groups for the prevention of the human immunodeficiency virus (HIV) in intravenous drug users who were patients in the emergency room.

Although there is little empirical evidence to guide the social worker when planning the duration of a group, one general rule could be stated: More is not necessarily better. At the least, a closed-ended group means that a termination date has been established a priori; the establishment of an end point facilitates movement toward goals.

Frequency and Length

Across models of group work, the most common frequency for group meetings is once a week and the average length of a group session is one to three hours. Although there is little to no empirical evidence to support this widespread practice, there are many practical reasons for this type of scheduling, including cost, the availability of a meeting space, and the coordination of the members' multiple schedules. Rose (1989) suggested that an optimal model for closed-ended groups would involve fading the frequency and duration of group meetings. Thus, when the group was first forming, there would be frequent meetings, but as the group moved closer to the final session, the time between group meetings would increase or the length of group sessions would decrease. This variability in the time schedule for a closed-ended group may be particularly valuable in the remedial model of groups.

Group Development

A variety of group development sequences have been offered to help the social worker understand changes in groups over time. These typologies have ranged from three stages (Schwartz, 1986) to nine (Beck, 1983). There is a considerable overlap in the labels applied to the stages and, more significantly, in the conceptualization of the stages. Tuckman (1965) suggested four stages of group development, which he summarized as forming, storming, norming, and performing. Tuckman's stages fail to include a termination phase; in keeping with Tuckman's rhyme, this author proposes a fifth and final stage: "adjourning." The crucial issue is not what the stages are, but the group worker's understanding of and skill in assisting the group to develop.

Although the concept of group development is of heuristic value, there are multiple problems with the current state of knowledge of group development. The problems identified in the group development literature include the failure to validate stages of group development empirically, the arbitrary division of the group into phases, the failure to realize that development is not *one* predetermined sequence, and the attribution of stages as group phenomena when what is actually being described may be the development of an individual member (Beck, 1983; Brower, 1988; Burlingame, Fuhriman, & Drescher, 1984; Glassman & Kates, 1990; MacKenzie, 1987; Tuckman, 1965). For example, Galinsky and Schopler (1989) pointed out that developmental patterns in open-ended groups are affected by the frequency of turnover among members and the extent to which membership is modified. On the one hand, open-ended groups with a frequent and extensive turnover of members would not be expected to move beyond the "forming" stage of group development. On the other hand, groups with an infrequent and small turnover would develop in a manner similar to closed-ended, fixed membership groups.

LEADERSHIP

It is axiomatic that group leaders should have the capacity, skills, values, and attitudes required of any social worker. It is also clear that group work necessitates a set of skills that caseworkers do not need. Schwartz (1966) summed up the difference in the requisite social work skills as follows:

> The group leadership role demands that the worker give up much
> of the interview control to which she has, often unconsciously,

become accustomed. Caseworkers have often told me that they had never realized how rigidly they controlled the client-worker interaction until they began to function as group workers, where changes of subject could be effected by anyone in the group, where people often turned to each other rather than to the worker for reinforcement and support, where clients could verify each other's "wrong" ideas, where mutually reinforced feelings could not be turned off when they became "dangerous," and where, in short, one's faith in the client's autonomy and basic strength was put to its severest test. (p. 575)

Aside from the group worker's skills, another important issue in leadership is whether to use one or two leaders. There is no consistent evidence in the empirical literature that two heads are better than one. In fact, Kolodny (1980) summarized the literature on coleadership by writing that "the requirement would seem to be that one's co-leader be someone whom one knows well and is compatible with, who agrees with one theoretically, possesses equal knowledge, and is similar to oneself in competence and professional stature, but is definitely not a friend" (p. 34). Having a coleader increases the financial cost to the agency or the clients. Another potential problem with coleadership is that the leaders may dominate the discussion, or to put it more strongly, two leaders typically talk too much. In groups with coleaders, Rose (1989) recommended that the leaders develop a "no back-to-back talking" rule, so they do not dominate discussions within the group.

There are four situations in which coleadership is desirable: (1) during training, when it is often helpful for social workers to colead their first group; (2) for groups that require specialized knowledge or skills, such as those for sexually abused children or people with AIDS; (3) when there are issues of physical or emotional safety, such as in groups of men who batter; and (4) in couples groups, when it is useful to have both male and female leaders. The danger in coleadership, particularly in groups with male and female leaders, is that there may be real or imagined differences in the leaders' status. Several studies have found that men are perceived as being of a higher status than are women when coleading groups of women. Similarly, when coleaders were members of different racial groups, clients have attributed more negative attributes to the group leader who was not from their racial group than to the same-race group leader (Davis & Proctor, 1989).

GROUP PROCESSES

The term "group processes," rather than "group process," is used in this section because many variables have been identified in the literature as belonging to the phenomena of group process. Therefore, it is more accurate, linguistically as well as conceptually, to discuss group process as a composite of phenomena, rather than as a single phenomenon (Fuhriman, Drescher, & Burlingame, 1984).

Novice group workers are often admonished for not paying attention to group processes. However, the problem usually is not that they ignore group processes, but that they do not know what is meant by group processes. Even when group workers are given an explanation of group processes, the definitions, such as "Process is everything in the group that is not content" (Yalom, 1985, p. 137), are often useless.

Unfortunately, no one clear definition of group processes exists. The following three definitions have been suggested: (1) "the way of working as opposed to the substance of the work" (Gitterman & Shulman, 1986, p. 42); (2) "changes that take place in group conditions" (Garvin, 1985, p. 203); and (3) "an aspect or characteristic of group behavior, the ecological characteristics of the group" (Fuhriman et al., 1984, p. 431). This author prefers the third definition because it is specific to group work, includes interpersonal relationship behavior, and also encompasses "characteristics" of the group that are more than individual transactions (Burlingame et al., 1984). Whichever definition of group processes the reader chooses to adopt, it is clear that a constellation of factors are necessary for the functioning of an effective small group, but are not sufficient for the group to achieve its goals. These "necessary but not sufficient" factors are collectively referred to as group processes.

Cohesion is an important process variable in group work, but as is the case with group development and group processes, there is little agreement on how to define it. Bednar and Kaul (1994) remarked that "Research on group cohesion . . . continues to be based on definitions and methods of measurement so impoverished [they] . . . can only produce a noncohesive body of literature" (p. 640). In spite of this criticism, whether one defines cohesion as attraction to the group (Lieberman, Yalom, & Miles, 1973), attraction to other members, or a common schema (Brower, 1988), it is clear that cohesive groups are more likely to achieve their purpose. High cohesiveness has been linked to change, whereas low cohesiveness has been shown to correlate highly with members dropping out of groups (Dies & Teleska, 1985; Lieberman et al., 1973). In group work, as in other methods of social work, dissatisfied clients drop out or terminate prematurely. Several suggestions have been made in the literature for maximizing group cohesion, including the use of a break with a snack, modeling, and reinforcing self-disclosure (Rose, 1977). In fact, intimacy in self-disclosure is associated with members' perceptions of group cohesion (Kaul & Bednar, 1986).

There is also general agreement that clients profit from self-disclosure (Kaul & Bednar, 1986). Wright and Ingraham (1985) concluded from their analysis of behavior in four interpersonal learning groups that self-disclosure is a function not only of individual differences but of the relationship among group members. This finding suggests that the quality of intermember relationships may affect the quantity of self-disclosure in a group.

Feedback, or what Yalom (1985) referred to as "interpersonal input," is a group process that has been shown to contribute to therapeutic change in groups (Dies & Teleska, 1985). There is widespread agreement that clients benefit from appropriate feedback under the right circumstances. The group leader, then, should encourage, if not teach, members to give feedback to each other. In a social goals group, feedback is essential for helping the members move toward the group's goal.

Although the evidence regarding the relative strength of group problem solving over individual problem solving is equivocal (see, for example, Davis & Toseland, 1987), it is clear that the mechanisms involved in group problem solving are central processes in group work. The components of group problem solving have been defined differently by group theorists (see Gitterman & Shulman, 1994; Yalom, 1985), but all agree that problem solving is important in group work.

As Table 9-1 indicates, the nomenclature used to label group processes varies by theorist, as well as by model of group work. A definitive list of group

Table 9-1. Common Group Processes in Remedial and Reciprocal Groups

Remedial Group Processes (Yalom, 1985)	Reciprocal Group Processes (Shulman, 1994)
Instillation of hope Altruism Cohesiveness	Mutual support Strength in numbers
Universality	All-in-the-same-boat phenomenon
Imparting information	Sharing data
Development of socialization techniques Imitative behavior	Rehearsal
Interpersonal learning	Problem solving Dialectical processes Mutual demand
Catharsis	Discussing a taboo area
Existential factors	Developing a universal perspective
Collective recapitulation of the primary family group	—[1]

[1]There is no exact parallel in reciprocal groups.

Sources: Shulman, L. (1994). Group work method. In A. Gitterman & L. Shulman (Eds.), *Mutual aid groups, vulnerable populations, and the life cycle* (2nd ed., pp. 29–58). New York: Columbia University Press; and Yalom, I. D. (1985). *The theory and practice of group psychotherapy.* New York: Basic Books.

processes is probably not possible, given that group processes are influenced by the group work approach, the stage of the group's development, forces outside the group, and individual differences within the group (Yalom, 1985).

The social worker who is able to identify group processes as they develop over the life of a group is in a position to harness their power in moving the group toward its goal or goals. A social worker who fixes his or her focus solely on the tasks or outcome of the group runs the risk that group processes will serve an inhibiting, rather than a facilitating, function.

PARTICIPATION

A fundamental aspect of the first group meeting is participation by every group member (Rose, 1977). One task of the group leader, unlike that of the caseworker, is to deemphasize his or her role and to stress the value of intermember relations within the group (Dies & Teleska, 1985). Coyle (1947), who wrote the first social work textbook on group work, addressed the issue of participation by writing that "a full orchestra can have no instruments that are silenced when they should be expected to come in. For that reason the . . . leader needs, first, . . . to have all participate and then to be aware of the extent of the existing participation. If his ear becomes trained to this, he is then in a position to encourage participation where it is inadequate" (p. 23).

The quality of participation is not the issue; the mere act of participating may be more crucial. Not only is participation, which is basically the development of socializing skills, one of the essential conditions of group membership, it can reduce the probability of members dropping out. For example, in a survey of practitioners, one of the most common reasons given for members dropping out was that they felt socially isolated and were less well integrated into the groups than were other members (Dies & Teleska, 1985). In addition, initial participation predicts later, and deeper, self-disclosure. Thus, MacKenzie (1987) reported that his analysis of "critical incident reports" revealed that the initial stages of groups were characterized by superficial self-disclosure, whereas the later stages of the group were characterized by deeper self-disclosure.

Although the social worker has the responsibility for maximizing members' participation in the group, certain forms of participation can be a problem. One of the most common types of problems is scapegoating (Shulman, 1994). Whereas Garvin (1986) suggested that scapegoating in a group is parallel to families seeking change in an identified patient, others, such as Tsui and Schultz (1988), consider it to be a reflection of larger societal tensions. Whatever the etiology of this form of communication, the group worker has the responsibility to provide help. The question, then, is What is most helpful when communication is a problem in the group?

Although the group worker may be inclined to "protect" the scapegoat, there is general agreement that this strategy only places him or her in conflict with the group (Gitterman & Shulman, 1994). One tactic is to empathize with the individual; another is to confront the group with its here-and-now behavior (Anstey, 1982). Another strategy is to find the common ground between the group and the scapegoat (Gitterman & Shulman, 1994); however, this approach has been criticized as taking too long to implement as well as being unrealistic (Anstey, 1982). Finally, Rose (1989) suggested treating scapegoating as a "group problem" and centering the intervention on defining the problem and engaging the group in a problem-solving process. Whichever strategy the worker uses, it should follow a careful assessment of the problem and be designed to promote the work of the group.

EFFICACY

Although the use of a specific group method should follow and be linked to assessment, there are several general advantages of group work. First, groups can relieve real or imagined isolation—a characteristic that Shulman (1994) referred to as the "all in the same boat phenomenon" (p. 44) and Yalom (1985) labeled "universality." Whatever the exact process, the group offers multiple opportunities for validation and reinforcement. Second, the group is a natural laboratory for learning and discussion. Clients or members are forced to deal with each others' attitudes, behaviors, and feelings, which helps them develop social skills either explicitly as part of the group contract or implicitly in the group interaction.

Toseland and Siporin (1986) examined the literature comparing individual and group interventions and asked, "Which is more effective?" In 24 of 32 studies, they found no statistical differences in the outcome of the modalities, but in the remaining eight studies, they found group treatment to be statistically more effective than individual treatment. Toseland and Siporin added that there was no clear pattern regarding the types of problems that are most effectively treated in a group setting. When this study is examined in terms of a "box score," it seems safe to conclude that the work done in groups is no worse than that conducted on an individual basis. However, the question to ask is not, Which is more effective? but, Which is more effective with these particular problems under these conditions? (Paul, 1967). Toseland and Siporin's inability to ask this question is a reflection of the failure of group workers to evaluate their practice systematically (Galinsky & Schopler, 1993). Furthermore, the more detailed question raised by Paul points to the need of social workers to move away from a focus on a "method" or "model" and to "start where the client is." If group workers think of themselves as social workers first, they will not prematurely confine themselves to working with one level of client system or one particular method of helping (Nelsen, 1975).

REFERENCES

Addams, J. (1960). *Twenty years at Hull House*. New York: Signet. (Original work published 1910)

Anstey, M. (1982). Scapegoating in groups: Some theoretical perspectives and a case record of intervention. *Social Work with Groups, 5*(3), 51–63.

Beck, A. P. (1983). A process analysis of group development. *Group, 7*(1), 19–28.

Bednar, R. L., & Kaul, T. J. (1994). Experiential group research: Can the cannon fire? In A. E. Bergin & S. L. Garfield (Eds.), *Handbook of psychotherapy and behavior change* (4th ed., pp. 631–663). New York: John Wiley & Sons.

Birnbaum, M. L., & Auerbach, C. (1992, February). *Group work in graduate social work education: The price of neglect.* Paper presented at the Annual Program Meeting, Council on Social Work Education, Kansas City, MO.

Brower, A. M. (1988). Group development as constructed social reality: A social-cognitive understanding of group formation. *Social Work with Groups, 12*(2), 23–41.

Burlingame, G., Fuhriman, A., & Drescher, S. (1984). Scientific inquiry into small group process: A multidimensional approach. *Small Group Behavior, 15,* 441–470.

Burlingame, G. M., & Fuhriman, A. (1990). Time-limited group therapy. *Counseling Psychologist, 18,* 93–118.

Council on Social Work Education. (1952). *Curriculum policy for the master's degree program in social work education.* New York: Author.

Council on Social Work Education. (1969). *Curriculum policy for the master's degree program in social work education.* New York: Author.

Coyle, G. L. (1937). *Studies in group behavior.* New York: Harper & Row.

Coyle, G. L. (1947). *Group experience and democratic values.* New York: Women's Press.

Davis, L. (1979). Racial composition of groups. *Social Work, 24,* 208–213.

Davis, L., & Toseland, R. (1987). Group versus individual decision making. *Social Work with Groups, 10*(2), 95–105.

Davis, L. E., & Proctor, E. K. (1989). *Race, gender and class: Guidelines for practice with individuals, families, and groups.* Englewood Cliffs, NJ: Prentice Hall.

Dewey, J. (1922). *Human nature and conduct.* New York: Random House.

Dies, R. R., & Teleska, P. A. (1985). Negative outcome in group psychotherapy. In D. T. Mays & C. M. Franks (Eds.), *Negative outcome in psychotherapy and what to do about it* (pp. 118–141). New York: Springer.

Flowers, J. V. (1987). Client outcome as a function of agreement or disagreement with the modal group perception of curative factors in short-term, structured group psychotherapy. *International Journal of Group Psychotherapy, 37,* 113–118.

Fuhriman, A., Drescher, S., & Burlingame, G. M. (1984). Conceptualizing small group process. *Small Group Behavior, 15,* 427–440.

Galinsky, M. J., & Schopler, J. H. (1989). Developmental patterns in open-ended groups. *Social Work with Groups, 12*(2), 99–114.

Galinsky, M. J., & Schopler, J. H. (1993, October). *Social group work competence: Our strengths and challenges.* Plenary address at the 15th Annual Symposium of the Association for the Advancement of Social Work with Groups, New York City.

Garvin, C. D. (1985). Group process: Usage and uses in social work practice. In M. Sundel, P. Glasser, R. Sarri, & R. Vinter (Eds.), *Individual change through small groups* (2nd ed., pp. 203–225). New York: Free Press.

Garvin, C. D. (1986). Family therapy and group work: "Kissing cousins or distant relatives" in social work practice? In M. Parnes (Ed.), *Innovations in social group work: Feedback from practice to theory* (pp. 1–15). New York: Haworth Press.

Garvin, C. D. (1987). *Contemporary group work* (2nd ed.). Englewood Cliffs, NJ: Prentice Hall.

Germain, C. B. (1983). Technological advances. In A. Rosenblatt & D. Waldfogel (Eds.), *Handbook of clinical social work* (pp. 26–57). San Francisco: Jossey-Bass.

Gitterman, A., & Shulman, L. (Eds.). (1986). *Mutual aid groups and the life cycle.* Itasca, IL: F. E. Peacock.

Gitterman, A., & Shulman, L. (Eds.). (1994). *Mutual aid groups, vulnerable populations, and the life cycle.* New York: Columbia University Press.

Glassman, U., & Kates, L. (1990). *Group work: A humanistic approach.* Newbury Park, CA: Sage Publications.

Kaul, T. J., & Bednar, R. L. (1986). Experiential group research: Results, questions, and suggestions. In S. L. Garfield & A. E. Bergin (Eds.), *Handbook of psychotherapy and behavior change* (3rd ed., pp. 671–714). New York: John Wiley & Sons.

Kolodny, R. (1980). The dilemma of co-leadership. *Social Work with Groups, 3*(4), 31–34.

Lang, N. (1979). A comparative examination of therapeutic uses of groups in social work and in adjacent human service professions: Part II—The literature from 1969–1978. *Social Work with Groups, 2*(3), 197–220.

Lewin, K., Lippitt, R., & White, R. (1939). Patterns of aggressive behavior in experimentally created "social climates." *Journal of Social Psychology, 10,* 271–299.

Lieberman, M. A., & Borman, L. D. (Eds.). (1979). *Self-help groups for coping with crisis.* San Francisco: Jossey-Bass.

Lieberman, M. A., Yalom, I. D., & Miles, M. B. (1973). *Encounter groups: First facts.* New York: Basic Books.

MacKenzie, K. R. (1987). Therapeutic factors in group psychotherapy: A contemporary view. *Group, 11*(1), 26–31.

Magen, R. (1991, May). *A comparison outcome study of parent training programs for aggressive children: Skills training versus problem solving.* Paper presented at the Seventh Empirical Group Work Conference, Chicago.

Middleman, R., & Wood, G. (1990). From social group work to social work with groups. *Social Work with Groups, 13*(3), 3–20.

Middleman, R. R. (1981). The pursuit of competence through involvement in structured groups. In A. N. Maluccio (Ed.), *Promoting competence in clients: A new/old approach to social work practice.* New York: Free Press.

Miller, W. R., & McCrady, B. S. (1993). The importance of research on Alcoholics Anonymous. In B.BS. McCrady & W. R. Miller (Eds.), *Research on Alcoholics Anonymous* (pp. 3–11). New Brunswick, NJ: Rutgers Center of Alcohol Studies.

Nelsen, J. C. (1975). Social work's fields of practice, methods, and models: The choice to act. *Social Service Review, 49,* 264–270.

Northen, H. (1982). *Clinical social work.* New York: Columbia University Press.

Ormont, L. R. (1969). Acting in and the therapeutic contract in group psychoanalysis. *International Journal of Group Psychotherapy, 11,* 420–432.

Papell, C. P., & Rothman, B. (1966). Social group work models: Possession and heritage. *Journal of Education for Social Work, 2*(2), 66–77.

Papell, C. P., & Rothman, B. (1980). Relating the mainstream model of social work with groups to group psychotherapy and the structured group approach. *Social Work with Groups, 3*(2), 5–23.

Paul, G. L. (1967). Outcome research in psychotherapy. *Journal of Consulting Psychology, 31,* 109–118.

Reid, K. E. (1991). *Social work practice with groups: A clinical perspective.* Pacific Grove, CA: Brooks/Cole.

Rose, S. D. (1977). *Group therapy: A behavioral approach.* Englewood Cliffs, NJ: Prentice Hall.

Rose, S. D. (1989). *Working with adults in groups: Integrating cognitive-behavioral and small group strategies.* San Francisco: Jossey-Bass.

Rubin, A. (1982). *Statistics on social work education in the United States: 1981.* New York: Council on Social Work Education.

Rubin, A. (1983). *Statistics on social work education in the United States: 1982.* New York: Council on Social Work Education.

Schopler, J. H., & Galinsky, M. J. (1993). Support groups as open systems: A model for practice and research. *Health and Social Work, 18,* 195–207.

Schwartz, W. (1966). Discussion of three papers on the group method with clients, foster families, and adoptive families. *Child Welfare, 45,* 571–575.

Schwartz, W. (1969). Private troubles and public issues: One social work job or two? *Social Welfare Forum* (pp. 22–43). New York: Columbia University Press.

Schwartz, W. (1986). The group work tradition and social work practice. *Social Work with Groups, 8*(4), 7–27.

Sherif, M. (1936). *The psychology of social norms.* New York: Harper.

Shulman, L. (1994). Group work method. In A. Gitterman & L. Shulman (Eds.), *Mutual aid groups, vulnerable populations, and the life cycle* (2nd ed., pp. 29–58). New York: Columbia University Press.

Toseland, R. W., & Rivas, R. F. (1995). *An introduction to group work practice* (2nd ed.). Boston: Allyn & Bacon.

Toseland, R. W., & Siporin, M. (1986). When to recommend group treatment: A review of the clinical and research literature. *International Journal of Group Psychotherapy, 36,* 171–201.

Tsui, P., & Schultz, G. L. (1988). Ethnic factors in group process: Cultural dynamics in multiethnic therapy groups. *American Journal of Orthopsychiatry, 58,* 136–142.

Tuckman, B. W. (1965). Developmental sequence in small groups. *Psychological Bulletin, 63,* 384–399.

Wright, T. L., & Ingraham, L. J. (1985). Simultaneous study of individual differences and relationship effects in social behavior in groups. *Journal of Personality and Social Psychology, 48,* 1041–1047.

Yalom, I. D. (1985). *The theory and practice of group psychotherapy.* New York: Basic Books.

10

Practice with Communities

Susan P. Kemp

S ocial workers have always been concerned with enhancing individual and social well-being through intervention in the community. Indeed, as earlier chapters have demonstrated, a concern with people's functioning in relation to their wider social and physical environment constitutes the particular jurisdictional claim of the social work profession. In community practice, social workers facilitate the empowerment of groups and communities, link people to resources and services, develop resources and services when they are lacking, nurture community development, and are an important voice for community and social change. In this practice, the social vision of the profession is most fully realized as social workers challenge social institutions to respond more effectively to community needs.

In community practice, the community is at once the context in which practice takes place; the target of intervention; and the vehicle, or means, by which change is effected (Kramer & Specht, 1975). As in practice with families or small groups, the community must be understood both as the setting within which intervention takes place and more immediately, as the unit of attention and action. This view requires, broadly, two kinds of knowledge: (1) knowledge about how communities are constructed, the functions they serve, and how they mediate between individuals and wider social structures and (2) knowledge of strategies for assessment and intervention at the community level.

PARAMETERS OF COMMUNITY PRACTICE

The most commonly used typology of community practice (Rothman, 1970) identifies three main approaches to change in the community: (1) locality (community) development, in which the focus is on enhancing participation and competence at the local community level through community service programs, self-help efforts such as the prevention of violence, and efforts to enhance social networks, among others; (2) social planning, which is a largely

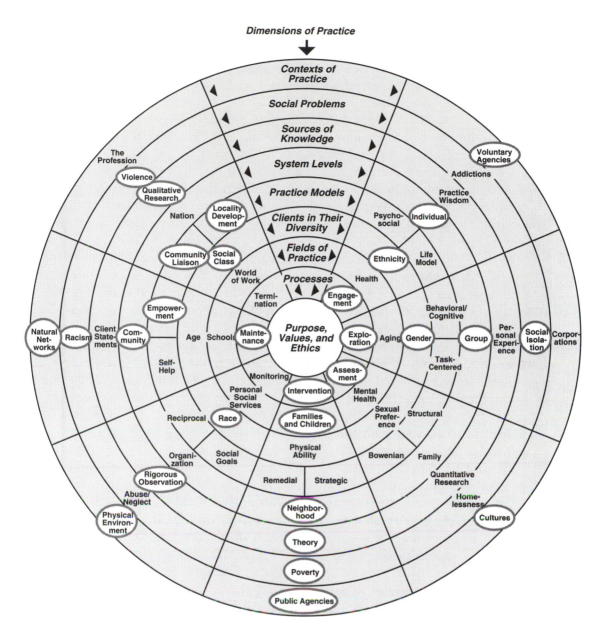

FIGURE 10-1. DIMENSIONS OF PRACTICE IN WORK WITH COMMUNITIES

technical process of problem solving with regard to substantive social problems (such as delinquency, inadequate housing, and mental illness); and (3) social action, in which the focus is on organizing disadvantaged groups to seek the redistribution of power or resources or to change the policies and services of formal organizations.

In an expansion of this typology, Rothman and Tropman (1987) grouped these community approaches with social policy and administration under the general rubric macro practice. Macro practice, Rothman and Tropman suggested, "deals with aspects of human activity that are nonclinical in nature, but rather focus on broader social approaches to human betterment, emphasizing such things as developing enlightened social policy, organizing the effective delivery of services, strengthening community life, and preventing social ills" (p. 3). From this perspective, community practice and clinical practice are distinct entities.

Taylor and Roberts (1985) differentiated five models of community practice: community development, program development and service coordination, social planning, political action, and community liaison. The community liaison approach is an important addition, for it brings into community practice the many community-related activities that social workers undertake in direct practice, including case management, with its central concern with accessing, coordinating, and monitoring community resources and relationships (Taylor, 1985).

In the 1990s the trend has been toward a "hybrid" model of community practice (Bradshaw, Soifer, & Gutierrez, 1994), characterized by flexible integration of macropractice strategies and those focused on the individual and small-group processes that are the building blocks of community empowerment (for examples of this perspective, see articles in the *Journal of Community Practice*). Emergent perspectives on community practice with women and communities of color endorse the feminist credo that the personal is political and point to the need for both individual and collective empowerment. These approaches challenge the construction of community practice in rational-technocratic, expert, and masculine terms and argue for interventions that emphasize process, diminish differentials in power and status, and empower vulnerable people and populations (Bradshaw et al., 1994; Weil, 1986, 1994).

Figure 10-2 summarizes the range of practice approaches that are typically included in community practice. Given the diversity, fluidity, and relative lack of conceptual development in this field (Rothman & Tropman, 1987), there is considerable overlap among different methods, which are "mixed and phased" in actual practice as situational needs shift and change.

With the goal of placing community practice within the reach of all social workers, particularly those in direct practice, this chapter focuses on locality or community development and community liaison activities (Rothman & Tropman, 1987; Taylor & Roberts, 1985). Although social administration and social policy are both highly relevant to community practice, these fields have their own bodies of knowledge and skills, and are not explored here. Nor are the more technical aspects of community practice, such as program development and social planning, discussed in depth. The purpose of this chapter is to provide an overview of the scope of community practice, concentrating on theory and skills that are of immediate relevance to entry-level social workers in a variety of settings and fields of practice.

This focus also fits the developmental nature of work with communities. In most communities, the initial challenge is to develop identity and connection (a sense of community) and to establish priorities among needs. Social workers in direct practice can support the development of community consciousness and competence in their ongoing work with individuals and small

Locality–Community Development

A dual focus on individual and community development. Empowerment is seen as both a process and a goal. Key activities are participation, conscientization, self-help, and leadership; emphasis is on the collaborative process. Clients are viewed as citizens. The practitioner is an enabler-catalyst, coordinator, teacher-learner, and advocate.

Community Liaison

Community activities are linked to goals and services of direct service agencies. Key functions are interorganizational relations, mobilization of community supports, and the redefinition of goals, functions, and programs in response to shifts in the environment. Administrative activities: coordination, community relations, environmental reconnaissance, and fundraising. Clinical staff activities: case management, community liaison, identification of needs, program development, and advocacy on behalf of clients.

Social Planning

Problem solving with regard to substantive community problems (such as physical and mental illness, inadequate housing, and the lack of recreational facilities). The use of the rational-technical approach to designing new programs and services, enhancing existing services, coordinating services, and reforming the human services systems. Clients are viewed as consumers. Roles of practitioners: fact gatherers and analysts, program implementers, facilitators, and coordinators.

Social Action

Actions designed to shift power relationships and resources and to create basic institutional change. Clients are viewed as victims of oppressive social conditions. Strategies include advocacy, conflict, confrontation, direct action, and negotiation. Roles of practitioners: activists, advocates, agitators, brokers, negotiators, and partisans.

FIGURE 10-2. MODELS OF COMMUNITY PRACTICE

Sources: Adapted from Rothman, J., & Tropman, J. E. (1987). Models of community organization and macro practice perspectives: Their mixing and phasing. In F. M. Cox, J. L. Erlich, J. Rothman, & J. E. Tropman (Eds.), Strategies of community organization: Macro practice (4th ed., pp. 3-26). Itasca, IL: F. E. Peacock; Taylor, S. H., & Roberts, R. W. (1985). The fluidity of practice theory: An overview. In S. H. Taylor & R. W. Roberts (Eds.), Theory and practice of community social work (pp. 3–29). New York: Columbia University Press; and Weil, M. (1986). Women, community, and organizing. In N. Van Den Bergh & L. B. Cooper (Eds.), Feminist visions for social work (pp. 187-210). Silver Spring, MD: National Association of Social Workers.

groups, as well as through interventions that are designed specifically for this purpose. These community-building efforts provide the foundation for effective action by the community to address identified issues. In this phase, the support, advocacy, brokerage, and negotiation skills of social workers become increasingly salient. Technical expertise also comes into play as social workers and communities attempt to structure services that more effectively meet the communities' needs.

THE DESIRE FOR COMMUNITY

The desire for community is deeply embedded in American life. In a society that is defined by individualism, the belief nonetheless persists that life was and is better when people are connected to one another in helpful ways. The term "community" is laden with the mythology of an idealized colonial past. It is a word that evokes nostalgic visions of small-town values and habits, of places where people know one another, look out for each other, and act together for the common good. The wish to recapture this mythic community has been a theme in American society at least since the late 19th century, when industrialization, mass migration and immigration, the growth of cities, and increased social mobility transformed a social structure that was previously defined by ties to blood and soil (Rupp, 1991).

The desire for community has continued to resonate in American life (Chavis & Wandersman, 1990), but recognition of the value of community ties is set against the even more compelling quest for individual fulfillment. In their landmark study of American culture, Bellah, Madsen, Sullivan, Swidler, and Tipton (1985) found a yearning for "meaning and coherence" in the midst of the pursuit of individualism. Although they suggested, as did the communitarian Etzioni (1993), that this yearning could be realized through a renewed commitment to community and civic responsibility, there is little evidence that Americans readily put the common good ahead of individual advancement. Therefore, efforts to develop community as a vehicle for social integration and shared meaning must confront the reality that the rhetoric of community cloaks deep ambivalence about the value of connection. As this ambivalence ebbs and flows, social workers find more or less opportunity to work effectively at the community level.

SOCIAL WORK AND COMMUNITY: A HISTORICAL NOTE

The early social workers in the settlement houses and the Charity Organization Societies (COS) were among the first to suggest that one solution for social disorganization was to re-create in U.S. cities the organic village community of the past (Halpern, 1993; Kemp, 1994). Both the friendly visitors and the settlement house workers attempted to revive the everyday contact between the social classes and the informal helpfulness of the rural village. Mary Richmond (1907), who systematized social casework, was a firm believer in the power of "neighborliness" and in the value of involvement in the daily life of the community. Likewise, Robert Woods (1893/1970), founder of Boston's South End Settlement, said of the settlements that they "take neighborhoods in cities, and by patience bring back to them much of the healthy village life, so that people shall again know and care for each other" (p. 91).

The COS and the settlement houses also worked to improve community life through vigorous involvement in social reform efforts, including public health, industrial safety, education, housing, and child labor. Both groups used their detailed knowledge of community conditions as a basis for lobbying and advocacy. Although much of this knowledge came from the daily experience of the settlement house workers and the friendly visitors, the need to develop systematic data on social conditions was recognized. Both the COS and the settlement houses conducted communitywide social surveys (such as the Pittsburgh Survey, funded by the Russell Sage Foundation, and the Hull House Survey in Chicago), which provided important information for use in local community planning and in reform activities (Garvin & Cox, 1987).

A broad-based commitment to the development of healthy communities thus has a long history in social work, with roots in both social casework and the settlement house movement. The community involvements of social caseworkers, however, changed markedly after World War I, when the mental hygiene movement, the influence of psychodynamic theory, and an inward turn in the wider society combined to move social casework toward a treatment approach. Caseworkers began to see clients in agencies, rather than in the clients' homes or in neighborhood settings, and casework practice became dominated by an individual treatment model borrowed from psychiatry.

The settlement houses also were transformed in the years after World War I, as community services were overtaken by machinery and the conservative interests of centralized funding sources (Reisch & Wenocur, 1986). The dominance of social casework in the field and in social work education placed community organizers at an increasing distance from the mainstream of social work. Many community organizers eschewed professional training; those who entered graduate education found themselves immersed in a system that was designed to produce caseworkers.

The social movements of the 1960s supported a revival of interest in community and neighborhood development. With significant federal support, both community action programs and jobs for community organizers proliferated. This resurgence of interest was reflected in the marked growth in the number of social work education programs that offered training in community practice and in significant efforts to carve out a recognized jurisdiction for community organization in the social work profession. These efforts often involved specific efforts to separate community organizing from interpersonal practice (Tropman, 1987), thus further widening the gap between community and clinical practice.

Not the flowering of federally supported community action programs, the ready availability of community organizing jobs, or the growth of interest in community practice in social work survived the Nixon administration. In the Reagan years, as the flow of federal dollars to community programs slowed to a trickle, interest in clinical practice grew steadily. By the 1970s and 1980s, the area of growth in community action had become self-help and grassroots organizations, supported mostly with nonfederal funds, and focused often on specific issues. The focus of community organization theory continued to be on changing large systems, however.

At the same time, new conceptual frameworks that were grounded in ecological and systems theory provided the basis for the development of integrated approaches to social work practice (Germain & Gitterman, 1980; Meyer, 1970, 1976; Middleman & Goldberg, 1974; Pincus & Minahan, 1973; Siporin, 1980). In the 1990s, largely through the efforts of practitioners who are committed to responding effectively to issues of diversity, multiculturalism, and oppression, the potential for an integrated approach to community issues is beginning to be recognized.

DEFINITIONS OF COMMUNITY
In general, community is defined as being a function of either a common geographic location or shared interests or concerns. To these definitions Heller (1989) added a third: community as collective political power or organized constituencies. For all three functions, it is assumed that people in a community have something in common that brings them together.

People belong to multiple communities based on where they live, their employment, interests, life experiences (such as belonging to Alcoholics Anonymous, being gay, or having a developmentally disabled child), and social and institutional memberships. Different kinds of community emerge, depending on whether people are linked primarily by affect (the ties of blood, land, religion, culture, ethnicity, or nationality) or by interest. Rubin and Rubin (1992) identified five major types of communities—neighborhoods, solidarity communities, social classes, networks, and communities of interest—each of which presents different issues and challenges for community practice.

Community as Locality
Many commonly used definitions of community (see, for example, Barker, 1995, p. 68; Warren, 1978) are grounded in a sense of place. From this perspective, a community is a group of people who live in a particular geographic area, or neighborhood, that affords ready access to key areas of daily life. In the neighborhood, social connections based on proximity, a shared lifestyle, and common local concerns are often reinforced by ties of ethnicity or culture.

Although in social work, much of community practice is locally based, there is a need for caution in defining communities in geographic terms. First, people who live near one another do not necessarily feel connected. Unless other areas of common ground exist, such as shared social class or racial, ethnic, or religious identity, territory may have little to do with the sense of community. Second, several communities often coexist in one geographic space. Many people develop a sense of investment in their local community more around specific issues than in a profound and ongoing way. Some, particularly those in urban neighborhoods, are invested more in being free of their community's demands than in developing ties with their neighbors. Heller (1989) noted that those who are the most connected to a locality tend to be "the very young or very old, women who do not work outside the home, and certain ethnic groups" (p. 7).

An accurate reading of what constitutes community is nonetheless often critical to the success of a program or intervention. Because social workers' perceptions as outsiders may be different from those of the local residents, it is important to ask local people how the boundaries of their community should be determined. Such boundaries may look nothing like city zoning plans, school districts, or other formal means of determining local "catchment areas" (many of which are imposed on agencies and programs through the way funding is structured).

Developing a community profile
Both Johnson (1992) and Sheafor, Horejsi, and Horejsi (1991) presented comprehensive outlines for developing a profile of a geographic community. The major domains include the physical setting, history, demographics of the population, cultural factors, the economic system, the political system, the educational system, the social-cultural system, the human services system, major problems and concerns of the community, and general aspects of community functioning (such as the sense of identity and belonging, decision-making structures, and autonomy). Much of the objective data for a community assessment is available from census data and materials compiled by state and local agencies that are involved in community planning (such as the United Way; local governments; and economic development, labor, and human services agencies). Supplemental data should include material developed from interviews with key community figures and local residents.

The value of local knowledge cannot be overemphasized. Regardless of their settings, social workers should be physically acquainted with the community in which they work. To do so, they must walk and drive around it, take the time to talk informally with local people, and generally explore. Often there is no substitute for the particular kind of environmental knowledge that comes from direct personal experience.

Solidarity Communities
Solidarity communities share a common heritage (Rubin & Rubin, 1992). Whether it is based on religion, ethnicity, culture, or nationality, this heritage provides members with a strong sense of identity and a common system of values and beliefs. Ties to the community tend to be deep seated and long lasting and are maintained in a variety of ways, including language, food, customs, traditions, and religious observances. Rivera and Erlich (1992) termed emergent ethnic communities "neogemeinschaft" communities and noted the importance of relationship-based social networks, informal exchange, and natural support systems. Although members of solidarity communities (such as Muslims who attend a particular mosque or refugee families who

cluster in one area) may live in the same neighborhood, they may also be spread over wide distances (for example, Mormons or Hasidic Jews) if their shared institutions maintain community ties.

In some instances, social solidarity is imposed on a group by the larger society (Rubin & Rubin, 1992), because there is a tendency to assume that people who share common demographic characteristics constitute a community (F. M. Cox, 1987). Thus, people speak of the Asian community, of African Americans, or of the urban underclass as though each is a homogeneous group. Such monolithic classifications can obscure both the rich diversity within such groups and the extent to which the level of identification is variable. For some people who are born into solidarity communities (for example, Catholics or upwardly mobile African Americans), the attempt to establish a separate identity may be more salient than any sense of connectedness or belonging.

Thus, a particular danger in using demographic indicators is the tendency to lump together groups of people who are extremely diverse. Again, a collaborative approach that involves local people in defining their community is recommended. Ethnographic data can then be set against data that are derived from broader demographic indicators, such as census data, public health statistics, uniform crime reports, or city planning data.

Social Class–Shared Power Relationships

Despite the rhetoric of the classless society, American communities are deeply defined by class divisions. Social class, based on income, education, and ownership of property, determines the degree of access to opportunities and resources of individuals, families, and communities. The members of a low-income community, such as an urban housing project, have little access to, and even less control over, a wide range of opportunities, including employment, education, housing, health care services, and public amenities. Upperclass communities, on the other hand, have ready access to and control over opportunities and services.

Although a concern with the distribution of power in communities has always been central to community practice, it has often focused on locating and influencing those in the community who already have power (F. M. Cox, 1987). An empowerment perspective suggests a more comprehensive approach that addresses power relationships not only in political terms, but at the personal and interpersonal levels (Dodd & Gutierrez, 1990). Activities that increase awareness of the ways in which the distribution of power is constitutive of life experiences are particularly important.

Practice strategy: Power analysis

Gutierrez (1990) suggested that a power analysis of a client's situation is a critical component of empowering practice. Such an analysis involves two key steps. First, it is important to analyze how conditions of powerlessness are affecting the client. Second, it is essential to identify the sources of potential power. This guideline for practice with individuals and groups can readily be extended to work with communities, where its use can both enhance critical consciousness of the distribution of power in the community and its consequences and provide important information on resources and strengths available to the community effort.

Social Networks

Rubin and Rubin (1992) defined a social network as "a pattern of linked relationships across which help and information flow on a particular issue" (p. 86). Networks may consist of family and kin, friends, workmates, church members, or people who come together around a shared concern. When need or affect is the primary basis for network ties, the focus of the network is likely to be on mutual aid. When the primary basis is shared interests, the network may be oriented more toward advocacy. In many networks, particularly those that are formed around issues of deep personal concern, both mutual aid and advocacy are integral functions (the National Alliance for the Mentally Ill is a powerful example).

Communities of Interest

Many communities are defined by shared concerns, rather than shared locale. These "communities without propinquity" (Webber, 1963) may be organized around shared interests (such as environmental issues, professional concerns, or gay rights), common needs (such as parents of children with rare diseases), or both. As this society becomes more mobile and more technological and people have access to multiple modalities for communication, communities of interest are becoming uncoupled from locality. In the information society of the 1990s, as computer networks such as the Internet become the modern equivalent of the village square, it will be increasingly possible for people to be connected without ever having physical or even verbal contact.

The understanding that a sense of community can develop without face-to-face contact encourages social workers to be more creative in determining what community means to their clients. Some clients who seem relatively isolated in their local neighborhoods may have connections with wider communities of interest. The awareness of new technologies also broadens possibilities for intervention. Just as successful groups have been established by teleconferencing (Wiener, Spencer, Davidson, & Far, 1993), computer networks also afford new possibilities for mutual aid and social support.

The Life Space

The terms *life space* (Lewin, 1936), and *lifeworld* (Husserl, 1970) have been used to describe the particular, individualized way in which each person experiences and constructs his or her social and physical world. Although collective experiences are similar in their broader contours, at the individual level they are shaped and colored by personal attributes and experiences. In ecological terms, the life space is described as a "niche" (Brower & Nurius, 1993; Germain, 1985), a sense of place in the world that is framed by experience, perception, personality, culture, and opportunity structures. People can occupy a variety of niches in the present, as well as across the life span. In community practice, as in practice at other systemic levels, it is important to understand the value and meaning that people attribute to these various niches and their experiences within them. In a tribal community, for example, a person's status may bear no resemblance to his or her class standing in Eurocentric terms. To work successfully within such a community, one must approach its members with the awareness that they occupy different niches in tribal society than they do in the wider community. Similarly, in a low-income housing project, whereas some women will feel defined by their status as recipients of Aid to Families with Dependent Children, others may give primacy to their experiences as members of an extended family network, as church leaders, or as community activists. Again, because the way that people perceive their place in the world frames their view of what is possible within it, community interventions should be responsive to the individual variations within aggregate experiences.

COMMUNITY PRACTICE: A GENERALIST APPROACH

From a generalist perspective, all social workers need knowledge of and skills in community practice, although they will use them to different degrees in different contexts. The generalist practitioner draws on a wide range of knowledge and skills and applies them flexibly in response to her or his assessment of the demands of particular situations. Intervention is based on the informed judgment of the practitioner, which, in turn, is shaped by the ecosystemic assessment of the situation, by the practitioner's knowledge and skills, by the resources and mandates of the practitioner's setting, by substantive professional knowledge relevant to the case, and by the purposes and values of the profession (Meyer, 1993). The social worker may enter the case at any systemic level; what remains constant is the intellectual structure that he or she applies to the tasks at hand.

Most often, given the complex interdependencies in the person–environment configuration, productive community intervention will involve more than one level of a system, as in the following example:

> In a neighborhood struggling with high levels of violence, a community worker who is assisting a group of parents to develop a block patrol uses sophisticated interpersonal and group process skills to engage parents and to facilitate their planning process. At the local child and family agency, a clinical social worker with many of these same parents in her caseload lobbies her agency for the resources to develop an empowerment group in which parents can explore the effect of the community environment on their families.

For interventions to have lasting effects (for people and communities to develop skills and competencies that will enable them to meet other, different challenges), they must develop structural connections between individuals, collectivities, and the broader social structure. Only multilevel interventions provide the opportunity for such linkages to develop.

Thinking Contextually

Although social workers in all settings learn a great deal about the environmental problems of their individual clients, they often fail to make connections between one case and another or, as Wood and Middleman (1991) put it, to "look beyond the client" (p. 57) to see whether others have the same problem. Faced with numerous depressed clients, for example, a social worker in direct practice may feel more of a need to develop more skills in treating depression than to think about whether a community issue is contributing to his or her clients' problems. A preoccupation with clinical methods and skills tends, however, to obscure the commonality of experience among clients and the impact of social and environmental conditions.

The ability to think flexibly from "case" to "cause" and back again forms the core of generalist practice. It is also the backbone of community practice, for it ensures that the needs of individuals are connected to broader efforts to construct effective and equitable social structures. Attention to community issues is constrained, in many instances, by the way individual social workers think about their practice and by the way that social agencies construct the work that social workers do. Because the cultural value that is placed on individual fulfillment is reflected in professional education, funding structures, and, by extension, agency practices, many social workers develop a view of practice that focuses their attention on clinical issues and relegates the social and environmental context to the background of the case. Rosen and Livne (1992), for example, demonstrated the prevailing tendency in clinical practice to attribute presenting problems more to psychological factors than to environmental factors, even when a client explains his or her problem in environmental terms. In a study of practice reasoning, Nurius and Gibson's (1994) finding that social workers tended not to include environmental variables unless they were explicitly prompted to do so suggests that this lack of attention to context is more than just an artifact of the worker–client interaction.

To respond effectively to environmental and community issues, social workers must develop habits of mind (cognitive maps) that support transactional and contextual practice approaches. Berlin and Marsh (1993) noted that stable cognitive structures, or schemata, have a powerful effect on the way people organize information. In effect, schemata influence the things that social workers attend to, the meanings they assign to these things, and the actions they choose to take. Social workers who interpret human problems primarily in terms of a psychological schema, or a worldview, are less likely to explore the social construction of their clients' difficulties. In the same way, those who are deeply committed to broader social change may screen out subjective and interpersonal issues (Burghardt, 1982).

Because social work encompasses both personal and social issues, it is important that practitioners develop complex and expansive habits of mind that direct their attention to the context, as well as to the client, and that readily encompass pluralistic perspectives. Furthermore, because a deliberate effort is needed to overcome bias (Nurius & Gibson, 1994), such habits of mind must be reinforced by the routine use of methods that open up issues for attention (many tools, such as clinical diagnostic systems, are designed to reduce complexity; see Mattaini & Kirk, 1991). Examples of reinforcers, or prompts, that encourage contextual mindfulness include the use of ecosystemic measures in assessment (such as ecomaps or social network maps), regular involvement in the daily life of the community, and efforts to ensure that consumers participate actively in the planning, delivery, and monitoring of services.

Using an Ecosystems Perspective

A generalist approach to community practice is most readily conceptualized from an ecosystems perspective (Germain, 1985; Meyer, 1983). As was discussed in chapter 2, the ecosystems perspective is a metatheoretical framework—a "wide-angle lens" that directs attention to the interdependence of people and their environments at multiple and interlocking levels of systems. It enables a holistic and organic approach to the issues that confront communities because the transactive and multilayered nature of person–environment relationships is recognized. It also allows for an integrative approach to method and skills. From the ecosystems perspective, Germain (1985) argued that

> the community is an integral part of the life space of individuals and collectivities that we serve. . . . Reciprocally, when the client is the community, then the individuals and collectivities within the community must be in the foreground of attention throughout the processes of assessment, intervention, and prevention. (p. 32)

Because the ecosystems perspective is nondirective, it accommodates a range of practice theories and methods. Although such openness encourages flexibility and creativity, it also carries the risk that social workers will choose methods that are incompatible with social work values and purposes. To balance this tendency, social workers are increasingly using empowerment theory to frame their practice and as a guide to the selection of appropriate interventive strategies. In contemporary community practice, this commitment to empowerment supports and informs an equally robust commitment to effective practice with diverse communities (Weil, 1994). The emergence of new ethnic communities, transitions in established communities of color, and the increasing visibility of the gay and lesbian communities have all contributed to the growing emphasis on multiculturalism and pluralism.

From an empowerment perspective, the goal of social work intervention is to enable people, organizations, and communities to gain mastery over their affairs (Rappaport, 1987). The concept of empowerment, as Zimmerman and Rappaport (1988) noted, enables social workers to link "individual strengths and competencies, natural helping systems, and proactive behaviors to matters of social policy and social change" (p. 726). Empowerment thus provides a common framework for social work activities at multiple systemic levels (Parsons, 1991).

Empowerment

Empowerment is most easily defined in its absence: as the lack of control, learned helplessness, alienation, or apathy (Rappaport, 1984). In positive terms, it is defined by competence and self-efficacy, connectedness, a concern for the common good, and a sense of commitment to and participation in the community (Zimmerman & Rappaport, 1988).

Solomon (1976) identified three sources of powerlessness: the negative self-evaluation of the individual, the negative experiences that people have in relation to external systems, and the environmental systems themselves. Research indicates that the objective experience of powerlessness has an impact on a person's view of himself or herself in relation to the world (Seligman, 1972). Real powerlessness is potentiated by perceived powerlessness, or the diminished sense of self that results (but also feeds into) the experience of powerlessness and oppression (Parsons, 1991). Passivity and resignation are typical responses to environmental conditions that are experienced as overwhelming or unlikely to change.

The process of empowerment thus involves a shift both in one's personal attitudes and in one's ability to act in the environment (Parsons, 1991). To become empowered is to perceive oneself as an effective and potent person and to develop the ability to act to change the conditions of one's daily life (Pecukonis & Wenocur, 1994; Simon, 1990). The relationship between personal competence and environmental action is reflexive; each reinforces the other (Zimmerman & Rappaport, 1988). Empowerment is thus both process and outcome—a state of mind and the ability to act differently in the outside world (Parsons, 1991).

Effective community practice requires an understanding of the developmental process of empowerment at the personal, group, and community levels (Dodd & Gutierrez, 1990; Kieffer, 1984). This understanding enables social workers to focus on the two major objectives of community practice: the empowerment of people and the redistribution of power and resources in the community (Mondros & Berman-Rossi, 1991).

ELEMENTS OF EMPOWERMENT IN COMMUNITY PRACTICE

Interpersonal effectiveness in community practice builds on the knowledge and skills outlined in chapter 7. As they work with people on community issues, social workers use their clinical skills in multiple ways: to build connections, to facilitate reflection and dialogue, to provide support, to reinforce existing coping skills and enhance new ones, and to encourage participation. Like empowering practice in general, however, community practice differs from clinical practice as it is traditionally constructed. At the interpersonal level, this difference is demonstrated by a commitment to clients' participation and ownership of the change process, an emphasis on mutuality and collaboration, a focus on the development of critical consciousness, and the use of dialogue as a primary strategy for change.

Participation

In empowering community practice, clients are regarded as citizens, consumers, members, or (from an activist perspective), victims of oppressive social conditions. Attention thus shifts from personal and interpersonal deficits to the relationship between people and their sociopolitical environment and to the rights of a community to opportunities, resources, and services.

Central to this perspective is the assumption that people should participate actively in defining their concerns and any action to be taken to address them (Maluccio, 1981). Indeed, Kieffer (1984) defined empowerment as participatory competence. Because participation is a prerequisite for any form of community action, efforts to enhance it constitute an important aspect of community practice (Mattaini, 1993a). Incentives for participation may be intrinsic (derived from the activity itself) or extrinsic (such as the offer of food, child care, or other benefits in return for participation).

Studies of community participation have demonstrated that active involvement and feelings of ownership contribute significantly to the psychological empowerment of individuals (Zimmerman & Rappaport, 1988) and result in more positive and durable outcomes of projects (Itzhaky & York, 1991; Mattaini, 1993a). Participation can take many forms, such as involvement in committees and coalitions, the contribution of a consumer voice in the development and delivery of services, participation in program planning and management, and involvement in participatory action research.

Unfortunately, the commitment to participation is often more rhetorical than real. In large-scale community projects in which a consumer presence is mandated by external funders and in which large institutional interests are represented, community involvement may be little more than tokenism. Participation may also be empty if the context in which it occurs (such as in poor communities) is unlikely to change as a result of the proposed action. Halpern (1993) rightly pointed out that in "depleted" communities, real change in opportunity structures depends on external social and economic structures. Although community development efforts are not wasted in such communities, goals and tasks must be constructed so that projects do not squander valuable (and scarce) human resources and further victimize members of the community by promising more than they can deliver. Careful work is required, both with consumers and the institutions and services in which they participate, to ensure that participation is meaningful and effective (Keenan & Pinkerton, 1991).

Mutuality and Collaboration
A shift in social workers' view of the person requires a concomitant shift in how the helping process is viewed and in practitioners' roles as helpers. Traditionally, social workers have been trained to maintain a neutral stance in interactions with clients. An empowerment approach, however, assumes an engaged worker who helps clients to construct their experience in political as well as personal terms. The social worker's ideological stance "lends a vision" and serves as a catalyst for the development of alternative ways of understanding among members of the community. Robust models for such engaged practice are readily available in feminist practice (Van Den Bergh & Cooper, 1986) and in the emerging literature on community practice with people of color (Rivera & Erlich, 1992).

In such practice, social workers replace paternalistic and elitist forms of intervention (those that assume that they know best) with approaches that maximize people's rights, strengths, and capabilities through careful attention to issues of power, social distance, and control. As far as possible, they use their expertise in ways that do not perpetuate oppressive social conditions. The professional skills and institutional resources available to them are both real and valuable, but must be applied within a relationship characterized by mutuality, rather than professional distance. Collaboration and consultation are thus key aspects of community practice. Appropriate social work roles are those of enabler, facilitator, teacher, resource provider, consultant, compatriot, organizer, advocate, broker, negotiator, and activist (Gutierrez, 1990; Parsons, Jorgensen, & Hernandez, 1994).

Development of Critical Consciousness

An essential foundation for empowerment is the development of what Freire (1973) called "critical consciousness" and others have labeled critical thinking (Parsons, 1991; Weick, 1993). Critical consciousness is the ability to reflect on one's everyday experience not just in personal terms, but with an awareness that individual experience is shaped by events and conditions in the social and political environment. Freire suggested that it is the development of critical consciousness that enables people to act to change oppressive social conditions. The process of consciousness-raising necessarily involves praxis, a mixture of reflection and action, to ensure that social action is grounded in critical analysis of the relationship between everyday experience and the wider social/structural context (Longres & McLeod, 1980).

Dialogue as a Basis for Community Action

Consciousness-raising is achieved through dialogue, whether with individuals, small groups, or larger collectives. Empowering dialogue differs from traditional therapeutic conversations in two ways. First, the social worker joins the conversation with the goal of helping individuals or groups to express, understand, and redefine their daily experiences in social rather than personal terms. Second, whereas traditional therapy tends to focus on enhanced personal and interpersonal functioning, empowering dialogue addresses the wider sociopolitical environment and enables issues of power and domination to be examined along with other experiences. Dialogical interventions help people to surface their individual and collective stories, to explore the meaning they give to these stories, and to develop new and more complex perspectives that incorporate social and political perspectives.

The use of dialogue and narrative to facilitate empowerment has sturdy roots in the women's and other grassroots movements. More recently, narrative techniques have emerged as a central aspect of dialogic and constructivist approaches to intervention in family therapy and social work (Allen, 1993; Anderson & Goolishian, 1988; Holland & Kilpatrick, 1993; Laird, 1993; Saleeby, 1994; White & Epston, 1990).

Strategies for facilitating dialogue build on core social work skills in engagement and exploration: empathy; trust; mutual respect; and active, nonjudgmental listening. In addition, the social worker becomes a participant-observer. Anderson and Goolishian (1992) suggested that the social worker functions as an ethnographer, a curious and respectful stranger (Laird, 1993) who does not make assumptions about how individuals and communities understand their social reality. The process is one of joint exploration (Holland & Kilpatrick, 1993). An early but still powerful example of such an approach can be found in the work of Auerswald (1968), who described the social worker's role in assessment as that of an "ecological explorer" in the client's physical and social environment.

Freire (1973) termed his dialogical strategy the "pedagogy of the question" (p. 35), a technique that encourages people both to find their own answers and to shape further questions (Simon, 1990). Using this technique, the social worker asks community members to question why things are as they are, what patterns they can see in their shared experiences, and what social and environmental factors contribute to their circumstances. The process of questioning creates a space in which alternative views can emerge (Holland & Kilpatrick, 1993). Dominant cultural and social interpretations are challenged, and groups are encouraged to develop explanations that reflect their particular identity and history. In this way, multiple realities and perspectives may emerge and be validated.

COMMUNITY PRACTICE WITH MEDIATING STRUCTURES

Berger and Neuhaus (1977) envisioned the community as a mediating structure between the person and the institutional and social structures of the wider society. In this sense, community is thought of as moderating the impact of social structures. It provides a buffer, or cushion, between people and social conditions that are often alienating and oppressive. Three aspects of community practice are particularly relevant to the mediating function of community: (1) the use of small groups, (2) the development of social networks, and (3) the construction of communities in social programs.

Use of Small Groups

Groups are the fundamental building blocks of neighborhood and community development (Mondros & Berman-Rossi, 1991; Ramey, 1992). Community workers interact with and facilitate many different kinds of groups, including issues groups, community meetings, planning groups, task groups, self-help groups, coalitions, neighborhood associations, and social action groups.

Groups are also critical to the process of empowerment (Brown & Ziefert, 1988; Gutierrez, 1990). As was discussed in chapter 9, small groups are an important context for the development of mutual aid, social support, critical (group) consciousness, the development of skills, and social action. It is within such multipurpose groups that the reflexive processes that are inherent in empowerment most readily occur. In a safe, nurturing, and supportive group environment, people can express and explore their realities and differences and develop the sense of common purpose that is necessary to collective growth and change. Empowering groups involve both collective dialogue and ongoing opportunities for "authentic" action in the environment. E. O. Cox (1991), for example, described the progressive empowerment of a group of mothers who received welfare as they worked together to solve problems related to the welfare system.

Mondros and Berman-Rossi (1991) stated that group work skills are particularly important in the initial stages of a community project, when the social worker brings members of the community together to explore and validate different perspectives, to develop shared understandings, to enhance commitment and motivation (and negotiate conflict), and to determine a plan of action. Noting that community organizers tend to focus more on the tasks to be accomplished than on the process of implementation, Mondros and Berman-Rossi contended that "organizers invite trouble for themselves if they don't attend to how and why people join groups, the meaning of group experience for individuals, and matters of group process during these beginning efforts" (p. 204). Knowledge of the stages of group development and skills in facilitating group process at different points in the life cycle of community projects are thus important aspects of community work practice.

Social Networks

At least since the 1980s social workers have been interested in identifying, supporting, and creating social networks as a source of support for clients and to buttress other interventions (Tracy & Whittaker, 1990; Whittaker, Garbarino, & Associates, 1983). There is growing recognition of the centrality of social networks to efforts to build community, particularly within emergent ethnic communities (Daley & Wong, 1994; Lewis & Ford, 1990). When they function well, social networks provide members with material assistance and services (caretaking), emotional nurturance and counseling, problem-solving advice and referral, and a forum for collective action and advocacy (Eng, Salmon, & Mullan, 1992). In ethnic communities, natural helpers and community healers provide culturally relevant help and support. Social networks are thus important buffers, or mediating structures, between individuals and broader social structures.

The social network map (Tracy & Whittaker, 1990) enables social workers and clients to assess the nature and availability of social supports. Developed primarily for use with individuals, it can be used with groups to determine patterns of support and isolation in communities. Although natural networks are an important resource in community practice, social workers must be careful not to overburden or disempower natural helpers. Furthermore, they should not assume that social networks are supportive; some, such as those in drug-ridden communities, are toxic to their members, and not all members perceive their social network in positive terms.

Program as Community

It is not always possible or reasonable to rely on informal networks. Some communities and their natural support systems, such as those in inner-city "war zones" (Garbarino, Kostelny, & Dubrow, 1991), are so depleted and overextended that little more can be asked of them. In such environments, it is important for social programs to offer the opportunities for connection, safety, support, recovery, and action that, in different circumstances, would have been given by networks of kin and friends. Provided they are culturally relevant, the social networks formed in community-based programs, such as the Head Start Family Support Centers (Lightburn & Kemp, 1994), are an important link in the chain from the empowerment of individuals to transformation of the community. Empowering community-based programs create a safe haven in violent and isolated environments, enable the development of individual and collective skills and resources, and provide a springboard for action in the wider environment. A commitment to developing, supporting, and working in such programs is thus an important, though neglected, dimension of direct practice and community development.

Community Assessment

Effective practice at the community level is grounded in a thorough understanding of the community and of its changing needs. The dimensions of community assessment should include the following:

- An understanding of different kinds of communities and of how a particular community is similar to and different from these general models.
- The use of multiple methods to generate data, including both objective-quantitative and participatory-ethnographic approaches. Although community practice has been dominated by rational-technical approaches to the collection and analysis of data (particularly in the social planning area), there is a growing emphasis on the importance of knowledge generated from the ground up. Recommended strategies for developing qualitative and experiential data include ethnomethodological approaches, such as participant observation, field observations, and informal interviews. The concerns report method developed by Fawcett, Seekins, Whang, Muiu, and Suarez de Balcazar (1980) is a structured approach to generating input from consumers. Practitioners should also develop the habit of using contextual assessment methods with all levels of systems (for a comprehensive overview of graphic assessment instruments, including nomothetic, or aggregate, ecomaps based on group data, see Mattaini, 1993b).
- The willingness to approach the community as a "respectful outsider" who is willing to learn about it from its members

and who does not impose externally constructed definitions. From this perspective, meaning is understood as local and historically situated.

- A focus on identifying strengths, competencies, and resources in the community, as well as needs and challenges (for material on a strengths approach to assessment see Parsons, 1991; Saleeby, 1992; Sullivan, 1992).
- A commitment to involving members of the community in the generation, analysis, and application of assessment material. The use of participatory action research models is particularly recommended in this regard (Curtis, 1989; Sarri & Sarri, 1992). Action research integrates research and practice by involving community members in the creation and use of knowledge about the community. Sarri and Sarri conceptualized it as a reflexive process involving the assessment of needs, planning action, implementing action, evaluation, and specifying learning (feedback).

Involvement in the assessment process educates members of a community (who often are not well informed about the parameters of particular issues), enhances their levels of participation and motivation by increasing their sense of ownership in the project, demystifies the planning process, and facilitates the development of collaborative relationships (Fagan, 1987). An action research approach also increases the probability that both the posing and solving of problems will be meaningful and appropriate. As people become active subjects, rather than just the objects of assessment and research, and develop capacities that can be used in other contexts, the likelihood of sustained change is increased.

Community Competence

At the community level, empowerment can be operationalized using the concept of community competence (Cottrell, 1977). Community competence refers to the ability of any kind of community to solve problems effectively and thus to master social and environmental challenges (Eng et al., 1992). Cottrell suggested that the process of enhancing community competence typically involves the following:

- engaging in activities that strengthen investment and commitment
- clarifying issues and interests in the community
- increasing the members' ability to articulate views, attitudes, needs, and intentions
- enhancing the members' communication skills
- developing the members' ability to negotiate differences and manage conflict
- encouraging members' participation in the community.

Groups in the community can achieve their goals only if their members have the knowledge and skills to negotiate effectively with those who control their access to needed resources and services. In groups in which these core skills are not available by virtue of the members' social class, education, or experience, they must be developed. Community members also need assistance to identify and strengthen the skills and resources they do have. Social workers make an important contribution, in small groups and community forums, when they model, teach, and support the identification and development of skills. The role of educator, though often overlooked in social work, is central to effective community practice (Lightburn & Black, in press).

Key areas for the development of skills include problem solving, assertive communication (public speaking, presenting issues, and chairing meetings), conflict management (collaboration, negotiation, and bargaining), political skills (influence and advocacy), and the technical skills associated with identifying, obtaining, and using resources (Cottrell, 1977; Mattaini, 1993a). Strategies for developing skills draw heavily on social learning theory and include didactic teaching; experiential approaches, such as coaching and role playing; and modeling effective behaviors. Leadership development is also a critical need in many communities. Because leaders may or may not be effective in negotiating with larger social systems, supporting the development of informed and effective indigenous leaders, particularly through participation in decision making, is an important aspect of community development efforts (Bradshaw et al., 1994).

Community competence is also predicated on the ability of community members to work together on areas of common concern. In this regard, social workers are challenged to help community members find common ground while recognizing that there is a value and strength in diversity (Bradshaw et al., 1994). Similarly, social workers play an important role in the development of coalitions of different interest groups and organizations in the community. At both levels, they must facilitate dialogue, "translate" different perspectives and expectations (a particularly important skill in cross-cultural practice), mediate power relationships to ensure equitable participation, and encourage an open approach to problem solving.

Challenging Social Systems
Although much work at the community level focuses on the development of consensus and collaboration, there are always instances in which such an approach does not meet the needs of individuals or the community. In these situations, social workers often become involved in advocacy and social action on behalf of community members (Mondros & Wilson, 1994). It is at this point that many social workers also become uncomfortable with community intervention.

Advocacy at the community level is universalistic, rather than exceptionalistic. That is, it is concerned with improving services and resources for people as a group, rather than for a specific client at a particular time. A helpful guideline for the use of confrontational tactics is to apply the principle of "least contest" in the choice of interventive strategies (Middleman & Goldberg, 1974); that is, less confrontational tactics should be used before those that escalate conflict. Middleman and Goldberg suggested a hierarchy of interventive roles, ranging from mediation to advocacy. McGowan (1978), who also promoted a strategic approach to the use of advocacy, listed the following six methods: (1) intercede (request, plead, persist), (2) persuade (inform, instruct, clarify, explain, argue), (3) negotiate (engage in dialogue, sympathize, bargain, placate), (4) pressure (threaten, challenge, disregard), (5) coerce (deceive, disrupt, redress administratively, take legal action), and (6) use indirect methods (educate clients, organize the community, dodge the system, construct alternatives). From this list, it can be seen that even when social workers decide to challenge social and institutional structures, they have recourse to a range of strategies from which they can select the most appropriate, depending on the developmental stage of the project, the community members' level of comfort with conflict, and the nature of the target system.

A Value Framework for Community Action

Although the choice of strategies for community action varies from situation to situation, social work practice with communities is always framed by the values and ethics of the profession. Fawcett (1991) suggested that community practice should also reflect the following principles:

- Social workers should avoid "colonial" relationships with community members, in which power, authority, and ownership of knowledge are vested in the worker, rather than in community members. Rather, they should engage in collaborative relationships, in which the contributions of both parties are valued equally.
- A project's goals should reflect the concerns, needs, and perspectives of the participants. Criteria for success (outcomes) should also be constructed in terms that are meaningful to community members (Rapp, Shera, & Kisthart, 1993).
- Both the selection of participants and the choice of interventions should reflect the "multilevel and systemic nature of community problems" (Fawcett, 1991, p. 625). Targets of change should include not only individuals (and their proximate environments) who experience a problem directly, but the institutional and social structures that create and sustain community problems.
- Social workers should plan for "small wins" at multiple levels of systems, while maintaining a vision of larger-scale change. In community practice, in which issues often seem overwhelming and intractable, it is particularly important to "think globally and act locally" and to accept that large changes in systems are likely to be achieved incrementally. Fawcett (1991) defined small wins as "those concrete outcomes of modest significance that attract allies and deter opponents" (p. 627).

- Interventions should be replicable and sustainable with local resources. That is, they should build on and enhance the capacities of the community.

At a more immediate level, Fawcett, Seekins, Whang, and Suarez de Balcazar (1984) recommended that the strategies selected for community intervention should, when possible, be inexpensive; demonstrably effective; decentralized (local and small scale); flexible; sustainable with local resources; simple; and compatible with existing customs, beliefs, and values.

References

Allen, J. A. (1993). The constructivist paradigm: Values and ethics. *Journal of Teaching in Social Work, 8*(1-2), 31-54.

Anderson, H., & Goolishian, H. (1988). Human systems as linguistic systems: Preliminary and evolving ideas about the implications for clinical theory. *Family Process, 27*(4), 371-393.

Anderson, H., & Goolishian, H. (1992). The client is the expert: A not-knowing approach to therapy. In S. McNamee & K. J. Gergen (Eds.), *Therapy as social construction* (pp. 25-39). Newbury Park, CA: Sage Publications.

Auerswald, E. H. (1968). Interdisciplinary versus ecological approach. *Family Process, 7*, 202-215.

Barker, R. L. (1995). *The social work dictionary* (3rd ed.). Washington, DC: NASW Press.

Bellah, R. N., Madsen, R., Sullivan, W. M., Swidler, A., & Tipton, S. M. (1985). *Habits of the heart: Individualism and commitment in American life.* New York: Harper & Row.

Berger, P. L., & Neuhaus, R. J. (1977). *To empower people: The role of mediating structures in public policy.* Washington, DC: American Enterprise Institute for Public Policy Research.

Berlin, S. B., & Marsh, J. C. (1993). *Informing practice decisions.* New York: Macmillan.

Bradshaw, C., Soifer, S., & Gutierrez, L. (1994). Toward a hybrid model for effective organizing in communities of color. *Journal of Community Practice, 1*(1), 25-41.

Brower, A. M., & Nurius, P. S. (1993). *Social cognition and individual change: Current theory and counseling guidelines.* Newbury Park, CA: Sage Publications.

Brown, K. S., & Ziefert, M. (1988). Crisis resolution, competence and empowerment: A service model for women. *Journal of Primary Prevention, 9*, 92-103.

Burghardt, S. (1982). *The other side of organizing: Resolving the personal dilemmas and political demands of daily practice.* Cambridge, MA: Schenkman.

Chavis, D. M., & Wandersman, A. (1990). Sense of community in the urban environment: A catalyst for participation and community development. *American Journal of Community Psychology, 18*, 55-81.

Cottrell, L. S., Jr. (1977). The competent community. In R. L. Warren (Ed.), *New perspectives on the American community: A book of readings* (3rd ed., pp. 546–560). Chicago: Rand McNally.

Cox, E. O. (1991). The critical role of social action in empowerment oriented groups. *Social Work with Groups, 14*(2), 77–90.

Cox, F. M. (1987). Communities: Alternative conceptions of community: Implications for community organization practice. In F. M. Cox, J. L. Erlich, J. Rothman, & J. E. Tropman (Eds.), *Strategies of community organization* (4th ed., pp. 232–243). Itasca, IL: F. E. Peacock.

Curtis, K. A. (1989). Help from within: Participatory research in a low-income neighborhood. *Urban Anthropology, 18*, 203–217.

Daley, J. M., & Wong, P. (1994). Community development with emerging ethnic communities. *Journal of Community Practice, 1*(1), 9–24.

Dodd, P., & Gutierrez, L. (1990). Preparing students for the future: A power perspective on community practice. *Administration in Social Work, 14*(2), 63–78.

Eng, E., Salmon, M. E., & Mullan, F. (1992). Community empowerment: The critical base for primary health care. *Family and Community Health, 15*, 1–12.

Etzioni, A. (1993). *The spirit of community: The reinvention of American society.* New York: Touchstone.

Fagan, J. (1987). Neighborhood education, mobilization, and organization for juvenile crime prevention. *Annals of the American Academy of Political and Social Science, 494*, 54–70.

Fawcett, S. B. (1991). Some values guiding community research and action. *Journal of Applied Behavior Analysis, 24*, 621–636.

Fawcett, S. B., Seekins, T., Whang, P. L., Muiu, C., & Suarez de Balcazar, Y. (1980). Involving consumers in decision making. *Social Policy, 13*(2), 36–41.

Fawcett, S. B., Seekins, T., Whang, P. L., & Suarez de Balcazar, Y. (1984). Creating and using technologies for community empowerment. *Prevention in Human Services, 3*, 145–171.

Freire, P. (1973). *Education for critical consciousness.* New York: Seabury Press.

Garbarino, J., Kostelny, K., & Dubrow, N. (1991). *No place to be a child: Growing up in a war zone.* Lexington, MA: Lexington Books.

Garvin, C. D., & Cox, F. M. (1987). A history of community organizing since the Civil War with particular reference to oppressed communities. In F. M. Cox, J. L. Erlich, J. Rothman, & J. E. Tropman (Eds.), *Strategies of community organization* (4th ed., pp. 26–63). Itasca, IL: F. E. Peacock.

Germain, C. B. (1985). The place of community work within an ecological approach to social work practice. In S. H. Taylor & R. W. Roberts (Eds.), *Theory and practice of community social work* (pp. 30–55). New York: Columbia University Press.

Germain, C. B., & Gitterman, A. (1980). *The life model of social work practice*. New York: Columbia University Press.

Gutierrez, L. M. (1990). Working with women of color: An empowerment perspective. *Social Work, 35*, 149–153.

Halpern, R. (1993). Neighborhood-based initiative to address poverty: Lessons from experience. *Journal of Sociology and Social Welfare, 20*, 111–135.

Heller, K. (1989). The return to community. *American Journal of Community Psychology, 17*, 1–15.

Holland, T. P., & Kilpatrick, A. C. (1993). Using narrative techniques to enhance multicultural practice. *Journal of Social Work Education, 29*, 302–308.

Husserl, E. (1970). *The crisis of European science and transcendental phenomenology*. Evanston, IL: Northwestern University Press.

Itzhaky, H., & York, A. S. (1991). Client participation and the effectiveness of community social work intervention. *Research on Social Work Practice, 1*, 387–398.

Johnson, L. C. (1992). *Social work practice: A generalist approach* (4th ed.). Boston: Allyn & Bacon.

Keenan, E., & Pinkerton, J. (1991). Some aspects of empowerment: A case study of work with disadvantaged youth. *Social Work with Groups, 14*(2), 109–124.

Kemp, S. P. (1994). *Social work and systems of knowledge: The concept of environment in social casework theory, 1900–1983*. Unpublished doctoral dissertation, Columbia University School of Social Work.

Kieffer, C. H. (1984). Citizen empowerment: A developmental perspective. *Prevention in Human Services, 3*(2–3), 9–36.

Kramer, R. M., & Specht, H. (Eds.). (1975). *Readings in community organization practice* (2nd ed.). Englewood Cliffs, NJ: Prentice Hall.

Laird, J. (1993). Family-centered practice: Cultural and constructionist reflections. *Journal of Teaching in Social Work, 8*, 77–109.

Lewin, K. (1936). *Principles of topological psychology*. New York. McGraw-Hill.

Lewis, E. A., & Ford, B. (1990). The Network Utilization Project: Incorporating traditional strengths of African-American families in group work practice. *Social Work with Groups, 13*(4), 7–22.

Lightburn, A., & Black, R. (in press). *Social workers as educators*. New York: Columbia University Press.

Lightburn, A., & Kemp, S. P. (1994). Family-support programs: Opportunities for community-based practice. *Families in Society, 75*(1), 16–26.

Longres, J. F., & McLeod, E. (1980). Consciousness raising and social work practice. *Social Casework, 61,* 267–275.

Maluccio, A. (Ed.). (1981). *Promoting competence in clients.* London: Free Press.

Mattaini, M. A. (1993a). Behavior analysis and community practice: A review. *Research on Social Work Practice, 3,* 420–447.

Mattaini, M. A. (1993b). *More than a thousand words: Graphics for clinical practice.* Washington, DC: NASW Press.

Mattaini, M. A., & Kirk, S. A. (1991). Assessing assessment in social work. *Social Work, 36,* 260–266.

McGowan, B. G. (1978). The case advocacy function in child welfare practice. *Child Welfare, 57,* 275–284.

Meyer, C. H. (1970). *Social work: A response to the urban crisis.* New York: Free Press.

Meyer, C. H. (1976). *Social work practice: The changing landscape.* New York: Free Press.

Meyer, C. H. (Ed.). (1983). *Clinical social work in the eco-systems perspective.* New York: Columbia University Press.

Meyer, C. H. (1993). *Assessment in social work practice.* New York: Columbia University Press.

Middleman, R. R., & Goldberg, G. (1974). *Social service delivery: A structural approach to social work practice.* New York: Columbia University Press.

Mondros, J. B., & Berman-Rossi, T. (1991). The relevance of stages of group development theory to community organization practice. *Social Work with Groups, 14*(3–4), 203–221.

Mondros, J. B., & Wilson, S. M. (1994). *Organizing for power and empowerment.* New York: Columbia University Press.

Nurius, P. S., & Gibson, J. W. (1994). *Practitioners' perspectives on sound reasoning: Adding a worker-in-context component.* Unpublished manuscript, Seattle, Washington.

Parsons, R. J. (1991). Empowerment: Purpose and practice principle in social work. *Social Work with Groups, 14*(2), 7–21.

Parsons, R. J., Jorgensen, J. D., & Hernandez, S. H. (1994). *The integration of social work practice.* Pacific Grove, CA: Brooks/Cole.

Pecukonis, E. V., & Wenocur, S. (1994). Perceptions of self and collective efficacy in community organization theory and practice. *Journal of Community Practice, 1*(2), 5–21.

Pincus, A., & Minahan, A. (1973). *Social work practice: Model and method.* Itasca, IL: F. E. Peacock.

Ramey, J. H. (1992). Group work practice in neighborhood centers today. *Social Work with Groups*, *15*(2–3), 193–206.

Rapp, C. A., Shera, W., & Kisthart, W. (1993). Research strategies for empowerment of people with severe mental illness. *Social Work*, *38*, 727–735.

Rappaport, J. (1984). Studies in empowerment: Introduction to the issue. *Prevention in Human Services*, *3*(2–3), 1–7.

Rappaport, J. (1987). Terms of empowerment/exemplars of prevention: Toward a theory for community psychology. *American Journal of Community Psychology*, *15*, 121–145.

Reisch, M., & Wenocur, S. (1986). The future of community organization in social work: Social activism and the politics of profession building. *Social Service Review*, *60*, 50–93.

Richmond, M. E. (1907). *The good neighbor in the modern city*. Philadelphia: J. B. Lippincott.

Rivera, F. G., & Erlich, J. L. (Eds.). (1992). *Community organizing in a diverse society*. Boston: Allyn & Bacon.

Rosen, A., & Livne, S. (1992). Personal versus environmental emphases in formulation of client problems. *Social Work Research and Abstracts*, *29*(4), 12–17.

Rothman, J. (1970). Three models of community organization practice. In F. M. Cox, J. L. Erlich, J. Rothman, & J. E. Tropman (Eds.), *Strategies of community organization: A book of readings* (pp. 20–36). Itasca, IL: F. E. Peacock.

Rothman, J., & Tropman, J. E. (1987). Models of community organization and macro practice perspectives: Their mixing and phasing. In F. M. Cox, J. L. Erlich, J. Rothman, & J. E. Tropman (Eds.), *Strategies of community organization: Macro practice* (4th ed., pp. 3–26). Itasca, IL: F. E. Peacock.

Rubin, H. J., & Rubin, I. S. (1992). *Community organizing and development* (2nd ed.). New York: Maxwell.

Rupp, G. (1991). Communities of collaboration: Shared commitments/common tasks. In L. S. Rouner (Ed.), *On community* (pp. 192–208). Notre Dame, IN: University of Notre Dame Press.

Saleeby, D. (Ed.). (1992). *The strengths perspective in social work practice*. New York: Longman.

Saleeby, D. (1994). Culture, theory, and narrative: The intersection of meanings in practice. *Social Work*, *39*, 351–359.

Sarri, R. C., & Sarri, C. M. (1992). Organizational and community change through participatory action research. *Administration in Social Work*, *16*, 99–122.

Seligman, M. (1972). *Helplessness*. San Francisco: W. H. Freeman.

Sheafor, B. W., Horejsi, C. R., & Horejsi, G. A. (1991). *Techniques and guidelines for social work practice* (2nd ed.). Boston: Allyn & Bacon.

Simon, B. L. (1990). Rethinking empowerment. *Journal of Progressive Human Services*, *1*(1), 27–39.

Siporin, M. (1980). Ecological systems theory in social work. *Journal of Sociology and Social Welfare*, *7*, 507–532.

Solomon, B. (1976). *Black empowerment: Social work in oppressed communities*. New York: Columbia University Press.

Sullivan, W. P. (1992). Reconsidering the environment as a helping resource. In D. Saleeby (Ed.), *The strengths perspective in social work practice* (pp. 148–157). New York: Longman.

Taylor, S. H. (1985). Community work and social work: The community liaison approach. In S. H. Taylor & R. W. Roberts (Eds.), *Theory and practice of community social work* (pp. 179–214). New York: Columbia University Press.

Taylor, S. H., & Roberts, R. W. (1985). The fluidity of practice theory: An overview. In S. H. Taylor & R. W. Roberts (Eds.), *Theory and practice of community social work* (pp. 3–29). New York: Columbia University Press.

Tracy, E. M., & Whittaker, J. K. (1990). The social network map: Assessing social support in clinical social work practice. *Families in Society*, *71*, 461–470.

Tropman, J. E. (1987). Introduction to part I: Common elements of practice. In F. M. Cox, J. L. Erlich, J. Rothman, & J. E. Tropman (Eds.), *Strategies of community organization: Macro practice* (4th ed., pp. 67–70). Itasca, IL: F. E. Peacock.

Van Den Bergh, N., & Cooper, L. B. (Eds). (1986). *Feminist visions for social work*. Silver Spring, MD: National Association of Social Workers.

Warren, R. L. (1978). *The community in America* (3rd ed.). Chicago: Rand McNally.

Webber, M. (1963). Order in diversity: Community without propinquity. In L. Wingo, Jr. (Ed.), *Cities and space: The future use of urban land* (pp. 23–54). Baltimore: Johns Hopkins Press.

Weick, A. (1993). Reconstructing social work education. *Journal of Teaching in Social Work*, *8*(1–2), 11–30.

Weil, M. (1986). Women, community, and organizing. In N. Van Den Bergh & L. B. Cooper (Eds.), *Feminist visions for social work* (pp. 187–210). Silver Spring, MD: National Association of Social Workers.

Weil, M. (1994). Editor's introduction to the journal. *Journal of Community Practice*, *1*(1), xxi–xxxii.

White, M., & Epston, D. (1990). *Narrative means to therapeutic ends*. New York: W. W. Norton.

Whittaker, J. K., Garbarino, J., & Associates. (1983). *Social support networks: Informal helping in the human services*. New York: Aldine.

Wiener, L. S., Spencer, E. D., Davidson, R., & Far, C. (1993). National telephone support groups: A new avenue toward psychosocial support for HIV-infected children and their families. *Social Work with Groups*, *16*(3), 55–71.

Wood, G. G., & Middleman, R. R. (1991). Advocacy and social action: Key elements in the structural approach to direct practice in social work. *Social Work with Groups*, *14*(3–4), 53–63.

Woods, R. A. (1970). The university settlement idea. In J. Addams, B. Bosanquet, F. H. Giddings, et al. (Eds.), *Philanthropy and social progress: Seven essays* (pp. 57–97). Montclair, NJ: Patterson Smith. (Original work published 1893)

Zimmerman, M. A., & Rappaport, J. (1988). Citizen participation, perceived control and psychological empowerment. *American Journal of Community Psychology*, *16*, 725–750.

11

Practice in Organizations

Meredith Hanson

Over 30 years ago Etzioni (1964) introduced his classic primer on modern organizations by writing: "Our society is an organizational society. We are born in organizations, educated by organizations, and most of us spend much of our lives working for organizations. We spend much of our leisure time paying, playing, and praying in organizations. Most of us will die in an organization, and when the time comes for burial, the largest organization of all—the state—must grant official permission" (p. 1). Fifteen years later Meyer (1979) observed that in modern society, "functions once thought to be private and belonging to the family and the intimate community have been transferred to institutions or organizations that are, in sanction and function, 'public'"(p. 1).

If this society can be described accurately as an organizational society in which many private functions have been taken over by public institutions, social workers can be characterized as organizational professionals who guide many of society's most vulnerable citizens through these institutions during times of personal crises. Most social workers carry out these duties as employees of social and human services organizations.

The social agency is "the hidden reality of social work" (Weissman, Epstein, & Savage, 1983, p. 3); it is "the locus of practice and professional services" (Vinter, 1959, p. 242). From the earliest days of the Charity Organization Societies and settlement houses, social work's existence has been tied closely to social agencies. "Unlike other professions, social work was almost exclusively a corporate activity, with little opportunity for independent practice. To carve out a niche, the social worker had to attain hegemony within the agency" (Lubove, 1965, p. 159).

Even though most social work practice occurs in social agencies, other human services organizations (Hasenfeld, 1983), and such nonservice host

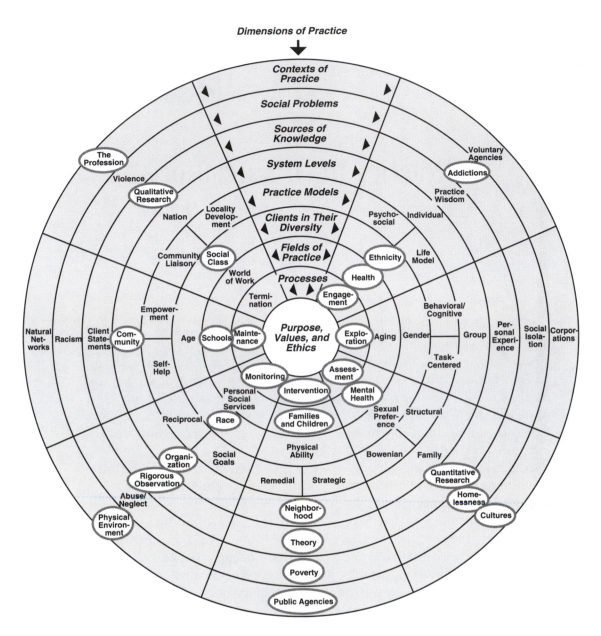

Dimensions of Practice

Contexts of Practice
Social Problems
Sources of Knowledge
System Levels
Practice Models
Clients in Their Diversity
Fields of Practice
Processes

Purpose, Values, and Ethics

The Profession
Violence
Qualitative Research
Nation
Locality Development
Community Liaison
Social Class
World of Work
Termination
Empowerment
Client Statements
Community
Schools
Maintenance
Age
Natural Networks
Racism
Self-Help
Monitoring
Intervention
Personal Social Services
Reciprocal
Race
Families and Children
Organization
Social Goals
Rigorous Observation
Abuse/Neglect
Physical Environment
Remedial
Strategic
Neighborhood
Theory
Poverty
Public Agencies
Physical Ability
Bowenian
Family
Quantitative Research
Homelessness
Cultures
Sexual Preference
Structural
Mental Health
Assessment
Exploration
Engagement
Aging
Gender
Task-Centered
Group
Personal Experience
Social Isolation
Corporations
Health
Ethnicity
Life Model
Behavioral/Cognitive
Psycho-social
Individual
Practice Wisdom
Addictions
Voluntary Agencies

FIGURE 11-1. ELEMENTS OF PRACTICE EMPHASIZED IN WORK WITH ORGANIZATIONS

settings as the military and business corporations (Dane & Simon, 1991; Kurzman & Akabas, 1993), professional social workers are relatively unaware of the extent to which organizational context affects practice. Consequently, they miss many opportunities to influence agency policies and procedures to make them more responsive to clients' needs.

Social work practice settings are powerful molders of social work practice (Zald, 1995). These practice settings provide legitimation and sanction for social services (Hasenfeld, 1983); they control many of the resources social workers need to assist clients (Toseland & Rivas, 1995); and, ultimately, they

206   The Foundations of Social Work Practice

are major sources of social workers' power (Hartman, 1993; Hasenfeld, 1987). Conflicts between agencies and professionals can lead to a loss of benefits and services for clients and low morale among staff (Lipsky, 1984; Marcos, 1988; Marriott, Sexton, & Staley, 1994).

This chapter is about social work practice in and with organizations. The chapter introduces readers to the work setting as both the context and target of professional influence, defines social and human services agencies, discusses several organizational components that are central to understanding the dynamics of agencies, and illustrates ways to assess and influence organizational structure and process.

Definitions

Social and Human Services Agencies

Social and human services agencies are formal organizations whose stated purpose is to enhance "the social, emotional, physical, and/or intellectual well-being of some component of the population" (Brager & Holloway, 1978, p. 2). They include such dissimilar practice settings as hospitals, schools, family service agencies, settlement houses, employee assistance programs, and victims' service agencies. They differ from other organizations with similar objectives in at least two key ways: (1) Their "raw materials" are people who become clients and are transformed or changed in some specified manner, and (2) they are mandated by society to serve the interests of their clients as well as those of society (Hasenfeld, 1983, 1992a).

Human services agencies are created to address social problems and injustices. As such, they are products of societal ideologies, which often are ambivalent and contradictory (Brager & Holloway, 1978; Sarri & Hasenfeld, 1978). They engage in "moral work" (Hasenfeld, 1992a) in that their services contain implicit and explicit meanings about the worth of clients as well as societal expectations of how people should behave and be treated.

Because their raw materials are people and they owe their existence to societal mandates, human services agencies are highly dependent on their external environments. Consequently, environmental pressures have profound implications for their operations. These agencies are accountable to multiple constituent groups with conflicting interests and agendas (Martin, 1987; Perrow, 1978; Taber, 1987), and their efforts to be responsive to one group may interfere with their ability to be accountable to another. For example, hospital clinic hours that are set to fit physicians' and social workers' schedules often create burdens for patients.

It is clear that although social agencies are established to serve particular client groups, their goals are not defined independently. Rather, they are produced by negotiations between human services organizations and their constituents. Furthermore, although professional codes of ethics may prescribe ideals of service that give primacy to clients' interests, human services agencies are not bound to place the interests of individual clients above their own (Gouldner, 1963; McGowan, 1978; Rhodes, 1991). As a result, the mechanisms that an agency creates to survive in uncertain environments may actually impede its capacity to meet the goals of service efficiently and effectively.

Formal Organizations

To understand fully the forces that affect social work practice settings, social workers must be knowledgeable about formal organizations. Literally hundreds of definitions of formal organizations have been proposed. Some of them overlap, others are contradictory, and all reflect particular theoretical perspectives (see Hasenfeld, 1992b; Hirschhorn & Barnett, 1993; Katz & Kahn, 1978; Morgan, 1986; Perrow, 1986; Scott, 1992; Shafritz & Ott, 1992). At the most basic level, an organization is any social unit with identifiable boundaries that has evolved or been created to attain some purpose or purposes. "Formal" organizations, like social and human services agencies, are social units that have been consciously designed a priori (Blau & Scott, 1962). Formal organizations are characterized by written policies, rules, and procedures that guide routine interactions, and they usually are complex, that is, they comprise personnel drawn from several professional disciplines who perform intricate tasks that require specialized education or training (Hage & Aiken, 1970).

Traditionally, formal organizations have been depicted as goal-oriented, rationally designed, thinking machines. The word "organization" is derived from the Greek word *organon*, which means tool or instrument (Morgan, 1986). Thus, it is not surprising that the first definitions of formal organizations emphasized their bureaucratic administrative structures and underscored such rational features as goals (purposes), hierarchical authority structures, divisions of labor, and specialized task arrangements (see, for example, Gerth & Mills, 1958; Weber, 1924/1947). Formal organizations were distinguished from other social systems in these classical formulations by their rational–legal nature and the priority they placed on the attainment of goals.

As knowledge about formal organizations developed, many scholars grew disenchanted with the mechanistic classical definitions, and new conceptualizations, which highlighted other organizational features, were crafted. For example, natural systems perspectives, like the human relations school, emphasized the relevance of noneconomic social rewards, informal communication, and leadership structures for understanding organizational dynamics (Etzioni, 1964). They drew attention to behavioral and normative patterns that emerged as organizational members attempted to minimize stress and organizations tried to survive and maintain themselves (Scott, 1992).

Open systems frameworks expanded on classical definitions by underscoring organizations' links with their environments. They depicted organizations as loosely coupled sets of interrelated, interacting subsystems (Buckley, 1967; Morgan, 1986). Proponents of these views argued that an organization's form is determined, to a large extent, by environmental exchanges (Lawrence & Lorsch, 1967; Scott, 1992).

Many other definitions of formal organizations, which attempt to integrate earlier perspectives and account for new knowledge, have emerged (see

Hasenfeld, 1992b; Scott, 1992). Each is a metaphor of sorts that provides an important, if incomplete, picture of reality. Taken together, they suggest that formal organizations are rationally based social entities characterized by predictable habitual patterns of interaction (organizational structures) that are explicitly arranged for the accomplishment of stated purposes. They are organic, dynamic, and open systems in which alliances form and re-form among organizational members and interest groups as they try to meet organizational goals and their own interests. Typically, organizations develop unique cultures (climates) and multiple formal and informal power centers that affect their operations. As open systems, they respond not only to internal institutional pressures, but to political, economic, and social pressures in the environment.

KEY COMPONENTS OF FORMAL ORGANIZATIONS

Organizational theorists (such as Leavitt, 1965; Scott, 1992) and students of human services agencies (such as Brager & Holloway, 1978; Hasenfeld, 1983; Weissman et al., 1983) suggest that to understand his or her practice setting, a social worker should attend to five key components of an organization: (1) its goals (stated mission or purpose) and any other external and internal demands it faces, (2) its internal structures, (3) its service programs and technologies, (4) the interests and characteristics of its membership, and (5) its environmental context, including the physical setting, prevailing mood, and resources.

Goals

An agency's goals represent its efforts to respond to multiple demands: to serve clients, to maintain smooth internal operations, and to adapt to changing environmental conditions. One would expect an agency's goals to be complementary. However, several factors can lead to the displacement of and conflict among goals. Consider, for example, the goals of service. An agency's service goals include official goals, as articulated in mission statements and other public pronouncements, and operative goals that outline actual operating policies (Perrow, 1961). Official goals usually are formulated in vague, overly broad terms to maintain maximum support among key constituent groups. Operative goals, on the other hand, are more precise and reveal how an agency makes daily decisions about its programs and allocates scarce resources. Operative goals reflect not only an agency's efforts to fulfill its mission but its attempts to respond to self-maintenance needs and to remain adaptive.

When responding to these competing pressures, an agency may subvert its official service goals, and other, sometimes covert, goals may emerge. For example, many mental health clinics establish waiting lists to prevent social workers' caseloads from getting too large and to ensure that clients receive all diagnostic evaluations before they are assigned to clinicians. Although these procedures may make the clinics' operations efficient and be consistent with professional standards, they can become organizational barriers to the delivery of services. It has been well-documented that long waiting lists prevent many people from receiving the assistance they need. Furthermore, long waiting lists and intake periods can serve latent purposes by enabling agencies to "cream off" pools of preferred clients who are most likely to accept the type of interventions the agencies offer (Brager & Holloway, 1978; Gitterman & Miller, 1989). Thus, agencies' decisions that are justified by self-maintenance needs can clash with service goals by interfering with the delivery of care to potential clients.

Internal Structures

Formal structures

Organizations' internal structures consist of role sets (networks of related role positions) and predictable patterns of interaction that exist among their members. They are the vehicles through which services are delivered to clients (Rothman, 1995). Formal organizational structures are most apparent in an agency's rules and regulations, task specializations, and hierarchical authority structures, as depicted in organizational charts and administrative manuals.

No particular formal structure is best suited to all agencies, and the structure that best fits a particular agency depends on such factors as the agency's mission, the nature of its services, environmental conditions, and the training of its staff (Netting, Kettner, & McMurtry, 1993). Decentralized, collegial structures may work well in smaller agencies such as family service centers that have highly professionalized staff who work independently of each other. More formalized, professional bureaucratic structures seem better suited to larger organizations such as public assistance offices that need expert knowledge yet require close coordination and communication among workers (Litwak, 1961). Matrix and project structures (Miles, 1975; Morgan, 1986), in which professionals work as members of interdisciplinary teams that are assigned to particular functions or projects (such as intake or community outreach), are better fits for agencies such as addiction treatment centers with many functional specialties that require input from employees who are drawn from several professional disciplines.

Informal structures

In addition to formal structures, all agencies have informal structures, which are more fluid and more closely linked with members' personal attributes than are formal structures (Etzioni, 1964). Informal structures include the unofficial interaction and communication patterns that develop as people adapt to their work settings and do their jobs. They can be thought of as work-based mutual aid networks, which are revealed by observing who people talk to, where they go for advice, and how they actually complete their work assignments (Weissman et al., 1983).

An important aspect of an agency's informal structure is its organizational culture, the learned and shared assumptions that regulate such behaviors as workers' communication styles and their cooperativeness. An agency's culture, or climate, reflects the values of the formal system and their reinterpretation in the informal system. Consequently, the informal culture, as expressed in the staff's daily activities, may differ greatly from the agency's purported values, as articulated in formal documents. An agency's culture is molded by many factors, including its history, its institutional and physical setting, its staff, its communication networks, and its authority structures (Albrecht, 1994; Katz & Kahn, 1978). This culture evolves over time as workers respond to the pressures of their jobs, establish social supports, and create comfortable work environments.

Informal norms can oil the wheels of an agency by providing incentives and explanations in areas in which the formal structure is deficient (Barnard, 1968; Perrow, 1986), or they can undermine the formal structure by furnishing competing arguments and legitimating individuals who are disillusioned with the agency's goals, programs, and procedures. How they evolve is affected by the exchanges that take place among formally designated authority figures, line workers, and their unofficial peer leaders. Thus, depending on staff members' experiences with the administrators and their interpretation of administrative motives, the same program initiatives may be viewed as either potentially useful innovations or more "busy work."

Consider, for example, the following. In response to a mandate from state regulators, the director of an addictions treatment facility ordered that all the workers must write "interdisciplinary biopsychosocial summaries" for clients. The purpose of these summaries, which were to be included in the clients' clinical records, was to document that staff from each professional discipline were involved in the development of comprehensive intervention plans for the clients. The workers in one clinic embraced the new procedure, whereas those in another clinic opposed it, citing increased paperwork and time constraints.

An examination of the two clinics revealed that the staffs' reactions were directly related to the clinics' cultures. In the first clinic, there was a history of collaboration between line workers and supervisors about procedural changes. Thus, when the new procedure was proposed, the line workers' opinions were sought, and the procedure was modified on the basis of their input. The line workers believed that they were treated fairly, and they incorporated the procedure into their routines. In the second clinic, there was a history of many procedural changes in which workers' opinions were not solicited. Thus, when the new directive was introduced, the staff members rallied around each other to oppose the change. Whereas in the first clinic an informal structure that reinforced collaboration and cooperation among the clinic members had developed, in the second clinic, an adversarial climate, which clashed with the formal structure, existed. In both clinics, the staff's access or lack of access to organizational decision making affected the organizational culture and contributed to the evolution of informal structures that had a marked impact on the clinics' process, the staff's morale, and the care that clients received.

Service Programs and Technologies

Human services technologies are the activities and tools (for example, hardware such as computers and other equipment and professional knowledge and skills) that agencies use to assist clients. Three of their characteristics have particular relevance for organizationally based practice. First, human services technologies are "intensive" in that they draw on a variety of techniques that are selected, in part, on the basis of feedback from clients (Thompson, 1967). Second, most human services technologies are indeterminate (their impact is variable and uncertain, and there is little consensus about desirable outcomes), and for many, there is no evidence of their effectiveness (Sarri & Hasenfeld, 1978). Third, although they are applied within an agency context, human services technologies are extremely sensitive to environmental pressures (Brager & Holloway, 1978).

These characteristics can cause dilemmas for social services agencies, which strive for technological predictability and certainty. To increase their control over their work, agencies try to seal off their core technologies from environmental and other influences (Mintzberg, 1979; Thompson, 1967) by developing routines (Lauffer, 1984) and ideological systems (Hasenfeld, 1992a) that support the use of particular practice approaches or models. Although the ideologies and routines fulfill an organizational self-maintenance function by reducing stress and uncertainty, they can become ingrained and resistant to change. Consequently, they may have unintended consequences: Clients who seek assistance may find that they receive what an agency has to offer, rather than what they need, and workers who question prevailing practice models may face deep-rooted, ideologically based, and structurally supported opposition.

To understand how an agency frames its practice, social workers should identify the core technologies that are central to agency operations. Then, they should locate the ideologies and routines that support these technologies. To increase their professional autonomy within an agency, social workers should develop their knowledge of the core technologies, appeal to an agency's own quality-control mechanisms to evaluate existing practice approaches, and emphasize responsiveness to clients' needs as a criteria for validating the helping process (see Lauffer, 1984).

Interests and Characteristics of Members
The work of human services agencies is carried out by "social actors" (members) who perform the agencies' tasks for monetary and other reinforcers. "Without them, there is no organization, no structure, no situation. . . . [They] are the instruments of both continuity . . . and change" in agencies (Scott, 1992, p. 19). Although all members may believe in an agency's mission, their views on its policies and their actions will vary, depending on such factors as their personal characteristics, job titles and functions, and involvement in other organizations and groups.

An agency's members are stakeholders who are interested in both the success of an agency's programs and their place in that agency. Thus, to understand their motives and actions, one should examine an agency's programs and goals and how any changes will affect different personnel. An agency's members generally act in their own self-interests, as well as in those of the agency and its clients. If a particular programmatic change adds to a worker's power, prestige, and security, he or she is apt to support it; if the same change threatens the worker's position, he or she is likely to oppose it. A hospital social worker, for example, may assume responsibility for coordinating discharge planning because she believes she will be able to help clients. Her enthusiasm for the task will increase if she perceives that her new role will add to her status and influence. Another social worker, who also believes that the change will aid clients, may be less supportive of it if he suspects that it will harm his organizational position by drawing resources away from projects with which he is involved.

Clearly, many variables must be considered to understand agency members' actions and motives. Although individuals usually act to protect their self-interests, it is difficult to define their interests. Thus, to clarify how agency members will act in particular situations, one must examine the positions they hold, the power and resources they control, and the impact of organizational processes on their work lives. If these factors are understood, one should be able to predict a worker's actions under different circumstances. If these factors remain unknown, it is more difficult to anticipate how agency members will react to different organizational practices (Brager & Holloway, 1978; Gummer, 1990; Mechanic, 1992).

Environmental Context
The environmental context consists of a multidimensional set of interacting political–legal, economic, technological, ecological, physical, and sociocultural forces that affect an agency's programs and structures. Its impact can be shown in several examples. First, hospitals have become more formalized (have many detailed and prescriptive written policies and procedures) because of directives from regulatory bodies and concerns about lawsuits. Second, the public's changed sentiment and the availability of fingerprinting technologies have supported an "administrative culture" (Bane & Ellwood, 1994) in some public assistance offices that value preventing fraud more than assisting vulnerable people. Third, whether social workers distribute condoms to high school students in groups that are geared to preventing the acquired immune deficiency syndrome (AIDS) is contingent on authorization from people in the community (such as parents).

An agency and its environment can be thought of as a set of concentric circles with the agency in the middle. The outer circle is the distal *environment,* the broad political, economic, and social conditions that affect all agencies. The *distal* environment changes slowly and cannot be altered by individual agencies. It sets the parameters for the types of services and programs that emerge in a society (Hasenfeld, 1983). The next circle is the *proximal geographic and sociocultural context.* The neighborhoods and communities in which agencies are located have a direct impact on service arrangements. Agency programs (such as health fairs and ethnic-sensitive services) are often based on community needs assessments; the way they are delivered may be shaped by input from community members and their representatives (see

Gutierrez, 1992). The third circle, and the one that has the most immediate impact on an agency's daily operations, is the agency's *task environment*—its beneficiaries (clients and their family members), funders, providers of nonfiscal resources, competitors, providers of complementary services, members of its service network, and legitimators (including advocacy groups and government bodies) (Lauffer, 1984). The task environment affects who an agency serves and how it serves them.

Several dimensions of an agency's environment help explain differences in programs (Brager & Holloway, 1978; Hahn, 1994; Hasenfeld, 1983; Perrow, 1986). First, the practice ideologies and rules that regulate different fields of practice limit what is permitted. Second, political trends and economic conditions affect the public's support for social services programs. Third, demographic changes, as well as competition for scarce resources (funding and clients), spur agencies to become innovative.

Answers to questions such as the following will help one discover how the environment affects an agency as well as its capacity to adapt to environmental pressures: What are an agency's funding sources, and what government bodies regulate its policies and programs? What client populations does it serve, and how does it attract new clients? What mechanisms exist to ensure that an agency is accountable to clients, funders, and other constituents? How does an agency get information about the environment? What is the quality of its communication (open or closed, friendly or hostile) with different environmental groups (local politicians, other agencies, the mass media, for example)?

ORGANIZATIONAL PRACTICE

Competent organizational practitioners see beyond the boundaries of individual cases. They maintain a shifting focus that allows them to understand how the troubles of individual clients represent larger practice issues in their agencies. When someone is referred to a social agency, several things can happen. In an ideal situation, the person's needs fit neatly within the agency's service structure and he or she receives help. Even in an agency that is carefully designed to be responsive to clients, however, there may occasionally be a poor match between a client's needs and the agency's capacity to fulfill them. When adequate services exist elsewhere and a social worker assesses that a client can be helped by another facility, he or she may refer the client to that agency. In other instances (for example, when the poor fit is an "isolated" case), the social worker may opt to advocate on the client's behalf, creatively interpret policies, and "stretch" existing programs so they help the client. When the poor fit represents more serious organizational dysfunctions that affect a class of clients, social workers have an ethical and professional responsibility to encourage organizational change. How they do so is a function of such factors as the nature and severity of the organizational problem, their assessment of conditions in their agencies, support from other staff, and their own resources.

There is an extensive social work literature on strategies for promoting innovation and change "from below" in social agencies (see, for example, Bargal

& Schmid, 1992; Brager & Holloway, 1978; Frey, 1990; Kettner, Daley, & Nichols, 1985; McGowan, 1978; Netting et al., 1993; Resnick & Patti, 1980; Rothman, Erlich, & Teresa, 1981). Although this literature cannot be reviewed in depth in this chapter, the following seven core practice tasks can be gleaned. To effect change in social agencies, social workers must (1) define the organizational problems that block the delivery of services; (2) "read" the agency; (3) pinpoint feasible solutions; (4) develop and select a strategy for organizational change; (5) prepare the agency and themselves for change; (6) initiate the strategy; and (7) monitor, evaluate, and revise the strategy, so the change will be institutionalized. The following case example illustrates aspects of these practice tasks.

Case Example

Two social workers employed at the Princeshire Clinic, an alcoholism treatment facility affiliated with a large medical school, identified a problem that troubled them:

> Over a three-month period, we noticed that 15 applicants were turned away because they had schizophrenia or bipolar disorder, which the intake workers said made them "inappropriate" for treatment in an alcohol clinic. All had serious drinking problems and would have been admitted if they did not have coexisting mental disorders.

Defining the problem

Organizational change begins when social workers determine that an organizational element is adversely affecting an agency's responsiveness to clients (Brager & Holloway, 1978; Resnick & Patti, 1980). Problem definitions focus the change effort and suggest its consequences for the agency, clients, and society. Useful problem definitions have seven features: (1) they are concrete and operational (make abstract concepts observable); (2) they are client centered (stress the significance of the problem for the care of clients); (3) they locate a problem in the agency by specifying whether it is structural (related to an agency's procedures), technological (arising from an agency's practice modalities), or personnel related (caused by the quality of the staff) (Brager & Holloway, 1978); (4) they do not confuse a problem with its solution; (5) they put a problem in context by suggesting why it exists (its history, sources, and adaptive functions); (6) they can be partialized; and (7) they suggest possible solutions. The two social workers' problem definition at the Princeshire Clinic was this:

> We discovered that a group home for patients who were discharged from the state psychiatric hospital recently opened near the clinic. Although the residents received medication and therapy, some began to drink heavily. The case managers referred those people to our clinic. Because we had no policy on applicants with mental disorders, the alcoholism counselors who conducted most

of the intake interviews declined to admit them. We clearly had a structural problem in the clinic. We also had a technological problem because we had no services for clients with dual diagnoses.

Because the clinic's resources were limited and there was resistance to admitting these applicants, we decided to partialize our plans. Specifically, we planned to request that one of us be assigned to intake and that we assess 15 dually diagnosed clients for admission. We hoped to develop and evaluate one treatment group that would be designed specifically for them.

Reading the agency

Once the initial problem definition has been formulated, social workers must read their agency (identify and assess the salient forces that affect its stability). They must ascertain how different constituent groups and individuals perceive the problem and how these groups and individuals may react to any proposal for change. They also must identify key individuals who must be involved in a change effort—critical decision makers who can give the go-ahead to a change; facilitators, who will support a change and who can influence other key actors; and resisters, who will actively or passively oppose a change (Brager & Holloway, 1978). Several useful tools, such as organizational ecomapping (Mattaini, 1993) and force-field analysis (Brager & Holloway, 1992), can be used to analyze the transactions among subsystems and to locate organizational supports and resistances for different change options. The two social workers at the Princeshire Clinic used these tools in their analysis:

> We completed an organizational ecomap in which we identified the relevant agencies and personnel that would affect our plans. They included the clinic director (the critical decision maker), our supervisor (facilitator), the alcoholism counselors (resisters), other social workers (most of whom were neutral), the clients, the group home, the medical school, and the state offices of substance abuse and mental health.
>
> A force-field analysis identified organizational and environmental forces that we could draw on to support our ideas. For example, the clinic director was committed to providing good care to clients and encouraged the staff to take the initiative. State and local pressure to assist deinstitutionalized patients was growing, and at least two other substance abuse clinics in the city had established small programs for dually diagnosed clients. The medical school was research oriented and urged the clinic to be innovative. The group home was interested in developing a joint initiative. The clinic had a strong service ideology.
>
> Counteracting these driving forces were restraining forces: The alcoholism counselors' practice ideology did not support a change. The clinic already had a waiting list for other applicants,

and there was no money available to expand services. Some clients were frightened by seeing people with obvious mental disorders in the waiting room. The clinic had no psychiatrist to consult on the care of such clients.

Pinpointing feasible solutions

On the basis of their preliminary analyses, social workers must develop potential solutions that are acceptable to their constituents and that will increase their agencies' responsiveness to clients. Agencies will resist any change (Frey, 1990). Practitioners can lower their agencies' resistance and increase the feasibility of proposed solutions in several ways. For example, partializing and introducing a change incrementally will make it more acceptable (Rothman et al., 1981). Feasibility also increases when potential solutions are directly relevant to the identified problem, are simple, do not depart radically from an agency's ideology, are reversible (can be undone), are operational, and are economical (their potential benefits justify the costs involved). The two social workers described the next steps they took:

> After we completed our assessment, we got our supervisor's permission to visit the two facilities that provide services for dually diagnosed clients; we also searched the professional literature. We decided that by modifying our ideas, we might be able to sell them to the staff. We opted to propose that the clinic should admit 15 group home residents on a trial basis and that these clients should be assigned to our team (an alcoholism counselor who backed the idea was on our team). To gain support, we suggested that our supervisor assess the applicants' needs to be certain we could manage them. We also proposed that a non-confrontational, skills-focused group should be formed for these clients. (The literature and the other facilities recommended this type of group for dually diagnosed clients.)

Selecting a change strategy

Social workers must make two decisions at this point. First, they must decide whether to intervene alone or with a task group. Because of the risks involved, the feelings evoked, line workers' relative lack of power, and the need to delegate tasks and responsibilities, organizational change from below usually involves group-based strategies. Individual strategies are more viable when a social worker is surer about views of or has direct access to the key actors.

The next decision is whether to use collaborative, mediatory, or conflict strategies (Brager & Holloway, 1978; McGowan, 1978). A collaborative strategy, characterized by open communication and joint action, works best when there is little disagreement about a problem and its solution, the participants' relative power is equal, and relationships are close. A mediatory strategy, distinguished by negotiation, persuasion, and political maneuvering, is used when a social worker hopes to reach a compromise despite some disagreement about the situation. A conflict strategy, which is coercive, is used only when there is fundamental disagreement between parties and a social worker decides that an agency will not respond to other strategies; because this strategy is volatile, it is rarely used to achieve internal change. In most situations social workers use collaboration and mediation to influence their agencies, as did the two social workers at the Princeshire Clinic:

> We decided to recruit our supervisor and the alcoholism counselor on our team and form an "ad hoc" dual-diagnosis study group to gain credibility and influence. Both agreed, and our supervisor informed the director that we were meeting to discuss clinical issues that arose in assisting clients with mental disorders. We worked collaboratively to develop our ideas. Our limited experience with a few dually diagnosed clients who "slipped through" the intake process suggested that we could help them. We were concerned about medication, but a case manager told us that the group home's psychiatrist would provide medication and case consultation.

> We decided to use mediation with the director, alcoholism counselors, and clients. We planned to appeal to the director's commitment to caring for clients and to point out how a creative program would impress funders and the medical school. To reach the alcoholism counselors, we considered discussing our positive experiences working with dually diagnosed clients at two of the weekly all-staff case conferences. We decided to address the clients' concerns by asking the agency to purchase informational pamphlets on alcoholism and mental illness. We also planned to have the alcoholism counselor on our team speak about psychiatric symptoms in his alcohol education groups.

Preparing the agency and staff members for change

For change to occur, agency members must become aware of the organizational problem, be dissatisfied with the status quo, and have hope that realistic options for correcting the problem exist. In short, a system that has organized itself around a problem must be destabilized. Awareness can be increased and stress can be induced in several ways. Social workers can raise their concerns at staff meetings and in discussions with individual staff members. A relatively safe and effective tactic is to ask "informational questions" without suggesting answers (Brager & Holloway, 1978). Stress also can be induced if social workers pick up on any "general" dissatisfaction that exists and use this mood to challenge the myth that "everything is OK" in an agency.

Besides inducing stress, social workers must position themselves personally and structurally to maximize their capacity to promote change (Brager & Holloway, 1978; Mechanic, 1992). They can increase their personal influence by appealing to the values and interests they share with other workers and by doing favors for them. They can gain credibility by developing knowledge and expertise on the problem situation. Structurally, they can increase their power by aligning themselves with authority figures in an agency, by forming coalitions with informal peer leaders, and by joining committees that allow them to work directly on the problem, as the two social workers at the Princeshire Clinic did:

> Once we decided that our plan was feasible, we tried to raise our coworkers' consciousness. At staff meetings we asked if anyone was familiar with state initiatives for treating dually diagnosed clients. We wondered aloud what happened to "all the clients" we sent away from the clinic. We also began to speak individually with some alcoholism counselors and offered to help those who were having trouble with some clients. Our supervisor met regularly with the clinic director and gave him written reports summarizing our visits to the other agencies and our literature search. She also described anecdotal impressions from our clinical work with dually diagnosed clients.

Initiating the change strategy

When agency members have been prepared, social workers can make their proposal public. Among the decisions they must make at this time are to whom to present the proposal and how to make the presentation. They also must divide tasks and prepare a negotiating strategy. They should anticipate that they may be asked to modify their plans and should think about how to do so. They must shape their arguments, develop alternatives and trade-offs, and identify any leverage they have. In this regard, the two Princeshire Clinic social workers did the following:

> We decided that our supervisor should bring the proposal to the director. The director respected our supervisor and had accepted her opinions on other matters. We and the alcoholism counselor on our team would float the idea without its specifics among our coworkers. Although we knew that it was risky to do so because one of them might argue against the plan before it was fully outlined for the director, we hoped to prepare our coworkers for change and uncover any opposition.

> Our supervisor proposed to the director that 15 group home residents be admitted to the clinic and assigned to our team. A social worker and the alcoholism counselor would form and lead a skills-focused group for them with the goal of helping them stop drinking. The group would meet twice a week. The group home's psychiatrist would continue to medicate the clients.

> Our supervisor suggested that we should monitor and make any indicated changes in the group over the next 12 months. At that time, we would write an evaluation report, so the director could decide whether to continue the program.

The director agreed with our plans. But, he agreed to only 10 admissions and cut the evaluation period to six months. He also directed the supervisor to give him biweekly reports on the clients' progress. He reserved the right to abort the program at any time.

Monitoring, evaluating, and revising the strategy
Once a proposal has been accepted, social workers implement their plans. Among the challenges they face during this stage are maintaining the commitment of superiors, nurturing members of the task group, maintaining links with other organizational operations, handling any new opposition that arises, altering the agency's and program's structures if necessary, and standardizing procedures to facilitate the generalization and dissemination of the findings (Brager & Holloway, 1978; Gummer, 1990; Resnick & Patti, 1980). The two social workers at the Princeshire Clinic desribed their experiences during this stage as follows:

> During the trial period, 15 dually diagnosed clients were admitted to the clinic. Five were rehospitalized, so there were never more than 10 such clients attending the clinic. Because 10 clients were too many to manage in one group, we formed two groups of five people. Some of the clients decompensated in the waiting room, upsetting other clients and staff, and we had to respond to the fear that was generated. One activity that was particularly helpful was having three dually diagnosed clients and the group home's psychiatrist come to a staff meeting to talk about the problems they faced in recovery.

> Our study group continued to meet weekly, and our supervisor gave regular reports to the director. We closely monitored the clients' attendance at group and individual sessions as well as their drinking status and general functioning. At three months, we wrote a draft procedure for working with dually diagnosed clients. At the end of six months, we delivered our final report, which the director presented at a staff meeting. Essentially, we learned that the presence of dually diagnosed clients did not disrupt the clinic's operations. Also, these clients seemed to benefit from our help. They attended regularly, six had been sober for four to five months, and their adaptation to the community improved.

> The director accepted and revised our draft procedures and authorized us to continue admitting dually diagnosed clients. He also began preparing a proposal with the medical school to get state funding to expand services for dually diagnosed clients.

CONCLUSION
Social workers are organizational professionals who must decide daily how to help clients humanely and effectively. Inevitably, they will encounter agency

arrangements that thwart their efforts. Thus, it is crucial that they be willing and able to look beyond casework and explore all options for aiding people in need. Much has been learned about human services agencies in recent years. "No longer are [they] a backdrop, but rather—for good or ill—they are a significant reality" in professional practice (Meyer, 1979, p. 12). To challenge dysfunctional organizational processes, social workers must develop a reflective skepticism about their agencies. They must be masterful clinicians who are knowledgeable about and skilled at organizational assessment and intervention. By starting with an attitude of helping people, they will find the opportunity and courage to use their knowledge and skills to improve their agency's responsiveness to clients.

REFERENCES

Albrecht, K. (1994). *The northbound train: Finding the purpose, setting the direction, shaping the destiny of your organization*. New York: American Management Association.

Bane, M. J., & Ellwood, D. T. (1994). *Welfare realities: From rhetoric to reform*. Cambridge, MA: Harvard University Press.

Bargal, D., & Schmid, H. (Eds.). (1992). Organizational change and development in human service organizations [Special issue]. *Administration in Social Work, 16*(3–4).

Barnard, C. (1968). *The functions of the executive*. Cambridge, MA: Harvard University Press.

Blau, P. M., & Scott, W. R. (1962). *Formal organizations: A comparative approach*. San Francisco: Chandler.

Brager, G., & Holloway, S. (1978). *Changing human service organizations*. New York: Free Press.

Brager, G., & Holloway, S. (1992). Assessing prospects for organizational change: The uses of force-field analysis. *Administration in Social Work, 16*(3–4), 15–28.

Buckley, W. (1967). *Sociology and modern systems theory*. Englewood Cliffs, NJ: Prentice Hall.

Dane, B. O., & Simon, B. L. (1991). Resident guests: Social workers in host settings. *Social Work, 36*, 208–213.

Etzioni, A. (1964). *Modern organizations*. Englewood Cliffs, NJ: Prentice Hall.

Frey, G. A. (1990). A framework for promoting organizational change. *Families in Society, 71*, 142–147.

Gerth, H., & Mills, C. W. (Eds.). (1958). *From Max Weber: Essays in sociology*. New York: Oxford University Press.

Gitterman, A., & Miller, I. (1989). The influence of the organization on clinical practice. *Clinical Social Work Journal, 17*, 151–163.

Gouldner, A. (1963). The secrets of organizations. In *Social welfare forum, 1963* (pp. 161–177). New York: Columbia University Press.

Gummer, B. (1990). *The politics of social administration.* Englewood Cliffs, NJ: Prentice Hall.

Gutierrez, L. M. (1992). Empowering ethnic minorities in the twenty-first century: The role of human service organizations. In Y. Hasenfeld (Ed.), *Human services as complex organizations* (pp. 320-338). Newbury Park, CA: Sage Publications.

Hage, J., & Aiken, M. (1970). *Social change in complex organizations.* New York: Random House.

Hahn, A. J. (1994). *The politics of caring: Human services at the local level.* Boulder, CO: Westview Press.

Hartman, A. (1993). The professional is political. *Social Work, 38,* 365–366, 504.

Hasenfeld, Y. (1983). *Human service organizations.* Englewood Cliffs, NJ: Prentice Hall.

Hasenfeld, Y. (1987). Power in social work practice. *Social Service Review, 61,* 469–483.

Hasenfeld, Y. (1992a). The nature of human service organizations. In Y. Hasenfeld (Ed.), *Human services as complex organizations* (pp. 3–23). Newbury Park, CA: Sage Publications.

Hasenfeld, Y. (1992b). Theoretical approaches to human service organizations. In Y. Hasenfeld (Ed.), *Human services as complex organizations* (pp. 24–44). Newbury Park, CA: Sage Publications.

Hirschhorn, L., & Barnett, C. K. (1993). *The psychodynamics of organizations.* Philadelphia: Temple University Press.

Katz, D., & Kahn, R. L. (1978). *The social psychology of organizations* (rev. ed.). New York: John Wiley & Sons.

Kettner, P., Daley, J. M., & Nichols, A. W. (1985). *Initiating change in organizations and communities.* Monterey, CA: Brooks/Cole.

Kurzman, P. A., & Akabas, S. H. (Eds.). (1993). *Work and well-being: The occupational social work advantage.* Washington, DC: NASW Press.

Lauffer, A. (1984). *Understanding your social agency.* Newbury Park, CA: Sage Publications.

Lawrence, P. R., & Lorsch, J. W. (1967). *Organization and environment: Managing differentiation and integration.* Boston: Harvard University Graduate School of Business Administration.

Leavitt, H. J. (1965). Applied organizational change in industry: Structural, technological, and humanistic approaches. In J. G. March (Ed.), *Handbook of organizations* (pp. 1144–1170). Chicago: Rand McNally.

Lipsky, M. (1984). Bureaucratic disentitlement in social welfare programs. *Social Service Review, 58,* 3–27.

Litwak, E. (1961). Models of bureaucracy which permit conflict. *American Journal of Sociology, 67,* 177–184.

Lubove, R. (1965). *The professional altruist: The emergence of social work as a career, 1880–1930.* New York: Atheneum.

Marcos, L. R. (1988). Dysfunctions in public psychiatric bureaucracies. *American Journal of Psychiatry, 145,* 331–334.

Marriott, A., Sexton, L., & Staley, D. (1994). Components of job satisfaction in psychiatric social workers. *Health and Social Work, 19,* 199–205.

Martin, P. Y. (1987). Multiple constituencies and performance in social welfare organizations: Action strategies for directors. *Administration in Social Work, 11*(3–4), 223–239.

Mattaini, M. A. (1993). *More than a thousand words: Graphics for clinical practice.* Washington, DC: NASW Press.

McGowan, B. G. (1978). Strategies in bureaucracies. In J. S. Mearig (Ed.), *Working for children: Ethical issues beyond professional guidelines* (pp. 155–180). San Francisco: Jossey-Bass.

Mechanic, D. (1992). Sources of power of lower ranking participants in complex organizations. In J. M. Shafritz & J. S. Ott (Eds.), *Classics of organization theory* (3rd ed., pp. 424–431). Pacific Grove, CA: Brooks/Cole.

Meyer, C. H. (1979). Introduction. In C. H. Meyer (Ed.), *Making organizations work for people* (pp. 1–12). Washington, DC: National Association of Social Workers.

Miles, R. E. (1975). *Theories of management.* New York: McGraw-Hill.

Mintzberg, H. (1979). *The structure of organizations.* Englewood Cliffs, NJ: Prentice Hall.

Morgan, G. (1986). *Images of organization.* Newbury Park, CA: Sage Publications.

Netting, F. E., Kettner, P. M., & McMurtry, S. L. (1993). *Social work macro practice.* New York: Longman.

Perrow, C. (1961). The analysis of goals in complex organizations. *American Sociological Review, 26,* 856–866.

Perrow, C. (1978). Demystifying organizations. In R. C. Sarri & Y. Hasenfeld (Eds.), *The management of human services* (pp. 105–120). New York: Columbia University Press.

Perrow, C. (1986). *Complex organizations: A critical essay* (3rd ed.). New York: McGraw-Hill.

Resnick, H., & Patti, R. J. (Eds.). (1980). *Change from within: Humanizing social welfare organizations.* Philadelphia: Temple University Press.

Rhodes, M. L. (1991). *Ethical dilemmas in social work practice.* Milwaukee: Family Service America.

Rothman, J., Erlich, J. L., & Teresa, J. G. (1981). *Changing organizations and community programs.* Newbury Park, CA: Sage Publications.

Rothman, J. (1995). Approaches to community intervention. In J. Rothman, J. E. Erlich, & J. L. Tropman (Eds.), *Strategies of community intervention* (5th ed., pp. 26–63). Itasca, IL: F. E. Peacock.

Sarri, R. C., & Hasenfeld, Y. (Eds.). (1978). *The management of human services.* New York: Columbia University Press.

Scott, W. R. (1992). *Organizations: Rational, natural, and open systems* (3rd ed.). Englewood Cliffs, NJ: Prentice Hall.

Shafritz, J. M., & Ott, J. S. (1992). *Classics of organization theory* (3rd ed.). Pacific Grove, CA: Brooks/Cole.

Taber, M. A. (1987). A theory of accountability for the human services and implications for social program design. *Administration in Social Work, 11*(3–4), 115–126.

Thompson, J. D. (1967). *Organizations in action.* New York: McGraw-Hill.

Toseland, R. W., & Rivas, R. F. (1995). *An introduction to group work practice* (2nd ed.). Boston: Allyn & Bacon.

Vinter, R. D. (1959). The social structure of service. In A. J. Kahn (Ed.), *Issues in American social work* (pp. 242–269). New York: Columbia University Press.

Weber, M. (1947). *The theory of social and economic organization* (A. H. Henderson & T. Parsons, Trans.). Glencoe, IL: Free Press. (Original work published 1924)

Weissman, H., Epstein, I., & Savage, A. (1983). *Agency-based social work.* Philadelphia: Temple University Press.

Zald, M. N. (1995). Organizations: Organizations as polities; an analysis of community organization agencies. In J. Rothman, J. E. Erlich, & J. L. Tropman (Eds.), *Strategies of community intervention* (5th ed., pp. 129–139). Itasca, IL: F. E. Peacock.

12

Generalist Practice: People and Programs

Mark A. Mattaini

A s is clear from the previous chapters, social work practice includes work with and for individuals, families, formed and natural groups, neighborhoods and communities, organizations, and even nations. The profession developed, in significant part, from separate professional groups that were working at each level; these groups came together as the National Association of Social Workers only in the 1950s. Until the 1970s, most graduate schools of social work were organized by "method"—casework, group work, community organization, and administration—and most students were trained for practice in only one of these areas. With the work of Bartlett (1970) and others in the late 1960s and early 1970s, the "common base" of social work knowledge and values at all systemic levels was clarified. Generalist practice is an effort to expand the social worker's knowledge base so he or she can choose the most promising interventive strategy at the most appropriate level.

There are three requirements for selecting the most effective and efficient approach to dealing with a client's problems: an understanding of the needs of the case, the skills of practice at multiple systemic levels (as reflected in the preceding chapters), and knowledge of how to mix and phase them effectively, which is the core of this chapter. Much of social work practice happens through organizations and "programs" that—at least ideally—emerge and evolve in response to the particulars of the social problems that they address. Therefore, basic skills in program development are an important facet of generalist practice and are presented in the final section of the chapter.

Generalist practice is an organic whole, not simply an aggregation of distinct roles. Although it may be necessary to learn practice in artificially discrete pieces, ideally graduate-level practitioners do not so much see themselves as being "group workers," "administrators," or "advocates" at different moments in time; rather, they recognize the coherence and flow among the activities they perform as social workers and see how they work together to address clients' needs.

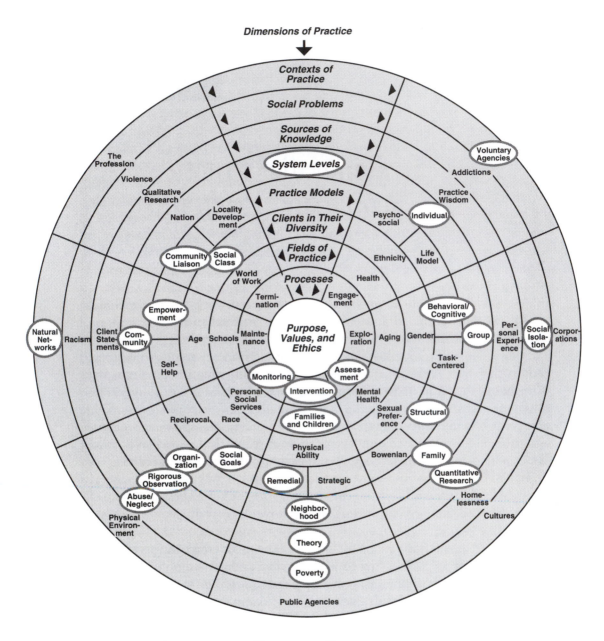

FIGURE 12-1. DIMENSIONS OF GENERALIST PRACTICE

Different functions require somewhat different skills (although many are useful at multiple levels). Ultimately, however, the goal is to achieve a professional identity as a generalist social worker who does what is necessary, in collaboration with a client, to engage the problem, *at whatever systemic level*. Figure 12-2, for example, is a Quick Scan (a form of ecomap, Mattaini, 1993) portraying the situation of a client, Robert, with multiple complaints and issues, including depression, what he defines as a "sexual addiction" for which he participates in a 12-step group (which he indicates has not worked well for

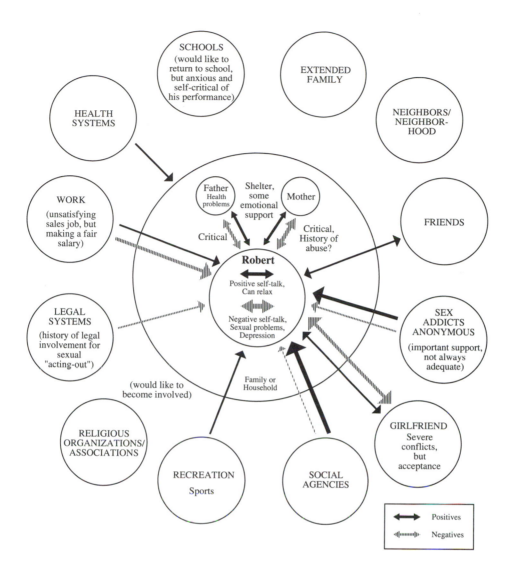

FIGURE 12-2. A QUICK SCAN OF ROBERT, A 32-YEAR-OLD CLIENT

him), limited and conflicted interpersonal relationships, and vocational and economic failure. (Note that all the arrows that represent interpersonal exchanges in the figure are thin, reflecting a high overall level of isolation.)

Even practitioners who defined themselves exclusively as "clinical social workers" might intervene with a client such as Robert individually, see him and his girlfriend together, have some contact with the parents, encourage him to try different Sex Addicts Anonymous groups, and refer him to other services. Generalist workers might identify additional potential points of intervention as well; they might design a new form of group service to address the needs of lonely and socially isolated individuals (Gambrill, in press) with ties to singles programs in synagogues, churches, and cultural organizations, or they might lead or participate in efforts to build new systems to improve clients' access to vocational and educational opportunities in the neighborhood. Any point on the ecomap, therefore, is "fair game" for a generalist practitioner as long as there is reason to believe that intervening at that point may help the client address his problems or achieve his goals.

The model of generalist practice presented in this chapter is rooted primarily in behavioral theory. Although the author's experience and a great deal of empirical data suggest that this model is particularly robust, there are other well-accepted ways to conceptualize generalist practice, including working from a psychosocial model, a task-centered model, or an ecological model. Responsible generalist practitioners will expose themselves to multiple options and decide what is best on the basis of their understanding of the available information.

CHANGING BEHAVIOR

All practice (even practice that focuses primarily on sustaining clients) is about change, and change always involves action—behavior—of some sort. In some cases, for example with people suffering from severe mental illness, the treatment goal may be stabilization or sustaining a current level of functioning, and avoiding deterioration. Even under these circumstances, if there is a need for social work, it is because someone must do something to help—to provide sufficient support for client action, or to change or support actions by others in the environment. The required action may be overt, such as acting more assertively, or covert, such as changing self-talk or learning to manage visceral activity. A finer-grained typology of behavior that goes beyond the common categories of overt behavior, affect, and cognition is presented in Table 12-1. As previous chapters have indicated, much is known about behavior and how to change it. Behavior is shaped by biology (genetic and physiological factors), one's idiosyncratic life experiences, and sociocultural forces (Skinner, 1981). Many of the same basic behavioral principles apply whether the social worker's goals are to affect the actions of an individual client, modify patterns of behavior in a family, or advocate that representatives of a social institution relate differently to clients. Specific practice tasks, however, as well as ways of understanding the multivariate matrix within which behavior occurs, vary considerably in each of these examples, partly because of the increasing complexity of the phenomena of interest, which reductionistic thought cannot capture.

If the service contract developed collaboratively with a client calls for helping him or her to feel better emotionally, the social worker may model, prompt, and reinforce more accurate self-talk ("cognitive therapy" which addresses covert verbal behavior). If the client's life situation is highly aversive, however, a further level of complexity may be indicated. Under these circumstances, the social worker may encourage and assist the client to "experiment" in his or her own life space, to begin to take control of the factors that lead to emotional struggles (an empowerment approach). Simply helping the client adjust to oppression would not be a responsible goal of practice.

In many cases, clients' (overt and covert) behavior is shaped, prompted, and maintained by the actions of others. Depression, for example, can be

Table 12-1. A Typology of Behavioral Modalities

Behavioral modality	Examples of overt behavior	Examples of covert behavior
Motoric	Slapping someone	Tensing or relaxing the muscles
Verbal	Speaking	Self-talk (for example, "I'm a real failure")
Visceral	Crying	Release of adrenaline
Observational	Turning one's head toward a sight or sound	Covert imaging

Note: Many activities consist of complex chains and composites across several modalities; for example, "seeking food" consists of at least motoric and observational behavior, it may be prompted by visceral activity, and in concert with others may proceed most effectively if action is coordinated verbally. As another example, a person may notice (covertly observe) that someone else seems less friendly than previously. This observation may result in "feeling badly" (covert visceral events), which the person observes in his body. Both the behavior of the other individual and the physiological stress may lead the person to tell himself, "This is terrible! It is critical that she approves of me!" This talk may lead to negative images, additional negative self-talk, and ultimately to increased or reduced motoric and visceral activity (feeling "tense" or "down").

Sources: Adapted with permission from Poppen, R. L. (1989). Some clinical implications of rule-governed behavior. In S. C. Hayes (Ed.), *Rule-governed behavior: Cognition, contingencies, and instructional control* (pp. 325–357). New York: Plenum Press.

deeply rooted in family (and other social) processes (Biglan, 1991; Brown & Harris, 1978), as well as in biological factors. Family therapists and those who work with people with severe behavioral problems have long recognized that if the behavior of one member of an interactive system changes, homeostatic forces tend to return that person and the overall system to the previous state; the problems associated with returning delinquents to their previous living situation are a common example (Wolf, Braukmann, & Ramp, 1987). If dramatic-enough change occurs, however, the effects may reverberate and be amplified through other parts of the system, resulting in a new configuration. Family treatment often seeks this sort of meaningful, and, it is hoped, irreversible, "restructuring" (Minuchin & Nichols, 1993). Even more complicated patterns are present at higher systemic levels.

But how do these abstract notions work in a more operationalized sense; that is, how does one construe them in the behavioral terms used here and determine analytically at what level to intervene? The concept of "interlocking contingencies" is the critical bridge. Individual actions that occur within any "cultural entity"—a family, school, or neighborhood—tend to be shaped by patterns of exchange among the people and forces who constitute the formal or informal group, often in conjunction with events outside the system itself. Networks of internal practices and exchanges among people and groups—like street gangs, residents of housing projects, and local police departments—ultimately result in aggregate outcomes:

Delinquency
Rate of 45%
in Neighborhood

This image (adapted from Glenn, 1988) conveys this concept, and suggests that interventions in such webs of contingencies (relationships between behavior and the antecedents and consequences of that behavior that affect its rate) are best selected by identifying those that are concurrently most powerful and most accessible. A similar diagram could be used to portray the interlocking contingencies within a family system that tend to maintain repetitive patterns of interaction (Minuchin's "structure," 1974), which may or may not have positive outcomes for the family as a whole. Such patterns constitute the culture of the group; the behaviors maintained by the group that, in the aggregate, constitute group culture are technically labeled "cultural practices" (Glenn, 1991).

MULTIPLE OPTIONS FOR CHANGING BEHAVIOR

An examination of the factors that maintain a problem behavior or factors that are missing that may support a behavior that is to be achieved can suggest possible interventive strategies on multiple levels. Look, for example, at the contingency diagram in Figure 12-3, which traces some of the factors related to instances of overly harsh, aggressive actions by a single parent toward a child.

A careful analysis of Figure 12-3 suggests that one could have an impact on this pattern in a variety of ways, including individual intervention (teaching the mother to respond to the child's provocation more effectively), family treatment (perhaps focused on reducing coercive exchanges and increasing the rate of positive exchanges), group work (say, for parenting skills or mutual aid), community organizing (to strengthen social networks and reduce specific environmental stresses that affect isolated single parents), or establishing programmatic responses on an organizational basis (broad-based family support programs). The generalist practitioner regards all these options as possibilities in planning services and often considers combinations that may produce synergistic effects. Examples of strategies at each level are discussed in the following sections.

Individual Work with Parents

When a parent is overwhelmed, it may well make sense to begin work with that individual. For example, in one case, a mother believed that her three-year-old daughter was disobedient and often became enmeshed in verbal

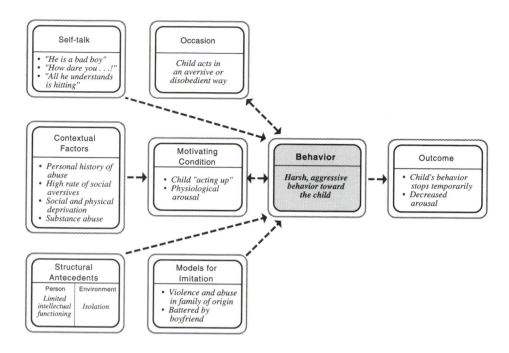

FIGURE 12-3. FACTORS INVOLVED IN THE HIGH RATE OF AGGRESSIVE, COERCIVE
ACTS TOWARD A CHILD BY A SINGLE MOTHER

arguments with the child. Observations of the mother and daughter at home, however, indicated that the daughter nearly always obeyed her mother and that the primary problem appeared to be that the mother displaced frustrations from other sources onto her child. If the pattern had continued, however, it is likely that the problems would have escalated because the child had begun to model her mother's verbal aggression, which could lead to an abusive spiral (Patterson, 1976). Interventions in this case focused on resolving those environmental issues that could be effectively addressed, developing new ways to cope with those that could not be changed, and building positive parent–child interactions characterized by positive reinforcement. Although individual intervention (with attention to environmental factors) was an efficient approach in this case, a primary focus on family interaction patterns may be indicated in other situations.

Family Treatment
Family intervention that includes work on restructuring interactional patterns within the family, as well as on building bridges to external supports and ameliorating stresses from multiple systems, is a demonstrably effective approach in families in which children are maltreated (Brunk, Henggeler, & Whelan, 1987). This interventive strategy can be differentially responsive to many of the multiple interacting factors that are associated with abuse (see Figure 12-3).

In family treatment, not only can parents learn new strategies for building relationships with the children in question and for managing behavior less coercively, but older children, in particular, can be coached to deal with parents differently, and problems with other systems can be directly addressed. If the family members are seen at home, they learn new behaviors in the setting in which these skills need to be used, which reduces the problem of generalizing what they have learned in the training situation to the home. Therefore, family treatment is a powerful and flexible strategy. However, it can be expensive to deliver and does not offer the potential for expanding social networks that some group and community approaches, discussed next, do. These approaches may be crucial for "insular" parents, a particularly challenging subgroup of maltreating parents (Dumas & Wahler, 1985; Wahler, 1980).

Group Work

Parenting groups are a common approach, partly because of their apparent cost-efficiency and partly because they sometimes offer advantages that other modalities may not. Parents who receive group training, for example, often find that the supportive network that develops can also help them find ways to resolve problems with other social systems (Brunk et al., 1987).

Parenting groups can be an effective approach for teaching both coping skills (Whiteman, Fanshel, & Grundy, 1987) and specific parenting techniques. Nevertheless, evidence suggests that skills that are learned in a group may not generalize well to the home unless in-home coaching is a component of the program (Howing, Wodarski, Gaudin, & Kurtz, 1989). Goldstein, Keller, and Erné (1985) found that with the addition of four specific "transfer-enhancing" techniques, generalization can be enhanced. The four techniques are (1) overlearning (the parent is given numerous opportunities to learn the skills to a high, almost automatic level of mastery), (2) stimulus variability (the parent learns to use the skills under an intentionally wide range of conditions, not simply in one way with one co-actor in a parenting group), (3) identical elements (skills learned in the group are practiced in exactly the same way with parent aides in the home at a later time), and (4) programmed reinforcement (parent aides are explicitly trained to note and reinforce the use of new skills in the home, which research suggests does not usually occur unless it is explicitly designed into the program). Without such additional elements, many parents do not consistently transfer what they learn in groups to the home.

Community Practice

There is strong evidence that the overall parental level of stress is a significant contributor to child maltreatment, both on a broad statistical level (Straus & Kantor, 1987) and from intensive observations of cases. For example, Wahler (1980) found that a mother's increased number of positive contacts with friends on a particular day was associated with reductions in mother–child problems and suggested that to achieve long-term success it is crucial to address this factor. In response to such findings, Wolfe (1991) and his associates incorporated informal activity groups in a community setting as a component of an abuse-prevention program that also includes individual behavioral training and guidance in parenting and the availability of respite care.

Lightburn and Kemp (1994) described a family-support program with which they have been associated for some time, which not only is deeply rooted in the community, but also emphasizes obtaining feedback from the community, developing community among the participants, and using an educational and mutual aid approach that builds consciously on historic roots in the settlement house movement. As Lightburn and Kemp reported, clients can learn a great deal in "learning collectives" that use resources in the group to develop and test alternative life strategies.

Even higher-level community interventions, such as those that target economic development or the reduction of drug-related problems, are likely to have an impact on the incidence of child maltreatment as well. Of course, if a family is referred because a child is in imminent danger, the social worker would ordinarily not devote most of his or her professional energies to economic development. Therefore, the need to "mix and phase" (Rothman & Tropman, 1987) multilevel strategies is clear. One may well see a parent in a skills-training group, as well as provide family-based intervention in the home, refer the parent to a support group, and advocate for the development of additional community-level resources. Of course, the social worker can do so effectively only if he or she understands the problem in depth and has the skills to intervene at these multiple levels. For this reason, training in generalist practice is crucial, even though it is not possible to be equally versed in everything. At the least, the social worker should know when to refer a client to a person with other skills or a program with other resources; ideally, she or he should know how to directly provide a rich array of services as well.

One way to begin thinking this way is to identify interventions at multiple levels that could benefit clients you are seeing now. Although the reader may find it valuable to complete this exercise individually, groups of students (who are likely to have different strengths and perspectives) may be able to develop a richer array of service options. Ideally, a social worker should be able to identify more than one possible interventive strategy at each systemic level (individual, family, group, community, or organization); further analysis should then help him or her to select the most potentially effective and efficient strategy.

An implicit case-to-class phenomenon is present in generalist practice. If the social worker sees or learns from others in the agency that all the social workers are seeing a number of similar cases, it may well make sense to step back and think about programmatic approaches that can efficiently respond to the issues that the class of clients is facing. A "planner" may also propose a programmatic response, but practitioners who are intimately familiar with the issues, in concert with clients (who are even more deeply embedded in the issues, although they may lack the practitioners' analytic understanding), may be more likely to develop programs that genuinely address the clients' needs. To design and develop excellent programs, practitioners must have an organic connection to the realities of the issues, as opposed to an exclusively abstract understanding of them.

Program Planning, Design, and Development

Program planning, design, and development are not the exclusive province of administrators or planners, who often have only limited knowledge of the realities and complexities of clients' lives. Effective programs that genuinely meet clients' needs and respond to social problems are much more likely to be designed by, or with extensive input from, practitioners who have been immersed in the issues for some time. Organizations and the programs they offer often do not work well for people (Meyer, 1979). Given the stubbornness of many social problems (and the current state of knowledge) even the best-designed and implemented programs may produce marginal results in many cases. The practitioner's involvement in program development is an effort to maximize the value of program activities for clients to the extent possible.

The following material presents the program development process in an idealized fashion. Not all programs develop in this way, and the process is usually recursive, circling back on itself. Furthermore, the social worker may be involved only in parts of this process, for example, joining a project after the needs assessment has been completed or being responsible only for developing a new program design if an evaluation indicates that the goals and objectives are not being satisfactorily achieved. A general framework for program development, adapted from Kettner, Moroney, and Martin (1990), is presented in Figure 12-4. Note that although a general direction is portrayed in the figure, it is common for program developers to circle back to earlier stages, particularly if the program appears not to be working as well as it might.

Problem Analysis

Programs emerge to address social problems, common difficulties experienced by a class of people, as opposed to unique "private troubles" affecting only an individual (Malagodi & Jackson, 1989). Program design should flow directly from an analysis and assessment of the problem. A problem should not be defined as the absence of services (as Kettner et al., 1990, emphasized). For example, the lack of foster care or of inpatient drug rehabilitation facilities is not a social problem. These services are *responses* to the problem, and beginning with such responses profoundly limits the consideration of alternative options (one would not even consider intensive home-based services to prevent and respond to family breakdown if the problem is defined as the lack of foster care).

Problem analysis proceeds by examining what is known about the problem, both locally by contact with the people who are affected and more globally by searching the literature to explore the etiology and epidemiology and available responses to the problem. The investigation of associated factors (such as social class, cultural factors that influence which responses are likely to be most acceptable, and the ways in which problems may interact with racism, sexism, and other issues) that may affect the program design and of available conceptual frameworks for understanding the issue is valuable at this stage.

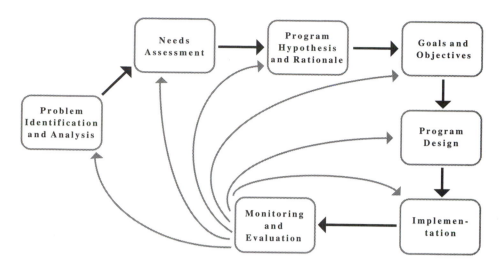

FIGURE 12-4. THE PROGRAM-DEVELOPMENT CYCLE

Needs Assessment

As the social worker and the agency learn more about the problem, it usually becomes clear that they need to know how many clients or potential clients the problem affects, and to what extent. If the agency is responsible for child protective services or preventive services in a large geographic area, with thousands of potential clients who are at high risk for abuse or neglect, its program will obviously need to be different from one designed to meet the moderate needs of a few families. Needs assessment provides the data that are required to answer questions about the extent of clients' needs. Although it is possible, and sometimes necessary, to implement complex and expensive needs-assessment strategies (Kettner et al., 1990), some needs assessment is better than none, and often a modest strategy produces adequate data from which to proceed. Neuber and Associates (1980) suggested the three-pronged strategy that has been adapted in Figure 12-5. They noted that to begin with, one can often obtain a fair amount of valuable information from existing data sources; although they emphasized statistical data, other information, including qualitative data, may also be of value.

Key informants, including professionals, community leaders, and others who are immersed in the local situation, can add information regarding the uniqueness of the problem in the service area, and consumers (clients) or potential consumers can often provide rich, grounded data that are often essential to understanding the problem and developing responsive programs. The approach of Neuber and Associates (1980) is firmly rooted in the community, without ignoring other types of information. There are, in fact, a range of available approaches to needs assessment that vary on dimensions of community involvement and empowerment, breadth, and rigor (Marti-Costa & Serrano-Garcia, 1983). It is valuable to think about multiple options (preferably with those who may be involved) before deciding how to proceed.

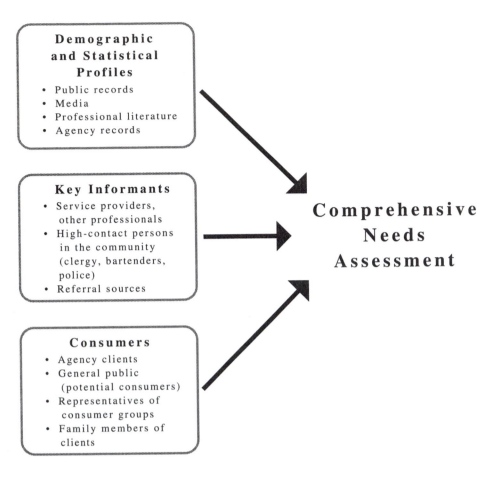

FIGURE 12-5. A COMPREHENSIVE NEEDS-ASSESSMENT FRAMEWORK
Source: Neuber, K. A., & Associates. (1980). Needs assessment: A model for community planning. *Newbury Park, CA: Sage Publications.*

The social worker may not always have the resources or sanction to complete a full needs assessment. An administrator may define the broad parameters of the program on the basis of long experience, essentially using herself or himself as the only key informant, and instruct the practitioner how to proceed. Even under these circumstances, examining the relevant literature to enrich the work is a low-cost strategy (and often an ethical imperative), and informal contact with other informants and consumers of services can often be incorporated seamlessly into planning in ways that do not threaten the administrator.

Establishing the Program Rationale
An effective program intervenes in the multicausal chain that produces and maintains the problem. Program developers who have not thought this chain through explicitly usually produce programs that fail to work well because they rely on doing the right thing essentially by accident. If an organization is charged with preventing child abuse, a social worker may decide, based on

his or her own interest, that the program should consist of a six-session educational group to teach parents who are at risk about child development and what they can realistically expect from their children. There is an implicit causal chain here, which suggests that the lack of knowledge and unrealistic expectations contribute significantly to abuse. As it happens, the available data do not generally support this model (Wolfe, 1991). Another social worker may decide to develop a dance group to prevent teenage pregnancy. Again, this may or may not be an effective approach; it is more likely to be effective, however, if it flows from an explicit and coherent conceptual rationale.

For example, it is known from the literature that isolation and poverty increase the risk of child maltreatment. Let us say that the needs assessment (which could in this case draw from the extensive literature) suggested that for a particular group of poor single mothers, the relatively common causal chain illustrated in Figure 12-6 leads to the emergence of child abuse and neglect.

As Figure 12-6 indicates, several factors contribute to having a child, including sexual activity and the failure to use contraceptives (which may involve the lack of knowledge, the lack of assertive-refusal skills, and motivational factors). The combination of having a child, high levels of environmental stressors, the lack of coping skills, and ineffective parenting lead directly to abuse, but limited social support, motivational factors, high levels of particular stressors, and the lack of knowledge of parenting skills also contribute to ineffective parenting (Wahler, 1980; Wolfe, 1991). Meanwhile, the effects of poverty are indirect, but pervasive.

Although it is oversimplified, Figure 12-6 begins to capture the complexities of the situation much more effectively than would a statement of a single cause. The image shows multiple points at which a program could intervene, once the strongest causal paths are identified. It may be that eliminating

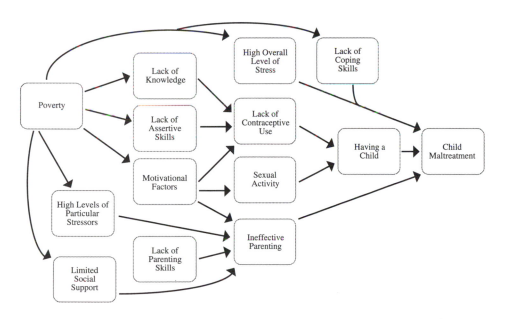

FIGURE 12-6. HYPOTHESIZED CAUSAL CHAIN, CHILD MALTREATMENT

poverty would be the most powerful intervention, but a single program cannot have a significant impact on that issue, so it may have to do whatever is second-best. If the data suggest that the lack of knowledge of contraception is significant, the appropriate response is clear. If the program is based on an assumption that the lack of knowledge is the issue, however, but motivational factors are actually the major contributor to the failure to use contraceptives, the program will fail. Thus, an accurate model is crucial.

In most social problems, contributing factors interact as well. For example, Wahler (1980) discovered that poor, insular, single mothers tend to be less effective with their children (even after training in parenting skills) on days when they experience negative interactions with kin and agency staff and more effective on days when they have many contacts with friends. This finding suggests that an effective program must not only teach skills, but help the client cope with social stressors and build support networks. Addressing only one of these factors probably will not have a substantial impact.

Goals and Objectives
Once the program rationale is clear, goals and objectives flow directly from the conceptual model. The range of real options is often constrained by contextual and organizational factors and limited resources; sometimes the program may be able to address only a subset of the relevant factors, and in some cases, for political reasons the program may need to include components that the social workers who are designing it do not believe are central, but that other crucial stakeholders do.

Goals are usually defined as general statements about what the program is meant to achieve ("to reduce the incidence of child maltreatment in Columbia County"), whereas objectives are more specific, measurable parts of the goals. Major types of objectives include the following:

- *impact* objectives, which target changes in the overall rate of a problem among a specific population (for example, "To reduce the rate of repeated reports of child abuse and neglect in the county by 20 percent by July 1, 1998")
- *outcome* objectives, which target (usually short-term) change among program participants (for instance, "To decrease the use of power-assertive discipline techniques among parents identified by the county child protective services agency by 70 percent after eight sessions, as measured by videotaped observations of parent–child interactions")
- *process* objectives, which describe program activities or inputs (such as, "To provide 270 home visits during 1997, as reported by the agency's management information system").

These types of objectives are hierarchical; impact objectives, which are not always practical, usually have one or more outcome objectives associated with them, and outcome objectives often have one or more process objectives associated with them. Note that each of these objectives, of whatever type, should be clear, specific, measurable, and time lined. Once goals and objectives have been determined, the program developer must determine exactly who will do what to achieve them—the process of program design.

Program Design

Once the goals and objectives have been established, the social workers involved can use them in at least two ways. First, they can use them as the basis of program evaluation, discussed later. Second, they can determine what activities must be performed to achieve them. Setting an objective related to reducing the rate of depression among a group of young single mothers, for example, provides valuable guidance to a program. But it does not tell one much about *how* the objective will be achieved. That decision is made on the basis of the conceptual framework developed as the program rationale, as guided by the needs assessment and problem analysis. If social isolation is hypothesized to be a major causal factor in maintaining the women's depression, for example, program activities that flow from this analysis may include support groups and case management to enhance positive connections with natural networks (and probably assist in reducing aversive factors from other systems as well).

Even these, however, are just overall strategies for addressing the issue; there is tremendous variation among "support groups," for example. An adequate program design clearly specifies who will do what, when; who will lead the group, who will attend, what the schedule and structure of the group will be, and what activities will take place in the group meetings. Although generally some relatively clear plans should be in place before the program begins, in most cases these activities will evolve over time, based on an ongoing evaluation of how well the program is approaching its objectives. This formative, or "developmental" (Berk & Rossi, 1990) evaluation can lead in a recursive fashion to improved programs; thus, evaluation should not simply be an add-on, but should be an integral part of the program development process.

Social workers often participate in ongoing programs that are designed by others. In many cases, they find that the programs are less effective than they believe the programs could be (this is a major professional and personal frustration in the field). In program redesign, the social worker must identify where the program development process has broken down. It may be at the level of problem specification and analysis; that is, the program may not really be clear about what problems it is trying to resolve or may have an inadequate, shallow, or out-of-date understanding of the issue. For example, unwed pregnancy in the 1990s is a different phenomenon, especially conceptually, from what it was in the 1920s, the 1940s, or even the 1960s (see Kunzel, 1993, for a discussion of the changing definitions of issues related to unmarried mothers), and programmatic responses to it should respond to advances in understanding. Or the program may have broken down at the needs-assessment stage; that is, the data that were collected may have been inadequate, or data may not have been gathered at all. Perhaps the most common breakdown, however, is in the conceptual understanding of the problem, its causes, factors that maintain it, and obstacles to its resolution—the program rationale stage.

Program Implementation

Program implementation generally requires the cooperative, coordinated effort of groups of people (line staff, supervisors, administrators, support staff, and clients). These individuals often function as members of task groups (staff groups, committees, or interdisciplinary teams) that must function effectively if the program is to be well-implemented. Social workers and others have studied effective task groups and have learned that it is possible for social workers, whether as group leaders or as members of groups, to work toward more effective team functioning (Toseland & Rivas, 1984). Specific techniques for encouraging effective teamwork and empowerment are now available, and every social worker who is involved in programming should be familiar with them (Daniels, 1994).

Staff who are involved in implementing the program also must be trained and supervised. It is usually a mistake to assume that they have the knowledge and skills required to implement a program and will apply them effectively. Every program is different, and some level of training is almost always required. One should assume that even highly competent staff have gaps in their knowledge and skills (Windsor, Baranowski, Clark, & Cutter, 1984) that must be addressed; even when they have the requisite skills and knowledge the staff may not apply them when and as the program requires unless they are trained to do so.

Effective supervision does not require speaking "longer, louder and meaner" (Daniels, 1994, p. 17) to obtain improved performance. Rather, it primarily involves the following steps:
- pinpointing (often with the staff involved) what must be done
- finding ways to track whether it is happening (measuring)
- providing feedback on performance
- reinforcing performance
- evaluating whether the staff's activities are leading to the achievement of objectives.

This model, drawn from Daniels, has broad applicability. By itself, it does not capture every situation, but this general framework can help social workers achieve excellence and resolve problems in most situations. The literature on social work supervision provides additional specific guidance. One important way to pinpoint what must be done clinically, for example, is to ask questions in supervision, such as these: "What does the client want help with?" and "What are you doing to help the client?" (Harkness & Hensley, 1991). Reinforcing what the person is doing right is much more effective than simply giving orders and criticizing inadequate performance. The concept of the "emotional bank account" is also important; supervisees respond better to corrective feedback if there are at least three times as many deposits as withdrawals (Latting, 1992).

Most graduate social workers develop programs that require staff training, effective team functioning, and supervision of other staff. These are yet other functions that generalist social workers must be ready to take on when the practice situation requires.

Program Evaluation

In an ideal world, if each of the previous steps has been implemented, all that remains to be done to complete at least a simple program evaluation is to organize the information and prepare the report. Because the program has been planned and implemented so the necessary information is collected on a routine basis, determining what the program is doing and how well it is doing it is a natural part of the process. Things are not always this simple in practice, of course, but it is useful to think about how little effort it would take to evaluate programs if they were designed from the beginning with a curiosity about and a commitment to finding out how they are doing.

Program evaluation is a field in itself, and some organizations and individuals specialize exclusively in performing evaluations, which can be complex and expensive. Most programs, however, do not need to expend so much effort to make a credible beginning. Although there are many ways that program evaluation can be subdivided, in general there are two primary types of evaluation: formative and summative. A formative evaluation is conducted as the program is beginning and is implemented, primarily to address questions such as, "Is the program reaching enough of the high-risk population?" "How much service is being provided?" and "How many resources, of what kinds, are being expended?" In a summative evaluation, one looks at how the program has fared over time and examines at least some of the following: process (program activities and inputs), outcomes for clients, and sometimes the impact on the target community. These factors can be combined with data about expenditures to perform cost-effectiveness and cost-benefit analyses as well.

A number of research-related questions clearly are important to think about while performing an evaluation, including how one reliably and validly measures services, outcomes for clients, and other variables of interest. Issues of design (such as the use of control groups or time-series analyses to enhance internal validity) also must be considered and can be complicated. Still, some evaluation is usually better than none, and although funders are increasingly demanding evaluation data—partly because everyone knows that many programs have not worked well in the past—they seldom require extremely sophisticated research-style designs. A relatively simple plan to track the number and types of services provided and to whom, clients' satisfaction, and task achievement (perhaps using Task Achievement Scaling; see Reid, 1992) would be a "high-end" evaluation in agency practice today. Demonstration projects require further emphasis on outcome and cost-effectiveness.

Program evaluation is really not about producing reports, of course. It is meaningless unless what is learned from it is fed back into the development process, to help sharpen goals and objectives and to improve services to clients. It is a common, but serious, mistake to think that one undertakes a program evaluation primarily to satisfy funders; rather, such an evaluation is primarily important to the program itself.

Proposal Writing

A good deal of funding for social work practice comes from contracts with government sources; grants from private and public sources; and, in public agencies, directly from budget allocations. These funds are generally provided on the basis of written proposals that are submitted in response to requests for proposals (RFPs) or proposals that are submitted as a regular part of the funding cycle. Proposal writing (and locating potential recipients of proposals) is an art and can be a full-time job, but most graduate social workers will be involved in the preparation of at least routine requests for funding. Excellent books on preparing proposals are available (see, for example, Coley & Scheinberg, 1990), but a few essential points can be summarized here.

Getting funding is not easy. Most proposals (except for regular continuation funding requests) are not funded, so it is essential not to become discouraged if a proposal is not funded. When proposals are not funded, it is important to consider any corrective feedback as nondefensively as possible, and to realize that the funding process is often highly politicized. Frequently, people submit proposals more to become known to funders, to become part of the network, and to test the waters for future submissions than to receive immediate funding. Funders tend to support the programs they know, and this tendency is not as irrational as it may seem because funders prefer giving money to those whom they are confident will use it well. A major objective of a proposal, then, is to build confidence in an organization and a program.

Although who one knows and the luck of the draw (the particular reviewers who read a submission) are important factors in funding decisions, a good deal can be done to enhance the chances that a proposal will be accepted. First, the proposal must be on time—extensions are rarely permitted. Therefore, back-up people, back-up computers, back-up copying machines, and so forth are necessary if the deadline is to be met. Second, the proposal must appear professional (with graphs and figures if appropriate) and be neat, grammatically correct, and pitched to the audience that will read it. Proposals geared to professional peers require a different approach than those to lay advisory boards, for example. Third, enthusiasm and genuine confidence in the suggested approach must be evident. Fourth, most funders have a particular format they require for proposals and it is essential to follow that format scrupulously. In general, the format is likely to include most of the elements of program design that have been discussed here; this fact suggests that if an organization has an effective program-development process in place, much of the necessary material will already be on hand.

All Things to All People?

Generalist practice can be overwhelming. There is so much to know—so many clinical, monitoring, programmatic, supervisory, and other skills to master— that social workers may be tempted simply to narrow their focus and learn one aspect well. Although there is a place for specialization, method is not it. Graduate social workers must be familiar enough to select interventive strategies that are based on clients' needs rather than on limitations of their knowledge, and to apply their skills effectively as part of organizational structures. In short, they need to be "masters of social work."

By this point it should also be clear that some practice processes are common across systemic levels, although interventive tactics and specific skills vary. The social worker must find some way to "engage," to "join" the system, thus potentiating his or her value as a support (reinforcer) and guide to potentially improved outcomes. One must, at every systemic level, gather information (exploration), organize that information analytically in a way that leads to collaborative interventive strategies (assessment), and selectively intervene at points and in ways identified by the assessment. In work with an individual, data collected may include emotions, levels of support and coercion within the household, and selected personal history because these data reflect the salient behaviors and the contingencies that shape them. In work with a neighborhood, one may be most interested in determining who the most powerful figures and organizations are and what the employment, economic, and educational levels of community residents are because these data tell one a great deal about current and potential contingency networks. In either case, one must first obtain the information, organize it, and understand its implications before one moves to interventive planning.

At the same time, social workers cannot be specialists in everything. They must know about the problems of clients that their organizations work with; about service structures, resources, and policies relevant to these problems; and about the variety of ways to intervene to address them. They may also be particularly skilled in some interventive modalities and may need to refer clients for specialized services (say, to groups for batterers or programs for autistic children). Still, a sense that one never knows enough may remain, and this is true. As long as clients come with problems that social workers are unable to help them resolve, individual practitioners and the field as a whole must continue the struggle to expand knowledge and deepen skills.

References

Bartlett, H. M. (1970). *The common base of social work practice.* New York: National Association of Social Workers.

Berk, R. A., & Rossi, P. H. (1990). *Thinking about program evaluation.* Newbury Park, CA: Sage Publications.

Biglan, A. (1991). Distressed behavior and its context. *Behavior Analyst, 14,* 157–169.

Brown, G. W., & Harris, T. (1978). *Social origins of depression: A study of psychiatric disorder in women.* New York: Free Press.

Brunk, M., Henggeler, S. W., & Whelan, J. P. (1987). Comparison of multisystemic therapy and parent training in the brief treatment of child abuse and neglect. *Journal of Consulting and Clinical Psychology, 55,* 171–178.

Coley, S. M., & Scheinberg, C. A. (1990). *Proposal writing*. Newbury Park, CA: Sage Publications.

Daniels, A. C. (1994). *Bringing out the best in people*. New York: McGraw-Hill.

Dumas, J. E., & Wahler, R. G. (1985). Indiscriminate mothering as a contextual factor in aggressive-oppositional child behavior: "Damned if you do, damned if you don't." *Journal of Abnormal Child Psychology, 13,* 1–17.

Gambrill, E. (in press). Loneliness, social isolation, and social anxiety. In M. A. Mattaini & B. A. Thyer (Eds.), *Strategic science: Behavior analysis and social issues*. Washington, DC: APA Books.

Glenn, S. S. (1988). Contingencies and metacontingencies: Toward a synthesis of behavior analysis and cultural materialism. *Behavior Analyst, 11,* 161–179.

Glenn, S. S. (1991). Contingencies and metacontingencies: Relations among behavioral, cultural, and biological evolution. In P. A. Lamal (Ed.), *Behavioral analysis of societies and cultural practices* (pp. 39–73). New York: Hemisphere.

Goldstein, A. P., Keller, H., & Erné, D. (1985). *Changing the abusive parent*. Champaign, IL: Research Press.

Harkness, D., & Hensley, H. (1991). Changing the focus of social work supervision: Effects on client satisfaction and generalized contentment. *Social Work, 36,* 506–512.

Howing, P. T., Wodarski, J. S., Gaudin, J. M., Jr., & Kurtz, P. D. (1989). Effective interventions to ameliorate the incidence of child maltreatment: The empirical base. *Social Work, 34,* 330–338.

Kettner, P. M., Moroney, R. M., & Martin, L. L. (1990). *Designing and managing programs: An effectiveness-based approach*. Newbury Park, CA: Sage Publications.

Kunzel, R. G. (1993). *Fallen women, problem girls*. New Haven, CT: Yale University Press.

Latting, J. K. (1992). Giving corrective feedback: A decisional analysis. *Social Work, 37,* 424–430.

Lightburn, A., & Kemp, S. P. (1994). Family-support programs: Opportunities for community-based practice. *Families in Society, 75,* 16–26.

Malagodi, E. F., & Jackson, K. (1989). Behavior analysts and cultural analysis: Troubles and issues. *Behavior Analyst, 12,* 17–33.

Marti-Costa, S., & Serrano-Garcia, I. (1983, Summer). Needs assessment and community development: An ideological perspective. *Prevention in Human Services*, pp. 75–88.

Mattaini, M. A. (1993). *More than a thousand words: Graphics for clinical practice*. Washington, DC: NASW Press.

Meyer, C. H. (1979). Introduction: Making organizations work for people. In C. H. Meyer (Ed.), *Making organizations work for people* (pp. 1–12). Washington, DC: National Association of Social Workers.

Minuchin, S. (1974). *Families and family therapy.* Cambridge, MA: Harvard University Press.

Minuchin, S., & Nichols, M. P. (1993). *Family healing.* New York: Free Press.

Neuber, K. A., & Associates. (1980). *Needs assessment: A model for community planning.* Newbury Park, CA: Sage Publications.

Patterson, G. R. (1976). The aggressive child: Victim and architect of a coercive system. In E. J. Mash, L. A. Hamerlynck, & L. C. Handy (Eds.), *Behavior modification and families* (pp. 267–316). New York: Brunner/Mazel.

Poppen, R. L. (1989). Some clinical implications of rule-governed behavior. In S. C. Hayes (Ed.), *Rule-governed behavior: Cognition, contingencies, and instructional control* (pp. 325–357). New York: Plenum Press.

Reid, W. J. (1992). *Task strategies.* New York: Columbia University Press.

Rothman, J., & Tropman, J. E. (1987). Models of community organization and macro practice perspectives: Their mixing and phasing. In F. M. Cox, J. L. Erlich, J. Rothman, & J. E. Tropman (Eds.), *Strategies of community organization: Macro practice* (pp. 3–26). Itasca, IL: F. E. Peacock.

Skinner, B. F. (1981). Selection by consequences. *Science, 213,* 501–504.

Straus, M. A., & Kantor, G. K. (1987). Stress and child abuse. In R. E. Helfer & R. S. Kempe (Eds.), *The battered child* (pp. 42–59). Chicago: University of Chicago Press.

Toseland, R. W., & Rivas, R. F. (1984). *An introduction to group work practice.* New York: Macmillan.

Wahler, R. G. (1980). The insular mother: Her problems in parent-child treatment. *Journal of Applied Behavior Analysis, 8,* 27–42.

Whiteman, M., Fanshel, D., & Grundy, J. F. (1987). Cognitive-behavioral interventions aimed at anger of parents at risk of child abuse. *Social Work, 32,* 469–474.

Windsor, R. A., Baranowski, T., Clark, N., & Cutter, G. (1984). *Evaluation of health promotion and education programs.* Mountain View, CA: Mayfield.

Wolf, M. M., Braukmann, C. J., & Ramp, K. A. (1987). Serious delinquent behavior as part of a significantly handicapping condition: Cures and supportive environments. *Journal of Applied Behavior Analysis, 20,* 347–359.

Wolfe, D. A. (1991). *Preventing physical and emotional abuse of children.* New York: Guilford Press.

13

Monitoring Social Work Practice

Mark A. Mattaini

Previous chapters have discussed social work practice with individuals, families, groups, organizations, and communities, as well as generalist practice, in which any or several of these systemic levels may be addressed. In each of these chapters, the need to monitor and evaluate practice has been identified, but the details have largely been deferred until this chapter to avoid repetition. Central questions that cut across practice at all systemic levels, questions with critical ethical and professional implications, are "How is the client doing?" and "Is my practice working (helping)?"

All social workers want to believe that they are doing well, as well as doing good, and need to project that message if they want financial support and community sanction. Still, believing they are effective is not the same as knowing that they are or being able to demonstrate it, both to themselves and to others. There has been a serious debate in the profession since the 1970s about the effectiveness of social work practice (Fischer, 1973, 1976; Gordon, 1983; Mullen & Dumpson, 1972; Reid & Hanrahan, 1982; Thomlison, 1984; Videka-Sherman, 1985; Wood, 1978). Without revisiting the details, one can say that there is considerable evidence that some practice "works" well and that some probably does not. And whether practice is effective or not matters.

Social workers are responsible to themselves, the community, and especially their clients to try to determine how their cases are progressing in as objective a way as possible. At a minimum, they simply must know whether a client is or is not doing better (or, for clients for whom the avoidance of deterioration or relapse is the objective, maintaining a particular level of functioning). It clearly matters if a parent is using alternatives to severe physical punishment, if an overstressed family achieves a more satisfying balance with its environment, if several depressed members of a treatment group are becoming less depressed, or if a neighborhood is achieving an increased level of empowerment that can lead to economic development and family stability.

When possible, one also likes to know whether one's practice is contributing to the change. There are, therefore, two important questions to be

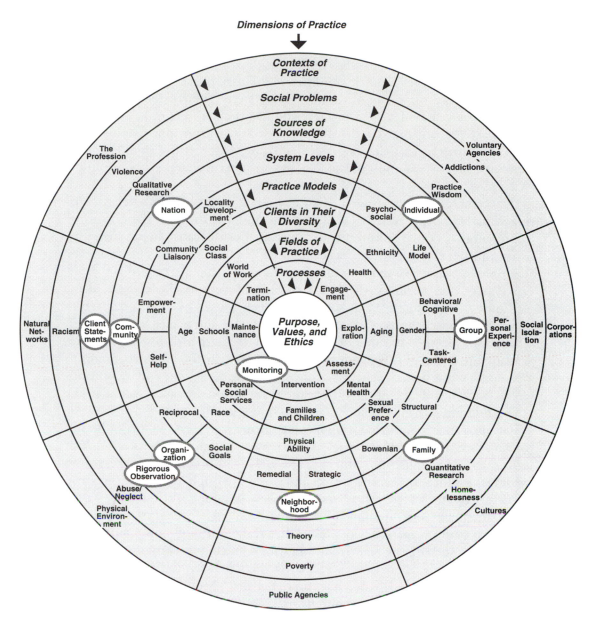

Dimensions of Practice

Contexts of Practice
Social Problems
Sources of Knowledge
System Levels
Practice Models
Clients in Their Diversity
Fields of Practice
Processes
Purpose, Values, and Ethics

The Profession
Violence
Qualitative Research
Nation
Locality Development
Community Liaison
Social Class
World of Work
Empowerment
Termination
Engagement
Age
Schools
Maintenance
Exploration
Self-Help
Monitoring
Assessment
Intervention
Personal Social Services
Reciprocal
Race
Families and Children
Organization
Social Goals
Physical Ability
Rigorous Observation
Remedial
Strategic
Abuse/Neglect
Physical Environment
Neighborhood
Natural Networks
Racism
Client Statements
Community

Voluntary Agencies
Addictions
Practice Wisdom
Individual
Psycho-social
Ethnicity
Life Model
Health
Behavioral/Cognitive
Personal Experience
Social Isolation
Corporations
Aging
Gender
Group
Task-Centered
Mental Health
Sexual Preference
Structural
Bowenian
Family
Quantitative Research
Homelessness
Cultures

Theory
Poverty
Public Agencies

FIGURE 13-1. ELEMENTS EMPHASIZED IN MONITORING PRACTICE

addressed in monitoring practice: Is the client system approaching its goals efficiently and satisfactorily? Is the intervention responsible for whatever change is being achieved (because knowing this fact is important to interventive planning and building one's practice knowledge)? Determining the extent to which the intervention is responsible for the change requires a level of control that may not often be easily available in practice settings; thus, compromises are often necessary. But it is always possible—though not always simple— to find some way to determine at least whether progress toward clients' goals is or is not being achieved.

Although monitoring has been addressed to some degree in many of the previous chapters, here it should be emphasized that the basic monitoring principles are the same regardless of the size or complexity of a client system. If focal issues (target problems and treatment goals) have been clearly specified and agreed on at any of these systemic levels, the creative, thoughtful practitioner can find a way to track whether they are being achieved in a manner that is organic to, rather than imposed on, the practice. The available evidence suggests that clients prefer that some clear method of monitoring outcome is used, as opposed to relying on practitioners' global opinion (Campbell, 1988).

Nevertheless, monitoring is often not straightforward. The behavior of individual clients is easier to measure, for example, than are the actions of representatives of large bureaucratic systems, both because better measures exist and because clients are easier to reach. If the issue is depression, for example, it may make sense to monitor the case using a standardized rapid assessment instrument like the Beck Depression Inventory (Beck, Rush, Shaw, & Emery, 1978). But if the depression is largely caused by situational factors over which the client has limited control (say severe and persistent battering), the lack of progress should not be attributed to the client's resistance, a personality disorder, or other factors that fail to take the full case situation into account. In this case, the client's depression is the focal issue and is appropriate to track, but intervention must be directed toward the causal factors in the social and physical environment (an assessment issue).

Granted that monitoring is important, there are at least two major bodies of knowledge with which social workers must be familiar before they can effectively accomplish monitoring. The first is approaches for measuring progress on focal issues, and the second is ways to apply these measures and structure treatment to track what is going on ("design"). Although the words "measurement" and "design" are research terms, no foreign, scientistic approach is being suggested here. Research is really nothing more than a rigorous way of seeking the answers to questions; in this case, the interest is in finding relatively rigorous ways to answer the practice questions, "Is the client doing better?" and "Am I helping the client?" Monitoring is an indivisible aspect of practice, not something extraneous that is layered onto it.

MEASUREMENT

There are many ways to measure the progress of people or systems toward achieving their goals. Some are more reliable and valid, some are narrow and some are broad, and some require more specific training than do others. Professional social workers who use any monitoring strategy must be familiar with technical details of measurement like reliability and validity (as physicians must understand how to read laboratory tests). Although it is not possible to review all the available approaches and practitioners may need to develop new ones to fit their situations, the discussion of a few approaches may help the reader think about possibilities that may fit a particular form of practice or a particular case.

The most accurate way to measure anything is through direct observation (especially, of course, if it is done by multiple observers). In many practice settings, such observations may be impractical, but this strategy is often dismissed too quickly. In working with parents to teach parenting skills, for example, social workers can often observe parents' and children's behavior directly, and such observations may provide extraordinarily useful data for ongoing interventive planning (see Mattaini, McGowan, & Williams, in press).

Various types of rating scales can be useful when direct observation is not realistic. One technique is Task Attainment Scaling (Reid & Epstein, 1972), in which the level of achievement of agreed-on tasks is rated on a scale of 1 (minimally or not achieved) to 4 (completely achieved) or "no" for no opportunity to attempt. This technique can be applied in every session, particularly in task-centered practice. The overall achievement of goals can also be rated using Goal Attainment Scaling, a general-purpose technique developed in community mental health settings (Kiresuk, 1973; Kiresuk & Sherman, 1968). Goal Attainment Scaling can be individualized for each case, or standard scales can be used for common problems. For example, Table 13-1 depicts a standardized Goal Attainment Scaling Follow-up Guide for the treatment of couples (Stuart, 1980).

Self-anchored scales, in which a client is asked to rate, for example, how sad he or she feels on a scale of 1 to 10, are relatively straightforward and have been used in a variety of situations, ranging from pathological jealousy (Slomin-Nevo & Vosler, 1991) to depression (Nugent, 1992). They are usually easy for clients to relate to and can have excellent psychometric properties (Nugent). Several such scales can be used together, as in the Mood Thermometers (Tuckman, 1988) (see Figure 13-2).

Clinician rating scales, such as the Clinical Rating Scale for family assessment (on which the clinician rates family functioning on six dimensions as well as overall) are also easy to use and can have excellent measurement properties (Epstein, Baldwin, & Bishop, 1983; Miller, Epstein, Bishop, & Keitner, 1985). Reliability and validity can be enhanced by adding behavioral descriptions to each or some points on a rating or self-anchored scale, to clarify what is meant by, say, a 5 on a 10-point scale of conflict containment in a family. See chapter 5, Figure 5-3, for instructions on preparing such behaviorally anchored rating scales (Daniels, 1994).

Graphing progress on such instruments is useful because both the client and the social worker may find it reinforcing to see progress or motivating not to see it. Graphing is also usually an integral part of self-monitoring, a strategy that clients often find empowering (Kopp, 1988, 1993). By graphing multiple self-anchored or rating scales concurrently, social workers may examine connections among various aspects of client and environmental functioning over time, which may help them to identify relationships and, not incidentally, to protect them from oversimplifying complex cases. For example, Figure 13-3 portrays multiple dimensions of the Marital Happiness Scale (Azrin, Naster, & Jones, 1973), as completed by one partner in a couples case. Plotting scores from each partner on each scale would enrich the available information even further.

Table 13-1. Generalized Goal Attainment Scale for Marital Therapy

X = level at intake (date:)
A = test after four weeks (date:)
B = test after eighth session (date:)
C = test at treatment termination (date:)
D = test at follow-up (date:)

Make marks in red for husband rating
Make marks in blue for wife rating

Score summary

Test	Husband	Wife
Intake		
A		
B		
C		
D		

Scale attainment levels	1. Commitment to marriage	2. Expressed desire for change	3. Follow-through	4. Prompt mate's change effort	5. Acknowledge mate's effort
Very poor level of treatment success (−2)	Decision by one spouse to divorce, no discussion	Refusal to state change is possible	Failure to interact with mate in any way	Continued acts that prevent change by mate	Continued complaints in old terms
Poor treatment success (−1)	Decision by one mate to divorce after discussion	Negative requests for change	First effort frustrated, no repeat	Maintain unfriendly distance from mate	No comment on effort by mate
Neutral level of treatment success (0)	Shared discussion leading to stay/divorce decision	Some vague but positive change requests	Partial follow-through on commitments	Maintain reasonable closeness	Comment on absence of negatives
Moderate success with treatment (+1)	Shared decision to stay with some expressed hope	Some specific and positive requests	Commitments met	Attempt to "change first" to help mate make changes	Comment on new positives
Marked success with treatment (+2)	Shared decision to stay with great hope	Many positive and specific requests	Commitment level met and exceeded	Mate's most difficult requests met before expected change by mate	Strong and regular comments on new positives

Source: Reprinted with permission from Stuart, R. B. (1980). *Helping couples change: A social learning approach to marital therapy* (p. 113). New York: Guilford Press.

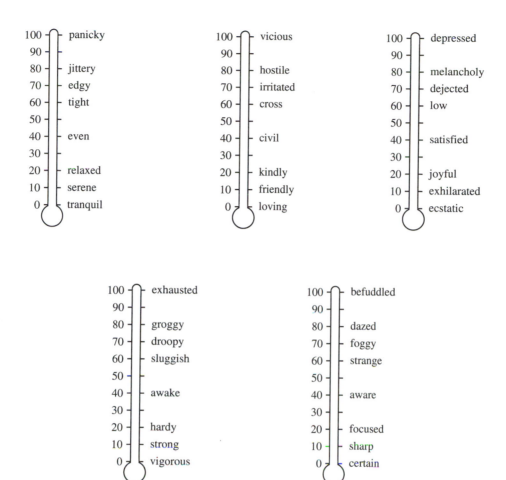

FIGURE 13-2. MOOD THERMOMETERS

Reprinted with permission from Tuckman, B. W. (1988). The scaling of mood. Educational and Psychological Measurement, 48, *p. 421. Copyright 1988 by Sage Publications.*

Note that some dimensions were never an issue for this couple, whereas others tended to be related; in particular, there seems to be a connection between communication and general happiness. A similar procedure could be used to examine concurrent changes among levels of support and aversives from environmental systems and a client's mood or family functioning, using data from a tool like the Visual EcoScan (Mattaini, 1993b), or paper-and-pencil rating scales.

Also available are a wide variety of rapid assessment instruments (RAIs), brief paper-and-pencil instruments that are designed to be completed quickly and often by a client. Such instruments have been used to measure moods, self-talk, assertiveness, family functioning, peer relations and social interactions,

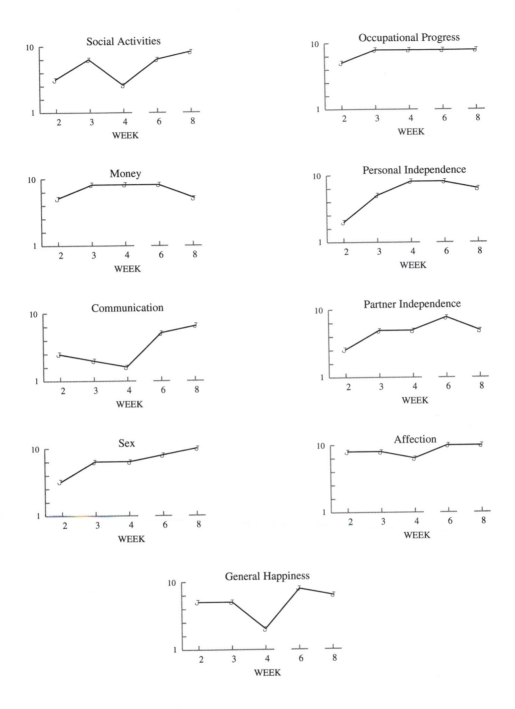

FIGURE 13-3. CONCURRENT GRAPHING OF DIMENSIONS OF THE MARITAL
HAPPINESS SCALE (AZRIN, NASTER, & JONES, 1973).

Note: Higher scores reflect greater satisfaction.

Source: Reprinted from Mattaini, M. A. (1993). More than a thousand words: Graphics for clinical practice *(p. 173). Washington, DC: NASW Press.*

SESSION 1

Member	1	2	3	4	5	6	7	8	9	10
Jill	○	○	○	○	●	○	○	○	○	○
George	●	●	○	○	●	○	●	○	●	○
Mary Kay	○	●	○	○	●	○	○	○	○	○
Ernie	○	○	○	●	○	○	●	○	●	●
Sarah	○	○	○	○	○	○	○	○	○	○
Kate	●	○	○	○	○	○	○	○	○	○
Sharee	○	○	○	○	○	○	○	○	○	○
Maxine	○	○	○	○	○	○	○	○	○	○

SESSION 2

Member	1	2	3	4	5	6	7	8	9	10
Jill	●	○	○	○	●	○	○	○	○	○
George	●	●	○	○	●	○	●	○	●	○
Mary Kay	●	●	○	○	●	○	○	○	○	○
Ernie	●	●	○	●	○	○	●	○	○	●
Sarah	○	○	○	○	○	○	○	○	○	○
Kate	●	○	○	○	○	○	○	○	○	○
Sharee	●	●	○	○	○	○	○	○	○	○
Maxine	●	○	○	○	○	○	○	○	○	○

SESSION 3

Member	1	2	3	4	5	6	7	8	9	10
Jill	●	●	●	●	○	○	○	○	○	○
George	●	●	○	○	●	○	●	○	●	○
Mary Kay	●	●	●	○	●	○	○	○	○	○
Ernie	●	●	●	○	○	●	○	○	●	●
Sarah	○	○	○	○	○	○	○	○	○	○
Kate	●	●	○	○	○	○	○	○	○	○
Sharee	●	●	○	○	○	○	○	○	○	○
Maxine	●	●	○	○	○	○	○	○	○	○

SESSION 4

Member	1	2	3	4	5	6	7	8	9	10
Jill	●	●	●	●	●	○	○	○	○	○
George	●	●	○	○	●	●	○	●	○	○
Mary Kay	●	●	●	●	●	○	○	○	○	○
Ernie	●	●	●	●	○	●	○	○	●	●
Sarah	○	●	○	●	○	○	○	○	○	○
Kate	●	●	●	○	●	○	○	○	○	○
Sharee	●	●	●	●	●	○	○	○	○	○
Maxine	●	●	●	●	○	○	○	○	○	○

SESSION 5

Member	1	2	3	4	5	6	7	8	9	10
Jill	●	●	●	●	●	●	●	○	○	○
George	●	●	●	●	●	○	○	●	○	○
Mary Kay	●	●	●	●	●	●	○	○	○	○
Ernie	●	●	●	●	●	○	●	○	○	●
Sarah	○	●	●	○	●	○	○	○	○	○
Kate	●	●	●	○	●	●	○	○	○	○
Sharee	●	●	●	●	●	●	●	○	○	○
Maxine	●	●	●	●	○	●	○	○	○	○

SESSION 6

Member	1	2	3	4	5	6	7	8	9	10
Jill	●	●	●	●	●	●	●	●	●	○
George	●	●	●	●	●	●	●	●	●	○
Mary Kay	●	●	●	●	●	●	●	●	●	○
Ernie	●	●	●	●	●	●	●	●	○	●
Sarah	○	●	●	●	○	○	○	○	○	○
Kate	●	●	●	○	●	●	●	●	●	○
Sharee	●	●	●	●	●	●	●	●	●	○
Maxine	●	●	●	●	●	●	●	●	○	○

FIGURE 13-4. TRACKING MATRIX FOR A SOCIAL SKILLS GROUP SHOWING SKILLS FOR WHICH GROUP MEMBERS HAVE MET THE CRITERION LEVEL
Source: Reprinted from Mattaini, M. A. (1993). More than a thousand words: Graphics for clinical practice (p. 163). Washington, DC: NASW Press.

magical thinking, and many other dimensions of human and social functioning (Fischer & Corcoran, 1994). It is important to learn how to select and use such instruments, usually through specific course content, because it is essential to understand their psychometric properties, cultural differences that may affect responses and interpretation, and how to integrate data from RAIs with other information to achieve a comprehensive clinical assessment. RAIs offer tremendous flexibility, however, and often have excellent reliability and validity. Hudson (1985) and his colleagues have developed a comprehensive computerized battery of such instruments that may be useful in a variety of settings and have recently incorporated them into an even more comprehensive assessment and clinical database system.

Many of these instruments can be used with clients who are seen in groups. Another strategy, useful at all systemic levels, but demonstrated here for use with a group, is the qualitative matrix (Miles & Huberman, 1994) used to track, for example, group members' progress in learning social skills in a structured skills training group (see Figure 13-4).

Other qualitative strategies may be useful in tracing the interventive process with individuals, families, groups, and communities. Reid's (1988) Case Process Chart is one approach to monitoring the progress of a case that relies primarily on rich narrative data, rather than numbers, but allows the relationships among events to emerge, using a matrix structure.

Although monitoring change at the community level may be more complicated, the same basic principles apply. Changes can be tracked by interviews or questionnaires, which may include many of the types of measures just described as well as others; by direct observation (for example, of the number of people hanging out on a street or the number of vacant buildings on a block); and by examining incidence data related to focal issues (for example, juvenile arrests or drop outs).

The list of tools discussed here is by no means exhaustive, and professional social workers will find that they often must adapt or even create tools that will adequately capture the critical data elements in a particular case or group of cases at whatever systemic level. The challenge is to find an approach that can capture the most important complexities of a case, rather than whatever is easiest. How often these measures are taken, and how, are design questions, which are discussed next.

DESIGN

Two general classes of design may be important for monitoring and evaluating practice: single-system designs and group designs. Practice is ultimately done with single systems (a person, a family, a community, or an organization); even in group work, the primary goal is to improve or maintain the level of functioning or quality of life of each member, and results for each may vary. For these reasons, the main emphasis here will be on what are called single-case or *single-system* designs. A brief consideration of group designs, which may be particularly valuable for some program evaluation purposes, especially when they are combined with single-system designs, is presented later in the chapter.

Many research courses focus on group designs. Although some of the concepts learned in such courses (like internal validity or generalizability) apply regardless of the type of design, group designs are generally inappropriate for the routine monitoring of practice, especially because most of them require a large number of similar clients and the use of untreated control groups, preferably with random assignment, or comparison groups who receive different treatments. Group studies also "wash out" differences among cases, which may not matter for research purposes, but does matter a great deal for clinical purposes. For example, on average a group of clients may improve, but this aggregate may consist of some clients who do much better, some who do a bit better, and some who deteriorate greatly. In practice, intervention should be varied for each case to achieve the best possible outcome, but this cannot be done without compromising group designs. For these and other reasons (Johnston, 1988), practitioners ordinarily use some form of single-case design instead, in which whatever controls are present are provided by the case itself.

Single-Case Designs

There are many types of single-case designs in use today, but only a few are highlighted here to demonstrate the range of designs that are available. The reader should refer to the specialized literature for further information (see, for example, Bloom, Fischer, & Orme, 1995).

In some circumstances, particularly in emergencies, the social worker simply starts to intervene and at the same time tracks the level of problems experienced. For example, with a severely depressed client, one would ordinarily begin treatment immediately and monitor the level of depression over time, using perhaps an RAI or a self-anchored scale. This approach is called a B design because the accepted convention is to label baseline phases (of which there is none here) "A" and to label intervention phases "B" (and "C", "D", and so forth if multiple types of interventions are used). Note that a B design is adequate for showing that depression is declining over the course of treatment, but does not provide a stable picture of how depressed the client was at the beginning (which would require baseline data collected before intervention begins). B designs also cannot demonstrate that the intervention was responsible for the change because something else may be the cause of the improvement, including artifacts—clients tend to enter treatment when things are at their worst, so data often improve to some extent because of "regression toward the mean."

In other cases, social workers can collect some baseline data, then continue to collect data during intervention and, ideally, at a later follow-up. Figure 13-5 is an example of such an AB design with a single follow-up point. It illustrates an interesting case, in which the client was disturbed by jealous thoughts about her husband's first wife, who had passed away before he and the client met (Slomin-Nevo & Vosler, 1991).

The extent of change in the client is clear in the figure, and it is reasonable to suppose that the intervention may have contributed to the change, although this assumption cannot be definitively proved. If the primary goal was scientific knowledge building, such uncertainty would be an issue, but for clinical purposes, these data are reasonably persuasive. In other cases, the first intervention does not have the desired effect, and the social worker may use a clinical analytic design with multiple sequential interventive phases, some of which may include combinations of several interventions, until a satisfactory outcome is achieved (Chapter 5, Figure 5-4).

Other more-involved designs enable social workers to untangle causality (for example, multiple baseline, changing criterion, or withdrawal designs [Mattaini, 1993a]), as well as to select the best of several possible interventive strategies to pursue with a particular case (for example, alternating treatment designs [McNight, Nelson, Hayes, & Jarrett, 1984]). What is perhaps most important is to clarify that designs and measurements are chosen because they fit the logic of a particular case and the treatment plan, rather than the other way around.

Single-system designs are applicable even when the system involved includes many people or groups. For example, if a neighborhood organization wished to reduce the rate of violent crimes on the street, it might test two different approaches, such as increased patrolling by the police (negotiated with the local precinct) and the use of citizen patrols, and determine the relative effectiveness of each. This strategy might involve establishing a baseline from data on violent crimes over the past year (A), followed by two months of increased

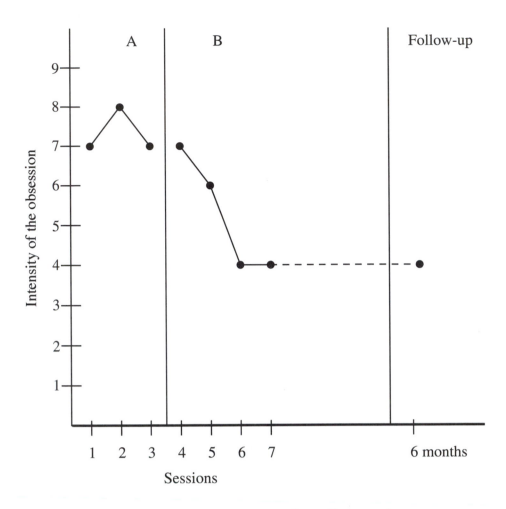

FIGURE 13-5. A SINGLE-SYSTEM EVALUATION OF BRIEF PROBLEM-SOLVING
THERAPY FOR OBSESSIVE JEALOUSY

*Source: Reprinted with permission from Slomin-Nevo, V., & Vosler, N. R. (1991). The use of
single-system design with systemic brief problem-solving therapy. Families in Society, 72, p. 42.*

patrolling (B), then two months of citizen patrols (C) or two months of both
(BC). Note that although the crime data involve multiple individuals, it is the
aggregate data for the neighborhood that the neighborhood organization
would trace—a single-system strategy.

Group Designs
There are times, however, when group designs may be useful, particularly at
the programmatic or community levels. For example, if an agency decided to
implement a new short-term treatment project, it might want to compare the
effectiveness of such a project with the standard open-ended approach currently being used. No clients would go untreated—this would be a contrast-
group, rather than an untreated control-group design. As long as the same measures (say, a package of RAIs) were used with both groups, and reasonable

decisions could be made about when to use them, such a design could be practical. Note, however, that there is no reason why single-case designs could not be incorporated within this group design, and they probably ought to be. It is really not enough to know that the average outcome is as good or better for the new program as it was for the old one, although that information is important. It is still critical for clinical purposes to monitor how each client is doing. One interventive stream would last longer than the other in this example, but what would happen during those periods, for each client, should be driven by the specifics of the case.

Comparison-group studies may also be useful if a social worker and a community group were working to prevent school dropouts, for example. They might establish a new tutoring and support program in one school and compare the dropout data for students in this school over a period of time with those in similar schools in which such a program is not in place. Although this is a weak design it provides at least some basis for comparison. It is important to examine such data because some "prevention" programs may have a range of benefits, but may not have any effect on the problem to be prevented. In a world of limited resources, it is essential to know this.

Monitoring at the programmatic level blends into program evaluation. Although evaluation is a specialized field and evaluation research can be extremely complex (Berk & Rossi, 1990), completing a simple evaluation that may include the clients' satisfaction and a measure of goal attainment or task achievement need not require major effort, particularly with the widespread availability of personal computers. Data that are routinely collected can often be used for simple evaluations that require few agency resources.

CONCLUSION

Monitoring practice need not be arcane and does not require advanced mathematical and research skills. There are risks if monitoring is poorly done because, for example, a requirement for monitoring may lead social workers to focus on what is easiest to see—often the behavior of clients, rather than what is most important—which may include larger systemic factors (Kagle & Cowger, 1984). But there is no choice. A professional cannot practice ethically while ignoring whether a client is achieving his or her goals. Therefore, social workers must learn the skills of monitoring. This is a special challenge because awareness of the importance of, and development of tools for, monitoring practice are recent. Some of the methods and instruments available are rough and need a good deal more elaboration. And many social workers, administrators, and supervisors in the field have limited knowledge in this area. In many settings, the demands by funders to document effectiveness and measure outcomes have become intense, another reason to develop expertise in this area. But the primary reason to struggle to find ways to track progress and outcome is that this is the only way in which one can know if a client is reaching his or her goals and if one is helping the client to do so.

REFERENCES

Azrin, N. H., Naster, B. J., & Jones, R. (1973). Reciprocity counseling: A rapid learning-based procedure for marital counseling. *Behaviour Research & Therapy, 11,* 365–382.

Beck, A. T., Rush, A. J., Shaw, B. F., & Emery, G. (1978). *Cognitive therapy of depression.* New York: Guilford Press.

Berk, R. A., & Rossi, P. H. (1990). *Thinking about program evaluation.* Newbury Park, CA: Sage Publications.

Bloom, M., Fischer, J., & Orme, J. G. (1995). *Evaluating practice: Guidelines for the accountable professional* (2nd ed.). Boston: Allyn & Bacon.

Campbell, J. A. (1988). Client acceptance of single-system evaluation procedures. *Social Work Research & Abstracts, 24*(2), 21–22.

Daniels, A. C. (1994). *Bringing out the best in people.* New York: McGraw-Hill.

Epstein, N. B., Baldwin, L. M., & Bishop, D. S. (1983). The McMaster Family Assessment Device. *Journal of Marital and Family Therapy, 9,* 171–180.

Fischer, J. (1973). Is casework effective? A review. *Social Work, 18,* 5–20.

Fischer, J. (1976). *The effectiveness of social casework.* Springfield, IL: Charles C Thomas.

Fischer, J., & Corcoran, K. (1994). *Measures for clinical practice: A sourcebook* (2nd ed., 2 vols.). New York: Free Press.

Gordon, W. E. (1983). Social work revolution or evolution? *Social Work, 28,* 181–185.

Hudson, W. W. (1985). *The clinical assessment system* [Computer program]. Tempe: University of Arizona School of Social Work.

Johnston, J. M. (1988). Strategic and tactical limits of comparison studies. *Behavior Analyst, 11,* 1–9.

Kagle, J. D., & Cowger, C. D. (1984). Blaming the client: Implicit agenda in practice research. *Social Work, 29,* 347–351.

Kiresuk, T. J. (1973). Goal attainment scaling at a county mental health service. *Evaluation* (Monograph No. 1), 12–18.

Kiresuk, T. J., & Sherman, R. E. (1968). Goal attainment scaling: A general method for evaluating comprehensive community mental health programs. *Community Mental Health Journal, 4,* 443–453.

Kopp, J. (1988). Self-monitoring: A literature review of research and practice. *Social Work Research & Abstracts, 24*(4), 8–20.

Kopp, J. (1993). Self-observation: An empowerment strategy in assessment. In J. B. Rauch (Ed.), *Assessment: A sourcebook for social work practice* (pp. 255–268). Milwaukee: Families International.

Mattaini, M. A. (1993a). *More than a thousand words: Graphics for clinical practice.* Washington, DC: NASW Press.

Mattaini, M. A. (1993b). *Visual EcoScan for clinical practice* [Computer program]. Washington, DC: NASW Press.

Mattaini, M. A., McGowan, B. G., & Williams, G. (in press). Child maltreatment. In M. A. Mattaini & B. A. Thyer (Eds.), *Strategic science: Behavior analysis and social issues.* Washington, DC: APA Books.

McNight, D. L., Nelson, R. O., Hayes, S. C., & Jarrett, R. B. (1984). Importance of treating individually assessed response classes in the amelioration of depression. *Behavior Therapy, 15,* 315–335.

Miles, M. B., & Huberman, A. M. (1994). *Qualitative data analysis: An expanded sourcebook.* Thousand Oaks, CA: Sage Publications.

Miller, I. W., Epstein, N. B., Bishop, D. S., & Keitner, G. I. (1985). The McMaster Family Assessment Device: Reliability and validity. *Journal of Marital and Family Therapy, 11,* 345–356.

Mullen, E. J., & Dumpson, J. R. (1972). *Evaluation of social intervention.* San Francisco: Jossey-Bass.

Nugent, W. R. (1992). Psychometric characteristics of self-anchored scales in clinical application. *Journal of Social Service Research, 15*(3–4), 137–152.

Reid, W. J. (1988). The metamodel, research, and empirical practice. In E. R. Tolson (Ed.), *The metamodel and clinical social work* (pp. 167–192). New York: Columbia University Press.

Reid, W. J., & Epstein, L. (1972). *Task-centered casework.* New York: Columbia University.

Reid, W. J., & Hanrahan, P. (1982). Recent evaluations of social work: Grounds for optimism. *Social Work, 27,* 328–340.

Slomin-Nevo, V., & Vosler, N. R. (1991). The use of single-system design with systemic brief problem-solving therapy. *Families in Society, 72,* 38–44.

Stuart, R. B. (1980). *Helping couples change: A social learning approach to marital therapy.* New York: Guilford Press.

Thomlison, R. J. (1984). Something works: Evidence from practice effectiveness studies. *Social Work, 29,* 51–56.

Tuckman, B. W. (1988). The scaling of mood. *Educational and Psychological Measurement, 48,* 419–427.

Videka-Sherman, L. (1985). *Harriett M. Bartlett practice effectiveness project: Report to NASW Board of Directors.* Silver Spring, MD: National Association of Social Workers.

Wood, K. M. (1978). Casework effectiveness: A new look at the research evidence. *Social Work, 23,* 437–459.

14

The Profession of Social Work

Barbara Levy Simon

1) that the essence of a profession is its work, not its organization
2) that many variables affect the content and control of that work
3) that professions exist in an interrelated system.
   (Abbott, 1988, p. 112)

To become familiar with the profession of social work in the United States, a profession in ongoing and active formation and re-formation since the 1890s, requires access to three crucial kinds of information, borrowed from the thinking of Andrew Abbott, a sociologist of professions and work: (1) the profession's actual work, the major tasks it has taken on; (2) the complex of factors that have helped shape the nature, direction, and leadership of that work; and (3) the interprofessional struggles, accommodations, alliances, and competitions that have influenced the profession's developmental course (Abbott, 1988).

THE WORK OF SOCIAL WORK

Organized social work in America during the past forty years [1899–1939] has been concerned primarily with protecting and raising the standard of living. Organized charity, one part of social work, has dealt with individuals and families who, because of physical disability or moral weakness or personal misfortune, are unable to solve their individual problems and therefore ask for help or at least need it. Other kinds of social work deal directly with more general needs, such as improved housing, community playgrounds, adjustment of immigrant groups, or old-age security. Generally in activities of this kind it includes both campaigns for the education of the public on the particular problem involved and securing an increase in the actual provision of needed facilities, either through legislation or through voluntary cooperation. (Devine, 1939, p. 150)

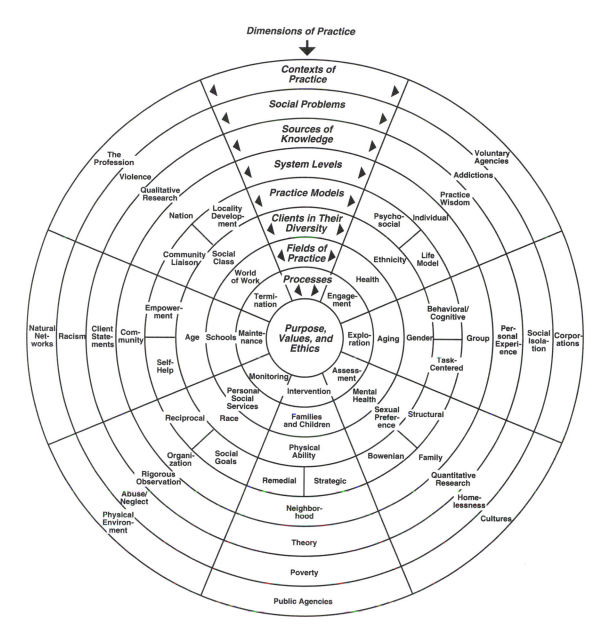

Dimensions of Practice

FIGURE 14-1. THE HISTORY OF THE SOCIAL WORK PROFESSION ENCOMPASSES ALL
DIMENSIONS OF PRACTICE

In this passage of his autobiography, Edward T. Devine, who was, like
Mary Richmond, a prominent founder of the social work profession, captured succinctly the two fundamental and concomitant projects of social work:
(1) enhancing the general welfare, and (2) helping individuals and families
who face some form of adversity to overcome it or, at the least, to find ways
to manage their relationship to it. Devine succeeded in embracing both tasks
throughout his long and remarkable career. So did many other architects of
the profession during its first 25 years before World War I.

Mary Richmond (1861–1928)
A leader of the Charity Organization Societies (COS) movement in the last decade of the 19th century and the first two decades of the 20th century, Mary Richmond codified and institutionalized the systematic practice of social casework. Her path-breaking books, *Social Diagnosis* and *What Is Social Case Work? An Introductory Description,* published in 1917 and 1922, respectively, constituted the first formal efforts to establish a theory and method of assessing and responding to clients' multidimensional issues and needs. Richmond became a nationally renowned professional educator in the course of developing teaching materials for COS workers across the country through the Russell Sage Foundation's Charity Organization Department.

Despite the structural and functional interdependence of these two primary jobs and their logical congruity, however, the history of American social work has been rife with fierce and, at times, prolonged battles over the question: Which is "actually" the core labor of the profession—responding to the immediate needs of vulnerable citizens and residents or transforming the whole society to make it more livable, safe, and just for all who live in it?

Although the answer, "both, of course," springs quickly to many social workers' lips, that is much more of an ideal of the profession than a realized record of performance. Most members of the profession's ranks since the close of the Progressive Era in 1917 have been respondents to clients' crises, whether working one-on-one with individuals, with families, or with small groups of people facing a common difficulty. Relatively few social workers since that time have been steady contributors to social reform movements while on "paid time," even though many have been episodic participants in social reforms on their "own time." Nonetheless, sustained controversy about "wholesale" versus "retail" priorities has raged over and over again among seasoned social workers with a deep investment in the success of both dimensions (Richmond, 1930). Indeed, this ongoing search for the proper lens through which to focus social work thought and action, the debate about the preferability of the telescopic versus the microscopic versus the kaleidoscopic approach to practice, has been a source of both internal renewal and of self-torment for the profession. To understand the contours of the debate about social work's central work, one must appreciate the profession's complex provenance.

The American social work profession is the offspring of a decidedly curious trio of urban reformers of the 1890s. Leaders of established philanthropic organizations, heads of the allied movements of settlement house work and adult education, and

Edward Devine (1867–1948)
Social worker and social reformer Edward Devine led and shaped several salient organizations, organs, and projects in early social work. Head of the influential New York COS from 1896 through 1916 and the person responsible for transforming the publication Charities into the Survey, the leading social work publication for four decades, Devine proved to be a master builder of professional institutions, as well as of professional education. He served as director of the first school of social work, the New York School of Philanthropy (now the Columbia University School of Social Work) from 1904 to 1907 and from 1912 to 1917.

independent reformers from universities and journalism initially formed a tripartite working alliance under the auspices of the National Conference of Charities and Correction. They had at least three reasons for coming together. First, they were all direct witnesses to the extreme misery brought about by the severe depression of 1893–1894. Second, they sought to modify and regulate the excesses of industrial capitalism, extremes that, they feared, could tear apart the American people, who were becoming increasingly fragmented along the lines of social-class affiliation, religion, nationality, and race. Third, they shared a common faith in the unique value of American democracy and a profound anxiety about that democracy's fragility in the face of, on the one hand, Marxism and anarchism, and, on the other hand, social Darwinism. Social Darwinism was a late 19th century social philosophy that opposed all forms of assistance to poor people on the grounds that philanthropy was a disruptive interference in the evolutionary process of natural selection, "the survival of the fittest" human beings.

Although these three founding groups occupied considerable common ground, they also evinced noticeable differences in the work that they emphasized in the fight against poverty. Organized philanthropy or charity, represented by such organizations as the Association for the Improvement of the Condition of the Poor, the Charity Organization Societies, Catholic Charities, and United Hebrew Charities, sought to help the poorest of the nation's individuals and families climb over whatever physical, emotional, linguistic, cultural, economic, vocational, legal, moral, or logistical barriers stood in the way of their general self-sufficiency and well-being. They relied on careful investigation of individual and familial need, merit, and environment; systematic record keeping; and regular visiting of needy families by paid

> ## Lillian Wald (1867–1940)
>
> Founder of the Henry Street Settlement in New York City, Lillian Wald helped shape a lasting tradition of community-based services for immigrants and social reform in social work. In so doing, she also created a worldwide program of visiting nursing services for home-bound individuals and families. Wald was an urban reformer of the first order; her social experiments with creating public playgrounds, school-based social and nursing services, tenement reform, and maternal and child health clinics spread rapidly throughout many cities in the United States.

agents and volunteers to determine the best use of their finite stock of material relief and caseworkers' time and skill. Although organized charities also published major reports on the conditions of poor neighborhoods gleaned from their staffs' direct work with poor people, their primary interest was in identifying and assisting the unfortunate victims of fate, God's will, or industrial capitalism. In the 1890s charity leaders considered such victims to be innocents who were deserving of help, unlike alcoholics, spendthrifts, and the shiftless, people they considered to be the primary agents of their own undoing (the "unworthy poor").

The second "parent" of social work, the settlement house and adult education (or university extension) movements, invested heavily in two kinds of work: providing group education and training in skills for immigrant adults and children in their own neighborhoods and conducting systematic neighborhood surveys on specific urban problems, such as contaminated milk, tuberculosis, and dangerous living conditions in tenements. The working poor were their primary constituency. Jane Addams, Lillian Wald, and many other settlement house leaders used their local studies, in turn, as empirical levers for launching multiple campaigns for model urban legislation and institutional reforms (Bulmer, Bales, & Sklar, 1991).

The final set of actors who helped found social work were university professors and journalists, who fought poverty and injustice primarily through the construction, dissemination, and mobilization of knowledge. Some, like journalist Paul Kellogg, conjoined social research in the social survey movement with writing and editing; Kellogg edited the widely read weekly journal of social work and social reform, the *Survey*. Other scholar-reformers, such as Sophonisba Breckinridge, who was a lawyer, political scientist, and economist, were antipoverty activists who used university-based research, publications, urban demonstration projects, and the development of social work education as their primary vehicles of reform.

> *Paul Kellogg (1879–1958)*
> Paul Kellogg headed a team of social researchers who studied the labor and living conditions of steelworkers in Pittsburgh. His team's work, published as The Pittsburgh Survey between 1907 and 1909, constituted the first comprehensive community study in the United States and inspired an entire research tradition. Kellogg then became editor of the widely read Survey magazine from 1909 until his retirement in 1952. The Survey, often called by contemporaries the "conscience of social work," championed numerous causes during his tenure at the magazine, including antilynching laws, women's rights, and occupational safety and health legislation.

Thus, three distinct definitions of what work social work is inspired the first uneasy confederation that became the modern-day profession. Each definition anchored a set of institutions and favored forms of practice; each was embodied and sustained by new technologies, updated ideologies, and evolving theories of practice.

The definition initially put forth by the spokespersons of charity organizations had two linked parts. The first segment, which has proved to be the dominant one within the profession in most decades of the 20th century since the early 1920s, defined social work as the differential assessment of and intervention with individuals and families in the context of their environments. Because charity leaders perceived that the resources needed to sustain such customized casework with individuals and families were scarce, they embedded in their vision of social work a second and secondary definition of social work. The work of social work, for charity leaders, was also the systematic administration and supervision of casework with individuals and families that was alert to issues of efficacy, efficiency, and the interagency coordination of social services and material relief.

The settlement house and adult education movements' definition of the work of social work also had two prongs, although different ones from those of organized philanthropy. The leaders of these movements viewed social work's work as the education and integration of new and marginal Americans into the mainstream polity and economy, using community-based group modalities. Concomitantly, settlement house and adult education leaders saw social work as neighborhood and civic development, an effort to reform local social conditions that were found to be unsafe and unhealthy and local institutions that were found to be inaccessible and unresponsive to their immigrant neighbors.

To the academic social scientists and journalists who helped found the profession, social work was the study of social problems, experimentation with possible remedies, and circulation of the knowledge gained thereby through publication, teaching, public testimony, and public education. The least local in their emphasis of the three founding groups, the university and media-based founders saw social work as a nationwide, if not global, endeavor to devise institutions and processes that would reduce social misery and oppression and enable all people to share more fully in the benefits of their respective societies.

From its earliest days, then, the social work profession has been a harbor of multiple ships whose captains have conceived of work in divergent ways. The majority of captains have commanded their crews to provide individualized casework to individuals and families who are embedded in multiple environments. That tradition is now configured in many forms, including individual, family, and group counseling; crisis intervention; case management; brief, episodic, and long-term treatment; skills development and training; and psychoeducational interventions. To maintain their vessels, those same leaders have called for the administration and supervision of "line" social workers. Meanwhile, different captains have required of their professional hands group work, adult education, and community organization. Still others have made social research and social policy formation their chief priorities, pursuing surveys of needs and resources; demonstration projects; ethnographic explorations of problems, populations, and institutions; and studies of clients' participation, social workers' interventions, action research, program outcomes, and policy implications. Social work, a century after its birth, remains much as it began—diverse in focus and method, rich in vision and commitment, and factious in its internal relationships.

INFLUENCES THAT SHAPED U.S. SOCIAL WORK

Myriad forces—economic, demographic, technological, and ideological—have had a major impact on the profession's development in the United States of the 20th century. This summary highlights six of the most potent influences.

Immigration

Successive waves of immigration, together with the reactions of native-born Americans to newcomers from Ireland, Eastern and Southern Europe, Asia and the Indian subcontinent, Africa, Central and South America, Mexico, and the Caribbean, have constituted one major influence on social work. Immigrants made up the majority of the clientele of turn-of-the-century charity organizations and settlement houses. The problems they and their offspring encountered in adjusting to the new terrain, language, and mores and in finding adequate housing, work, schooling, and health care rapidly became fundamental problems for the emergent profession of social work to tackle. Similarly, the xenophobia, racism, ethnocentrism, and anti-Semitism evoked by large-scale immigration to the United States were sufficiently widespread and enduring that they became defining parameters of and challenges to the profession's identity, value base, composition, constituencies, and mission (Jenkins, Sauber, & Friedlander, 1985; Said, 1979; Takaki, 1989).

Immigration to the United States slowed in the period of restrictive immigration legislation between 1917 and 1965. Nonetheless, the struggles of immigrants and their families to survive, adapt, and succeed in the American context were a fundamental focus of the profession's work during those decades. And they have remained so since then as millions more immigrants and refugees from disparate regions and traditions continue to settle here in the wake of the liberalizing effects of the Immigration and Nationality Act Amendments of 1965. Social workers in family and children's services, workplaces, mental health agencies, hospitals and health clinics, programs for elderly people, jails and prisons, schools, community centers, and public welfare organizations grapple daily with the concerns and dreams of new Americans, just as social workers have done since the 1890s.

Race and Ethnicity

Equally fundamental in the shaping of social work as a profession has been the phenomenon of American race relations. Social work was founded in the era of Jim Crowism, the systematic practice of segregating and suppressing African Americans through law, community custom, institutional racism, and vigilante violence in both the North and the South. It is not surprising, therefore, to find that early social work, like every other established and emergent profession of the time, welcomed few African Americans or other people of color into its midst as either colleagues or clients. Even the massive migration of African Americans from the rural South to the industrial centers of the North during World War I and the 1920s sparked relatively few white initiatives to assist newly arrived African Americans in finding their way in northern cities.

Consequently and necessarily, African Americans and Latino Americans created their own institutions of community and professional development. The National Association for the Advancement of Colored People, the Urban League, and the Insular Society of Social Workers, founded in 1935 by Puerto Rican professionals, are a few examples. Atlanta University and Howard University created schools of social work dedicated to preparing professionals for service in unserved and underserved African American rural and urban communities. Atlanta and Howard universities also sought to educate white America about its impact on black America and, therefore, on the country and culture as a whole. The College of Social Workers of Puerto Rico was started in 1940 to fulfill similar purposes in Puerto Rico and on the mainland.

Slowly, white social work practitioners and educators in the United States gained a greater awareness of some of the ways in which cultural biases about and prejudices toward African Americans, Latino Americans, Caribbean Americans, and Asian Americans permeated and contorted their own practice and profession. Educated by many events and movements, among them the lynching of African Americans, the genocide committed by the Third Reich, the forced internment of Japanese Americans in World War II, and the civil rights and black liberation movements, social work since the 1970s has intensified its efforts to attract more people of color to its membership and leadership. The pursuit of an authentically multicultural profession, one that is sufficiently diverse, knowledgeable, competent, and attuned to resonate with an increasingly heterogeneous United States, remains a central challenge of social work.

Changing Family Forms and Gender Roles

Changing family forms and gender roles have been another important influence on the development of the profession since the 1890s. Industrial and postindustrial capitalism have effected a dramatic decline in the proportion of women working at home as full-time homemakers and mothers. The average family size has diminished markedly. Divorce rates have escalated in comparison with figures from the 1950s and soared in comparison with rates from the 1900s. The great majority of women in the United States since the 1970s have combined full- or near full-time paid work with homemaking and mothering. A rapidly increasing number of widowed, divorced, abandoned, or never-married women are heading households. Domestic abuse of women and children has become epidemic. Reduced rates of infant mortality and enhanced average life spans result in many more woman-years of providing care to young, aged, and sick dependents than just a century ago.

As a result the list of presenting problems that lead the clients and patients of social workers to seek professional help or that trigger the mandating of services has expanded and become considerably more complicated since the 1960s. All the old problems remain, such as poverty and economic insecurity, chronic and acute illness, disability, unemployment and underemployment, addictions, domestic violence, crime, juvenile delinquency, discrimination, and marital difficulties. In addition, newer burdens are imposed by the spread of the postindustrial service economy and attendant technological changes. Conflicts between the imperatives of work and family life multiply; struggles between men and women and generations in families proliferate; uncertainty about jobs and income has become a stock worry among breadwinners, regardless of the levels of their occupational skills and social class. The work of social work has been defined, in part, by these structurally induced troubles.

Rise of the Welfare State

Another principal influence in shaping the social work profession in the United States has been the rise of the welfare state. When social work came into being, "the state," meaning government, was an extremely modest affair in both size and function. The government—federal, state, and local—was no more than the "night watchman," protecting private citizens, property, and businesses from harm. The concept of the activist or interventionist state was alien to the American tradition, except as an unpleasant and vague association to the British Crown from which the 13 colonies had taken considerable trouble to free themselves. Notions of what one would now term social safety nets were distant Prussian ideas, understood by most Americans to be irrelevant and unnecessary threats to the integrity of the free marketplace of ideas, services, and commodities. The regulation of commerce, industry, the environment, and professions was in its infancy, created begrudgingly by legislators to contain the worst damage done by those who were deemed to be aberrant capitalists, the greedy few who gave a bad name to an otherwise honorable cadre.

Forty years and a Great Depression later, the New Deal embodied both a new ideal and a new reality of a limited welfare state. The social work profession in the United States, like the country, was irrevocably transformed by the Roosevelt administration's social welfare innovations, changes promoted by many social workers for decades before they were realized. The creation of public jobs programs for those without work; income supports for dependent children and their mothers, blind people, and disabled people; and social insurance for retired and unemployed people meant that the state was no longer a mere night watchman. After 1935, with the passage of the Social Security Act, it had become the good uncle who makes certain that none of his many relatives, no matter how remotely related, slips between the cracks into penury.

In the place of social work agencies, the government became the court of last resort for material relief and jobs for the desperate. Although a substantial number of social workers helped staff the New Deal's public welfare functions, most professional social workers worked in voluntary human services organizations that, after the consolidation of the New Deal, became providers mainly of information, solace, and psychosocial assistance for the dispossessed, the dislocated, and discomfited. Whereas earlier social work had prided itself on responding holistically to clients' needs with both concrete aid and various social, psychological, educational, and cultural supports, social workers, after the passage of the Social Security Act, found their functions halved. If they worked in the public sector, most were charged with concentrating on economic want. If they were employed in the voluntary sector, their assignment was to relieve all other forms of distress that clients brought forward. The mind-body dualism of Western culture was thereby reinstated in the work of a profession that had sought to transcend it.

Suburbanization of the United States

A fifth salient influence on the profession's development was the planned suburbanization of the United States in the four decades following World War II and the correlative neglect of cities and rural areas. Confronted with a serious housing shortage in the period immediately following the war, federal and state officials during the Truman and Eisenhower years made a series of interrelated policy choices that acted as catalysts for suburban housing starts and auto transportation and as disincentives for the restoration of older rural and urban housing stock and mass transportation within cities and between rural regions. Four federal policies, in particular, enacted between 1946 and 1953, underwrote the rise of the American suburb. Federal, low-interest housing loans to returning veterans, federal fiscal stimulants for real estate developers who built modestly priced housing, the decision to construct a comprehensive federal interstate highway system, and a tariff system that heavily favored long-distance trucking and penalized railroad freight traffic reconfigured the American panorama within a mere quarter century.

At least five consequences followed, only the first two of which were intended: (1) the rapid growth of residential suburbs, a trend accelerated by the flight of whites in the 1950s and 1960s from older cities to which an increasing number of African American families had migrated after the mechanization of southern cotton farming during the 1940s; (2) the subsequent movement to suburbs by many industries and corporations; (3) the growing indispensability of automobiles in far-flung suburban areas with scanty public transportation; (4) increased isolation, unemployment, and poverty in rural and urban areas; and (5) the creation of entire regions of economic depression in those inland areas that had grown up as freight railroad entrepôts.

What impact did these changes make on the profession of social work? First, two of its historical client populations, poor people and new immigrants, were, for the first time in American history, almost completely removed from daily contact with middle-income and wealthy residents, many of whom had moved to homogeneous suburbs by the 1960s. Neighborhoods in American cities had long clustered along lines of income levels, race, religion, and ethnicity. Nonetheless, wealthy, middle-income, working-class, and poor city dwellers in earlier eras had intermingled regularly in travel, work, and commerce.

The suburbanization of residential communities and major employers, with the resultant reliance on family cars, made cross-class, cross-racial, and even cross-religious understanding a rarer element because interpersonal contact across demographic groups grew less frequent. Workplaces still provided considerable exposure to people different from oneself demographically, but suburban residential communities, malls, schools, and travel no longer did. Consequently, social work's urban and rural clients and their concerns became less recognizable and legitimate in the eyes of middle-class communities than had been true in the decades before World War II. The results were tax revolts, reduced funding for social work programs and for the development of urban communities, and heightened mistrust of vulnerable populations and of the professionals who worked with them.

Second, the profession itself began to mirror in a new way some of the same divisions that were occurring in the broader culture. Some social workers have chosen to become full-time private psychotherapists to middle-class patients, exclusively. Their abandonment of the profession's original mission of serving historically underserved and marginalized citizens and residents is the functional equivalent of the flight of white residents and corporations to homogeneous suburbs.

A second group of social workers, in contrast, has remained immersed throughout their careers in public or voluntary sector work with stigmatized, especially vulnerable, or poor clients and neighborhoods or with the policies that affect those clients. Such agency-based practitioners continue to make up the preponderance of the profession and to perform path-breaking work with a variety of distressed populations, such as migrant workers and refugees, abused children, adults and children with the human immunodeficiency virus and the acquired immune deficiency syndrome, homeless individuals and families, substance abusers, and people with severe and persistent mental illness. They work in social work organizations and in a wide variety of host settings, such as schools, hospitals and community health clinics, hospices, prisons and jails, rape crisis centers, and government offices. After years of refining their interventive skills in agency service, some social workers choose to supplement their income and experience with part-time, sliding-scale, clinical practices of their own in the evenings and on weekends.

A third group of social workers has chosen to work in corporate or union settings, where employees or retired employees frequently seek help that they might not otherwise pursue if they were referred to more traditional (and therefore more stigmatized) human services programs. Social work in the workplace has been of particular importance to workers who have experienced difficulties in their familial or supervisory relationships; have suffered from alcoholism, clinical depression, or other mental illnesses; have endured major losses, such as the death of a child or partner; have been subject to minor or major physical disabilities; have grappled with unemployment or underemployment; and have contemplated retirement.

> *Bertha Capen Reynolds*
> *(1885–1978)*
> An outstanding direct practitioner, educator, theoretician, and activist, Bertha Capen Reynolds embodied in her own person and career the case-to-cause approach to enhancing human welfare. Her books, among them Between Client and Community (1934), linked social casework with group leadership and social reform in as seamless a manner as her life did. Associate director of the Smith College School for Social Work from 1925 through 1938, she was dismissed from her position for supporting the labor organizing of rank-and-file social workers. In 1943 she created the prototype for contemporary employee assistance programs at the National Maritime Union.

Incompatible Job Demands

According to Pernick (1985), "the attempt to resolve incompatible job demands may well prove to have been one hitherto overlooked critically important driving force in explaining the historical evolution of professionalism" (p. 248).

The sixth influential factor is an internal phenomenon, unlike the other five just discussed. Also shaping social work's development have been the profession's ongoing struggles with two sets of incompatible job demands. Both forms of incompatibility emanate from the same root cause.

A leitmotif in the history of American social work has been the collision between the profession's occupational imperative to be client centered and the necessity of being cost-efficient. Throughout U.S. history, providing relief for poor and unfortunate people has been a collective responsibility exercised through the church; village and county administrations; organized philanthropies; and, more recently, federal and state governments. To no one's surprise, each of these authorities historically has sought to offer maximal succor for minimal cost. Social workers, as a consequence, have been faced since the 1890s with a perpetual juggle. At the same time that they have sought to respond fully and carefully to each client, they have constantly had to attend to "bottom-line" considerations to be accountable fiscally to the taxpayers and donors who fund their services.

For example, contemporary social workers in the realm of child protective services bear one of the heaviest social and professional responsibilities imaginable—that of identifying and protecting children who are at risk of neglect or abuse. The entire citizenry relies on child welfare professionals to succeed in guarding the health and welfare of the most vulnerable of the newest generation of Americans. However, accompanying this important charge is another: to reduce social service expenditures and increase caseloads; in sum, to do more with less. This particular double-bind has dogged social work since its inception.

Similarly, another kind of internal incompatibility has accompanied social work throughout its first century of existence. Social work's funding sources, whether public or private, have, on many occasions, created social programs to promote social peace and cohesion, to hasten the integration of marginal groups, and to strengthen the social order in the face of societal fragmentation and strife. Indeed, the profession of social work in the United States was created, in large part, for those purposes.

Meanwhile, the client-centered social worker has understood his or her central charge to be that of contributing to the self-empowerment of his or her clients and their communities. Self-empowerment activities by individual clients and groups, as the liberation and self-help movements since the 1960s have indicated, often necessarily perforate social cohesion and calm. They frequently entail sustained advocacy, the staking of new and old claims, and the purposeful disruption of long-established and exclusionist patterns of privilege and domination. How does the professional social worker honor both masters? How does she or he remain a loyal agent of auspices that seek to consolidate the social whole in situations in which clients' welfare and development require challenges to prevailing arrangements of rights, prerogatives, and resources?

How, for example, does one help a battered woman whose repeated beatings may well be at the hands of her spouse or the father of her children? The well-being of the woman and children may well hinge on immediately ending all contact between the assailant and his wife and children, either through removing the husband from the household or through assisting the wife and children to leave. The laws of most states and localities make the latter far more feasible than the former. If one's sponsoring agency is committed to the strengthening of the family, the slowing of the divorce rate, and the reduction of the welfare rolls, then helping battered women to leave their abusers may be an act that is incompatible with key organizational priorities, although necessary in light of social work values. Tensions such as these characterize the work of many social work professionals because that work is often paid for by actors and interests whose location in the social and economic structure is far removed from those of social workers' clients.

A Profession in a Sea of Other Professions

Interprofessional rivalries, alliances, and battles have informed and complicated social work's development and possibilities as long as the profession has existed. Securing a reliable market for its wares, an occupational niche all its own, a knowledge base and set of skills that attract "customers," and a reputation that ensures durable financial backing and government licensing and accreditation have been necessary activities for every profession in the United States, including social work (Abbott, 1988; Larson, 1977; Rothman, 1971). Far more so than in Western Europe, professions in the United States must become and remain compelling to the marketplace, to philanthropists (also known as foundations and donors), and to the state if they are to survive and endure. It follows, therefore, that all American professions incessantly have jockeyed with each other for leverage, clientele, jurisdictional control, and legitimacy. Medicine, law, the ministry, public health, nursing, public administration, urban planning, psychiatry, psychology, teaching, applied sociology, family therapy, marital counseling, and addictions counseling are some of the key professions with which social work has at times collaborated, at other times sparred, and often competed.

The classical ethos of professionalism has trumpeted the centrality of knowledge, skills, and altruism and muted the salience and ubiquity of market, status, and territorial imperatives. As a result, interprofessional rivalries within society and particular institutions remain cloaked competitions, conflicts represented as disinterested pursuits of the best interests of clients and patients, not as battles that involve the self-interest of professions or professionals. The more prestigious and powerful the profession, the more costly would be its acknowledgment of its own commercial, competitive, and acquisitive elements.

Consequently, conscientious professionals, among them social workers, must equip themselves with a repertoire of capacities for understanding and working constructively in institutions that are deeply influenced by competitive market forces. One necessary skill is that of "reading between the lines," of remaining alert to subtexts of self-interest and ambition that are encoded within stated or written texts about professional altruism. Just as in work with clients, collegial relations demands a constant search for latent as well as manifest content.

Second, social workers who desire to serve clients to the best of their ability must become astute assessors of the culture, dynamics, and structures of the institutions in which they work. Comprehending both the institutional and occupational niches, interests, leverage, and "track records" of colleagues from other professions is as important as learning from their knowledge bases and grasping fully their long-term goals and stated intentions regarding their clients, projects, or departments.

Because social work is frequently conducted on interdisciplinary teams, interprofessional collaboration is a third crucial skill for social work professionals to refine. Collaboration in interprofessional contexts calls for steady translation, extrapolation, and interpolation. Interprofessional collaboration is an art of mediation and negotiation, a craft of discerning common ground amid diversity. It is, above all, a search for the meanings that others hold dear, rather than a hunt for their motives.

Social work in the United States mirrors, represents, and influences the pluralistic, dynamic, and conflictive society of which it is a part. Small wonder, then, that it is a profession that is strikingly diverse, rapidly changing, and frequently at odds with itself. It is a profession with numerous parts and functions. Fortunately, for both its clients and itself, the whole that is social work is far greater than the sum of its parts.

REFERENCES

Abbott, A. (1988). *The system of professions: An essay on the division of expert labor.* Chicago: University of Chicago Press.

Bulmer, M., Bales, K., & Sklar, K. K. (1991). *The social survey in historical perspective, 1880–1940.* New York: Cambridge University Press.

Devine, E. T. (1939). *When social work was young.* New York: Macmillan.

Immigration and Nationality Act Amendments of 1965. P.L. 89-236, 79 Stat. 911.

Jenkins, S., Sauber, M., & Friedlander, E. (1985). *Ethnic associations and services to new immigrants.* New York: Community Council of Greater New York.

Larson, M. S. (1977). *The rise of professionalism.* Berkeley: University of California Press.

Pernick, M. (1985). *A calculus of suffering: Pain, professionalism, and anaesthesia in nineteenth-century America.* New York: Columbia University Press.

Richmond, M. E. (1930). *The long view: Papers and addresses.* (J. C. Colcord & R. Z. S. Mann, Eds.). New York: Russell Sage Foundation.

Rothman, D. (1971). *The discovery of the asylum.* Boston: Little, Brown.

Said, E. (1979). *Orientalism.* New York: Vintage Books.

Social Security Act of 1935. Ch. 351, 49 Stat. 620.

Takaki, R. (1989). *Strangers from a different shore: A history of Asian Americans.* New York: Penguin.

NASW Code of Ethics

PREAMBLE

This code is intended to serve as a guide to the everyday conduct of members of the social work profession and as a basis for the adjudication of issues in ethics when the conduct of social workers is alleged to deviate from the standards expressed or implied in this code. It represents standards of ethical behavior for social workers in professional relationships with those served, with colleagues, with employers, with other individuals and professions, and with the community and society as a whole. It also embodies standards of ethical behavior governing individual conduct to the extent that such conduct is associated with an individual's status and identity as a social worker.

This code is based on the fundamental values of the social work profession that include the worth, dignity, and uniqueness of all persons as well as their rights and opportunities. It is also based on the nature of social work, which fosters conditions that promote these values.

In subscribing to and abiding by this code, the social worker is expected to view ethical responsibility in as inclusive a context as each situation demands and within which ethical judgment is required. The social worker is expected to take into consideration all the principles in this code that have a bearing upon any situation in which ethical judgment is to be exercised and professional intervention or conduct is planned. The course of action that the social worker chooses is expected to be consistent with the spirit as well as the letter of this code.

In itself, this code does not represent a set of rules that will prescribe all the behaviors of social workers in all the complexities of professional life. Rather, it offers general principles to guide conduct, and the judicious appraisal of conduct, in situations that have ethical implications. It provides the basis for making judgments about ethical actions before or after they occur. Frequently, the particular situation determines the ethical principles that apply and the manner of their application. In such cases, not only the particular ethical principles are taken into immediate consideration, but also the entire code and its spirit. Specific applications of ethical principles must be judged within the context in which they are being considered. Ethical behavior in a given situation must satisfy not only the judgment of the individual social worker, but also the judgment of an unbiased jury of professional peers.

This code should not be used as an instrument to deprive any social worker of the opportunity or freedom to practice with complete professional integrity; nor should any disciplinary action be taken on the basis of this code without maximum provision for safeguarding the rights of the social worker affected.

The ethical behavior of social workers results not from edict, but from a personal commitment of the individual. This code is offered to affirm the will and zeal of all social workers to be ethical and to act ethically in all that they do as social workers.

The following codified ethical principles should guide social workers in the various roles and relationships and at the various levels of responsibility in which they function professionally. These principles also serve as a basis for the adjudication by the National Association of Social Workers of issues in ethics.

In subscribing to this code, social workers are required to cooperate in its implementation and abide by any disciplinary rulings based on it. They should also take adequate measures to discourage, prevent, expose, and correct the unethical conduct of colleagues. Finally, social workers should be equally ready to defend and assist colleagues unjustly charged with unethical conduct.

NASW Code of Ethics

I. The Social Worker's Conduct and Comportment as a Social Worker

A. Propriety—The social worker should maintain high standards of personal conduct in the capacity or identity as social worker.
   1. The private conduct of the social worker is a personal matter to the same degree as is any other person's, except when such conduct compromises the fulfillment of professional responsibilities.
   2. The social worker should not participate in, condone, or be associated with dishonesty, fraud, deceit, or misrepresentation.
   3. The social worker should distinguish clearly between statements and actions made as a private individual and as a representative of the social work profession or an organization or group.
B. Competence and Professional Development—The social worker should strive to become and remain proficient in professional practice and the performance of professional functions.
   1. The social worker should accept responsibility or employment only on the basis of existing competence or the intention to acquire the necessary competence.

2. The social worker should not misrepresent professional qualifications, education, experience, or affiliations.
3. The social worker should not allow his or her own personal problems, psychosocial distress, substance abuse, or mental health difficulties to interfere with professional judgment and performance or jeopardize the best interests of those for whom the social worker has a professional responsibility.
4. The social worker whose personal problems, psychosocial distress, substance abuse, or mental health difficulties interfere with professional judgment and performance should immediately seek consultation and take appropriate remedial action by seeking professional help, making adjustments in workload, terminating practice, or taking any other steps necessary to protect clients and others.

C. Service—The social worker should regard as primary the service obligation of the social work profession.
1. The social worker should retain ultimate responsibility for the quality and extent of the service that individual assumes, assigns, or performs.
2. The social worker should act to prevent practices that are inhumane or discriminatory against any person or group of persons.

D. Integrity—The social worker should act in accordance with the highest standards of professional integrity and impartiality.
1. The social worker should be alert to and resist the influences and pressures that interfere with the exercise of professional discretion and impartial judgment required for the performance of professional functions.
2. The social worker should not exploit professional relationships for personal gain.

E. Scholarship and Research—The social worker engaged in study and research should be guided by the conventions of scholarly inquiry.
1. The social worker engaged in research should consider carefully its possible consequences for human beings.
2. The social worker engaged in research should ascertain that the consent of the participants in the research is voluntary and informed, without any implied deprivation or penalty for refusal to participate, and with due regard for the participants' privacy and dignity.
3. The social worker engaged in research should protect participants from unwarranted physical or mental discomfort, distress, harm, danger, or deprivation.
4. The social worker who engages in the evaluation of services or cases should discuss them only for professional purposes and only with persons directly and professionally concerned with them.
5. Information obtained about participants in research should be treated as confidential.
6. The social worker should take credit only for work actually done in connection with scholarly and research endeavors and credit contributions made by others.

II. The Social Worker's Ethical Responsibility to Clients

F. Primacy of Clients' Interests—The social worker's primary responsibility is to clients.

1. The social worker should serve clients with devotion, loyalty, determination, and the maximum application of professional skill and competence.

2. The social worker should not exploit relationships with clients for personal advantage.

3. The social worker should not practice, condone, facilitate, or collaborate with any form of discrimination on the basis of race, color, sex, sexual orientation, age, religion, national origin, marital status, political belief, mental or physical handicap, or any other preference or personal characteristic, condition, or status.

4. The social worker should not condone or engage in any dual or multiple relationships with clients or former clients in which there is a risk of exploitation of or potential harm to the client. The social worker is responsible for setting clear, appropriate, and culturally sensitive boundaries.

5. The social worker should under no circumstances engage in sexual activities with clients.

6. The social worker should provide clients with accurate and complete information regarding the extent and nature of the services available to them.

7. The social worker should apprise clients of their risks, rights, opportunities, and obligations associated with social service to them.

8. The social worker should seek advice and counsel of colleagues and supervisors whenever such consultation is in the best interest of clients.

9. The social worker should terminate service to clients, and professional relationships with them, when such service and relationships are no longer required or no longer serve the clients' needs or interests.

10. The social worker should withdraw services precipitously only under unusual circumstances, giving careful consideration to all factors in the situation and taking care to minimize possible adverse effects.

11. The social worker who anticipates the termination or interruption of service to clients should notify clients promptly and seek the transfer, referral, or continuation of service in relation to the clients' needs and preferences.

G. Rights and Prerogatives of Clients—The social worker should make every effort to foster maximum self-determination on the part of clients.

1. When the social worker must act on behalf of a client who has been adjudged legally incompetent, the social worker should safeguard the interests and rights of that client.

2. When another individual has been legally authorized to act on behalf of a client, the social worker should deal with that person always with the client's best interest in mind.

3. The social worker should not engage in any action that violates or diminishes the civil or legal rights of clients.

H. Confidentiality and Privacy—The social worker should respect the privacy of clients and hold in confidence all information obtained in the course of professional service.

1. The social worker should share with others confidences revealed by clients, without their consent, only for compelling professional reasons.
2. The social worker should inform clients fully about the limits of confidentiality in a given situation, the purposes for which information is obtained, and how it may be used.
3. The social worker should afford clients reasonable access to any official social work records concerning them.
4. When providing clients with access to records, the social worker should take due care to protect the confidences of others contained in those records.
5. The social worker should obtain informed consent of clients before taping, recording, or permitting third-party observation of their activities.

I. Fees—When setting fees, the social worker should ensure that they are fair, reasonable, considerate, and commensurate with the service performed and with due regard for the clients' ability to pay.

1. The social worker should not accept anything of value for making a referral.

III. The Social Worker's Ethical Responsibility to Colleagues

J. Respect, Fairness, and Courtesy—The social worker should treat colleagues with respect, courtesy, fairness, and good faith.

1. The social worker should cooperate with colleagues to promote professional interests and concerns.
2. The social worker should respect confidences shared by colleagues in the course of their professional relationships and transactions.
3. The social worker should create and maintain conditions of practice that facilitate ethical and competent professional performance by colleagues.
4. The social worker should treat with respect, and represent accurately and fairly, the qualifications, views, and findings of colleagues and use appropriate channels to express judgments on these matters.
5. The social worker who replaces or is replaced by a colleague in professional practice should act with consideration for the interest, character, and reputation of that colleague.
6. The social worker should not exploit a dispute between a colleague and employers to obtain a position or otherwise advance the social worker's interest.
7. The social worker should seek arbitration or mediation when conflicts with colleagues require resolution for compelling professional reasons.
8. The social worker should extend to colleagues of other professions the same respect and cooperation that is extended to social work colleagues.

9. The social worker who serves as an employer, supervisor, or mentor to colleagues should make orderly and explicit arrangements regarding the conditions of their continuing professional relationship.

10. The social worker who has the responsibility for employing and evaluating the performance of other staff members should fulfill such responsibility in a fair, considerate, and equitable manner, on the basis of clearly enunciated criteria.

11. The social worker who has the responsibility for evaluating the performance of employees, supervisees, or students should share evaluations with them.

12. The social worker should not use a professional position vested with power, such as that of employer, supervisor, teacher, or consultant, to his or her advantage or to exploit others.

13. The social worker who has direct knowledge of a social work colleague's impairment due to personal problems, psychosocial distress, substance abuse, or mental health difficulties should consult with that colleague and assist the colleague in taking remedial action.

K. Dealing with Colleagues' Clients—The social worker has the responsibility to relate to the clients of colleagues with full professional consideration.

1. The social worker should not assume professional responsibility for the clients of another agency or a colleague without appropriate communication with that agency or colleague.

2. The social worker who serves the clients of colleagues, during a temporary absence or emergency, should serve those clients with the same consideration as that afforded any client.

IV. The Social Worker's Responsibility to Employers and Employing Organizations

L. Commitments to Employing Organization—The social worker should adhere to commitments made to the employing organization.

1. The social worker should work to improve the employing agency's policies and procedures, and the efficiency and effectiveness of its services.

2. The social worker should not accept employment or arrange student field placements in an organization which is currently under public sanction by NASW for violating personnel standards, or imposing limitations on or penalties for professional actions on behalf of clients.

3. The social worker should act to prevent and eliminate discrimination in the employing organization's work assignments and in its employment policies and practices.

4. The social worker should use with scrupulous regard, and only for the purpose for which they are intended, the resources of the employing organization.

V. The Social Worker's Ethical Responsibility to the Social Work Profession

M. Maintaining the Integrity of the Profession—The social worker should uphold and advance the values, ethics, knowledge, and mission of the profession.

1. The social worker should protect and enhance the dignity and integrity of the profession and should be responsible and vigorous in discussion and criticism of the profession.
2. The social worker should take action through appropriate channels against unethical conduct by any other member of the profession.
3. The social worker should act to prevent the unauthorized and unqualified practice of social work.
4. The social worker should make no misrepresentations in advertising as to qualifications, competence, service, or results to be achieved.

N. Community Service—The social worker should assist the profession in making social services available to the general public.

1. The social worker should contribute time and professional expertise to activities that promote respect for the utility, the integrity, and the competence of the social work profession.
2. The social worker should support the formulation, development, enactment, and implementation of social policies of concern to the profession.

O. Development of Knowledge—The social worker should take responsibility for identifying, developing, and fully utilizing knowledge for professional practice.

1. The social worker should base practice upon recognized knowledge relevant to social work.
2. The social worker should critically examine and keep current with emerging knowledge relevant to social work.
3. The social worker should contribute to the knowledge base of social work and share research knowledge and practice wisdom with colleagues.

VI. The Social Worker's Ethical Responsibility to Society

P. Promoting the General Welfare—The social worker should promote the general welfare of society.

1. The social worker should act to prevent and eliminate discrimination against any person or group on the basis of race, color, sex, sexual orientation, age, religion, national origin, marital status, political belief, mental or physical handicap, or any other preference or personal characteristic, condition, or status.
2. The social worker should act to ensure that all persons have access to the resources, services, and opportunities which they require.
3. The social worker should act to expand choice and opportunity for all persons, with special regard for disadvantaged or oppressed groups and persons.

4. The social worker should promote conditions that encourage respect for the diversity of cultures which constitute American society.
5. The social worker should provide appropriate professional services in public emergencies.
6. The social worker should advocate changes in policy and legislation to improve social conditions and to promote social justice.
7. The social worker should encourage informed participation by the public in shaping social policies and institutions.

As adopted by the 1979 NASW Delegate Assembly and revised by the 1990 and 1993 NASW Delegate Assemblies.

Sample Exercises

Introduction

Following are some examples of exercises that can be used in class sessions. Because the foundation course covers so much content, it is important that students have an opportunity to "process" what they are learning. There are many approaches to this kind of experiential learning, and the illustrations here are merely suggestive. Teachers and students likely will find a style that works for a particular class. It might be role play, small group discussion, or some other kind of participatory presentation. What is important is that students act on or express their grasp of the class content so that they experience some of the dilemmas and ambiguities that are inevitable in their practice. These exercises do not lead to "right answers," and thus they help students to become more comfortable in taking risks, in using their judgment, and in living with uncertainty.

EXERCISE 1

Your own life experiences mold and influence not only your personal life but your professional practice as well. If you had a strong family background, for example, you will draw a great deal of emotional strength from those experiences, but it may be more difficult for you to deeply understand experiences of clients with very different histories. Or, if you come from a family in which substance abuse was a factor, this will have multiple effects on your practice. It is crucial that you deepen your self-awareness, including knowledge of areas about which you need to be particularly sensitive, as well as strengths you draw from your personal history. This exercise is designed to help you begin such exploration, which you will want to continue throughout your career, because you will periodically discover new facets of yourself in your work.

In a small group of four to six people, take a moment to individually write down answers to these questions:

- In what two areas of my practice do I need to be especially sensitive to possible interference from my personal history?
- What are two particular strengths I bring to practice from my personal history?

Do not surface issues that you do not feel comfortable sharing (although you should process such issues yourself or preferably with someone you trust). When everyone in the group has completed this, take turns going around the circle, first discussing your responses to the first question. Use a Native American talking circle method: Each person takes his or her turn and speaks without interruption; when that person is done, the next person takes his or her turn. Save general discussion until everyone has taken a turn. Be sure to listen to and support each other in this exercise; avoid self-absorption! After you have processed the first question, use the same procedure to examine the second question.

EXERCISE 2

Divide the class into three groups, each of which is to draw an ecomap on the chalkboard to describe the dynamics of the following case:

Case Example

An 18-year-old single mother of a two-year-old daughter was referred to child protective services (CPS) by the emergency room physician of X hospital. The girl was brought in by her mother because the child was crying in pain from severe burns on her buttocks. The mother's explanation was that the child had backed into the open oven door when the mother was removing cookies she had just baked. The mother was extremely agitated and fearful.

The social worker at CPS learned from the mother that she had few social supports—the father of the child visited occasionally, her parents lived in another city, she did not work or socialize outside her apartment house, and she had no real friends except for one neighbor who was an elderly woman living alone. The mother had not finished high school because she had become pregnant; she had no job skills; and although she seemed intelligent and aware of the seriousness of her situation, her affect was flat and she seemed to be severely depressed. The child appeared to be developmentally normal, affectionate with her mother, and outgoing in the social worker's presence.

The mother was worried that her description of the accident would not be believed and that CPS would remove her daughter from her care. The social worker had the impression that the mother was concerned about her daughter's welfare and that this might have been a true accident, not an instance of child abuse. Yet, when the social worker later talked with the neighbor who knew the mother, she learned that the mother often lost her temper and hit the child.

The social worker had to make a decision about the immediate health and welfare of the child: Did this case require immediate placement to protect the child? Was this a woman who would respond to help, and what would the interventions be?

Creating the Ecomap

In drawing the ecomaps, consider the interrelatedness of the case variables, what is known and not known about the case, and what limitations and potentials for help are present in the case. The three ecomaps may emphasize different points for intervention, depending on the way they are drawn.

A typical ecomap will include

1. a circle depicting the case variables in sectors
2. lines—broken and unbroken—to depict strong or weak connections among the variables
3. shading or colors to identify the point or points of intervention indicated by the perspective on the case.

EXERCISE 3

Skills Exercise in Ethics and Values

Case Example

The social worker in the psychiatric outpatient clinic of a general hospital served as a member of the treatment team with a psychiatrist and a psychiatric nurse. The psychiatrist attended the clinic irregularly, primarily to prescribe medications for patients. Most of the direct work with the patients was done by the social worker and the nurse. Although the social worker and the nurse had the freedom to carry out their own professional treatment plans, the psychiatrist, as director of the clinic, had a strict rule that patients were required to come to the clinic and that home visits were not permitted.

One day a patient called the social worker to say that she could not come to the clinic and that she was so depressed that she was contemplating suicide. The social worker could not convince the patient to come to the clinic, and because the patient lived alone, the social worker was concerned about the patient's welfare. When she discussed with the nurse her plan to visit the patient, the nurse cautioned her about the strict rule against doing so. Despite the rule, and in the face of the nurse's warning, the social worker made the home visit.

Class Exercise
Divide the class into three groups, each group taking one of the following positions to debate:
1. The social worker should not have made the home visit. Argue the reasons.
2. The social worker did the right thing in making the home visit. Why?
3. The social worker should have contacted the psychiatrist to get his permission to make the home visit. Why?

EXERCISE 4

Before you begin this exercise, it is important that everyone in the group recognize the need for mutual respect and curiosity when discussing core personal and cultural values. Start by giving each member of the class the opportunity to answer the question, How do you self-identify culturally? The instructor or group leader usually should go first, to act as a model. It is important that each person be allowed to define himself or herself in his or her own way; for many students, race and religion may be the most salient factors, but for others, sexual orientation or cohort factors may be the most important. (It may be necessary to remind the class of this fact because on occasion, one member of the class may interrupt another to question whether the other is using the right categories.)

As each person provides her or his self-identification, it is listed on large sheets of paper or on the chalkboard. The instructor or group leader then breaks the larger group into smaller groups that have one or more central features in common. Those who do not fit into any simple system of grouping can form their own "diversity caucus."

Each small group is then given 20 minutes to discuss the following questions and to prepare a report to give to the larger group:
1. What messages did you receive in childhood about your own group?
2. What messages did you receive in childhood about those who are not of your group?
3. Which of your most important values came primarily from the microculture of your family, and which came from larger cultural entities or groups?

4. How may your cultural background and values affect your practice—now and in the future?

After 20 minutes, each group sends a reporter to participate in a panel discussion in front of the larger group. After the reporters summarize the group discussion, the instructor and other members of the class are given the opportunity to ask members of the panel questions, to clarify and deepen mutual understanding—like a television talk show.

Source: Nakanishi, M., & Rittner, B. (1992). The inclusionary cultural model. *Journal of Social Work Education, 28,* 27–35.

EXERCISE 5

Case Example

Mr. P is a 28-year-old graphic artist who is seeking help at the community mental health center because he has been experiencing anxiety and depression. Since he recently learned that he has acquired immune deficiency syndrome (AIDS), he has been unable to concentrate on or to complete his work assignments, sleep at night, or eat regularly. Before his marriage, Mr. P took drugs, and his physician assumes that that is how he contracted AIDS. Although he is presently asymptomatic, Mr. P is concerned about his health, his job status, and his ability to care for his family. However, his most immediate concern is that he cannot disclose either his past drug use or his health condition to his wife or his parents.

In spite of his good health, Mr. P has missed days at work and has received several warnings from his supervisors, who are baffled by the recent deterioration in his work performance. Mr. P and his wife have two toddlers. Mrs. P is also concerned about his lack of motivation at work and his "hypochondria." At home, he makes excuses for not being near his children or his wife. Mrs. P does not know of his AIDS diagnosis. Mr. P's parents and younger brother live in a small town far away, and he knows that they would never understand how he got AIDS, so he is also afraid to tell them.

Divide the class into two groups, and ask each group to discuss the following questions in order to arrive at a beginning focus with Mr. P.

1. What do the facts so far tell us about Mr. P?
2. What are his strengths and limitations?
3. What is known about AIDS?

On the basis of this discussion, each group should role-play a social worker and Mr. P during the first interview. Engagement and contracting should be the focus.

After both presentations (which may emphasize different issues), the class should determine if the interviews flowed from an understanding of the case and should then analyze what occurred during the interviews and why.

EXERCISE 6

Choose one of these exercises:
1. Divide the class into two groups, each of which will present one example of
   a. family-friendly agency policies
   b. family "unfriendly" agency policies.
   What are the policies? How are the policies evident? Identify the impact of these policies on case examples.
2. Divide the class into three groups. Each group should plan and role-play a family therapy session with the Gutierrez family from one of the three perspectives presented in chapter 8, with the rest of the class observing. Following the role plays, the students can discuss and compare their experiences from the perspectives of clients, the social worker, and observers.

EXERCISE 7

Putting the Group Together
1. Compose a group or groups according to the following description of the applicants. Justify your decisions on the basis of the principles of group composition and research on small group behavior. If any clients are eliminated from the group, justify this decision. What would you say to them?
2. You must also decide how many leaders to use. Justify this decision on the basis of the literature on leadership in small groups.

Applicants
Thirty clients applied to participate in a group that was advertised to deal with issues surrounding parenting primary school-aged children. Of the 30 clients, 10 were men and 20 were women. Two of the men and seven of the women were African American, five of the women listed their ethnicity as Hispanic (two were Cuban and three were recent immigrants from Central America), and the rest were Caucasian.

Two of the Caucasian women were recently discharged from a 28-day alcohol detoxification and treatment program, which referred them to the group. Three of the Caucasian women

Note: Exercise 7 was developed by Sheldon D. Rose, professor, School of Social Work, University of Wisconsin–Madison.

and one of the African American men were referred by the local child protective services agency after a substantiated report of child abuse. One of the Caucasian men had no recent group experience and stated in a pregroup interview that he was hesitant about participating in the group.

Four leaders were available to lead the group or groups—two men and two women. All the group leaders were Caucasian. Three of the leaders were parents, the one nonparent was a social work graduate student in her field placement.

Schematically, the foregoing information looks like this:

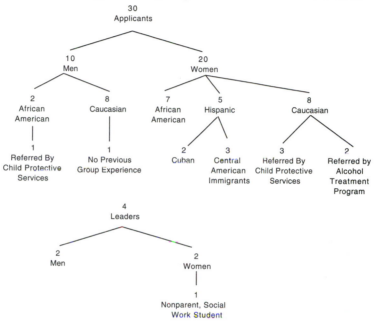

Suggested Reading

Acosta, R., & Yamamoto, J. (1984). The utility of group work practice for Hispanic Americans. *Social Work with Groups, 7*(3), 63–74.

Aries, E. (1976). Interaction patterns and themes of male, female and mixed groups. *Small Group Behavior, 7*(1), 7–18.

Bertcher, H. J., & Maple, F. (1985). Elements and issues in group composition. In M. Sundel, P. Glasser, R. Sarri, & R. Vinter (Eds.), *Individual change through small groups* (2nd ed., pp. 180–202). New York: Free Press.

Davis, L. (1979). Racial composition in groups. *Social Work, 24,* 208–213.

Davis, L. (1984). The significance of color. *Social Work with Groups, 7*(3), 3–6.

Davis, L. (1984). Essential components of group work with black Americans. *Social Work with Groups, 7*(3), 97–110.

Davis, L. (1985). Group work practice with ethnic minorities of color. In M. Sundel, P. Glasser, R. Sarri, & R. Vinter (Eds.), *Individual change through small groups* (2nd ed., pp. 324–343). New York: Free Press.

Kahn, L. S. (1984). Group process and sex differences. *Psychology of Women Quarterly, 8,* 261–281.

Kolodny, R. (1980). The dilemma of co-leadership. *Social Work with Groups, 3*(4), 31–34.

Martin, P. Y., & Shanahan, K. A. (1983). Transcending the effects of sex composition in small groups. *Social Work with Groups, 6*(3–4), 19–32.

Reed, B. G. (1985). Gender issues in training group leaders. In M. Sundel, P. Glasser, R. Sarri, & R. Vinter (Eds.), *Individual change through small groups* (2nd ed., pp. 70–86). New York: Free Press.

Rose, S. D. (1989). Preparing for group therapy. In S. D. Rose (Ed.), *Working with adults in groups: Integrating cognitive-behavioral and small group strategies.* San Francisco: Jossey-Bass.

Rose, S. D., & Edleson, J. L. (1987). Planning treatment and orienting children and parents. In S. Rose & J. L. Edleson (Eds.), *Working with children and adolescents in groups: A multimethod approach.* San Francisco: Jossey-Bass.

EXERCISE 8

Role-Play Exercise on Scapegoating

You are the leader of a group of female ninth and 10th graders (15 and 16 year olds) in a school-sponsored group for underachievers (students who do not do homework, talk a lot in class, or do not concentrate on schoolwork). These students do not have many friends in school and have been identified by classroom teachers as those who make trouble for other students. These students hang out together after school and outside the group.

The purpose of this group is to help these students develop skills and attitudes that will lead them to succeed in school. The group was formed three or four months ago and is now in the work or ongoing phase (Tuckman's, 1965, "performing" stage of group development). For example, in recent sessions, the group members have talked about their families and discussed how to respond when they are angry with other students and teachers.

Several of the group members went dancing at a club on Saturday night, and this is the first group meeting since the

---

Note: Exercise 8 was developed by Renée Solomon, associate professor, Columbia University School of Social Work, New York.

dance. While she was dancing with Ellen, Jane said to her, "You look gorgeous. I could really go for you." Ellen left abruptly and did not return to the dance.

At the next meeting Ellen came in a little late. Upon seeing her, several group members immediately asked her, "Where did you disappear Saturday?" Ellen responded, pointing to Jane, "Ask her!" Jane said, "What are you talking about?" There is some arguing back and forth, but finally Ellen is persuaded to tell her story. Then the group members criticized and "dumped on" Jane.

Instructions for Role Plays
1. Assign the roles of (1) the leader, (2) Ellen, (3) Jane, and (4) two to three other members.
2. There are two ways to begin this role play:
   • Begin the group where the scenario left off.
   • Have Ellen leave the room and start the role-play with her coming to the group late.
3. The leader and the members (especially the leader) must respond to this interpersonal obstacle. The members should stay in their roles. The role play should last five to seven minutes. After that time, one leader and one member should switch roles and continue the role play. However, before the switch, the members should give feedback to the leader about what helped and what did not help.
4. Finally, one group member should serve as a recorder who will report back to the class the feedback given to each leader.

Suggested Reading
Shulman, L. (1967). Scapegoats, group workers, and preemptive intervention. *Social Work, 12,* 37–43.

Eliciting Multiple Perspectives
In any community group there will be a wide range of perspectives on issues facing the community, even when there seems to be a high level of shared concern. For the social worker, this situation raises the problem of how to ensure that multiple perspectives, particularly those that are typically silenced, get heard and validated. In the following exercise, students use their everyday experiences to learn a strategy for providing all members with a voice in the process. The exercise uses Freire's "pedagogy of the question" to elicit various perspectives and to encourage critical reflection on their meaning.
1. Select a topic that is part of the everyday experience of all students in the class (such as some aspect of their experience in the class or as students in the school).

2. Pose the topic to the class in the form of a question, for example, "How do you experience issues of race (or gender, class, participation, or another thematic issue) in this class (school)?

3. Ask the students to spend 15 to 20 minutes responding to the question in writing. Tell them *not* to put their names on the paper (this is an anonymous exercise).

4. After 15 to 20 minutes, collect the papers and shuffle them. Distribute them to the class, so that each person has someone else's response.

5. Go around the class and have each person read out loud the response he or she has.

6. Have the class discuss what they heard in the responses. Use newsprint and marker pens (so a record exists) to record the various points of view. Ensure that both minority and majority perspectives are captured. Also focus on what people are learning about what other people think. Encourage critical reflection on both content and process. Note any general (or generative) themes that connect the students' experience to wider institutional, social, and political issues. Encourage discussion of these issues from multiple perspectives.

7. Close by exploring with the class ways in which the material might be used as a basis for further discussion and action. How can the multiple voices that emerge from this process be nurtured and encompassed in the longer term?

8. Evaluate the exercise: What did it achieve, and what were its limitations? Consider constraints, such as the assumption that all participants can read and write. Could the exercise be adapted for groups in which literacy is an issue? Does the exercise violate any cultural norms?

This exercise is useful at three levels: It generates thematic material from the students' experiences that will be similar to content they will encounter in the community, it models a strategy that students can use in their own practice, and it provides a vehicle for enhancing students' empowerment (if material relevant to the class gets a response). Each of these three levels should be identified by the instructor in the discussion that follows the exercise.

EXERCISE 10

The Impact of Agency Context on Social Work Practice

At your fieldwork agency, your supervisor asked you to help Ms. G, a 48-year-old, single, homeless woman with no known relatives. Ms. G was referred to your agency after she was picked up by the police following a mugging in which she was beaten severely. She told the police, "I just want to be left alone—by everyone."

Until five years ago, when she was hospitalized for six months for what she called a "nervous breakdown," Ms. G worked as a lab technician in a local hospital. For the past four years, she has lived on the streets near the bus depot. She has been beaten frequently by people she has befriended and has been hospitalized for brief periods for medical treatment. The police regularly pick her up and bring her to hospital emergency departments because she seems disoriented or injured. She has consistently refused all efforts to engage her at any agency. She has missed follow-up appointments and has refused to live in a public shelter.

Outreach workers have observed Ms. G raving and ranting at pedestrians. She also has a history of drinking heavily (she has been detoxified at least once). She has sustained no extended period of sobriety in the past four years. When she is asked about her drinking, she says, "I drink because I have problems."

Questions for Discussion

1. What are the salient issues in this case? What leaps out at you?
2. What systems and agencies will be most relevant to your work?
3. How will your practice setting affect the definition of this client's needs? Consider its mission, service goals and arrangements, the resources and technologies it uses, its task environment, and other agency members.
4. What options are available in your agency to assist Ms. G?
5. What potential barriers are present?
6. Compare your answers to those of students who work in other practice settings and fields of practice (such as hospitals, homeless shelters, addictions agencies, victim services programs, protective services, and mental health clinics).
7. What inferences can you draw about the impact of your agency on your practice, as well as options for using professional influence in the agency?

EXERCISE 11

Duration: 45 to 60 minutes
Materials needed: felt-tip markers and large sheets of paper

Conceptualizing Practice at Multiple System Levels

A social worker can, and sometimes must, respond to a client's needs in many ways and at multiple system levels. The material in chapter 12 discussed such responses to the problem of child abuse and neglect, but a similar approach is important in working with many social problems. This exercise is designed to encourage creativity and analytic thought in deciding on effective interventive strategies.

In small groups of four to six persons, choose one type of case that at least one student in that group is currently working with (if possible, choose something other than child maltreatment). In each small group, do the following:

- On large pieces of paper, draw a hypothesized causal chain involved in maintaining the problem in at least some cases. Do not aim for perfection; spend no more than 10 minutes developing this conceptual model. And remember, artistic excellence is not important.
- On another large sheet of paper, develop a three-column table. In the first column, list systemic levels (individual, family, group, neighborhood, community, organization). In the second column, list at least one possible interventive strategy for each systemic level in the first column. In the third column, note the reasons why you have identified each strategy, based on the conceptual model of the problem you have sketched. Spend no more than 15 minutes on this table.
- Next, a reporter from each small group briefly explains the conceptual model and table of interventions to the full group without interruption. When all the groups have reported, open the floor for general discussion, with particular emphasis on areas of contrast among the small groups.

Index

Cognitive processes
    critical consciousness, 191
    ethical decision making, 35–37
    exploratory history taking,
        117–118
    generalist approach to community assessment, 187–188
    systemic thinking versus linear
        thinking, 20–21
Cognitive therapy, 78, 80, 107
Communication
    community dialogue for empowerment, 191–192
    double bind, 145
    paradoxical, 146
    strategic family theory, 144–145
Community practice
    advocacy in, 196–197
    agency design and functioning,
        213–214
    assessment, 194–195
    on behalf of families, 133–137
    characteristics of, 176
    community as locality, 182–183
    community-building in, 178–180
    community competence concept,
        195–196
    community liaison activities in,
        178, 179
    community of interest, 185
    community profile for, 183
    conceptual and practice development, 180–182
    contextual thinking in, 187–188
    current status, 182
    development of critical consciousness in, 191
    dialogue for empowerment,
        191–192
    ecosystems perspective, 188
    empowerment in, 188–192
    generalist approach, 186, 187
    goals of, 186
    life space concept, 185–186
    locality–community development, 176, 178, 179

mediating structures in, 192
monitoring change in, 253–254
multiple perspectives in, sample
    exercise for eliciting, 291–292
needs assessment, 235
parameters of, 176–180
for parenting behavior change,
    232–233
power analysis in, 184–185
professional trends, 269–270
shared power relationships as
    basis for community, 184
social class as basis for community, 184
social goals model of group
    work, 160
social networks in, 185, 193
social planning in, 178, 179
social programs as community,
    194
social work tradition, 176
solidarity communities, 183–184
types of community, 182–186
use of small groups in, 192–193
value framework for, 197–198
Confidentiality, 34
Consciousness-raising, 164, 191
Constructionism, in family therapy,
    147
Contract, therapy, 116
    in group work, 165
Cost of care
    current policy environment, 111
    group work and, 158–159
    social work funding, 242
    social work profession and,
        270–272
Council on Social Work Education
    curriculum development, 158
    on fields of practice, 86, 88–90
Court-ordered treatment, 112
Critical thinking, 191

D

Deconstructionism, 61
Demographic trends, 42–43

Depression, 248
Development
    family relatedness and, 128–129
    group therapy, 166
Devine, Edward, 261, 262
Double bind, 145
Duration and frequency of therapy
    Bowenian family therapy, 142
    episodic interventions, 113–114
    group work, 165–166
    open-ended, 114
    planning considerations, 112–113
    short-term approaches, 113
    structural family therapy, 143

E

Eclectic practice, 9–10, 78, 80
    mainstream model of group
        work, 161–162
Ecobehavioral approaches, 80, 107
Ecomap
    application, 11–12, 18, 19, 25, 26
    casework example, 108–109
    community, 24
    comparisons, 26
    data sources, 117
    generation of, 25
    sample exercise, 284–285
Economic status
    African Americans, 46
    Asian Americans, 48–49
    Latino Americans, 46
    Native Americans, 49
Ecosystems perspective
    application, 10
    case representation in, 18
    casework assessment, 108–109
    community practice in, 188
    conceptual evolution, 16–18
    culturally sensitive practice in, 52
    ecological science in, 75
    family functioning in, 132
    family intervention in, 148

general systems theory in, 19, 23
integrated practice in, 78
intellectual basis, 19
in multicultural practice, 44
practice application, 105
role of, 18, 19
Education and training for social
        work
    common core approach, 86, 102,
        225
    community practice in, 181
    CSWE curriculum, 158
    fields of practice approach, 86,
        88, 102
    fields of practice training, 95
    program implementation, 240
    sample exercises, 283–294
    values and ethics in, 32–33
Educational system, 49
Empathy, 8–9
Empirical research
    monitoring programs, 249
    practice decision making and, 30
Employment issues
    for Asian Americans,
        48–49
Empowerment. *See also* Client
        empowerment
    community competence concept,
        195–196
    through groups, 192–193
Engagement
    in casework, 116–117
    in culturally sensitive practice,
        51–52
Enmeshment, 142
Ethics and values in social work
    addressing dilemmas in, 35–37
    characteristics of, 31–32
    common base, 225
    in community practice, 197–198
    conceptual evolution, 5–6,
        30–31, 40
    conflict with personal values, 64
    deontological analysis, 37

ethical rules screen, 38–40
generic consistency approach,
    37–38
legal issues and, 33–35
practice decision making and,
    28–30, 40
professional code of ethics,
    30–31, 33, 34, 35–36, 39, 40,
    275–282
sample exercise, 285–287
social work education and, 32–33
sources of conflict in, 35–37
systems of decision making in,
    37–40
utilitarian view, 37
Evaluation of programs and prac-
    tice. *See also* Outcome research
accountability and, 246
challenges in, 257
common features, 248
design considerations, 239, 241,
    254
group designs, 256–257
measurement techniques,
    248–249, 251–254
obstacles to, 248
role of, 246–247, 257
single-case designs, 254–256
skills for, 257
social work professional develop-
    ment and, 246
Event shape, 11
Expectations, in group therapy, 165
Experimental research
group designs, 69–70, 256–257
role of, 69
single-case designs, 70–72,
    254–256

F

Families. *See also* Family function-
    ing; Family intervention;
    Family structure
assessment, 249

conceptualizations of, and social
    work profession, 267
developmental issues and related-
    ness in, 128–129
ecosystemic relationships, 132
incompatible job demands for
    social workers, 271–272
intergenerational effects,
    131–132, 140
in non-systems perspective, 136
organization and structure,
    130–132
organizational and community
    work on behalf of, 133–137
practice knowledge, 126
recent sociocultural trends, 126
theories and concepts, 127–128
Family functioning
communication patterns in,
    144–145
community context, 137
conceptual trends, 147–148
disengagement, 142
interlocking contingencies in,
    230
strategic theory and therapy, 145
structural theory, 143
systems perspective, 229
theoretical models, 81
triangles, 140, 142, 145
Family intervention
agency environment, 135
Bowenian approach, 139–142
case example and analysis,
    139–147
conceptual development, 25,
    137–138, 147–149
major theoretical concept-
    ualizations, 138–139
for overly harsh parent, 230–232
program flexibility, 136–137
social worker roles in, 134
social worker self-awareness in,
    146–147
strategic approach, 144–146

structural approach, 142–144
in systems perspective, 136
Family structure
  African American, 46
  Asian American, 48
  boundaries, 130, 140, 142, 143, 145
  family mapping, 143
  hierarchy concept, in structural family therapy, 145
  intake assessment, 135
  Latino American, 47, 48
  parental child in, 142
  structural theory, 142
  underorganization in, 142
Feedback, 168–169
Feminist thought
  Bowenian approach in, 142
  on strategic family theory, 146
  on structural family therapy, 144
Fields of practice
  analytical framework for identifying, 90–92
  assessment framework, 96
  conceptual development, 86–92, 102
  current conceptualization, 92–95
  definition, 86, 92
  as domain of social work, 7–8, 86
  historical development, 96–98
  implications for practitioner, 102–103
  legislative and political context, 99
  maintaining expertise in, 102
  models of practice in, 101
  new, 95
  personal social services as, 93–94
  program models, assessment of, 99–101
  research practices, variation in, 101–102
  in social work education, 86, 88, 95
  staffing structure, assessment of, 101

targets of, 96
variations within, 95

G

Gay and lesbian population, 42
  demographics, 50
  diversity within, 50
  identity formation, 51
  living arrangement, 50
  support systems, 51
Gender issues, 267
General systems theory
  characteristics of systems in, 21–24
  closed and open systems, 21–22, 23
  in ecosystems perspective, 19
  entropy in, 21–22
  equifinality in, 23
  interaction of systems in, 22–23
  multifinality in, 23
  social work application, 23
  system boundaries in, 21
Generalist practice
  advantages of, 233
  assessment in, 243
  basic skills for, 225
  behavior change strategies for overly harsh parent, 230–233
  behavioral change in, 228–230
  coherence of, 225–227
  contributions of, 225
  good qualities in, 242–243
  intervention planning, 227–228
  program planning and development, 233–243
  theoretical basis, 228
  typology of behavior for, 228
Generic consistency, 37–38
Genetics, behavior and, 73–75
Genogram, 140–141
Goal Attainment Scaling, 249
Government social welfare programs
  current, 94
  development of fields of practice and, 94, 96–97

program rationale, establishment of, 236–238
proposal writing, 242
psychosocial approach, 110–111
resource considerations, 121–122
role of theory, 77–78
termination phase, 122
Involuntary clients, 112

K

Kellogg, Paul, 264
Knowledge base
behavioral and social sciences, 75–76
biological science, 73–75
case-specific, 72–73
conceptual issues, 59–61
conceptual model, 5
ecological science, 75
experimental research, 69–72
generalist practice, 225
integration of sources in practice, 81–82
liberal arts, 66–67
naturalistic research, 67–68
personal experience, 63, 146
practice wisdom, 62–63
psychosocial approach, 110
quantitative versus qualitative research, 68–69
social and cultural diversity, 7
for social work with families, 126
sociopolitical context, 65–66
sources for practice, 6–7, 61–62
theory and conceptual analysis in, 76–81, 107–108

L

Latino Americans
current sociocultural experience, 47–48
diversity among, 45
family patterns, 47
family stress, 48

Learning theory, 107
Legal issues
confidentiality, 34
court-ordered treatment, 112
duty to tell the truth, 34
field of practice assessment, 99
social work values and ethics and, 33–35
social worker loyalty, 34–35
Life model concept, 80, 107
Life space concept, 185–186
Linear thinking, 20–21

M

Macro practice, 177–178
Managed care, 111, 158–159
Marital Happiness Scale, 249
Mediators in family work, 134
Medical science, 75–76
Mental health
biological etiology, 73–75
Native Americans, 49–50
Mexican Americans, 47–48
Minority populations
challenges for, 42
community practice with, 178
cultural sensitivity in practice with, 51–53
demographic trends, 42–43
diversity among, 45–46
principles of social work practice, 44–45
See also specific racial or ethnic group
Monitoring. *See* Evaluation of programs and practice
Mood Thermometers, 249
Motivation for change, 121
Multicultural practice, 43–45, 51–53
Mutual aid model, 161

N

Narrative construction, 191–192
National Association of Social Workers

therapy group membership,
288–289
Scapegoating behaviors, 170,
290–292
Self-disclosure, 64-65
client, in group, 168
Self-help groups, 162
Self-rating, 249
Settlement house movement, 156,
180–181, 263–264, 264–265
Short-term therapy, 11, 111, 113
Social and cultural context
African American experience,
46–47
assessment and, 120
authority of social work, 33
challenges for minority populations, 42
changes in family service needs,
136–137
definitions of community,
182–186
desire for community, 180
development of social work
profession, 265–272
family functioning in, 137
historical development of group
work, 158
interlocking contingencies in
system functioning, 230
intervention planning in, 121–122
of minority populations, 45–46
of organizational practice, 213–214
origins of social work profession,
262–263
principles of social work practice,
44–45
restraints on social work practice,
111–113
sensitivity in social work practice,
51–53
structural family therapy, 144
Social constructionism, 61
Social sciences, 75–76
Social services, 92
accountability, 207

organizational characteristics,
207–208
Social Services Block Grant, 94
Social welfare, 92–93
Social work practice
basic processes, 8–9
common core, 89, 124, 225
conceptual basis, 262, 264–265
conceptual model, 5
conceptual net, 11–13
cultural sensitivity, 51–53
elements and structure, 3–5
epistemological basis, 61
fields of practice, 7–8, 92–96
historical development, 105–106
implementation of social work
values in, 7, 32
integration of sources of knowledge in, 81–82
multicultural, 43–44
origins of social work profession,
263–265
resolving ethical dilemmas in,
35–37
role of values in decision making,
28–30
significance of context, 10–11
sources of knowledge for, 6–7,
61–62
strategy design, 8, 9–10
systemic thinking versus linear
thinking, 20–21
systems of ethical decision
making, 37–40
systems perspective in, 10, 25–27
unique features of, 108
Social work values, 5–6
Sociobehavioral approaches, 80, 107
Staff design
for family work, 135–136
field of practice assessment, 101
program implementation and, 240
Strategic family theory and therapy,
144–146
Structural theory and therapy,
142–144

Supervision, program implementa-
    tion, 240
Support system
    considerations in intervention
        planning, 121–122
    family assessment, 144
    mutual aid groups as, 161
    social network map for assess-
        ment of, 193
Systems perspective. *See also* Ecosys-
        tems perspective; General
        systems theory
    assessment in, 10
    cognitive processes in, 20–21
    family functioning in, 130–132
    family work in, 136
    functioning of formal organiza-
        tions, 208–209
    individual behavior in, 228–230
    interlocking contingencies
        concept, 229–230
    purpose of social work in, 1
    in social work practice, 10, 25–27

T

Task Attainment Scaling, 249
Task-centered interventions, 78–80
Termination of treatment, 122
Theory
    basis for practice models, 9
    Bowenian, 139–142
    family development, 128–129
    family therapy, 137–139

generalist practice, 228
of knowledge and knowing,
    59–60
role of, 6
in scientific method, 76
selection for casework, 109–111
selection of, 77–78
in social work knowledge base,
    76–77, 107–108
for social work with families,
    127–128
strategic family, 144–145
structural approach to family
    therapy, 142, 143, 144
types of, 78–80
use of, 80–81
Title XX programs, 93, 94

U, V

Urban areas
    policy trends, 268–269
    social work practice in,
        269–270
Values. *See* Ethics and values in
        social work

W

Wald, Lillian, 263
Women's issues, Latina American,
    47–48
Workplace intervention, 98, 270

About the Editors

Mark A. Mattaini, DSW, ACSW, teaches the foundations of social work practice, and family and neighborhood practice, at the School of Social Work, Columbia University, New York. His writing and research focus on the visualization of practice theory and events; behavioral analysis of human systems; and prevention of and intervention with emerging social issues including violence, homelessness, and substance abuse. He continues to do part-time clinical and community practice.

Carol H. Meyer, DSW, is Norman Professor of Family and Child Welfare, School of Social Work, Columbia University, New York. She has long been interested in social work practice theory and has written extensively on eco-systems theory and assessment. Her practice experience has been in public and voluntary family and child welfare agencies.

About the Contributors

Meredith Hanson, DSW, is associate professor, School of Social Work, Columbia University, New York, where he teaches courses in clinical practice, program design and development, advanced generalist practice, and social work practice in alcoholism and other drug abuse. His research and practice interests are in program design and evaluation, addictions, and people with dual diagnoses.

Peg McCartt Hess, PhD, ACSW, is associate dean, School of Social Work, Columbia University, New York. She previously was on the faculties of the Universities of Indiana, Tennessee, and Alabama schools of social work. Her direct practice, teaching, research, and publications have focused on social work practice with families with children.

Aurora P. Jackson, PhD, is assistant professor, School of Social Work, Columbia University, New York. Her research interests and publications have focused on employment, family processes, women's well-being, and children's development in poor, single-parent, and minority families. She teaches in the direct practice area.

Helene Jackson, PhD, is assistant professor, School of Social Work, Columbia University, New York. Her teaching and research interests include severely disturbed and abused children and adolescents and their families. She has published books and articles on sexual abuse, rape, and clinical decision making.

Sheila B. Kamerman, DSW, is professor of social policy and planning, School of Social Work, Columbia University, New York, where she also codirects the Cross-National Studies Research Program. She teaches social policy and local social services and has published widely on U.S. and comparative child and family policies and programs.

Susan P. Kemp, PhD, is assistant professor, School of Social Work, University of Washington, Seattle. She was formerly a member of the practice faculty, School of Social Work, Columbia University, New York. Dr. Kemp's research interests include community-based and environmental social work practice and social work history.

Randy H. Magen, PhD, is assistant professor, School of Social Work, Columbia University, New York. His research interests include group work and domestic violence. He has recently published book chapters and articles on parent training, support groups for cancer survivors, and group interventions to manage stress.

Brenda G. McGowan, DSW, is professor, School of Social Work, Columbia University, New York, where her primary teaching responsibilities are in the areas of clinical practice, program development, and family and children's services. Author or coauthor of four books and a number of articles on delivery of family and children's services, she is currently a member of the National Association of Social Workers's National Committee on Inquiry.

Josie Palleja, DSW, is in private practice and is adjunct associate professor, School of Social Work, Columbia University, New York. She also serves as a consultant to family services agencies. Her interests include practice with people from ethnic minority groups.

Barbara Levy Simon, PhD, is associate professor, School of Social Work, Columbia University, New York. Her research and writing concentrate on the history of social welfare, philanthropy, and the human services professions in the United States and Western Europe.

The Foundations of Social Work Practice

Designed by Anne Masters Design, Inc.

Composed by Wolf Publications, Inc., in Galliard and Industrial 736.

Printed by Boyd Printing Company on 60# Windsor.